# INTERNATIONAL CHANGE AND THE STABILITY OF MULTIETHNIC STATES

# International Change and the Stability of Multiethnic States

## *Yugoslavia, Lebanon, and Crises of Governance*

*Badredine Arfi*

INDIANA UNIVERSITY PRESS

Bloomington and Indianapolis

This book is a publication of
Indiana University Press
601 North Morton Street
Bloomington, IN 47404-3797 USA

http://iupress.indiana.edu

*Telephone orders* 800-842-6796
*Fax orders* 812-855-7931
*Orders by e-mail* iuporder@indiana.edu



The paper used in this publication meets the minimum requirements of American National Standard for Information Sciences—Permanence of Paper for Printed Library Materials, ANSI Z39.48-1984.

Manufactured in the United States of America

Library of Congress Cataloging-in-Publication Data

Arfi, Badredine.
International change and the stability of multiethnic states : Yugoslavia, Lebanon, and crises of governance / Badredine Arfi.
p. cm.
Includes bibliographical references and index.
ISBN 0-253-34488-3 (cloth : alk. paper)
1. State, The. 2. Ethnic conflict. 3. Pluralism (Social sciences) 4. International organization. 5. Security, International. 6. World politics—1945-1989. 7. World politics—1989- 8. Yugoslavia—Politics and government—1945-1980. 9. Yugoslavia—Politics and government—1980-1992. 10. Lebanon—Politics and government—1946-1975. I. Title.
JC131.A73 2005
321.09—dc22
2004014519

1 2 3 4 5 10 09 08 07 06 05

# Contents

# Acknowledgments

Over the long course of researching and writing this book I have undoubtedly acquired a number of significant debts.

The book is an outgrowth of a dissertation that was essentially conceived at Ohio State University (Mershon Center), almost completed at the University of Illinois at Urbana-Champaign, and then finalized at Southern Illinois University at Carbondale. I am grateful for the time and support provided by all these institutions. I have especially benefited from the advice of my teachers and friends Edward Kolodziej, Richard Lebow, and Peter Katzenstein.

I remember in the spring of 1993 admitting to Edward Kolodziej that I had yet to decide on the topic for a term paper that he required his graduate-level class on international security to submit at the end of the semester. He suggested that I look into the problem of state collapse. That simple suggestion ended up having far-reaching consequences for my intellectual development as a political scientist for the next decade. As I was immersing myself in the literature on state collapse and failure, Paul Diehl asked whether I would be willing to be a discussant for a panel on constructivism-related works at the Midwest Political Science Association meeting in fall 1995. This "routine" role of a discussant opened the door for me to a vast area of knowledge —constructivism and much beyond—the horizon of which keeps enlarging, much like the boundary of the known universe as the physicist hypothesis of the expanding universe has it. This book in part reflects this expanding universe of my intellectual venture into the vast land of political governance and social theory in general.

Along the path I have accumulated much debt to many of my colleagues at the University of Illinois, the Mershon Center at Ohio State University, and Southern Illinois University.

I have most prominently benefited from long discussions with Edward Kolodziej, who never refrained in sharing with me his deep and vast understanding of international relations and security; Gerry Munck, who introduced me to the challenging issues and methods of comparative politics; Ned Lebow, who patiently listened to me and shared with me his understanding of domestic and international politics; and Peter Katzenstein, who continuously encouraged me to finish the whole project and provided me with much-needed feedback on various aspects of the book approach and ideas.

These friends and colleagues and many other scholars provided valuable comments, without which this book might have not been finished. Edward Kolodziej, Ned Lebow, Peter Katzenstein, and Michael Barnett read most (if not all) of the various manuscripts related to the book and sometimes many iterations of the same chapters. Many other people provided help and guidance in one way or another as well. They include Douglas Foyle, Gerry Munck, Paul Diehl, Carol Leff, Rick Hermann, Edward Mansfield, Ted Hopf, Ian Lustick, Henry Nau, William Zartman, Stephen Cohen, Roger Kennet, Marvin Weinbaum, and probably many others to whom I can only apologize for forgetting to acknowledge their input and feedback. The book is much better for all this help.

At Indiana University Press, Marilyn Grobschmidt, Janet Rabinowitch, Jane Lyle, and their colleagues' enthusiasm and constant support for the project helped me go beyond my often convoluted texts to a prose without which this book could not have been turned into a tangible vision and readable reality. Marinus van Kuilenberg, my graduate research assistant at Southern Illinois University, did a wonderful job in compiling the index for the book in record time. I thank him for this and for much more assistance in my research.

I am especially grateful to my parents, Rabah and Zelikha; my sisters, Najat, Nadia, and Hanifa, and my brothers, Abdelwahab, Cherif, Farid, and Mounir; and my parents-in-law, Mohammed and Fatima, who instilled in me from a young age the thirst for knowledge and deep inquiry, which are partially reflected in this book.

My wife, Khadidja, supported me all these years and made our marriage a happy source of love and enjoyment. I thank her from the deepest quarks and gluons of my heart and the highest stages of my soul for her love and for always being there for me even when I did not seem to be asking for it. My daughter supported me with her love and belief in me all throughout the project and constantly looked forward to reading the finalized book. She and her husband, Noureddine Tayebi, are a constant source of joy for the whole family, without which my intellectual abilities would surely be impaired.

I dedicate this book to all my teachers and mentors who contributed to make me who I am today, from a tender age till this day and for more to come, God willing.

# INTERNATIONAL CHANGE AND THE STABILITY OF MULTIETHNIC STATES

# PART I

# Theoretical Framework

# One

# Introduction

This book is about the transformation of multi-communal states under conditions where fundamental changes are occurring in the international environment. Its central proposition is that the transformation of state governance in this kind of society is the combined result of fundamental changes in international order and in the character of domestic intercommunal relationships and politics. The argument is as follows.

As fundamental changes in the international order develop, the polity as a whole becomes confronted with two basic questions: (1) whether to transform the existing form of state governance in order to adapt it to the changes occurring in international order, and (2) if yes, what form of state governance would emerge. First, fundamental changes in the international order would induce domestic debates about transforming state governance if the international order is a constitutive element of the existing form of state governance, that is, if the international order contributes to defining and legitimizing the existing practices and rules of domestic politics. If that were the case, fundamental changes in the international order would then induce domestic political debates about the legitimacy and authority of the existing system of state governance. Second, the outcome of the political debates on state governance (which could, for example, lead to a failed or consolidated state) depends on a combination of intercommunal vulnerability and trust and on the distribution of institutional power among the major domestic communal groups.

This chapter begins by discussing why the question raised in this book is an important one, particularly in the post–Cold War era, and more so in the era of U.S.-led "war" against international terrorism and "mission" of regime change of post–September 11, 2001. It then briefly summarizes the argument and introduces the dependent and independent variables. It ends with a summary of the empirical cases and findings of the study.

## Understanding the Transformation of States

The transformation of state governance in deeply divided societies at a time when the international political environment is in flux and changing is a question of vital interest to both theorists and practitioners in international relations and security, especially in the post–Cold War era, where ethnic conflicts have become more visible. The dissolution of the Soviet Union into fifteen republics and the ensuing interstate and armed civil conflicts that it has spawned; the collapse of the Lebanese, Yugoslav, and Somali states and the prospect that other states may be on the brink of similar fates; and the Soviet invasion of Afghanistan, the war, and the ensuing civil and ethnic war in post-Soviet occupation, as well as the rise of the Taliban regime and its demise under the U.S.-led coalition, all demonstrate the importance of state failure and consolidation for international security and relations. Civil strife in Algeria, the bloodshed in Sri Lanka, communal tension in India, the genocide in Rwanda, and Kurdish resistance in Turkey and Iraq further illustrate a problem that appears to be enlarging in scope and complexity.[1] Failing states such as Somalia and Afghanistan evolved to become breeding grounds for international terrorism as we moved into the twenty-first century. The situation is as depicted in the following metaphor:

> A ship which is sinking is kept alive and floating by the acts of some crew, passengers and passing ships . . . other members of the crew and passengers are busily tearing the ship apart for material for another ship. Passengers on other ships observe, shout advice, may throw life-lines or may assist some groups against others. Conflicts . . . are not only about the ship's course or the distribution of benefits and authority within an ongoing enterprise, but include most fundamentally the ship itself—whether it ought to be kept afloat and how it ought to be rebuilt or destroyed even as conflicts over allocations rage. (Marenin 1987, 68–69)

Contemporary security studies and international relations (IR) theory hence need to devote an even closer look to this problem. The oversight in theory building cannot be justified in terms of today's dominant IR schools. Prominent schools of international relations, such as realism (and neorealism), neoliberal institutionalism, and constructivism (Waltz 1979; Keohane 1986; Baldwin 1993; Wendt 1999), all build their respective theories of international politics and security on the assumption that the state is a stable unit of analysis. None of these approaches offers a theory of state transformation under changing international conditions. Yet understanding and explaining state and regime changes is a critically important issue. Rapid changes in international practices and norms driven by the end of the Cold War and many processes of globalization taking place today make the analysis of this problem at both the international and the state levels critical for building a theory of the state and regime. Such a study is also important for informed empirical analysis and surer policy formulation and execution at a time when international security and politics landscapes are in flux. This undoubtedly makes explaining and understanding the transformation of states in changing international environments a central problem as we move into the twenty-first century. From this perspective, the casual assumption of much of extant IR scholarship that the state is stable and somehow unchanging is deceptive. The scholastic discourse on this assumption remains highly underdetermining and unsatisfactory. This book's enterprise is to suggest a corrective that views the process of state and regime as a ceaseless bargaining and negotiating relationship, notably in deeply divided societies.

Nor have theories of comparative politics provided satisfactory theories for issues of state and regime stability and transformation under changing international conditions. Students of ethnic politics have made substantial progress in understanding the conditions, sources, and variations of interethnic and group-state relations when the system of state governance changes. Likewise, students working in the institutionalist tradition have also made much progress in understanding the role that state institutions play in the process of governance transformation. Yet these two bodies of literature often do not speak to one another, and when they do, two related problems remain. These problems ensue in part from the difficulty of studying the process of transforming state governance. No single work or approach can fully remedy these problems. Nevertheless, these problems continue to limit further progress in understanding the mutually supportive or undermining roles that ethnic politics and state institutions play in the transformation of state governance in multi-communal societies.

First, scholars mostly continue to work within separate theoretical domains and fail to appreciate or build upon common political problems and independent variables. This is by and large true both in the literature that relies on institutional factors and mechanisms to explain the transformation of state governance and in the literature that takes ethnic politics as a framework of analysis. In practice, however, all deeply divided societies are concerned with the mutual feedback between state institutions and ethnic politics, particularly at times when state governance is fundamentally changing. Second, despite the focus put on the variation of ethnic politics and institutional factors, scholars fail to give adequate consideration to the full range of "solutions" available to the communal groups. For example, scholars focus on the collapse or consolidation of state governance but fail to ask how, in what ways, and to what extent these "solutions" or constructions are substitutes for one another, or can be incorporated in the same explanatory framework. Any full explanation must compare all alternative outcomes of the process of governance transformation. For example, explaining why state collapse occurs in certain multi-ethnic societies would remain insufficient if one does not simultaneously explain why state consolidation did not occur. Nor would the explanation be satisfactory if it does not deal with the question of why the failure or consolidation of a particular state occurred when it did.

A strong need for a closer look at the problem of state transformation also arises in terms of immediate policy and urgent practical concerns. State failure, for instance, invariably triggers intense policy debates in neighboring and sometimes global powers, as well as in international organizations such as the United Nations and humanitarian nongovernmental organizations such as Amnesty International and Human Rights Watch. State collapse can cause shifts in the balance of power, alter the pattern of international alliances, threaten to undermine diplomatic agreements and international treaties, and create opportunities for other states to aggressively pursue their national interests in the failing state. State collapse can also threaten the stability of a whole region and become a source of spillover effects of communal conflicts and waves of refugees and a breeding ground for international terrorism. Despite the obvious relevance of this problem for policy makers on security, political, economic, and humanitarian grounds, only limited efforts have been made to assemble hypotheses and evidence that might advance the debate. The need for more informed debate is also apparent from the poor record of states' foreign policies that have dealt with various cases of state failure, whether in the Balkans, in the former Soviet Union, or in Africa (Herbst 1996–97; Howe 1996–97; 2001; Rotberg et al. 2000). In most cases policy makers have had difficulty in fully understanding the problems they encountered when confronting the issue of failing or collapsed states. This highlights even more the need for informed policy guidance.

Moreover, in the post–Cold War era, states are still major players in international politics and security, even if they are increasingly more integrated in the world economy. Most states are multi-communal, with a diversity of ethnic, racial, religious, and linguistic divisions. Most of these divided states are stable enough and able to effectively govern their respective populations and manage many differences and adversities among local groups. Yet many other states suffer from a deficit of stability and run the potential, if not yet actual, risk of succumbing to ethnic and religious strife and conflict. These potential risks are more visible in the post–Cold War world. Many of these potentially, if not actually, weak or failing states fell within a region under the influence of one or the other side of the Cold War struggle. Superpowers and their respective clients and allies were more inclined to intervene in those weak states to prevent any domestic instability, preserve their respective spheres of influence, or prevent the opposed side of the Cold War from getting a foothold in a coveted weak or failing state. In some sense, weak and unstable states benefited from the interventionist logic of the Cold War. In the post–Cold War world, Russia is neither capable nor even willing to project its power far abroad. Likewise, the United States is much more selective in projecting its power and extending its interests into different regions of the world.[2] As a result, many of these failing, or would-be failing, states find themselves almost left to their own means to sustain a functioning level of governance over their domestic arenas. Not surprisingly then, the first decade of the post–Cold War world witnessed many cases of ethnic conflict and sometimes genocide that resulted from, or created, a situation of state failure. Many of these cases could not adapt or live up to the pace of international changes of the post–Cold War era. Understanding why and how, as well as under what conditions, a multi-communal state might succumb to internal conflict partly as a result of the changing post–Cold War world is an important issue, both for the international community and for the local populations, before the latter become enthralled in hard-to-resolve problems and conflicts.

Therefore, despite its theoretical challenge and policy importance, the transformation of multi-ethnic states is a topic that is surprisingly understudied, especially from a perspective that incorporates both international and domestic factors. In an effort toward filling this gap in the international relations and security literature, this book offers a study of the process of transforming states in multi-communal societies. It specifically offers a theory concerned with changes in the form of state governance when the international environment is in flux. I conceptualize state governance as a continuous process of negotiating and enacting the rules and practices that define and organize domestic politics. Different forms of state governance correspond to different *degrees of state consolidation.* The degree of consolidation is measured by the extent to which the rules and practices of state governance are taken for granted, that is, perceived as the normal way of playing politics. Put differently, the "degree of consolidation" is the extent to which the political actors automatically enact as well as commit themselves to the existing rules and practices defining "normal politics"—termed *constitutive rules and practices.* The more these rules and practices are perceived as defining "normal politics," that is, legitimately defining, prescribing, and proscribing political action, the more consolidated is state governance.

Empirically, state governance in deeply divided societies takes a variety of forms, some relatively consolidated, such as Switzerland and Malaysia, others relatively failing, such as many sub-Saharan states. Most recent theoretical works typically concentrate on a very limited range of forms of state governance in multi-communal societies, studying failing and consolidated states, for instance, but rarely both together. In order to offer a satisfactory explanation of governance transformation of multi-communal states under an international environment in flux, the full range of alternative forms of state governance must be specified and their respective degrees of consolidation compared. Even when concerned with only a single form of state governance, one must place that form of state governance into a spectrum of possibilities. By artificially truncating the range of variation in the form of state governance in multi-communal polities, analysts significantly curtail their assessments of the transformation of state governance in these polities.

State governance in deeply divided polities can in fact take many forms and vary along a continuum from collapsed to consolidated states. In a collapsed state, the major domestic actors (individuals and groups) no longer conceive of or play the game of politics according to existing rules and practices—the degree of consolidation of state governance is nil. This category encompasses a variety of instances of state collapse, extending from peaceful and orderly state dissolution such as in Czechoslovakia in 1993 to extremely violent and chaotic disintegration such as in Yugoslavia in 1991, or protracted civil war such as in Lebanon in 1975. State collapse is different from a breakdown of civil society but does not exclude it. Yet the latter is not necessarily coterminous with the former.[3] The state can sometimes collapse without a breakdown of civil order (e.g., Czechoslovakia). Nor is bad governance a sufficient cause of state collapse. If that were the case, state collapse would be occurring much more often than what has actually been the case in the modern states system.[4] Likewise, territorial disintegration is not a necessary feature of state collapse. As the cases of Lebanon, Somalia, Afghanistan, and Liberia (to name a few) evidence, the state can collapse without the territorial integrity of the country becoming a central issue among the belligerents. Nor is violent conflict such as ethnic wars or genocide a necessary outcome or cause of state collapse.

In consolidated state governance, most political actors take the rules and practices of the domestic game of politics as "normal." That is, most domestic actors do not seek to undermine the rules and practices of the game of politics. These rules and practices thus define what counts as the normal game of domestic politics—they define and regulate relations, govern political conduct in public life, and delimit the types of behaviors and actions that are prescribed, prohibited, or desirable. The case of Malaysia in the 1960s is illustrative. The 1969 parliamentary elections provided a climate within which communal violence quickly developed, thereby threatening peaceful cohabitation of ethnic Malays, Chinese, and Indians. The constitutional contract that had regulated the communal relations since independence was at stake, thereby menacing the legitimacy and integrity of the existing form of state governance. The incumbent deputy prime minister was able through a dual strategy of coercion and reward to defuse an imminent spread of ethnic violence. The regime devised an institutionalized preferential treatment of the Malay community to partly alleviate the Malays' concerns about their economic welfare and access to higher and better education. For the same reason, the regime enlarged the governing coalition to include most of the opposition parties. As a result, state governance was consolidated.

In between the two extremes of collapsed and consolidated state governance is a variety of intermediate forms of governance wherein the rules and practices of the game of politics more or less define what counts as "normal politics." In failing state governance, the major domestic actors are increasingly disputing the rules and practices of "normal politics," if not proposing alternative rules and practices. The challenging actors constantly attempt to push the limits of what is "normal politics" through various ways and methods. The more they succeed in challenging what counts as "normal politics," the less the "normal" rules and practices of domestic politics are taken for granted. The instability of the Burundi state is illustrative. The regime ruling Burundi attempted to launch democratic reforms in 1988, which resulted in violence between historically dominant Tutsis (85 percent) and Hutu (14 percent) challengers. When Hutu opposition forces managed to win the first ever multiparty presidential and legislative elections in 1993, disaffected Tutsi military forces revolted and assassinated the Hutu president. This initiated a series of three subsequent waves of armed clashes and massacres between Tutsis and Hutus. The Burundi polity has since then been embroiled in the thrall of failing state governance (Lemarchand 1994; Reyntjens 1995).

In consolidating state governance, the actors endeavor to "normalize" the rules and practices of domestic politics. The more domestic politics evolves according to these rules and practices, the more the latter would define what counts as "normal" political action. The case of Algeria during the period 1988–2000 is illustrative. Faced with worsening economic conditions, the regime sought to carry out economic reforms in the mid-1980s. However, these reforms quickly became unpopular within the circles of the state clientele. The latter closed ranks with the army top leadership to oppose and undermine the economic reforms. The incumbent regime therefore faced a hard-to-resolve dilemma between the rationality of would-be free market economy and preserving a system of clientelism that had supported it for many years. The regime sought to democratize the state in an effort to strengthen the momentum for economic reforms. This, however, proved to be as problematic as trying to maintain the old regime. Ultimately, the army opted for stopping the democratization process in 1992 and subsequently eradicating any form of genuine political opposition. Algeria has since then adopted a new constitution in 1996 and held presidential and parliamentary elections three times. State governance, however, is still in the process of being consolidated. Many political groups and actors are still attempting to play politics through other ways or push the outer limits of what the 1996 Constitution defines as "normal politics" (King 1999; Martínez 1998; Addi 1995; Charef 1994; Roberts 2003).

As the above examples suggest, negotiations among domestic actors can lead either to a collapsed state or to a form of governance with varying degrees of consolidation. Therefore, if inquiring "Why do states collapse?" is an interesting question in itself, a more comprehensive approach for analysts and practitioners alike is to pose the two following questions.

1. Why would fundamental changes in international order induce domestic debates on the form of state governance?
2. Why do some divided societies end up consolidating their system of state governance whereas others end up in a failing system of state governance?

To answer these two questions and hence explain the transformation of state governance in multi-communal societies when the international environment is in flux, I draw on insights from the social-constructivist (interactionism) school at both the international and the intercommunal levels. Using this doubly constructivist approach, I answer the above two questions in two steps.

First, the international environment can shape states in one of two ways. It can have a regulative effect on states by providing opportunities for and constraining the power and scope of state institutions and practices of domestic politics (Gourevitch 1978; Finnemore and Sikkink 1998). This implies that the international environment is something like a billiard table, constraining state behavior and policies, internally and externally. The international context can also play a constitutive role in the formation and functioning of state institutions and political practices (Jackson 1990; Finnemore 1996; Wendt 1999). The international environment would in this case help to define and legitimize what counts as "normal politics" in domestic politics by contributing to the constitution of state institutions, policies, and practices. Fundamental changes in the international order would deprive state institutions, policies, and practices from such constitutive and legitimating elements. Such a condition would then induce pressures for domestic debates about reconfiguring state governance. The outcome of these debates, as discussed at length in chapter 2, falls on a continuum of forms of state governance, extending from collapsed states to strongly consolidated forms of state governance.

Second, three primary factors combine to determine the outcome of the domestic political debates: intercommunal vulnerability, trust, and distribution of institutional power. These three variables are discussed at length in chapter 3. All three variables are necessary elements of a complete explanation of governance transformation in deeply divided states. The following briefly summarizes the general contours of the argument.

To begin with, debating state governance, which is the basis of the sociopolitical order including intercommunal relations, threatens to destabilize the intercommunal status quo as well as state-group relations. It implies the possibility of opening up opportunities for certain communal groups and not for others and threatening certain communal groups and not others. Consequently, some (if not all) communal groups might fear becoming more vulnerable to one another. In 1987–91, Yugoslavia faced a major crisis of state governance. Serbian leader Slobodan Milosevic called for new constitutional amendments that would restore Serbia's hegemony over Kosovo and Vojvodina by abrogating the autonomous status of the two provinces. In parallel, Milosevic-controlled media in Belgrade launched a propaganda campaign against the Croats, accusing them of nurturing a conspiracy against the Serbs. Croatian leaders in turn accused Milosevic of "Stalinist" and "unitarist" tendencies after he reduced the autonomy of Kosovo. The Croatians henceforth began calling for more political decentralization at the federal level, alleging that Serbian politicians were aiming at destabilizing Croatia. The more the debates lingered, the more the Serbs and Croats (as well as other groups) became vulnerable to each other's verbal attacks and accusations.

Intercommunal vulnerability can take the form of intercommunal abandonment, exploitation, or exclusion. Abandonment stands for defection from, or abrogation of, intercommunal understandings, agreements, and commitments. Exploitation occurs when a group takes advantage of the others. Exclusion occurs when a communal group is banned from the domestic political space. Therefore, as the communal groups engage in the debate about state governance, they increasingly face the prospects of seeing their mutual commitments breached or exploited and of suffering exclusion from decisive moments in the life of the polity. The more the communal groups dispute the rules and practices of the existing form of state governance, the higher will be intercommunal vulnerability.

To address this vulnerability, the debating communal groups can use, I argue, one of two devices (alone or in tandem), namely, intercommunal trust and institutional power. Intercommunal trust exists as a shared belief among two or more actors who, in spite of having a degree of freedom to disappoint each other's expectations, expect one another to act with "goodwill." Reliance on institutional power becomes a possibility when an asymmetry of institutional power exists among the communal groups. Institutional power enables the beholder to address intergroup vulnerability to its own advantage.

Intercommunal vulnerability, trust, and distribution of institutional power all interact to determine the outcome of negotiations and debates on the form of state governance, that is, whether the outcome would be a collapsed or consolidating state and, in the latter case, the degree of consolidation of state governance. State collapse would most likely ensue when there is high intercommunal vulnerability, high reliance on institutional power, and very low or vanishing intercommunal trust. The debating communal groups will most likely stop viewing the existing rules and practices of state governance as "defining normal politics" when they share little or no trust and face high mutual vulnerability. Consolidating state governance is most likely when there is a moderate and decreasing vulnerability, a low and decreasing reliance on institutional power, and a moderate and increasing trust. Consolidated state governance is more likely when there is a low and significantly declining vulnerability, a low and significantly falling reliance on institutional power, and a high and significantly increasing intercommunal trust.

As this discussion implies, none of the three explanatory variables can alone satisfactorily explain the process of state transformation in multi-communal societies. High levels of trust, for example, cannot exist concurrently with a strong reliance on institutional power. Likewise, a low intercommunal vulnerability will not correlate with a high reliance on institutional power. State governance will not consolidate enough if some communal groups fear to become too vulnerable to other groups that have more control over state institutional power. Failing state governance is hence most likely when both intercommunal vulnerability and reliance on institutional power increase while intercommunal trust falls.

## Summary of Cases and Findings

The theory outlined above implies that four questions should drive the process of transforming state governance in the four historical cases considered in later chapters.

1. Were there fundamental changes in the (constitutive) rules and practices of the international environment? If yes, did these changes induce domestic debates on state governance?
2. How vulnerable did the communal groups feel, or fear becoming?
3. How much did any of the debating communal groups rely on institutional power to address intercommunal vulnerability?
4. What was the level of intercommunal trust among these communal groups?

These four basic questions constitute the core of the research design used to test the theory in the four chosen cases, as discussed in chapters 2 and 3. In each case, a plausible reading of the four primary variables—fundamental changes in international order, intercommunal vulnerability, intercommunal trust, and reliance on institutional power—appears to be consistent with the origin of, and outcome that eventually emerged from, the debates on state governance.

I consider the following selection of case studies: Yugoslavia (1947–53, 1987–91) and Lebanon (1957–58, 1973–75). All periods examined correspond to crises of state governance in the respective histories of the two states under a variety of international conditions. The Yugoslav cases respectively unfolded during the emergence, consolidation, and end of the Cold War in Europe. The two Lebanese cases both correspond to the aftermath of an Arab-Israeli war (the 1956 Suez Canal War for the 1958 crisis, and the 1967 Six-Day War and

1973 Ramadan War for the 1975 crisis) and subsequent reconsolidation of regional order. The first Lebanese crisis in addition unfolded at a time when the U.S.-Soviet Cold War rivalry was extending its tentacles to the Middle East, whereas the second Lebanese crisis unfolded at a time when inter-Arab politics and Arab-Israeli relations were fundamentally in flux.

The two Yugoslav case studies focus on the 1947–53 period, during which Yugoslavia consolidated its state governance, and the 1987–91 period leading to the disintegration of the federation. During the period (1947–53), Yugoslavia fundamentally redefined its international role within the surrounding Cold War environment to become the first European communist country to split with the Soviet Union. The result was a major transformation and consolidation of state governance. A low and decreasing intercommunal vulnerability as formulated in the 1953 Constitutional Law framework, a somewhat stagnating intercommunal trust, and a moderate and decreasing reliance on institutional power all combined to produce somewhat rapidly consolidating state governance in the mid-1950s after the formulation of the 1953 Constitutional Law. In contrast, the period 1987–91 culminated in a complete collapse of state governance and a territorial disintegration of the Yugoslav federation. After Tito's death in 1980 and the subsequent emergence of a new style of republican leadership that did not hesitate to revive and utilize intercommunal fears and threats in pursuit of political goals (as epitomized by Slobodan Milosevic of Serbia), Yugoslavia was confronted with a waning Cold War within difficult global economic conditions. The Yugoslav federation was losing an international buffer role that had privileged it in the policies of both camps of the Cold War. Absent the Cold War, privileges such as economic assistance were lost. More importantly, the Yugoslav state found itself immersed in new international conditions that it was ill prepared to deal with. The dire economic conditions of the federation compounded such difficulties and generated divisive and heated debates on the future of state governance. The outcome of the debates was a collapse of the federal state and a territorial dismemberment of Yugoslavia. The major Yugoslav communal groups increasingly refused to take for granted then-existing rules and practices of state governance and failed to reach any agreement on any new practices and rules of governance due to a combination of three elements. First, intercommunal vulnerability was somewhat high and increased as the republican leaders relied increasingly more on ultranationalistic agendas and rhetoric. Second, intercommunal trust was low and quickly decreased as the debates raised more doubts about the existing form of state governance. Third, reliance on institutional power increased quickly (for the Serbs) as the debates turned more heated.

The two Lebanese case studies compare the period 1957–58, leading to the 1958 crisis, and the period 1973–75, ending with the eruption of the 1975–76 civil war and state collapse. During the first period (1957–58), the Lebanese

**Table 1.1. Summary of Cases and Findings**

DCSG: Degree of Consolidation of State Governance

| *Observed Outcome: State Governance* | *Intercommunal Vulnerability* | *Intercommunal Trust* | *Reliance on Institutional Power* |
|---|---|---|---|
| **Yugoslavia 1: 1947–53** | | | |
| **International Environment: Emergence and Consolidation of the Cold War and the Rule of International Bloc Politics in post-1947** | | | |
| Consolidating:<br>DCSG increasing after the 1948–49 Tito–Stalin split and more so after the 1953 Constitutional Law. | Low, somewhat increased as the national question began to reemerge. | Moderate, increased significantly with the formulation of the 1953 Constitutional Law. | Low, somewhat stagnated as the national question began to reemerge. |
| **Yugoslavia 2: 1987–91** | | | |
| **International Environment: Waning and End of the Cold War in 1989–91** | | | |
| Collapsed:<br>DCSG low, rapidly vanishing, particularly after Slovenia and Croatia initiated unilateral moves toward independence in June 1990. | High, increased rapidly with the stalemate within the Collective Presidency and the polarization of the YNA. | Low, decreased rapidly with the stalemate within the Collective Presidency and the polarization of the YNA. | High, increased rapidly with the stalemate within the Collective Presidency and the polarization of the YNA. |
| **Lebanon 1: 1957–58** | | | |
| **Regional Environment: The Rise of Nasserism, the 1957 Eisenhower Doctrine, and the Formation of the United Arab Republic (UAR) in 1958** | | | |
| Consolidating:<br>DCSG moderate, significantly rising, particularly after the emergence of Fuad Shihab as president. | Moderate, increased significantly in summer 1958 but then decreased significantly with the emergence of Fuad Shihab as president. | Moderate, decreased rapidly in summer 1958 but then increased significantly with the emergence of Fuad Shihab as president. | Moderate, increased somewhat with Chamoun's attempt to rely on state institutions but then decreased with the emergence of Fuad Shihab as president. |

| Lebanon 2: 1973–75 | | | |
|---|---|---|---|
| **International Environment: 1967 Six-Day Arab-Israeli War, 1970–71 Black September Episode in Jordan, 1973 Ramadhan War** | | | |
| Collapsed:<br>DCSG low, rapidly vanishing, particularly after the Maronites and other groups began to form strong paramilitary units in the post–May 1973 crisis. | High, increased rapidly after the 1971 exodus of Palestinians to Lebanon from Jordan, and subsequent paralysis of the army, the Parliament, and the government, and the polarization of the presidency in the post–May 1973 crisis. | Low, decreased rapidly after the 1971 exodus of Palestinians to Lebanon from Jordan, and subsequent paralysis of the army, the Parliament, and the government, and the polarization of the presidency in the post–May 1973 crisis. | High, increased rapidly after 1971 exodus of Palestinians to Lebanon from Jordan, and subsequent paralysis of the army, the Parliament, and the government, and polarization of the presidency in the post–May 1973 crisis. |

state descended toward a crisis that culminated in violence in 1958. State governance was reinforced, however, as the Lebanese polity passed through the crisis successfully. A consolidating form of state governance resulted (as General Shihab launched a process of reconstructing state legitimacy and authority) due to a combination of three elements. First, intercommunal vulnerability was moderate and decreased. Second, intercommunal trust was increasing. Third, reliance on institutional power decreased. In contrast, the Lebanese polity became increasingly unable to surpass a major crisis in the early 1970s, eventually leading to a complete collapse of state governance and a civil war in 1975–76 due to the combination of three elements. First, intercommunal vulnerability was high and increased as the sectarian leaders relied increasingly more on unilateralist agendas and rhetoric. Second, intercommunal trust was low and quickly decreased as the debates raised more doubts on the state governance. Third, reliance on institutional power increased quickly (for the Maronites) as the debates turned more heated.

# Two

# Debating State Governance

The present chapter presents a typology of possible outcomes of the debates on state governance induced by fundamental changes in the international environment. In other words, this chapter discusses at length the dependent variable of the causal argument.[1] The following chapter seeks to explain these outcomes of the domestic political debates.

In this book, I deal with multi-communal societies where politicized communal groups are important political actors. A deeply divided society is one in which ascriptive ties generate segmentation in the society based on identities with political saliency, sustained over a substantial amount of time and a wide variety of issues (Lustick 1979, 325). The divisions can occur along religious lines such as in India and Lebanon, racial and ethnic ones such as in Malaysia and South Africa, and tribal ones such as in Congo. These divisions often overlap and mutually reinforce one another. Yet, as a minimum condition, boundaries between the groups must be sharp enough so that communal membership is clear and expected to be enduring and stable (Lustick 1979, 325).

Yugoslavia was a deeply divided country, with no dominant ethnic group. Out of a total population of 22.4 million in 1981, for example, the Serbs represented 36.3 percent and the Croats 19.7 percent (Woodward 1995a, 21–46; Ramet 1992b). Significant similarities in terms of language, ethnic origin, and customs existed among the Yugoslav national groups. The overall ethnic makeup of Yugoslavia did not change in the seventy years after its creation in 1918, except for a marked increase in the Albanian population and a sharp decline in the numbers of Jews, ethnic Germans, and Hungarians after World War II. Most nationalities were not located within the borders of the Yugoslav republics or provinces, thereby making the ethnic landscape very complicated. In 1981, about 98 percent of all Yugoslavia's ethnic Slovenes lived in Slovenia, and about 96 percent of its ethnic Macedonians lived in Macedonia. In comparison, only 60 percent of ethnic Serbs lived in Serbia, and only 70 percent of ethnic Montenegrins lived in Montenegro. Croatia had a substantial Serb minority of about 12 percent. Serbo-Croatian, Slovenian, and Macedonian were official state languages.

Lebanon is also a deeply divided country along religious and sectarian lines. More than 95 percent of the population is Arab, with some pockets of Armenians (4 percent), Kurds, and Jews. The religious landscape includes a variety of Muslim and Christian sects. Muslims constitute about 70 percent of the population with five legally recognized groups—Alawite or Nusayri, Druze, Ismaʿilite, Shiite, and Sunni. The rest of the population is mainly Christian, with many legally recognized groups—Maronites, Greek Orthodox, Greek Catholics, Roman Catholics, Jacobites, Armenian Orthodox, Assyrians, and Protestants. Arabic is the official language, with French, English, and Armenian widely used.

## Debating State Governance: The Variety of Outcomes

In order to offer a satisfactory explanation of governance transformation in multi-communal states in a changing international environment, one needs to specify the full range of possible forms of state governance as well as compare the respective degrees of consolidation of these forms of governance. As argued earlier, state governance is essentially a never-ending process of negotiating and renegotiating the rules and practices that define, organize, and regulate domestic politics. The collective debate in the polity may result in consolidated state governance, a collapsed state, or some intermediate forms of state governance characterized by varying degrees of consolidation. The degree of consolidation is a function of the *scope of collective intentionality*, that is, the extent to which the major political actors take for granted—accept, enact, and abide by—the constitutive rules and practices of state governance.[2]

Intentionality is the term given to the mind's striking capacity to have mental states that are about features in the world. Davis states that "Having an intention involves forming a commitment to action, and intentional action occurs only when an agent aims to bring something about by acting in a purposive way" (Davis 2002, 13). Put differently, a mental state can have the property of being about something, and intentionality is the *directedness* of the mind toward a content or object that allows thoughts to be about other things. People believe that such-and-such is the case, intend to do something, think about or mean a particular object. This property of "*aboutness*" is an intentional one. For example, fears and beliefs are directed toward their objects.

Intentionality can be of two sorts—individual and collective. Individual intentionality is held by an individual, and collective intentionality is held by a collectivity such as a team, ethnic group, community, or nation. Collective intentionality is expressed in statements such as "*I* am doing something only as part of *our* doing something" (Searle 1995, 23; original italics). Collective intentionality is about "a sense of doing (wanting, believing, etc.) together, and the individual intentionality that each person has is derived *from* the collective intentionality that they share" (Searle 1995, 24–25; original italics). For example, exclusive territoriality has become so deeply ingrained in the practice of international politics that actors (both states and non-states alike) almost no longer think of this "fact" as a constructed "fact" at all. However, the practice of "exclusive territoriality" is durable and reified as long as it remains based on collective intentionality (Ruggie 1998, 873). Absent collective intentionality, the "fact of exclusive territoriality" would become obsolete. Likewise, slavery was abolished worldwide through an act of collective intentionality.

A key question is, where is collective intentionality "located"? Is it a property of the individuals making up the collectivity? Or, alternatively, is it the manifestation of some sort of supermind or Hegelian spirit? Following John Searle's view (1995), this book adopts the perspective that individual intentionality and collective intentionality are both "primitive" and cannot be reduced to one another. However, agreeing with a number of Searle's critics,[3] the book rejects Searle's ontological position that both individual intentionality and collective intentionality are "located" in the minds of individuals—that is, are features of the individual. The book instead adopts the view that collective intentionality is an inextricable (intersubjective) combination of beliefs held in the minds of the individuals participating in the collectivity and the (social) relations among these individuals—collective intentionality is fundamentally intersubjective, "social." What makes collective intentionality very attractive as conceptualized in this book is that it helps to explain how it is possible for an individual to think and act as a member of a large group (such as a communal group or a nation) without being a mere "component" of some supra-individual entity with a "supermind." Indeed, without being reducible to sets of individual intentions, collective intentionality is an integral part of the individual intentional activity and not the other way around. As stated by Davis (2002, 12), "individuals attribute intentions to the groups of which they are members, and participate in this attribution by using 'we' language. In this sense, we-intentions are shared. . . . We-intentions are individually expressed intentions, though of a special kind in making the group rather than the individual their subject." Thus, for example, car drivers act collectively insofar as they individually "we-intend" to get by each other collision-free and legally, and therefore choose "right" as their individual contribution. In Searle's theory, the "we" is not a matter of my taking myself and your taking yourself to be a member of the team plus some common knowledge about each other's self-understanding. Collective intentionality is a primitive phenomenon, for the sense of "we-intend" cannot be reduced to the aggregated sum of individual "I-intend." It is of course true that for our "we-intending" to succeed, the relevant others have to "we-intend," too. But this does not mean that we individually "decide" whether to "we-intend," dependent on our belief about the relevant other's collective intentionality. In sum, "collective intentionality exists both in the form of cooperative behavior and in consciously shared attitudes such as shared desires, beliefs, and intentions. Whenever two or more agents share a belief, desire, intention, or other intentional state, and where they are aware of so sharing, the agents in question have collective intentionality" (Searle 2003, 5).[4]

Collective intentionality is necessary for the creation of any form of social reality and social facts (Searle 2003, 5). Put the other way around, a social fact is any fact involving the collective intentionality of two or more human agents (Searle 2003, 5). More specifically, collective intentionality creates, maintains, and negates the constitutive rules of politics. It is not easy to fully understand and explain the recurrent character of politics without considering the constitutive rules that underpin politics.[5] These rules are said to be "constitutive rules" because they "constitute" the political fact itself.[6] For example, the rules of chess are the conditions of possibility of the game. It is possible to change the size, material, or shape of the characters, or change the colors of the squares on the chessboard. Yet we will have a chess game still, insofar as we use the proper set of rules. This means that the proper answer to the question "What is a chess game?" is not "The game played by such and such at such and such time or place" or "The game created by John Doe." The proper answer is that it is "The game that is played in such and such a way, according to such and such rules." For example, the rook is the chessman that can, whatever its color, shape, size, or material, move only in a straight line. The game itself is constituted by a set of constitutive rules, and each piece is constituted in the game by these rules. It must be noted that constitutive rules are not just conventions, because "convention" implies arbitrariness, and constitutive rules are not arbitrary.[7] Searle (1995, 28) explains the difference using the following example: "It is a rule of chess that we win the game by checkmating the king. It is a *convention* of chess that the king is larger than the pawn." A rule is constitutive according not to the form it has but to the function it plays. The formulation of a constitutive rule is not the answer to the question "What counts as a pawn in this match?" Rather, it is the answer to the question "What is a pawn?" What constitutive rules are "constitutive of" is the idea (or form) of the object of which they are rules. Put in somewhat more formal terms, collective intentionality plays an essential role in the constitutive rule "X counts as Y in context C" by imposing the property "Y" on "X" in the context "C." The "counts as" locution imposes a function "Y" on "X" by way of collective intentionality (Searle 1995, 44).

In other words, collective intentionality imposes a special status on some phenomena, and with that status, a function. The function in turn requires the status in order that it is performed, and the status requires collective intentionality, including a continued acceptance of the status with its corresponding function.

In the realm of politics, the constitutive rules and practices of state governance define and legitimize what counts as a part of the game of domestic politics (Bukovansky 1997; Searle 2003).[8] State governance is hence a never-ending process of negotiating and renegotiating the constitutive rules and practices that are to govern domestic relations among various groups (Barnett 1998, 6–15). These rules of the political game constitute and regulate relations and political conduct in public life. The rules delimit the types of behaviors and actions that are prescribed, prohibited, or desirable. Under conditions of political stability, the elites and public alike would normally resist, if not prevent, a redefinition of the constitutive rules and practices of state governance. The polity becomes "entrapped" in the existing political game, which in turn is defined by the constitutive rules and practices. The latter help to define what is feasible and acceptable, that is, the realm of state discourse and behavior that most of the elites and public alike come to perceive as legitimate and authoritative. Even if domestic actors realize that the existing constitutive rules and practices of the state are part of a spectrum of possibilities, they cannot easily change the collective stand toward them. It may be politically too risky to raise questions about the existing constitutive rules and practices. This is especially true for incumbent politicians and elites who might fear losing their power positions and roles, should the constitutive rules and practices change or be seriously challenged. Building and reconstructing state governance is not an easy task; it is not part of normal politics.

Fundamental changes would occur in domestic politics if the constitutive rules of domestic politics change. The debate in Israel about the Palestinian-Israeli peace process is partially explainable in these terms. An important fraction of the Israeli polity views a transfer of more territory to the Palestinians as a redefinition of constitutive rules and practices of the state. Conversely, others argue that not to cede more territory now to the Palestinians and instead to keep large numbers of Palestinians as potential Israeli citizens might eventually redefine the constitutive rules and practices of the state of Israel (Lustick 1993, 352–438; Ezrahi 1997; Peleg 1997).

In most situations, though, societies do not fully (or, at least, do not always fully) take for granted the constitutive rules of politics. The process of creating, maintaining, and changing the constitutive rules and practices of domestic politics is indeed never final—the constitutive rules and practices are always in process. At a fundamental level, negotiating the constitutive rules and practices is creating, changing, undermining, or reinforcing a form of collective action. And all successful collective actions are rooted in collective intentionality. The variation of the extent to which the constitutive rules and practices are taken for granted means that those constitutive rules and practices are underpinned by different scopes of collective intentionality. This means that collective intentionality is in itself always undergoing a process of construction, deconstruction, and reconstruction. To put it differently, the constitutive rules and practices of politics are underpinned by a collective intentionality, the scope of which can increase or decrease. The higher the scope of collective intentionality, the less likely it is that the constitutive rules and practices of politics will be challenged. Conversely, the lower the scope of collective intentionality, the more likely it is that the constitutive rules and practices might be challenged and changed.

Of course, speaking of collective intentionality among a set of actors does not necessarily imply that all actors play the same role in the construction of this collective intentionality. Yet regardless of how actors instantiate (i.e., produce and reproduce) collective intentionality, the latter is necessary for any form of state governance.[9] A high scope of collective intentionality is necessary for a consolidated form of governance; otherwise the constitutive rules and practices might remain seriously contested. The latter in turn would deplete the degree of stability of the domestic game of politics.

Nor does a high scope of collective intentionality necessarily imply power parity among the actors instantiating the collective intentionality. Stronger parties can sometimes induce weaker ones to develop a sense of "we-intend," that is, to engage in public behavior that produces and reproduces the game of politics. Put differently, collective intentionality is not always necessarily consistent with the individual intentionalities of all participating actors when taken one by one. Conflict between collective intentionality and individual intentionality is quite common in societies, a social phenomenon that Kuran (1995) aptly termed the coterminous existence of "private truths" and "public lies." The rapid fall of the communist regimes of Eastern Europe in the late 1980s illustrates both how a high scope of collective intentionality is necessary for governance stability and how a weak scope of collective intentionality undermines the system of governance. The fall of communist governance in the late 1980s followed many decades during which East Europeans cheered leaders whom they despised, keeping quiet in the face of tyranny. To prove their public loyalty to communist governance, they turned in to the government any citizen who dared criticize the political status quo (Kuran 1995, 266). However, when the East Europeans decided to abrogate the collective intentionality that underpinned the communist system of governance, the communist regimes simply collapsed. When the masses descended into the streets, the support of communist governance in Eastern Europe vanished.

This example and many others in cases of fully developed states illustrate how a high scope of collective intentionality underpins stable state governance regardless of the nature of the regime. Neither liberal democracy anchored in popular legitimacy and consent nor totalitarian regimes based on oppression and repression can exist and remain stable without an underpinning collective intentionality (Searle 2003). The two types of regime, however, differ on how they create collective intentionality as well as maintain it. In a liberal democracy, the people consensually participate in the process of forming and sustaining collective intentionality, whereas a totalitarian regime coerces its people into a process of forming and sustaining collective intentionality. To focus on collective intentionality is hence to emphasize the inherently social nature of the process not only of forming governance and maintaining it, but also of undermining it. Forming and sustaining, as well as transforming, collective intentionality is a social process that is fundamental to the creation, reproduction, and erosion of all forms of state governance.

Thus, when major domestic actors neither conceive of nor play the game of politics according to existing constitutive rules and practices, nor renegotiate these rules and practices, this amounts to a *collapse of the existing form of state governance.* The scope of collective intentionality (underpinning state governance) becomes nil. This category encompasses a variety of instances of state collapse, extending from peaceful and orderly state dissolution such as in Czechoslovakia in 1993 to extremely violent and chaotic disintegration such as in Yugoslavia in 1991, or to protracted civil war such as in Lebanon in 1975. In contrast, in *consolidated state governance,* the scope of collective intentionality underpinning the rules and practices of the domestic game of politics is very high and continuously reinforced. In this scenario, the rules and practices of state governance define what counts as a part of the normal game of domestic politics, and most domestic actors do not think of seriously undermining the rules and practices. Playing the game of politics according to the constitutive rules and practices makes the latter even more "normal" and taken for granted and increases their underpinning scope of collective intentionality.

In between the two extremes of collapsed and consolidated states there are a variety of intermediate forms of state governance with varying scopes of collective intentionality. In *failing state governance,* the major domestic actors are increasingly disputing the rules and the practices, if not looking for alternative rules and practices. The challenging actors constantly attempt to push the limits of what is normal politics through various ways and means. The more they succeed in challenging what counts as "normal politics," the lower would be the scope of collective intentionality underpinning the existing rules and practices of domestic politics. In *consolidating state governance,* the actors instead endeavor to "normalize" even more the rules and practices of domestic politics. The more major political actors play domestic politics according to these rules and practices, the higher the scope of collective intentionality would become. The difference between a consolidating form of governance and a failing one resides in the *direction of change* in the scope of collective intentionality; the latter increases in the case of consolidating governance and decreases in the case of failing governance.

The cases of Tadjikistan in the immediate aftermath of the Soviet era and Malaysia after the 1969 riots following the parliamentary elections are respectively illustrative of failing and consolidating forms of state governance. From the first years of independence, politics in Tajikistan emerged as long struggles for political power between, on the one hand, groups that sought Soviet-style dominance of power and privilege and, on the other hand, a variety of opposition forces seeking to establish a new government. In the first half of 1992, the opposition reacted to increased state repression by organizing ever-larger pro-reform demonstrations. When in May 1992 President Nabiyev stopped negotiating with the opposition and went into hiding, the confrontation became a bloody one. Conditions improved temporarily with the formation of a coalition government in which the opposition held one-third of the cabinet posts. However, for most of the rest of 1992, opponents of reforms worked hard to overturn the coalition and block the formation of a new legislature wherein the opposition could have a voice. In the summer and fall of 1992, vicious battles resulted in many casualties among civilians and combatants. In August 1992, demonstrators in Dushanbe captured Nabiyev and forced him to resign. The speaker of the Supreme Soviet, Akbarsho Iskandarov, became acting president. Iskandarov sought a negotiated resolution of the conflict, but to no avail. The conflict continued through fall 1992.

In contrast, Malaysia provides a good example of a rapidly consolidating form of state governance after the 1969 riots. The incumbent regime feared that should the situation degenerate further, state legitimacy might suffer some irreparable damage. High levels of paranoia and communal animosity created a crisis of confidence over the capacity of the government to keep order and meet minimal demands of competing, politically mobilized communal constituencies. Government policies aimed at restructuring the economic control of the country in a communally equitable fashion became a major concern of the regime, and greater encouragement of the *bumiputera* economic participation in Malaysia became official policy. A major positive step toward that end was the creation in July 1969 of the Department of National Unity (Jabatan Perpaduan Negara). The department's first action was to recommend a new national identity based on Rukunegara (principles of nationhood) doctrine anchored in a number of basic principles, such as the belief in God, loyalty to the king and country, upholding of the Constitution and rule of law, and displaying good public behavior and morality. The acceptance of this "racial bargain" became a prerequisite for participation in the political life of the country (Grouch 1978). Parliamentary government became fully operational in February 1971 (Means 1991).

## Studying Debates on State Governance

As the previous section shows, failing and consolidating forms of governance are a matter of degree, and elements of failure and consolidation can coexist in both of these "pure" types. Moreover, the processes that lead to more failure (or consolidation) are reversible; societies can reverse course along the path toward either more state failure or consolidation. It is only after the fact that we can ascertain with the benefit of hindsight that state governance has clearly collapsed. Conversely, it is after a long process of consolidation that we can ascertain that a state has established a strongly consolidated form of governance.

Hence, one must be careful in applying the definition of collective intentionality as developed in the previous section. One should not draw conclusions about the scope of collective intentionality from the processes through which the governance system emerges. The processes of creation do not always define the scope of collective intentionality. Different paths can produce a similar scope of collective intentionality. Stable liberal democracies create and maintain a strongly consolidated governance system through trust. A strongly consolidated system of governance can alternatively emerge through coercive institutional power, as in former communist European states, or through a combination thereof. The shift from individual (group) intentionality to collective intentionality (or from an almost vanishing scope of collective intentionality to a higher one) is what defines the degree of consolidation (or, conversely, failure) of state governance, irrespective of whether the governance system is created or sustained through more coercion or more free consent. In sum, estimating the scope of collective intentionality is a necessary step in the analysis but is insufficient to differentiate between failing and consolidating states. The difference can be made only by estimating both the scope of collective intentionality and its direction of change.

Generally, discerning the scope of collective intentionality underpinning a system of state governance is also a difficult and imperfect process. Changes in collective intentionality can be of two "pure" analytical types, minor or radical. These two types of change differ in terms of their implications. Because collective intentionality is always in process, minor changes tend to occur often. Minor changes are part of the day-to-day political negotiation-renegotiation routines and thus are not of major importance to the issues of governance transformation. Nonetheless, an accumulation of minor changes in the scope of collective intentionality could negate or lead to a new collective intentionality through a tipping process. However, these changes tend to occur very slowly and hence are difficult to trace empirically. Instead, this book focuses on changes that occur over relatively shorter time spans such as during crises. All four case studies revolve around more or less important crises that pose a potential, if not always actual, threat to state governance. The empirical analysis therefore focuses solely on radical changes in the scope of collective intentionality during crises of a relatively short duration.

Measuring changes in the scope of collective intentionality is a tricky enterprise, however. Group leaders and other politically influential actors can easily use their power positions and influence within the state and society to "deceive" the observer through self-serving statements, discourses, and practices. The ideal would be to conduct a widespread probe of the system of collective belief of as many members as one can, and then infer from that what is collectively held constant or changes. However, since the focus is on collective and not individual beliefs, there are other ways, though more indirect, to trace changes in collective intentionality. I thus use public discourses by leaders, intellectuals, activists, writers, religious and cultural establishments, and members at large. I also rely on popular literature and poetry, educational curricula, and communal commemorations and rituals, and on voting polls when available. This approach does not necessarily ignore the possibility of dissenting members or members who might support the same collective belief for different reasons. This is not a problem because collective beliefs are just like social norms. Deviant behavior does not invalidate a norm. It might, in fact, indirectly reinforce the norm (Wrong 1994, 37–69). If a norm were never challenged, it might go unnoticed and become taken for granted, to a point where people might even forget that a particular norm exists.

Moreover, collectively enacting a norm does not necessarily imply that every individual within the collectivity believes in the norm. It means that the members are socially constrained to abide by the norm. It could also mean that the field of action is constituted by the norm in such a way that acting otherwise is either socially "unthinkable"—beyond socially allowed options—or very costly, or both. Similarly, probing for collective beliefs does not imply that every communal group has to hold these beliefs. Nor does it imply that only those public proclamations believed to be genuine personal beliefs count as evidence. Collective beliefs are held by many members, and hence a good (if not the best) way to probe changes in collective beliefs is to process-trace how they are socially upheld and challenged. This is what the case studies do.

# Three

# A Theory of Debating State Governance

This chapter develops the theory of the book at length. The theory is designed to be applicable in a variety of circumstances of state transformation under changing international conditions. The chapter concludes with a discussion of the research design. The argument of the book draws upon insights from the social-constructivist school at both the intercommunal and international levels.[1] As explained in the previous chapter, state governance is in effect a never-ending process of negotiating and renegotiating the rules and practices that define and organize the domestic political space. In negotiating the form of state governance, the polity—political leaders and subjects of the state—may produce either a collapsed state or a form of state governance that lies on a continuum of possibilities characterized by differing degrees of consolidation. The latter is defined by the scope of collective intentionality, which is a function of three primary factors: intercommunal vulnerability, trust, and distribution of institutional power. All three factors are necessary elements of a complete explanation of governance transformation in multi-communal states.

The logic of the argument is as follows. Fundamental changes in the international environment induce domestic political debates about the system of state governance. These debates threaten to destabilize the intercommunal status quo as well as state-group relations. Hence some (if not all) communal groups might feel (or fear becoming) too vulnerable to others. Intercommunal vulnerability increases as the existing form of state governance comes increasingly into question. To address this vulnerability, the debating communal groups can use two devices (alone or in tandem), namely, intercommunal trust and institutional power. Intercommunal trust reduces the negative effects of intercommunal vulnerability because the debating groups expect a mutual behavior based on "goodwill" and communicative persuasion. Institutional power enables the beholder to address intergroup vulnerability in one of two ways, which are both to the advantage of the dominant actor: (1) coercion leading to capitulation of the subordinate actors to the dominant one or (2) manipulation of the debates. Although intercommunal trust and institutional power can both be effective in addressing intercommunal vulnerability, they shape the intercommunal debates in opposite directions. A greater reliance on institutional power arguably correlates with a lesser reliance on mutual trust, whereas a lesser reliance on institutional power correlates with a greater reliance on mutual trust. Together, intercommunal vulnerability, trust, and distribution of institutional power interact to determine, first, whether changes in political arrangements will result in state collapse or consolidation, and, second, the degree of consolidation in the latter case. I explicate the various parts of this argument in this chapter. Any theory of political behavior makes a number of core assumptions that create limitations for the theory. Mine is no exception. A comprehensive presentation of the theory would remain impaired without explicitly addressing the most important assumptions and limitations of the theory. Being clear about the assumptions and limitations of a theory can only improve its value to explaining the phenomenon at hand.

## Assumptions and Limitations

In developing the theory, I make several assumptions. First, politicized communal groups not only are motivated by self-interest in coacting with other groups, but are also interdependent on, and mutually susceptible to, other actors (Arfi 2000). One actor often depends on the support and participation of others in achieving its self-motivated goals. The actors (i.e., groups and their leaders and members) do act purposively to achieve their goals. Yet both their choice-sets and the processes through which these purposes form and evolve are "social" in character. The goals partially emerge during the process of social interaction—collectively formed, confirmed, disconfirmed, or changed. In other words, the contents and issues of intercommunal debates on state governance are always social, in-process, and emergent. The actors have the ability to be forward-looking, that is, to anticipate their mutual reactions to each other's actions. They hence endeavor to ground their own decisions and choices in such expectations. Yet they inherently face emerging elements of social contingency during their mutual interactions. In short, I posit the social-constructivist assumption that groups' preferences and leaders' strategies endogenously emerge, or at least change, in the interaction milieu during the debates. No single group has sole control over the issues, preferences, and strategies of the debates on state governance. Issues, preferences, and strategies are socially constructed during the debates.

Second, intercommunal politics during the debates drive domestic politics. The major politicized communal groups possess concrete organizations that constitute the main protagonists in the collective debates on state governance. I assume that the leaders of these concrete organizations speak for their respective politicized communal groups. That intercommunal politics drive the debates is a consequence of the deeply divided character of the society, which infuses the political process for two reasons. First, the collective understandings that underpin the political process are rooted in communal politics (Horowitz 1985; Esman 1994; Mozaffar 1995). Hence, communal elites can easily frame political issues in communal terms and resort to enlisting the support of their communal fellows. That is, the elites may focus on intercommunal relations for instrumental reasons such as preserving their leadership roles or as a way to fend off in-group challengers. The elites may also focus on intercommunal relations because they genuinely perceive a threat to, or an opportunity for, their community. This then calls for and facilitates the enlisting of communal support. Second, debating the constitutive rules and practices entails a challenge to the intercommunal status quo, which the existing governance system helps to define, organize, and perpetuate. Because intercommunal status quo is at stake, communal elites frame the issues in communal terms.

That the major politicized communal groups possess concrete organizations that constitute the main protagonists is a common feature of deeply divided societies (Esman 1994; Horowitz 1985). However, making this assumption does not imply that dissent within communal groups is irrelevant, or that each communal group is supposed to rally around one organization. In many cases, intercommunal competition takes place precisely through the emergence of multiple organizations, each claiming to speak for the communal group, or at least an important fraction of it. The African National Congress, the Inkatha Freedom Party, and the PAC-AZAPO (a coalition between the Pan Africanist Congress and the Azanian Peoples Liberation Organization) were different organizations that emerged and often competed with one another within the African community in South Africa. In the empirical assessment, I thus focus on the major organization representing a communal group, and when relevant for the analysis I do consider additional organizations that compete, or claim to represent different factions, within the same communal group.

An additional complication occurs in the analysis when the leadership becomes multiple and divided as elites and challengers compete with one another for positions, group ideology, agenda setting, goals, strategies, and resources. However, I assume that the leaders are (more or less) the perfect agents for the communal group whenever it is plausible to do so. This would of course produce a highly stylized view of intra-communal relations, but it allows one to treat communal groups as more or less unitary actors. This assumption does not imply that *intra-communal* politics and debates are not important. It is important only for keeping the theoretical framework focused, since I do consider *intra-communal* debates and politics in the empirical assessment of the theory.

Third, leaders' strategies and decisions shape the behavior of their respective politicized communal groups and the collective behavior of the groups. The latter, in turn, shape the leaders' decisions and actions. Political leaders aim at creating and increasing their legitimate authority while competing with in-group challengers. However, these "brokers" of loyalty might entrap themselves in self-legitimating strategies that they use to rally the support of their respective communities. Even if the elite strategically manipulates its followers, the latter becomes a constraint on the elite's actions and strategies by framing the kind of appeal to which most group members would positively respond—leaders and followers become stuck in self-fulfilling prophecies.

Fourth, politicized communal groups and their leaders are acting within social structures that they produce and reproduce, and at times attempt to change. These social structures in turn define the agency of the groups and their respective leaders, as well as provide resources that become useful in the process of debating state governance (Giddens 1984, 1–40). This assumption is quite consequential. It underlines the claims that the outcomes of the debates on state governance are necessarily "collectively" (or socially) constructed and that *any attempt to reach an outcome of the debates is in fact the construction (or deconstruction) of collective intentionality.* The aggregation of preexisting preferences of individual groups does not determine the outcome. This implies that the problem is not one of incomplete information regarding each other's intentions. Rather, what crucially determines the form of state governance is how collectivized is the intentionality sustaining it—that is, the scope of collective intentionality.

Fifth, I do not "reify" state institutions. That is, I assume that members from one or more communal groups produce, maintain, and possibly change the institutions. Hence, communal politics and state institutions are mutually constitutive, and their fates are inextricably linked (Mozaffar 1995). In the case of the former Yugoslavia, ethnicity "was reinforced by a system of ethnic 'keys' within each republic which determined the distribution of certain positions by ethnic identity according to the proportion of each group in the republic's population. This political reification of ethnicity, along with the suppression of expressions of ethnic sentiment, combined to reinforce the historical construction of political identity in terms of ethnic identity, and made ethnic issues politically relevant when the political system opened up to include the wider population" (Gagnon 1994–95, 140–41).

These assumptions are important for the development of the theory but do pose important challenges for the empirical assessment of the argument. I address these difficulties more closely at the end of the chapter when I discuss the research design.

## Logic of Debating State Governance

In this section, I explicate the causal mechanisms through which the major politicized communal groups collectively construct the outcome of the process of transforming state governance. The outcome—characterized by a scope of collective intentionality—is principally a function of intercommunal vulnerability, trust, and distribution of institutional power.

### *Intercommunal Vulnerability*

Debating state governance, which is the basis of the sociopolitical order, including intercommunal relations, threatens to destabilize the intercommunal status quo as well as state-group relations. This creates a fear of intercommunal vulnerability, that is, the possibility of opening up opportunities for certain communal groups and not for others and of threatening certain communal groups and not others. In a deeply divided polity, politicized communal groups face three kinds of intercommunal vulnerability: abandonment, exploitation, and exclusion. A communal group fears being abandoned; that is, other politicized communal groups may shirk by formally or informally defecting from or abrogating prior intercommunal agreements and commitments. A politicized communal group fears exploitation when one (or more) dominant group takes advantage of it or designs the rules and practices of the political game to benefit the dominant groups. A politicized communal group also fears or faces exclusion from participating in the domestic political game of state governance.

Fears of intercommunal abandonment, exploitation, and exclusion can possibly emerge in "normal politics" but become much more important during the process of debating state governance. As the politicized communal groups begin to raise questions about and debate the existing form of state governance, existing collective intentionality becomes at stake. A high scope of collective intentionality means that the major politicized communal groups fully take for granted the constitutive rules and practices of state governance. This implies that they do not fear mutual abandonment, exploitation, or exclusion from the political space. It also means that they act as if they were sure that the game of state governance would remain the same, among the same actors, and with the same rules. Conversely, not fully taking the existing governance game for granted means that the politicized communal group faces a potential (if yet to be actual) threat of seeing their mutual commitment breached, being exploited, or being excluded from the game of governance. This in turn helps to erode the collective intentionality underpinning the system of governance itself. Hence, intercommunal vulnerability manifested as fears of abandonment, exploitation, or exclusion increases with decreases in the scope of collective intentionality.

The desire to reduce one's vulnerability motivates, shapes, and constrains the debates. The greater the level of vulnerability, the more likely the politicized communal groups would engage one another in debates about transforming or preserving state governance. Strong fears of vulnerability can thus have a paralyzing effect on the game of politics. Vulnerability arises from three mutually reinforcing sources: intercommunal information complexity, predictability, and strategic interdependence. In brief, as the complexity of intercommunal information increases, predictability decreases, and interdependence increases, some (if not all) communal groups become (or fear becoming) more or less vulnerable to one another. To understand the logic of this argument, we first need to discuss these three sources of vulnerability.

### INTERCOMMUNAL INFORMATION COMPLEXITY

During the political debates on state governance, a group might raise questions about the nature and amount of information that it has on the intentions and capabilities of other groups. Each group also faces the prospect that the information provided by other groups might be fraudulent or unreliable—other groups could be withholding information that might actually supply information about their true intentions and capabilities. Incomplete information on intentions and political capabilities and the possibility of misrepresenting this information can hence become major concerns during the debates on state governance. This creates what I call a problem of information complexity.

Demography and economic, symbolic, and other resources available to a group, as well as the group's capacity to organize effectively, determine its political capabilities (Esman 1994, 36).[2] However, information on these capabilities is not always available to other groups. More generally, intercommunal interactions often occur under a condition of incomplete information on each other's intentions and capabilities. Yet the communal groups are dependent on or forced to interact with one another. This makes information a constant concern for these groups, especially given the fact that gathering information on other groups is always costly and most often remains incomplete. The impact of incomplete information can be compounded by deliberate misrepresentation (or distortion) of private information about one's intentions and capabilities. Private information is anything known by one group but not the others. This includes a group's preferences about its specific policy objectives, as well as how cohesive the group is, or would be, when faced with a challenge. It also includes how group leaders would use their organizational power should the intercommunal relationship come to be at stake (Lake and

Rothchild 1998, 12–13). Incentives to misrepresent this kind of information occur in at least two situations because revealing true information might undercut a group's ability to realize its goals and protect its interests. First, misrepresentation occurs when interacting groups believe they can gain by bluffing. By exaggerating their strengths, minimizing their weaknesses, or misstating their preferences, groups seek to achieve favorable outcomes. Second, a group may refrain from revealing information necessary to reach a mutually satisfactory outcome if it fears becoming a victim of exploitation.

Hence, the problem of information complexity—incomplete information compounded by a misrepresentation of private information—is a major source of intercommunal uncertainty and shapes in important ways the emergence and evolution of vulnerability. Information complexity is low when the interacting groups do not attempt to misrepresent their intentions toward one another and honestly "display" and provide reliable and verifiable information on their respective capabilities. High information complexity occurs when intentions are opaque and groups cannot reliably estimate each other's capabilities. The less information on intentions and capabilities of other groups a group is able to collect, the more vulnerable it fears becoming. A resort to misrepresentation of private information, if believed to be occurring, can create a fear of vulnerability. Therefore, each group may begin to feel vulnerable because the information that it has on other groups is incomplete, and other groups might have distorted the disclosed information—that is, the higher the level of information complexity is, the more uncertainty this would create. The latter in turn makes the groups more liable to abandonment, exploitation, or exclusion from the political process.

#### INTERCOMMUNAL PREDICTABILITY

Communal groups and leaders do often possess some discretion over their decisions and behavior, despite being constrained by state power structures and institutional rules (and societal norms and expectations). One implication of this freedom is the possibility of frustrating each other's expectations for addressing concerns of mutual vulnerability through cooperation or conflict. Such contingencies cannot be completely resolved using available information on intentions and capabilities, however perfect the information might be. This is more so in times of political instability, when institutional constraints and mutual obligations could be at stake, such as during debates on state governance in deeply divided societies. Put differently, groups are concerned with assessing the reliability of today's intercommunal information as an indicator of their future strategic environment. I call this a problem of intercommunal predictability. This is an important issue because it shapes the credibility of intercommunal commitments. Communal groups cannot simply assume that commitments made to them today or in the past are, or will remain, credible under fluid conditions, such as during debates on state governance. The credibility of commitments depends on the reputation of the communal leaders making those commitments. It also depends on the confidence-building measures created between the groups such as institutions and procedures as well as within the communal groups themselves. The reputation of leaders and intergroup as well as intra-group confidence-building measures are useful sources of information on the level of intercommunal predictability.

One can generally hypothesize that intercommunal predictability depends on the balance of political power between the groups, their beliefs about their mutual intentions and likely behavior, and shared understandings about the groups' rights and responsibilities and political privileges. Two sorts of change would thus undermine intercommunal predictability in important ways. First, problems of intercommunal predictability would arise whenever the balance of intercommunal power shifts. As the influence of one side of the balance declines, previously held commitments become less reliable as a source of predicting each other's likely intentions and behavior. The less powerful group might fear that the more powerful group will use its power advantage in unpredictable ways. Second, uncertainty over previously shared understandings and beliefs about intercommunal relations can generate problems of predictability that are independent of changes in the intercommunal balance of power. Groups might begin to "interpret" situations differently, which would create unpredictability about their most likely mutual intentions and behavior. Interpreting situations differently potentially engenders different strategic responses and hence problematizes intercommunal predictability.

#### INTERCOMMUNAL STRATEGIC INTERDEPENDENCE

Even if the debating groups were to solve almost completely the problem of uncertainty coming from information complexity and attain a high degree of intercommunal predictability, this would not preclude the possibility of another element of uncertainty regarding intercommunal relations, namely, strategic interdependence. Communal groups become strategically interdependent when they mutually share control over the outcome of their interactions—the outcome of the debate depends on all, and the fates of all depend on the outcome of the debate.

How is strategic interdependence important to the debates? Groups engage in a process of debating state governance to adapt to a new international context. Adaptation to outside changes is, however, not sufficient to entice the groups to debate state governance; without a heightened sense of intercommunal interdependence, the groups may either reject any transformation of state governance or attempt to unilaterally deal with the challenge. Hence, the higher the sense of intercommunal interdependence among groups facing pressure to adapt state governance to international changes, the more likely they would be to seek to engage in a collective debate on whether and, if yes, how to transform state governance. Put differently, no group can "go it alone."

To summarize the argument up to this point, state governance is a never-ending process of negotiating and renegotiating the rules and practices that organize domestic politics. The result of the debates may be a consolidated form of state governance, a collapsed state, or some intermediate forms of state governance characterized by varying degrees of consolidation. The degree of consolidation is defined in terms of the scope of collective intentionality, that is, to what extent the polity takes the constitutive rules and practices of state governance for granted, as "the normal way of playing politics." Debating state governance forces the communal groups to consider the problems of information complexity, predictability, and strategic interdependence. These elements can vary across polities (and in time) and thus combine to create different levels of intercommunal vulnerability. To address this issue, the debating communal groups use one of two devices (individually or in tandem): intercommunal trust and institutional power. Intercommunal trust and institutional power shape the meanings of intercommunal information complexity and predictability and transform the uncertainty effects of strategic interdependence into a risk that the groups can more or less tolerate, as discussed next.

### *Intercommunal Trust*

Intercommunal trust exists as a shared belief among two or more actors who, in spite of having a degree of freedom to disappoint each other's expectations, do expect one another to act with "goodwill." Mutual trust is thus a situation wherein two or more actors are both mutually trustworthy and trusting. Trustworthiness is the attribute of a party who would choose to act with goodwill. Trust is the attribute of a party who believes that the partner will act with goodwill.

The following three propositions summarize the relationship between intercommunal trust and vulnerability. First, the more the groups debating state governance trust one another, the less these groups will fear abandonment. Second, the more the groups trust one another, the more they will reciprocate goodwill toward one another and hence refrain from exploiting one another. Third, the more these groups trust one another, the greater is the chance that they will not exclude one another from participating in the game of state governance. In sum, the higher the level of intercommunal trust, the lower will be the level of intercommunal vulnerability. Mutual trust solves the problem of intercommunal vulnerability—abandonment, exploitation, and exclusion—by reducing the uncertainty coming from the three sources of vulnerability, namely, information complexity, predictability, and interdependence.

First, mutual trust facilitates the emergence of shared meanings about intercommunal information and, hence, helps to resolve the issue, or at least diminish the adverse effects, of information complexity. The higher the level of mutual trust among the actors, the more these actors will expect reciprocated goodwill to be the basis for processing information, and the more they will act as if they did not face a problem of information complexity. Second, mutual trust shapes intercommunal predictability, since mutually trusting groups will refrain from opportunistic behavior and fulfill the mutual expectation of acting with goodwill. The more mutually trusting the groups are, the more mutually predictable their behavior toward each other will be.[3] Third, mutual trust transforms the uncertainty created by intercommunal interdependence into an *ex ante* tolerable risk. Mutual trust creates the expectation of reciprocated goodwill, which henceforth will create more or less *ex ante* assurance that the actors will not *ex post* "abuse" their mutual interdependence, but will rather act with goodwill toward one another. The higher the level of mutual trust becomes, the more tolerable this risk will be.

This discussion of trust is based on a key assumption underlying the rationale for using intercommunal trust to explain intergroup relations, which is that trust is a variable; that is, different groups under different conditions can bestow different levels of trust on one another. In other words, the level of intercommunal trust is socially constructed. To understand how this occurs, I next explicate how intercommunal trust arises through processes strongly shaped by a "structural lock-in." I first discuss this concept of structural lock-in and second analyze the processes through which intercommunal trust emerges and evolves.

### STRUCTURAL LOCK-IN

Structural lock-in stands for a symbiotic relationship, an "informal" and hard-to-surmount linkage, between state institutions and domestic social structures.[4] Stable and well-functioning state institutions create inertia to change and henceforth encourage domestic actors to adapt to the existing institutional environment. As put by North (1990, 99), "the increasing returns characteristic of an initial set of institutions will create organizations and interest groups with a stake in the existing constraints." Institutions encourage various social and political actors to make commitments drawing on the incentives and within the constraints created by existing institutions. Once such commitments are consolidated, the difficulty of exiting from these arrangments rises rapidly as the range of possible paths and outcomes narrows over time (Arthur 1994; Pierson 2000). The further into a process the actors are, the harder it becomes to move collectively from the current path to another.

In Lebanon, the structure of sectarian cleavages (Maronite, Sunni, Shiite, Druze, etc.), the fabric of sectarian memories, and the constitutional arrangements of the French mandate period (1920–43) combined to produce a structural lock-in. The latter became encapsulated in the so-called 1943 National Pact (al Mithaq al Watani), the effects of which shaped the Lebanese polity for decades. The National Pact revolved around four principles. First, Lebanon is a completely independent state. The Christian communities should primarily identify with Lebanon, not with the West. The Muslim communities should protect the independence of Lebanon and prevent its merger with any Arab state. Second, Arab Lebanon should preserve its spiritual and intellectual ties with the West. Third, Lebanon, as a member of the family of Arab states, should cooperate with the other Arab states, and in case of conflict among them, it should not side with one state against another. Fourth, public offices should be distributed proportionally among the recognized religious groups, but preference should be given to competence without regard to confessional considerations in technical positions.

In socialist Yugoslavia, the Tito regime decided to adapt the Soviet 1936 solution to the nationalities problem to the Yugoslav context by designing the new political system as a federation that would reconcile the communist ideal and the realities of the national question. The combination of the realities of the national question and the constitutional and institutional solutions to it became a structural lock-in that shaped the evolution of state governance in socialist Yugoslavia in the aftermath of the war of national liberation. The lock-in reinforced the importance of nationalities below the federal level in the day-to-day political practice both within and outside the Communist Party. Even though in the Politburo the policy of national proportional representation did not play a great role, Yugoslav federalism was severely constrained with the centralism that characterized the structure of the Communist Party itself. The party leadership, making its decisions in the Politburo, had to rely on a large bureaucracy with main sections that reached down to the republic and local levels. Yet the local party members were still largely provincial in their habits and approach to the national question, in spite of being loyal to the party leadership and to the larger aims of the Communist movement. The dichotomy created many distortions in regions of mixed nationality, reflecting local prejudices, the strong resistance of certain groups to participating in the system, or both.

As the Lebanese and Yugoslav cases illustrate, structural lock-in takes different forms depending on the peculiarities of each society, that is, depending on the social structures that emerge, or become politicized, in response to institutional incentives and constraints. Two types of social-structural organization are particularly important in the case of multi-communal societies —salient historical memories and the structure of communal cleavages. These two elements in combination with state institutional arrangements engender a structural lock-in, which, if consolidated, in turn strongly shapes the social construction of intercommunal trust. In the following section, I introduce each of these elements.

*Salient Collective Memories*

As widely recognized in the literature on ethnicity and nationalism, collective memory plays an important role in the definition of communal groups as well as intercommunal relations. Collective memory is a shared recollection and interpretation (or reinterpretation) of historical experiences (Halbwachs 1992; Pennebaker 1997; Hosking and Schöpflin 1997). It originates in the works of poets, narrators, writers, politicians, historians, and most powerfully in the oral and written stories and legends of common peoples handed down through generations. Holiday celebrations, festivals, monuments, memorials, songs, stories, plays, and educational texts all continuously compete or concur with scholarly appraisals of the past in constructing collective memory (Carr 1961; Collingwood 1956; Lewis 1975; Connerton 1994; Gillis 1994; Ram 2000). Each act of commemoration is an opportunity for introducing new interpretations of the past, yet the recurrence of commemorative performances also contributes to an overall sense of continuity of the community (Anderson 1992; Connerton 1994). This makes ideologically motivated and mediated reexamination of history a common practice among politicians and intellectuals seeking historical legitimacy (Davis and Gavrielides 1991; Dawisha and Parrot 1994; Starr 1994; Ram 2000). Even in day-to-day activities, decision makers resort to a reexamination of history when faced by unanticipated circumstances to find affinities with or seek moral support and justification from past circumstances and events (Lowenthal 1985; Neustadt and May 1986; Mosse 1990; Gillis 1994; Reiter 1996; Lewis 1975; Streich 2002; Derderian 2002; Lambrose 2002). These collective notions of the past help to form the values that shape people's views on, and consent to, prevailing or changing intergroup and group-state relations.

By using collective memory as an explanatory variable, I am attempting to capture the extent to which widely held notions of the past (and interpretations thereof) come to shape the parameters within which intergroup and group-state relations are defined, anchored, or challenged. Because collective memory is inescapably interpretive, differences of interpretation of it are inherent even in societies with high degrees of homogeneity. Hence, it is not surprising that in deeply divided societies collective memory becomes a battleground for interethnic politics.

Salient collective memories can become strong determinants of intergroup and group-state relations when translated into political myths. Leaders and followers would use these political myths to challenge or reinforce prevailing collective meanings that underpin intergroup and group-state relations. The elites imbue the political myths with a quality of "oughtness" by anchoring them in salient collective memories (or in interpretations thereof) of their respective communities. Such political myths become "a significant factor in conditioning the limits of the possible, in establishing the cognitive field and in underpinning the rule-boundedness which makes politics work" (Schöpflin 1997, 24). Communal collective memory becomes even more salient under conditions where existing shared meanings that underpin the polity face a serious challenge. This, as argued earlier, occurs when various domestic actors begin to question the constitutive rules and practices underpinning state governance. Under such conditions, communal collective memory would provide a source of symbolic discourse that might enhance a community's integrity and give communal leaders strong tools to achieve communal solidarity.[5] Through myths, "communication within the community is intensified, making it far simpler to transmit the messages" from the elites to group members and enhancing the trust between the two parties (Schöpflin 1997, 24).

### *The Structure of Communal Cleavages*

The structure of communal cleavages in a deeply divided society can assume a determining role in intergroup and group-state relations. For example, the segmentation of Bosnia-Herzegovina into regions with high concentrations of Muslims, Serbs, and Croats was quite strong (Ramet 1992a; Cohen 1995). The territorial distribution of communal groups played a major role in determining the fault lines in events that unfolded in the 1990s when Bosnia became the theater of communal cleansing among Serbs, Croats, and Muslims.

Extant literature on the impact of communal cleavages on intergroup relations is rather mixed. For example, more than two decades ago, Lijphart (1977) argued that communal territorial segmentation is a necessary condition for successful consociationalism because the resulting lack of direct intercommunal contact on a daily basis works to enhance each community's political solidarity. This would increase the leaders' autonomy and hence their ability to compromise with one another at no risk of losing the support of their respective constituencies. In contrast, Duchacek (1991, 31) argues that communally mixed regions have a potential "calming effect" in federal states. For Horowitz (1985, 574, 598), it is more likely that intra-communal elite competition would occur in territorially segmented multi-communal societies than not. The way that this competition evolves within the state institutions in turn shapes the potential for intercommunal elite cooperation. Should crosscutting cleavages occur, they would provide an incentive for intercommunal cooperation because such a pattern of divisions has the potential to foster intercommunal competition over non-communal issues. However, in cases where crosscutting cleavages are not effectively mobilized (or absent), intercommunal competition could turn into outbidding on communal issues, thereby limiting the freedom of the communal elite (including previously moderate ones), sometimes forcing it to capitalize on inflammatory intercommunal issues. Despite their differences, these and other works all agree that communal cleavages do, more often than not, shape intercommunal interactions both within and outside state institutions.

Moreover, the structures of communal cleavages and salient collective memories mutually reinforce one other. For example, when the structure of communal cleavages facilitates intra-communal outbidding, the outbidding entrepreneurs would use collective memory to create political myths that support their agenda. Collective memory would therefore become a battleground among communal outbidders (Kaufman 2001). Conversely, preserving the structure of communal cleavages also helps to keep the "vividness" of collective memories through various ways, such as communal holiday celebrations, commemorations, popular songs and poetry, and a variety of community-specific social, cultural, religious, and political rituals (Gagnon 1994–95).

### *State Institutional Arrangements*

Institutional arrangements shape both the impact of collective memory and the structure of communal cleavages on intergroup relations. Institutions empower actors with political, material, and both physical and symbolic resources (Mozaffar 1995). Multi-communality in Yugoslavia "was reinforced by a system of communal 'keys' within each republic which determined the distribution of certain positions by communal identity according to the proportion of each group in the republic's population. This political reification of communality, along with the suppression of expressions of communal sentiment, combined to reinforce the historical construction of political identity in terms of communal identity, and made communal issues politically relevant when the political system opened up to include the wider population" (Gagnon 1994–95, 140–41). Similarly, in Czechoslovakia the two major constituent nations—Czechs and Slovaks—were unable to definitively resolve their dispute about an institutional arrangement best suited for the state (Leff 1988). In view of their historical aspiration and struggle for political autonomy, if not statehood, the Slovaks would not be satisfied with any institutional arrangement that ipso facto did not facilitate achieving their self-styled historical goals (Kirschbaum 1995). The Slovaks did not rest until they achieved institutional parity with the Czechs after federalization of the communist regime in 1968–69. However, establishing institutional parity between the two nations consolidated even more the underlying division of the country into Czech and Slovak sub-polities and diminished the sociopolitical cohesion of the Czechoslovak polity as a whole. Establishing political communal parity "institutionalized" the binational character of the country. Slovak and Czech Parliaments became more representative of their respective nations, while the federal Parliament had to follow whatever Czech and Slovak leaders would agree on.

### EFFECTS OF STRUCTURAL LOCK-IN

Communal memories and the structure of ethnic cleavages in combination with state institutional arrangements engender a structural lock-in that has two important effects on the process of transforming state governance. First, the lock-in defines the social criteria of political success among domestic actors as well as selects potential candidates for political entrepreneurship and leadership. That is, because the legitimacy of political entrepreneurship is defined by the structural lock-in, potential entrepreneurs who would not want to be displaced or marginalized by eventual challengers consider only the kind of political agendas that fall within the parameters defined by the structural lock-in. Hence, the latter delimits the realm of feasible agendas that these entrepreneurs may opt for, if they want to retain their entrepreneurial roles and remain legitimate. For example, ethno-federalism is not only a structural lock-in wherein federal institutions become entangled with communal divisions so the federal divisions match very closely the communal ones. Ethno-federalism also selects only those leaders who are sensitive enough to its criteria for popular appeal and legitimation. In the former Soviet Union, federalism "distributed mobilizational resources such as entrepreneurial skills and means of communications in a manner that eventually shaped its incidence and agendas. . . . The politicization of communality has been the work of political entrepreneurs created by Soviet federalism" (Roeder 1991, 228–31). Put differently, the structural lock-in defines the agency of communal elites and entrepreneurs.

Second, the lock-in endows actors with political and organizational resources, since only those political entrepreneurs who are sensitive to the social criteria of success embodied in the structural lock-in are "selected in." To use a metaphor, a political entrepreneur is like a surfer who skillfully rides the ocean waves (that are transporting him or her) to execute spectacular maneuvers. The surfer would not be able to appear as defying the logic of gravity without effectively channeling the energy stored in the waves. Likewise, skilled political entrepreneurs know how to "surf" the society by "riding" the structural lock-in.

These two effects of structural lock-in are probabilistic only, not deterministic, in nature. Although the structural lock-in selects, empowers, or constrains the key political entrepreneurs and generally defines political practice in the polity, the political entrepreneurs still have some degree of freedom to build their mutual relationships within the contours of politics as shaped by the structural lock-in. This is a defining element of the social process of constructing (or deconstructing) intercommunal trust, as discussed next.

### SOCIAL (DE-)CONSTRUCTION OF INTERCOMMUNAL TRUST

These effects of structural lock-in determine in important ways the process of constructing (or deconstructing) intercommunal trust through three successive stages: (1) the construction of a set of political myths that fundamentally challenge the status quo relations with particular communal groups, (2) widespread internalization of these myths, and (3) a reciprocated confirmation of emerging intercommunal meanings and practices.

*Emergence of Political Myths*

As argued earlier, in a deeply divided society the constitutive rules and practices underpinning state governance reflect and, in turn, stabilize intercommunal relations. When the groups begin to question the viability of the current form of state governance, existing intercommunal relations become at stake, thereby prompting the groups to reevaluate intercommunal trust. This process of reassessing intercommunal trust divides the political and communal elites into two "ideal" categories of entrepreneurs: revisionist and conservative. Revisionist elites engage in a process of reevaluating the existing level of intercommunal trust, whereas conservative elites endeavor to reproduce and reinforce it.

To achieve their goals, revisionist political entrepreneurs and communal activists begin by constructing new or reviving old political myths that challenge the status quo of intergroup relations, group-state relations, or both—a politicization of salient collective memory (Edelman 1971; Kertzer 1988; Hosking and Schöflin 1997). Using these political myths, the revisionist elites increase their ability to present an alternative to the shared understandings underpinning the constitutive rules of the governance game. Put differently, the revisionist elites are challenging the collective intentionality that underpins state governance—promoting political myths has the potential to do precisely that. However, not every political myth can seriously threaten to destabilize the foundations of intercommunal trust. Only those political myths anchored in collective memories that are salient enough to acquire historical legitimacy would evoke emotional attachments and communal solidarity and sacrifice and hence become a serious challenge (Smith 1997, 56–58). Using self-styled selective criteria, the elite divides the group's history into major stages, reducing complex historical events to a set of images that are presented as core elements of the group's collective memory (Stein 1996). A reification of these images into political goals, that is, the apprehension of these images as if they were something other than human constructions, produces a set of political myths (Berger and Luckmann 1966, 89). The myths are powerful symbols through which the elite molds its group's understanding of the current conditions and rationalizes chosen goals, strategies, and courses of action (Bennett 1980, 168; Kaufman 2001). Using the political myths, the elite thus becomes able to describe the conditions of the community in such a way that causes and effects appear simple and remedies unambiguous (Edelman 1971, 83).

While both activists and political entrepreneurs participate in this process of constructing political myths, political entrepreneurs aim, in addition, at creating and preserving enough legitimate authority for themselves. The entrepreneurs use the political myths to simultaneously compete with other communal groups and defeat in-group challengers (Snyder and Ballentine 1996; Gagnon 1994–95). This process begins to unfold as "A political elite deploys myth in order to preserve its power by erecting barriers to comprehension, by stressing myth to ensure that its actions cannot be challenged because the means of making that challenge are not there. The very language of contest is made to seem unavailable as words acquire the very particular, constricted meanings with which myth invests them, and the range of understanding is greatly narrowed" (Schöflin 1997, 26). The political myths become a powerful framework that defines the kind of appeal to which most group members would positively respond. These "brokers" of political myths, however, entrap themselves in the very self-legitimating strategies that they use to rally the support of their respective communities. The political myths become constraints on the kind of strategies that the leaders could adopt to mobilize the masses or sustain the mobilization momentum. The relationship between leaders' strategies and collective memory is thus neither linear nor purely instrumental, but rather one of codependence.

### *Internalization of Political Myths*

The response of the group membership to the political myths determines how the communal elites evaluate their strategies. The revisionist elites would become more assertive and demanding in their bid to challenge the intercommunal status quo if their constituencies internalize the political myths. Political myth internalization occurs when group members accept and identify with the political myths. The vision and goals that the elite articulates would hence acquire a quality of "oughtness." The political myths become a collective framework (or lens) through which the communal group would conceive of its relations with other communal groups and as well as its conception of state governance. The political myths provide essential conceptual and analytical tools for collective acts, such as "we-think," of the communal group. However, constructing political myths through a manipulation of collective memory does not guarantee that the communal group will internalize them. Skillfully constructing political myths may be necessary, but it is insufficient to ensure their wide acceptance. Therefore, the communal elites have to induce their respective communities into internalizing the political myths. This can occur through various ways, some of which are ritualization, stereotyping, fear- or empathy-arousing discourses, ideological indoctrination, coercive inducement, and various combinations thereof as well.

Political myth internalization occurs through ritualization when group members accept the elite-promoted political myths through ritual practices or communally standardized and repetitive symbolic behaviors (Kertzer 1988, 57–101). Ritualization proceeds through a repetitive use of emotionally charged acts in symbolically significant locations at symbolically appropriate times (Bennett 1980). Demonstrations, rallies, collective commemorations, holiday celebrations, festivals, construction of monuments, memorials, songs, stories, and plays are different ways of ritualization. Rituals are powerful means of political myth internalization because they provide a way to tie together particular political myths and strong emotions.

Political myth internalization occurs through stereotyping and fear-arousing discourses when the elite generates or exaggerates real or potential threats to the group.[6] The elite would stress the importance of cohesion and unity to withstand these challenges and threats. The elite can even go as far as actually provoking a threat to the economic or physical survival of its own group to convince the group to "stick" together and discredit or eliminate any eventual internal opposition. In other words, the elites realize the very conditions that would self-fulfill their prophecies and hence vindicate their strategies. Conversely, the elite can not only highlight or exaggerate real or potential threats to a sense of common fate with the target group but also minimize the threats that this target group might constitute now or in the future. In this case, internalization of the political myths occurs through empathy-arousing discourses. The elite would also eliminate (or at least contain) any in-group challenge that could be interpreted as signals of belligerency by other communal groups.

The elite may also propagate an ideology that "normalizes" the political myths by increasing the cognitive appeal of the political myths to the community and making them appear "natural." In this scenario, political myth internalization occurs through ideological indoctrination. To this effect, the elite would use various educational and propaganda media such as schools, print media, television and radio broadcasting, conferences, and so on.

The elite could also use coercion to induce the group to adopt the political myths, both through incremental change and adjustment of their political values. Internalization of political myths hence would occur through coercive inducement. The elite can psychologically pressure the members of the community who closely identify with the elite to accept the political myths. The members would espouse the political myths in order to minimize cognitive dissonance between identifying with the elite while not espousing the political myths that the elite promotes. A search for cognitive consistency between identifying with the elite and preserving one's beliefs prompts the members to internalize the political myths. The greater the impact of dissonance on individual experiences, the stronger is the pressure to reduce it. Alternatively, if not concurrently, the elite can resort to other forms of coercive measures such as peer pressure, threat of being ostracized, economic deprivation, or physical punishment, depending on the circumstances and, more precisely, on the power structure within the community. The more coercive power the elite possesses, the more it will be inclined to use it, especially if it cannot propagate its political myths through less explicitly coercive mechanisms. However, too much coercion might backfire and lead to stiff resistance and opposition (Kuran 1995).

### *Routinization of Intercommunal Presentation*

As group members internalize the political myths in increasing numbers, the political entrepreneurs and communal activists thenceforth seek to mobilize large segments of their followers into rejecting the status quo and challenging existing intercommunal relations (Gurr 1993; Goodwin 1994). However, by doing so, the communal groups entice one another to imitate and learn from each other and reciprocate such practices. The construction/deconstruction of intercommunal trust crucially depends on this process of mutual emulation and representation across communal boundaries through recursively reciprocated practices (Perinbanayagam 1985, 9–10). Yet the process of reciprocating practices is neutral as to the kind of intercommunal relations that might result from it—mutual reciprocation can reinforce as well as undermine the status quo relations. The nature of the practices that are recursively reciprocated is what determines the level of intercommunal trust eventually constructed.

As argued earlier, intercommunal trust is a situation wherein two or more actors are both trustworthy and trusting. The level of trust is the combined result of both the level of trustworthiness of the "Other" and the level of one's readiness to be trusting. A high level of intercommunal trust would result if, and only if, there are high levels of both trustworthiness and trusting behavior. Therefore, intercommunal trust *decreases* if

1. the political myths anchored in salient communal collective memories (or interpretations thereof) entail conflicting political actions and positions across communal lines;
2. the communal groups demonize one another;
3. such a dynamic slowly becomes a routinized way to relate to the "Other" as untrustworthy and creates a self-image as untrusting.

Conversely, intercommunal trust *increases* if

1. the political myths anchored in salient collective memories (or interpretations thereof) entail cooperative political actions and positions across communal lines by, for example, positively highlighting shared values and historical experiences;

2. the communal groups praise one another and empathize with, as well as justify, each other's actions and positions;
3. this dynamic slowly becomes a routinized way to relate to the "Other" as trustworthy and creates a self-image as trusting.

This discussion implies that not every situation of intercommunal interaction is one of trust, or distrust, for that matter. Trust emerges between two interacting communal groups within three important facilitating conditions: strategic interdependence, *ex ante* agency, and *ex post* agency.

1. Trust emerges among strategically interdependent actors. Absent strategic interdependence, individual actors would have no need to trust one another (Lewis and Weigart 1985, 969). That is, actors develop mutual trust only if they are either attracted or constrained into recurrently interacting with one another and mutually codetermining the outcome of the interaction.
2. The actors have some discretion to avoid or engage in a potentially risky situation of trust—what I call *ex ante* agency. For example, there is no mutual trust in a state completely dominated by an oppressive communal group that does not leave much room of maneuver to the other groups. The subordinate groups do not have much freedom to be able *ex ante* not to interact with the dominant one, or even to shape the relationship in other ways.
3. Trust is a relationship among actors that have a degree of freedom to be able to "breach" the trust—what I call *ex post* agency. The groups would not have to expect each other to act with goodwill—to trust—if they cannot even entertain the thought of defection, or breaching each other's expectations.

Conditions 2 and 3 mean that actors have a degree of "free will." In a situation where the actors do not bestow much trust on one another, the actors might try to overcome the lack of trust not only by restricting the feasible set of alternatives *ex ante* open to others, but also by enlarging their own *ex post* option set. Conversely, for actors who do not enjoy a certain degree of "free will," trust becomes meaningless. Yet arguing that *ex ante* agency and *ex post* agency are two facilitating conditions of trust does not entail that trust would exist only in situations where there is a parity of institutional power among would-be trusting and trusted groups. Disparity in the distribution of institutional power can indeed impede the emergence of mutual trust due to a fear of exploitation of the weak by the strong. Conversely, the institutionally powerful group can also win the trust of the less powerful through strategies of self-restraint and gestures of assurances toward the weak. More generally, though, as argued next, institutional power and mutual trust are two complementary ways to address the strategic vulnerability that emerges within the debates on state governance.

*Institutional Power Leverage*

In all polities, including multi-communal ones, the distribution of institutional power is an important determinant of domestic politics. Institutions shape the interaction environment because the institutions constrain the groups' options, enhance their lot of opportunities and resources, or both. Hence, reliance on institutional power is another device that communal groups can use to address the problem of intercommunal vulnerability during the debates over state governance. Should an institutional power asymmetry exist among the groups, one (or more) of them might be tempted to use it to favorably shape the debates to its advantage. Institutional power would enable the beholder to address intergroup vulnerability in one of two ways (or a combination thereof): coercion leading to capitulation of the subordinate actors to the dominant one or manipulation of the debates by the institutionally empowered group.

In a process of *capitulation,* the dominant group controls the debates, for example, by setting the agenda and scope of the debates and by deciding on the list of participants in the debates. The dominant group seeks in effect to control the impact of intercommunal vulnerability on the unfolding debates. This would alienate the subordinate groups and enhance their fear of abandonment, exclusion, or exploitation by the dominant group. In these situations, reliance on institutional power during the debates inhibits the construction of collective intentionality, or at least produces a low scope of collective intentionality. Hence, the more the dominant group relies on its institutional power to control the debate, the lower the scope of collective intentionality will be.

In a process of *manipulation,* the dominant party distorts the debates to secure consent from the subordinate party. As long as the dominant group can "disguise" its true intentions, it can more or less secure the consent of the subordinate groups not to abandon it. Conversely, as long as this consent lasts, the subordinate groups will not fear exploitation by the dominant groups or exclusion from the debates. In this case, relying on institutional power does not directly translate into a low scope of collective intentionality. Yet the scope of collective intentionality would not reach a high level, for its basis is rather precarious. As long as the dominant group can distort the debates successfully, the subordinate groups will consent to participate in the construction of collective intentionality. This is a tenuous situation at best. It is not only the elites of different subordinate groups who are sensitive to the issue and might challenge the "cover-up" of the distortion. Intra-group outbidding might in addition force the debating elites from the subordinate groups to challenge the "sincerity" of the dominant group. This in turn might undermine the formation of collective intentionality or produce at best a low scope of collective intentionality.

In sum, reliance on institutional power is more likely to produce a low scope of collective intentionality. However, in the worst-case scenario it might even inhibit the emergence of collective intentionality in the first place. Therefore, although the debating groups can use both intercommunal trust and institutional power to address intercommunal vulnerability, these two devices shape the debates in opposite directions. Reliance on mutual trust economizes on the resort to the use of institutional power, since such a relationship would be constructed and sustained through a communicative process of mutual persuasion. Conversely, in situations shaped by institutional power, the dominant group manipulates or coerces the subordinate ones to accept its views, thereby making mutual persuasion either superfluous or irrelevant.

More generally, the effects of relying on intercommunal trust and institutional power are complementary. This is possible because the relationship between relying on power and relying on mutual trust is dynamic. A dominant group can use its institutional power to increase the level of mutual trust if the dominant group chooses strategies that would enhance its trustworthiness in the eyes of the subordinate groups. Were the subordinate groups to respond positively to such strategies, the result would be a higher level of mutual trust between dominant and subordinated group. Conversely, mutual trust would decrease or become irrelevant were the dominant group to rely more exclusively on its power and not attempt to embellish its trustworthiness in the eyes of the subordinate groups. The more the dominant group resorts to power, the less trustworthy it becomes for the subordinates, and the less trust there will be between dominant and subordinate groups. This in turn would prompt the dominant group to resort even more to power to safeguard its preferred kind of intercommunal relationship.

Alternatively, the subordinate groups could choose to "abuse" any "overture" made by the dominant group, thereby prompting the dominant group to become less trusting toward them. The more the subordinate groups behave untrustworthily, the more the dominant group will become untrusting toward them, and the more the dominant group will rely on its power to shape the intercommunal relations. Hence, for a given level of intercommunal vulnerability, the level of reliance on institutional power increases as the level of reliance on trust decreases, and vice versa. Figure 3.1 schematically summarizes the causal path along which the game of debating state governance unfolds.

## Outcomes of Debating State Governance

Intercommunal vulnerability, trust, and distribution of institutional power combine to determine whether the outcome of the debates over state governance will be a collapsed state or a consolidating state, and in the latter case, the degree of consolidation of state governance. None of the three explanatory variables—vulnerability, trust, and institutional power—can alone satisfacto-

Figure 3.1. The Process of Transforming State Governance

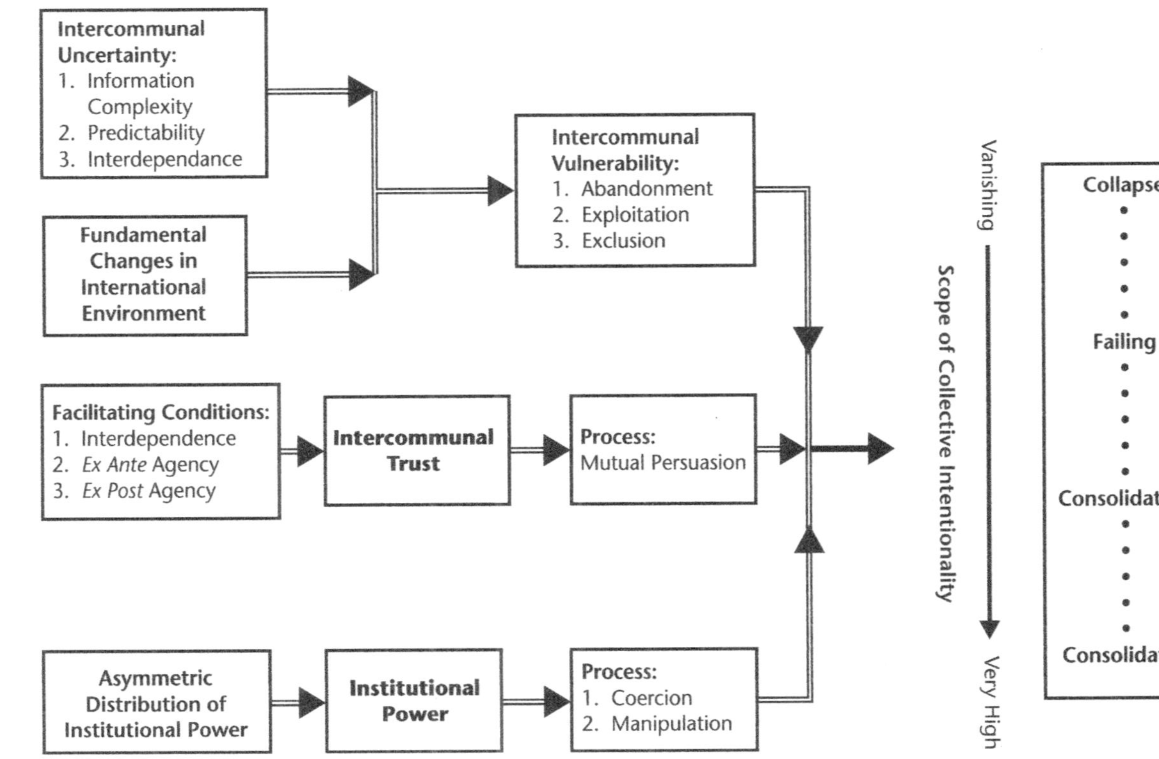

rily explain the outcomes of the negotiations about state governance. Moreover, the combination needs to be done in a consistent way because, as explained below, the three variables may under certain conditions reinforce each other's effects or may weaken each other's effects under different ones. For example, high intercommunal trust cannot exist concurrently with high reliance on institutional power. Likewise, low intercommunal vulnerability will not correlate with high reliance on institutional power. State governance will not consolidate enough if some communal groups fear to become too vulnerable to other groups that might use too much of their institutional power. In the following, I discuss how the three independent variables combine to produce a certain outcome of the intercommunal debates on state governance. I summarize the discussion along the way in a number of hypotheses to facilitate the testing of the theory.

### *Logic of the Game and Hypotheses*

The hypotheses are organized in such a way as to explore the different dimensions (variables) of the overall argument, first one by one, and then in pairs, both statically and dynamically. The overall organization of the hypotheses is thus a "blueprint" for the empirical parts of the book. One key element of the theory and subsequent empirical analyses is to consider the key variables—intercommunal vulnerability, trust, and institutional power—as dynamic. Not only is it important to establish whether each of these three variables is necessary to a satisfactory explanation of the outcomes of the debates. It is also equally important to explore how the rate and direction of change of each variable affect the overall outcome as well as the coevolution of the variables themselves.

More specifically, the empirical study needs to start first by looking at the intercommunal interdependence as the starting point of discussion; this is highlighted in hypothesis 1. Having explored the occurrence and degree of intercommunal interdependence, the next step is to look at the occurrence and degree of intercommunal vulnerability; hence, hypothesis 2. Exploring whether there is intercommunal vulnerability is important to understanding how the communal character of the polity shapes the debates over state transformation. However, this is insufficient since the responses of different communal groups to each other's strategies and actions also depend on how fast and in which direction intercommunal vulnerability changes; this is summarized in hypothesis 3. Having explored the nature and degree of intercommunal vulnerability leaves one with the important question of how the various communal groups would respond to it. As explained earlier, the groups would rely on one or two mechanisms, namely, intercommunal trust and institutional power. Hence, hypothesis 4 explores whether the groups would (or could) rely on intercommunal trust as a response to the perceived vulnerability. Again, how the rate and direction of this reliance on intercommunal trust change (either by increasing or decreasing) shapes the debate and might either reduce or increase the fear of intercommunal vulnerability. These two aspects of intercommunal trust are summarized in hypotheses 4 and 5. The following three hypotheses (6, 7, and 8) explore how institutional power shapes the groups' responses to perceived intercommunal vulnerability. As in the case of trust, looking at whether institutional power is used is an important explanatory factor but is insufficient if considered alone. Both the rate and direction of change of this reliance on institutional power are important factors to understanding how the debates evolve. Having explored the two variables—institutional power and trust—in "isolation," hypothesis 9 explicitly looks at their mutual relationship since these two mechanisms can produce the same result, as discussed earlier. This kind of exercise is very important for the empirical testing of the theory, as one needs to be able to delineate as clearly and sharply as possible the effects of both variables in "isolation" as well as in tandem. The final hypothesis (10) summarizes basically the overall argument by looking at how the rates of changes in relying on institutional power and intercommunal trust combine to shape the final outcome of the debates. In the following, I discuss the logic of these hypotheses one by one.

To begin with, communal groups engage in a process of debating state governance to confront the challenge posed by the fundamental changes that have occurred in the international environment. The latter is, however, not a sufficient reason to entice the groups to begin a debate on whether to transform the existing form of state governance. Without a heightened sense of intercommunal interdependence—that is, a strong sense that they share control over their fates—the communal groups may individually opt for unilateral exit policies. Alternatively, the strongest groups may attempt and could succeed in forcing a preservation of the existing form of state governance. Hence:

*Hypothesis 1: Role of intercommunal interdependence*

> The greater the sense of intercommunal interdependence among the politicized communal groups, the more likely it is that they will seek to debate the existing form of state governance to deal with the fundamental changes occurring in the international environment.

During the process of exploring the possibility of whether to debate the existing form of state governance, the groups fear or face a potential of intercommunal vulnerability. As argued earlier, debating the existing status quo system of governance has the potential to make some, if not all, groups feel or fear to become vulnerable to abandonment, exclusion, or exploitation. Intercommunal vulnerability can vary from being low to high, depending on how information complexity and intercommunal predictability combine to "soften" or "magnify" the effects of interdependence. Thus, the groups weigh contributing to a debate over the existing form of state governance against the vulnerability that could ensue from the very process of debate itself. The groups would be more reluctant to engage in a debate if they fear to become too vulnerable. Hence:

*Hypothesis 2: Role of intercommunal vulnerability*

> The greater the expected intercommunal vulnerability among the politicized communal groups, the less likely they will be to engage one another in debates about the existing form of state governance to deal with the fundamental changes occurring in the international environment.

Intercommunal vulnerability might change when the groups begin to debate the existing form of state governance. Vulnerability might increase or decrease depending on the existing scope of collective intentionality in the polity, that is, on the extent to which the debating groups continue to abide by the existing constitutive rules and practices of state governance in addressing the challenges coming from the international environment. The less likely it is that any one particular group would seek to exploit, abandon, or exclude the others, the more the existing rules and practices of state governance would be taken for granted, and the more consolidated state governance would be. The expected vulnerability thus would rapidly decrease with increases in the degree of consolidation of state governance. Hence:

*Hypothesis 3: Rate of change in intercommunal vulnerability*

> The more rapidly the expected vulnerability declines with the scope of collective intentionality, the more likely the politicized communal groups are to construct a form of state governance with a higher degree of consolidation.

Faced with vulnerability, the groups can alternatively rely on mutual trust, institutional power, or both to shape the debate. Mutual trust emerges and develops through mutual persuasion about reciprocated goodwill. This facilitates the construction of a strong sense of "we-ness" among the various debating groups. Thus, the more these groups trust one another, the more likely they are to opt to participate in an intercommunal debate on state governance. Hence:

*Hypothesis 4: Role of intercommunal trust*

> The higher the intercommunal trust among the politicized communal groups, the more willing they will be to participate in a debate on the existing form of state governance as a response to the fundamental changes occurring in the international environment.

As the groups begin the process of debate, the scope of collective intentionality might increase or decrease, which implies that the degree of consolidation of state governance might accordingly increase or decrease. However, the more the groups trust one another (i.e., the more the debating groups act with goodwill toward one another), the more likely it is that they will not seek to exploit, abandon, or exclude one another from the process of debating the existing form of state governance. That is, an increase in mutual trust decreases intercommunal vulnerability, which then reinforces the collective intentionality underpinning the constitutive rules of state governance. A reinforced collective intentionality then would mean a consolidation of state governance. In other words, rapidly increasing intercommunal trust thus correlates with higher degrees of consolidation of state governance. Hence:

*Hypothesis 5: Rate and direction of change in intercommunal trust*

> The more rapidly intercommunal trust increases, the more likely the communal groups are to construct a form of state governance with a higher degree of consolidation.

However, should an institutional power asymmetry exist among the debating groups, one (or more) of them might be tempted to use it to favorably shape the debates. They do so by either controlling or distorting the process of debate on state governance. The larger the disparity of institutional power is, the more likely the dominant group is to rely on its institutional power to control or distort the process of debate. The subordinate groups will contribute to the debate either because the powerful group coerces the weaker into capitulation, or because the dominant group manipulates the process to make it look as if the dominant group is playing a fair game of debate. In both cases, the outcome is not the result of reciprocated expectations of goodwill, but rather the result of institutional power that seeks to protect the interests of the dominant group, first, and those of the subordinate groups, second. The dominant group can opt for one of two strategies. It might attempt to prevent a debate on state governance from occurring in the first place by forcing on the subordinate groups the existing form of state governance and resisting any move toward any challenges thereto. Alternatively, the dominant group might accept to debate the form of state governance but then would rely on its institutional power to address any fear of intercommunal vulnerability to its liking. Hence:

*Hypothesis 6: Role of institutional power*

> The stronger the institutional power of the dominant group, the less likely the dominant group will be to seek to transform state governance to deal with the fundamental changes occurring in the international environment.

*Hypothesis 7: Intercommunal vulnerability and institutional power*

> In the event that the dominant group accepts to debate state governance, the greater the expected intercommunal vulnerability, the more likely the dominant group is to rely on institutional power to shape the outcome of the debates.

In the event that the dominant group accepts to debate state governance, the debating groups still need to address the question of what degree of consolidation of state governance they will be able to construct. As the groups begin to debate the existing form of state governance, the more the dominant group relies on its institutional power, the harder it becomes to achieve a high scope of collective intentionality. This means that the more the dominant group seeks to control or distort the debate and thus exploit, abandon, or exclude the subordinate groups, the less consolidated state governance will be. A rapidly increasing reliance on institutional power thus would lead to a decreasing degree of consolidation of state governance with a lower scope of collective intentionality. Thus:

*Hypothesis 8: Rate and direction of change in institutional power*

> The more rapidly the reliance on institutional power among the politicized communal groups increases, the more likely they are to construct a form of state governance with a lower degree of consolidation.

Having said this, intercommunal vulnerability, trust, and distribution of institutional power are all necessary; none alone is sufficient to explain the construction of a given scope of collective intentionality. It is thus important to explore how the two variables "intercommunal trust" and "reliance on institutional power" combine at any given level of vulnerability. As discussed earlier, mutual trust and institutional power can functionally be equivalent. Each can reduce information complexity, increase intercommunal predictability, and transform the uncertainty effects of strategic interdependence into a tolerable risk. However, trust and institutional power shape the intercommunal relationship in opposite directions. Intercommunal trust economizes on the resort to power since such an intercommunal relationship would be constructed and sustained through a communicative process of mutual persuasion. Conversely, in situations shaped by institutional power, the dominant group manipulates or coerces the subordinate groups to accept its views, thereby making mutual persuasion either marginal or even irrelevant. A greater reliance on institutional power correlates with a weaker intercommunal trust, whereas a lesser reliance on power correlates with a greater intercommunal trust. A strong reliance on institutional power would be expected to weaken the possibility or feasibility of intercommunal trust since it would undermine any recourse to (or usefulness of) mutual persuasion. Hence:

*Hypothesis 9: Intercommunal trust versus institutional power*

> The higher intercommunal trust is, the less likely it is that the politicized communal groups will rely on institutional power, and vice versa.

Combining the effects of *intercommunal trust and institutional power* on *the scope of collective intentionality* leads to one additional hypothesis. The reliance on institutional power for a given level of vulnerability depends on the ability of the dominant group to either coerce or manipulate the debates at the expense of the subordinate groups. This ability is in turn a function of the level of trust between the dominant and subordinate groups. The more rapidly the reliance on institutional power increases, the lower the scope of collective intentionality will be. Because the dominant group is relying on its institutional power, it can either coerce the subordinate groups to capitulate to its choices or manipulate the debates to protect its needs and interests. Hence, the dominant group will not depend on or seek much consent from the subordinate groups. Nor will the latter consent to the dominant group, for they do not have much influence on the debates anyway. Conversely, a stronger trust between the groups will generate a high level of consent because mutual trust develops through a communicative process of mutual persuasion. Hence, combining this discussion with that leading to hypothesis 9 leads to the last hypothesis:

*Hypothesis 10: Combined effect of institutional power and intercommunal trust*

> The more rapidly the reliance on institutional power increases (decreases), the more rapidly intercommunal trust decreases (increases), and the more rapidly the scope of collective intentionality decreases (increases).

Although these hypotheses are stated in comparative static terms, the collective construction of a form of state governance (defined by the scope of collective intentionality) is the result of the combined effects of the three independent variables.

Table 3.1 outlines the conditions under which four "ideal" types of state governance—collapsed, failing, consolidating, and consolidated—are most likely to occur. Collapsed state governance corresponds to high vulnerability, very low trust, and high reliance on institutional power. The groups unilaterally "opt" for the exit option even if they do face a condition of strategic interdependence. Because the dominant groups rely heavily on their institutional power, debating the existing form of state governance ends up eroding the existing scope of collective intentionality. This would occur because the subordinate groups would not trust the dominant ones, as the latter are relying heavily on their power. The dominant groups in turn would not feel a

**Table 3.1. Outcomes of the Process of State Transformation**

| | *SCI* | *Outcome* | *Most Likely When* |
|---|---|---|---|
| Scope of Collective Intentionality (SCI) | Nil | Collapsed | • Very high intercommunal vulnerability<br>• Very strong reliance on institutional power<br>• Very low intercommunal trust |
| | Rapidly Vanishing | Rapidly Failing | • High intercommunal vulnerability, rising rapidly with a decline in scope of collective intentionality<br>• Strong reliance on institutional power, rising rapidly with a decline in scope of collective intentionality<br>• Low intercommunal trust, falling rapidly with a decline in scope of collective intentionality |
| | Decreasing | Moderately Failing | • Moderate intercommunal vulnerability, rising moderately with a decline in scope of collective intentionality<br>• Moderate reliance on institutional power, rising moderately with a decline in scope of collective intentionality<br>• Moderate intercommunal trust, falling moderately with a decline in scope of collective intentionality |
| | Increasing | Moderately Consolidating | • Moderate intercommunal vulnerability, falling moderately with an increase in scope of collective intentionality<br>• Moderate reliance on institutional power, falling moderately with an increase in scope of collective intentionality<br>• Moderate intercommunal trust, rising moderately with an increase in scope of collective intentionality |
| | Rapidly Increasing | Rapidly Consolidating | • Low intercommunal vulnerability, falling rapidly with an increase in scope of collective intentionality<br>• Weak reliance on institutional power, falling rapidly with an increase in scope of collective intentionality<br>• High intercommunal trust, rising rapidly with an increase in scope of collective intentionality |
| | Very High | Consolidated | • Very low intercommunal vulnerability<br>• Very weak reliance on institutional power<br>• Very high intercommunal trust |

need to trust the subordinate groups. Nor would the dominant groups believe it possible to trust the subordinate groups anyway. The lack of mutual trust would not only undermine the legitimacy of existing rules and practices of state governance. It would also prevent the emergence of any new collective intentionality, without which state governance cannot exist.

In a consolidated state, the fates of the communal groups are highly intertwined due to a very high level of strategic interdependence, but the level of intercommunal vulnerability is very low. Under such conditions, the groups can either trust one another or rely on institutional power to address intercommunal vulnerability. However, only a very weak reliance on institutional power combined with a very high intercommunal trust would lead to a very high scope of collective intentionality. Consolidated state governance thus corresponds to the combination of very low intercommunal vulnerability, very high intercommunal trust, and a very weak reliance on institutional power.

In between these two extremes lies a continuum of either failing or consolidating forms of state governance. State governance would be failing if the scope of collective intentionality declines as intercommunal vulnerability increases, reliance on institutional power increases, and intercommunal trust decreases. Conversely, state governance would be consolidating if the scope of collective intentionality rises as intercommunal vulnerability decreases, reliance on institutional power decreases, and intercommunal trust increases. Whether one obtains a failing state (corresponding to a decreasing scope of collective intentionality) or a consolidating state (corresponding to an increasing scope of collective intentionality) is thus determined by the direction of changes in the three variables—intercommunal vulnerability, trust, and reliance on institutional power. Moreover, one obtains a moderately or rapidly failing (consolidating) state depending on the pace of changes in the three key variables (as shown in table 3.1)

## Method and Evaluation

This book is an exercise in theory-driven analysis of four major crises that occurred in two deeply divided societies, two Yugoslav and two Lebanese cases. The principal criterion for evaluating the four cases is the ability of the theory to shed new light on the historical reality, to reveal new dimensions and causes, and to allow the reader to see events from a different standpoint. The theoretical framework was essentially developed before effectively undertaking its empirical evaluation. The cases and periods were chosen to ensure variation in the dependent variable—the outcome of the debates on state governance. It is important to highlight the fact that these cases were selected before collecting empirical data on the independent variables. Every effort has been made to avoid reasoning "backward" from the empirical data to the framework and hence adjusting the theoretical arguments to exactly fit the empirical discussion. Although this is important for the overall process of explanation, it can sometimes become self-fulfilling and become the source of a sense of a "good fit," which in effect is no more than a manipulation of both the data and theory to preempt potential negative reviewers' critiques. My overall strategy has been to keep the consistency and cogency as well as logic of the theoretical framework as tight as I could, even if the fit between empirical cases and theory is not as perfect as one would like it to be. For example, when estimating the value of intercommunal trust in the first Yugoslav case, I readily admit that the fit is not easy and it is hard to reliably estimate this independent variable in this specific case. I believe that it is important to report this part of the actual empirical analysis as part of clearly evaluating the weaknesses of one's work. For this reason, I decided to keep this empirical case in spite of this "weakness." However, when all the cases are taken together, the fit between empirical data and theoretical expectations (as discussed in the various empirical chapters and summarized in the conclusions chapter) provides confidence that the theory does indeed capture important aspects of the real world.

An appropriate assessment strategy (for this kind of theory-driven empirical exercise) is to examine the comparative static predictions (hypotheses 1–10) of the theory. This makes it possible to observe the direction and rate of change in the independent variables as well as probe the range of possible variation in the process of transforming state governance. Of course, this implicitly assumes that one is able to consider as well as fully explicate the counterfactual values of the dependent variable. Although this is a very difficult task, the cases should nonetheless contain enough evidence to identify the direction of change in the dependent variable and point toward the range of most likely outcomes. This is a problem inherent in any empirical testing enterprise that uses the case study method when the causal theories allow for variation in the dependent variable. A few case studies do not allow an exploration of a full range of variation in the dependent variable. The method does nevertheless allow an exploration of the plausibility level of theory. In each case, I look for evidence that would identify the direction and rate of change in the independent variables. I then predict the range of likely values of the dependent variable. This requires estimating the most likely, if unobservable, ranges of the independent variables. To minimize the bias of "self-fulfilling prophecies," I try to be as explicit as I can about how and why I draw the estimates of the independent variables that I do. In the following, I discuss how I measure the impact of change in the international environment on the constitutive rules of state governance. I also discuss how I measure changes in intercommunal vulnerability, trust, and distribution of institutional power. I have already presented the method of how to measure changes in the scope of collective intentionality in chapter 2.

*Measuring the Impact of Changes in the International Environment*

As discussed in chapter 2, the constitutive rules and practices of state governance are in effect a process of drawing analogies between past, present, and future situations through negotiation and renegotiation among relevant actors. Likewise, international politics is also a never-ending process of negotiating and renegotiating the constitutive rules and practices that define a system of international governance (Rosenau 1992, 4–7). For example, the emergence of the Cold War between the United States and the Soviet Union in 1947 meant major changes in the constitutive rules and practices of the international political-economic order, especially in Europe. The new order emerged through two elements. First, the international context had completely changed with the Allies' victory led by the conjoint efforts of the United States and the Soviet Union. The latter powers became de facto the two new main reorganizers of the post–World War II order. Second, each of the emerging superpowers had its own agenda on how to protect and promote its interests through the creation of a new world order thenceforth, slowly making it impossible to continue playing international politics according to the pre–World War II rules of the game. The two superpowers began to create new patterns of practices, with each of them attempting to justify its choices, contest the other's choices, and persuade the other to abandon its own vision. The Cold War was thus increasingly unfolding through the constitutive rule of postwar bloc politics that bounded the practice of politics throughout the international system (Koslowski and Kratochwil 1994, 232–33). This constitutive rule was rooted in the practice of communist conquest by subversion and by the United States practice of communism containment initially embodied in the Truman Doctrine and the Marshall Plan in 1947–50 (Leffler 1984; Gaddis 1987; Cohen 1993).

Although international politics is conventionally thought of as separate from domestic politics, these two realms are not hermetically sealed off from one another. The international context can shape states in one of at least two ways. First, it can have a regulative effect on states by providing opportunities for or constraining the power and scope of state institutions and practices of domestic politics or both (Gourevitch 1978; Finnemore and Sikkink 1998). This implies that the international environment is something like a "billiard table," constraining state behavior and policies internally and externally.

Second, the international context can play a constitutive role in the formation and functioning of state institutions and political practices (Jackson 1990; Finnemore 1996; Wendt 1999).[7] The international environment would in this case help to define and legitimize what counts as "normal politics" in domestic politics by contributing to the constitution of state institutions, policies, and practices. Once a state has opted for such an institutionalization track, which is strongly shaped and legitimated by the international context, "the costs of reverse are very high. There will be other choice points, but the entrenchments of certain institutional arrangements obstruct an easy reversal of the initial choice" (Levi 1997, 28). When the international context becomes part of the elements that legitimize and define the processes of institutionalization, the entrenchment is hard to reverse. What becomes legitimate state practice in domestic politics is then "inherently" dependent on the support provided by the international context.[8] Leaders and public alike would come to perceive the existing entrenchment with the international context as "normal." The international system can thus be a defining context of the constitutive rules and practices underpinning the state institutions. The constitutive rules and practices of the international system can be part of the context under which the constitutive rules and practices of the state institutions are defined, enacted, and legitimated.

Conversely, that domestic politics can have far-reaching consequences on the constitutive rules and practices of international politics is not surprising since states are very important actors of international politics. Great powers play a leading role in the construction as well as maintenance of the constitutive rules and practices of international politics. Hence, their domestic politics have far more impact on international politics than those of weaker states (Richter 1992; Koslowski and Kratochwil 1994; Hall 1999).

Fundamental changes in politics occur when the constitutive rules that underpin (international or domestic) politics change in one of two ways. First, changing the context, wherein a constitutive rule is enacted, would negate the constitutive character of the rule because constitutive rules are always contextual. Hence, fundamental changes in international politics can lead to major transformations in domestic politics, that is, a change in the constitutive rules and practices underpinning the state institutions. Changes in the constitutive rules and practices of the international context undermine the facticity and legitimacy of the state institutions, which would thereby become the object of domestic debates among various actors. Whether the existing institutions should continue to constitute the state as they have done so far in the absence of the previous international context becomes an overriding issue in the polity.

In 1948 Yugoslavia was the first country to break away from Stalin's monolithic communist bloc. The country subsequently maintained an independent international role that made it a prototypical postwar "nonaligned nation." Sustaining such an independent international role in the midst of the Cold War rivalry between the two superpowers made it imperative to reconstruct the Yugoslav political, economic, and ideological systems. This occurred during the period 1948–53, during which the Yugoslav state underwent an overall transformation away from the rigid Stalinist line that Tito and his comrades had opted for in the immediate aftermath of World War II. The effects of the new Yugoslav international role on the domestic arena continued well into the sixties and even seventies, becoming a constraint on Tito's attempts to address a variety of political and socioeconomic challenges in the late 1960s and early 1970s, and more so after Tito's demise in 1980.

Second, "collective intentionality" among relevant actors is the basis for constitutive rules. A change in collective intentionality thus entails a change in the constitutive rules because, as argued in chapter 2, collective intentionality creates, maintains, and negates constitutive rules.

To summarize, changes in the constitutive rules of state governance can have two sources: changes in the international context and changes in the collective intentionality within the polity itself. This implies that measuring the process of transformation of state governance amounts to measuring changes in the international context and changes in the collective intentionality. I have already discussed the method to measure changes in the scope of collective intentionality in chapter 2. Thus, I discuss in this section only how to measure changes in the international environment. I am interested only in fundamental changes in the international environment, that is, changes in the constitutive rules and practices of the international order.

Using the above discussion on constitutive rules of politics in tandem with that of chapter 2, I operationalize a constitutive rule using John Searle's (1995) definition, that is, *a constitutive rule typically has the form "X counts as Y in context C."* This can be recast less formally as *a constitutive rule stipulates that a generalized practice X takes the form or counts as a specific activity Y over a range of situations C.* In the specific example of the Cold War, we have a constitutive rule of the Cold War was that X [X = great power politics] took the form of Y [Y = bloc politics that bounded the practice of politics] throughout C [C = the post-1947 international system]. How paper money acquires the role that it does in the society is another good illustration of this way of operationalizing a constitutive rule. The constitutive rule assumes the form "Bills issued by the Bureau of Engraving and Printing (X) count as money (Y) in the United States (C)" (Searle 1995, 28). Paper money acquires the important economic role that it does as follows:

> Certain sorts of bits of paper are widely circulated in the United States. These pieces of paper satisfy certain conditions that constitute satisfying the X term. The pieces must have particular material ingredients, and they must match certain set of patterns (five dollar bill, ten dollar bill, etc.). They must also be issued by the Bureau of Engraving and Printing under the Authority of the US Treasury. Anything that satisfies these conditions (X term) counts as money, i.e., US paper currency (Y term). But to describe these bits of paper with the Y term "money" does more than provide a shorthand label for the features of the X term; it describes a new status, and that status, viz. money, has a set of functions attached to it, e.g., medium of exchange, store of value, etc. In

virtue of the constitutive rule, the paper counts as "legal tender for all debts public and private." And the imposition of this status function by the Y term has to be collectively recognized and accepted or the function will not be performed. (Searle 1995, 45–46)

Thus, a change in a constitutive rule would occur either when the rule loses its character as a generalized practice X, or when the context C of the rule changes so much that it is not possible to find a specific activity Y that would meaningfully represent or be a manifestation of the generalized practice X. Hence, to measure changes in the constitutive rules of international politics I ask the following two questions:

1. Is a given international constitutive rule not a generalized international practice anymore?
2. Did the context of the constitutive rule change in such a way that it does not allow for a meaningful representation of the generalized practice through a specific activity?

I answer these two questions by exploring the behavioral and discursive dimensions of constitutive rules (Klotz 1995, 27–33; Finnemore 1996, 23–24). The analysis specifically is done by process-tracing changes in patterns of state practices and discursive articulations such as justification, contestation, or persuasion that characterize a given constitutive rule.

Two "pure" types of change occur in this respect. On the one hand, a minor change in international constitutive rules would not threaten the validity of state governance. In this case, state governance can be adapted to the changes occurring in the external conditions (as opportunities or constraints). On the other hand, a fundamental change in international constitutive rules would mean a major challenge for state governance. Only an overhaul of the state institutional makeup could transform state governance to reconcile it with the new external environment. As argued in chapter 2, the adaptation or preservation of the constitutive rules and practices of the domestic political game occurs through a process of domestic political debates about state governance. These negotiations are particularly pronounced when a major external event (e.g., the end of the Cold War and the collapse of the Soviet Union, the collapse of the Ottoman Empire, the drop of the gold standard for monetary exchanges, a severe global economic recession) forces domestic actors to reconsider the suitability and legitimacy of a constitutive rule of state governance. The event or shock thus triggers intensified exchanges among domestic groups and individuals about the rules that constitute the game of domestic politics. Conversely, should a fundamental transformation of the constitutive rules and practices of international politics not lead to major debates about whether to adapt state governance to the external environment, such an instance would constitute a partial falsification of the theory.

One still faces the task of deciding which international constitutive rules are relevant for a given state. This is an empirical question that I answer by process-tracing the evolution of the state in question. To this effect, I consider the evolution (construction and transformation) of the most important institutions of the states under consideration such as the constitution, coercive institutions (e.g., the armed forces), political institutions (e.g., parliament, national assembly), economic institutions (e.g., the banking and fiscal system), and the legal system. The impact of international constitutive rules is explored by process-tracing how domestic actors respond to the international constitutive rules and practices when constructing and maintaining or transforming these state institutions—that is, how domestic actors adapt, transform, and attempt to reconcile the domestic rules and practices of state governance with the international constitutive rules and practices.

Domestic debates about a profound adaptation—radical transformation—of the rules of the domestic political game are expected to arise when there are fundamental changes in the international constitutive rules and practices that had helped to shape the building or consolidation of state governance in important ways. Conversely, when the international constitutive rules and practices did not strongly shape the construction or transformation of state governance, it is not expected that a serious need for adaptation of the domestic rules would arise. In this case, the international environment is effectively not part of the context that underpins and legitimates the domestic system of governance. Changes of this second kind of international rules and practices are not expected to produce a domestic debate about state governance. To sum up, the impact of international constitutive rules on state governance is probed in three consecutive steps:

1. Carry out a "constitutive" analysis to examine whether the constitutive rules of international politics have indeed shaped the construction or transformation of state governance. That is, the analysis should explore whether domestic coalitions of actors transformed the institutions of state governance to adapt them to the international constitutive rules.
2. Examine whether these international constitutive rules have changed over time. This is done by process-tracing the practices of a core set of states (and their agents) that have discretion over the creation, enactment, and transformation of these constitutive rules. In general, whether the state under study is one of these core states is an empirical question.
3. Having established that changes have occurred in the international constitutive rules, examine whether these changes have induced domestic debates on state governance and, if yes, how they shaped these debates.

*Measuring Intercommunal Vulnerability*

The level of intercommunal vulnerability is operationalized in terms of three elements: abandonment, exploitation, and exclusion. It is very low when the communal groups do not expect abandonment, exploitation, or exclusion from the debates on state governance. Increasing prospects of abandonment, exploitation, or exclusion augment the level of vulnerability. As discussed earlier, vulnerability arises from a combination of information complexity, predictability, and interdependence. Information complexity is operationalized in terms of intentions and capabilities. Information complexity is low when intentions are transparent to the "Other" to avoid misjudgments and capabilities are "displayed." Information complexity increases when information on intentions or capabilities becomes increasingly incomplete or misrepresented. High information complexity occurs when intentions are opaque and actors cannot reliably estimate each other's capabilities. The more information complexity confronts the politicized communal groups, the more vulnerable they become.

Predictability is operationalized in terms of the credibility of intercommunal commitments and transparency of intergroup processes of decision making. The credibility of intercommunal commitments depends on the reputation of the group leaders and agents making those commitments as well as on the confidence-building measures created between the groups. The ability to predict the nature of future contingencies also depends on the degree of transparency (or, conversely, opacity) of intergroup decision-making processes. The more transparent the intergroup processes of decision making are, the easier it is for other groups to understand how positions and decisions are formed, and hence to estimate more or less realistically the intentions and actions of the group in question. Intercommunal commitments and decision-making processes are mutually related, for the latter shape the leaders' ability to make intercommunal commitments, the difficulty (or easiness) of reversing those commitments, and the capability of groups to monitor each other's adherence to the commitments. Therefore, high predictability would correspond to very credible intercommunal commitments reinforced by transparent intergroup processes of decision making. Conversely, transparent processes of intergroup decision making are not a sufficient condition for intercommunal commitments to be credible or sustained.

Intercommunal interdependence occurs between groups when they share control over the outcome of their interaction. Interdependence varies with the level of mutual control over the outcomes of the interaction. Intercommunal vulnerability occurs only under conditions of strategic interdependence. Increases in strategic interdependence lead to increases in vulnerability. However, as argued earlier, strategic interdependence is a necessary but insufficient condition for intercommunal vulnerability to occur.

*Measuring Intercommunal Trust*

An important step in empirically probing the importance of mutual trust as an independent variable is to examine whether and to what extent the three facilitating conditions—strategic interdependence, *ex ante* agency, and *ex post* agency—discussed earlier in the chapter are present in the case studies.

Trust can be measured by process-tracing how it evolves through intercommunal interactions. The process of creating and maintaining, or deconstructing, trust is partly a problem of how a communal group successfully presents itself both as trustworthy and trusting. A group can do this by displaying a willingness to link more tightly its fate to the relationship with the other communal groups. Three sets of indicators help in tracing such processes.[9]

First, because trusting others is linking one's fate to theirs, identifying *intercommunal policies and actions that tie the fates* of the groups provides a measure of the extent to which the groups behave both trustworthily and trustingly toward one another. The more groups design their policies and actions to link their respective fates together, the higher should be the mutual trust. Also, the wider and more far-reaching the scope of these policies and actions is, the higher should be the level of mutual trust.

Second, because mutual trust is based on creating and communicating as well as sustaining shared meanings, an exploration of *the discursive explanations of the groups' positions* toward each other as well as *their mutual descriptions* provides another set of indicators on the level of trust among the groups. The more the groups explain and justify their mutual relations in terms of mutual trust, the more this indicates mutual trust between them. Likewise, the more the groups identify one another as trustworthy and trusting, the more this indicates the relevance of trust for their mutual relations.

Third, the type of *safeguard mechanisms* used by the groups to monitor compliance with mutual commitments also provides a set of indicators on the level of mutual trust. The more these safeguard mechanisms shift from being *ex ante* preemption to *ex post* detection of "breach of trust," the higher should be the level of mutual trust. In addition, the larger the scope of these safeguard mechanisms is, the more this would indicate the existence of mutual trust among the groups. Whereas context-specific mechanisms would indicate that the groups do not trust each other very much, broadly designed mechanisms are more consistent with relationships based on mutual trust.

*Measuring Reliance on Institutional Power*

Reliance on institutional power becomes important in situations where there is an asymmetry of institutional power among the communal groups. I use three indicators to measure reliance on institutional power. First, I look for the existence of an institutional power asymmetry. Second, I examine the role that this asymmetry in institutional power plays in the process of debating state governance. I hence examine whether, and the extent to which, the dominant group seeks to distort as well as control the process of debating state governance. Third, I examine how the dominant group seeks to divide the rights and obligations among the dominant and subordinate groups during the debates process.

Chapters 4 through 7 use these various assessment strategies to test the theory in two Yugoslav and two Lebanese case studies.

# PART II:

# CASE STUDIES

# Four

# Yugoslavia and the Emerging Cold War, 1947–53

During the period 1948–53, Yugoslavia fundamentally redefined its international role to become the first European communist country to split with the Soviet Union and remain independent from both sides of the Cold War. This occurred through a series of domestic debates that resulted in a major transformation of state governance. The debates were dominated not only by a concern of preserving its status as a communist state that is independent from the Soviet Union, but also by a concern that the form of state governance established during the few years after the war had to be radically transformed so soon. The new form of state governance eventually consolidated with a scope of collective intentionality that slowly increased after 1949, and more so after the formulation of the 1953 Constitutional Law. The period was a turning point in the history of the state, many effects of which were to become defining features of the Yugoslav polity. This outcome was the result of a combination of three mutually reinforcing elements. First, intercommunal vulnerability was low and somewhat increased as the national question began to reemerge in the late 1950s. Second, intercommunal trust was moderate and somewhat stagnated after the formulation of the 1953 Constitutional Law and as the national question began to reemerge in the late 1950s. Third, reliance on institutional power was low and somewhat decreased in the 1950s.

This and the three subsequent chapters begin by discussing the expectations of the theory developed in chapter 3 for each of the four case studies analyzed in the book. Each chapter then explores the role that changes in the international order played in the evolution of state governance during the relevant period. The next section evaluates the dependent variable, the degree of consolidation of state governance. In the remaining part of each chapter, I organize the analysis of the case study around the three key independent variables: vulnerability, trust, and institutional power.

### Theoretical Expectations

The emergence of the Cold War between the United States and the Soviet Union in 1947 signified major changes in the constitutive rules and practices of the international order, especially in Europe. The two superpowers began to create new patterns of practices, with each of them attempting to justify its choices, contest the other's choices, and persuade the other side to abandon its vision. The Cold War thenceforth developed into a rule of postwar bloc politics that increasingly bounded the practice of politics throughout the international system. These fundamental changes in international constitutive rules and practices induced Yugoslavia not only to seek a new international role. The new environment also induced domestic political debates about the form of state governance in socialist Yugoslavia that the communists had only recently established. The new international environment seriously undermined the collective intentionality that had underpinned the form of state governance established in the aftermath of the war—to maintain itself, the Tito regime had to reconstruct the collective intentionality underpinning socialist Yugoslavia.

Transforming state governance once again, which had yet to be fully consolidated only a few years after the end of the war of national liberation, threatened to revive the old national question, an issue the Tito regime was priding itself on having permanently resolved. The ethnic "understanding" reached in the immediate aftermath of the war was at stake. Yet when the period of radical transformation began after the 1948 split with Stalin, the constituent nations of Yugoslavia were interdependent enough to realize that it was in their common interest to remain united against the Soviets' subversive maneuvers. The theory outlined in chapter 3 suggests that for this case the outcome of the debates on state governance in the period 1948–53 is most likely to be a reconsolidation of state governance of the federation.

First, intercommunal vulnerability remained low during the period 1948–53, if somewhat increasing as the divisive national question began to reemerge in the late 1950s. Under these conditions, the major communal groups had no serious fear of intercommunal abandonment, exploitation, or exclusion from participating in the debates that transformed state governance. Low vulnerability was the result of low to moderate information complexity, moderate to high intercommunal predictability, and a heightened sense of intercommunal interdependence. Information complexity was low to moderate because, as primary participants in the Communist Party and other state organs, the major communal groups had more or less reliable information on each other's intentions and capabilities. Predictability was moderate to high since there was enough reliable intercommunal commitment to the communist arrangement. In contrast with the interethnic massacres that occurred during the war, a respite on the national question for the most part characterized the immediate aftermath of the war. After the war, most people were reluctant to revive the old national question. The Yugoslav Communist Party succeeded in turning the principles of national equality, respect for national differences, and an end to the exploitation of one nationality by another into basic rights. The postwar understanding did face a challenge when the members of the Cominform organization attempted to use the national question as a means for dividing the Yugoslav party in its support for Tito. Yet this effort failed in spite of the fact that in a number of cases the national issue played a role in motivating people to break with the Yugoslav party and defect to the Cominform side. Hence, a heightened sense of strategic interdependence among the major communal groups in the Yugoslav polity greatly strengthened the incentives for the Yugoslav communal groups to transform state governance in dealing with the fundamental changes occurring in the international environment (hypothesis 1). As the Yugoslav communists increasingly succeeded in surpassing the 1948 crisis, intercommunal vulnerability in the Yugoslav polity decreased with increases in the scope of collective intentionality in the polity, that is, as the communal groups increasingly took for granted the emerging rules and practices of state governance encapsulated eventually in the 1953 Constitutional Law (hypothesis 3).

Second, intercommunal trust increased significantly with the formulation of the 1953 Constitutional Law. The state was a federation with extensive decentralization and a right of political self-determination, including in principle the right of secession. This created a fear of mutual vulnerability—abandonment, exploitation, or exclusion—which helped the major communal groups realize that it was in their common interest to remain united against the Soviets' subversive maneuvers. The Yugoslav leaders understood that the intercommunal trust that had been emerging since the end of the war was an important device that they should use to preempt and prevent any increase in the level of vulnerability. In fact, intercommunal trust increased with the emergence of a new form of state governance, and the scope of collective intentionality increased during the post-1948 debates (hypothesis 5).

Third, the fear as well as the fact of Soviet subversive maneuvers induced the Tito regime to resort somewhat to coercion and a centralization of institutional power to preempt any possible overthrow of, or widespread dissension from, the regime. However, as the Soviet threat receded, the Yugoslav leaders slowly opted for a return to more devolution of institutional power across the intercommunal landscape. The regime reliance on institutional power henceforth was low and stagnated somewhat when the national question began to reemerge in the late 1950s. Therefore, overall reliance on institutional power decreased as intercommunal trust increased (hypothesis 9).

In sum, as the period ended with the formulation of the 1953 Constitutional Law, vulnerability remained low and decreased somewhat with increasing institutionalization of the stipulations of the Constitutional Law. Intercommunal trust was moderate and stagnated somewhat in the 1950s as the national question began to reemerge under the form of a national economic question. The Tito regime was also able to maintain a more or less even distribution of institutional power among the constituent nations, thereby not allowing institutional power to become a device through which the communal groups might attempt to address any concern about intercommunal vulnerability.

These estimated values of the three key variables—vulnerability, trust, and institutional power—are close to the "most likely conditions" for a moderately consolidating form of state governance with an increasing scope of collective intentionality, as explicated in table 3.1 (chapter 3). Hence, that the Yugoslav polity was able to reconsolidate its state governance conforms to the expectations of the theory outlined in chapters 2 and 3 (hypothesis 10). These theoretical expectations are summarized in table 4.1.

## Changes in the Constitutive Rules of International Environment

The emergence of the Cold War between the United States and the Soviet Union in 1947 signified major changes in the constitutive rules and practices of the international order in Europe. The new order emerged in two ways. First, the international context had completely changed with the Allies' victory led by the conjoint efforts of the United States and the Soviet Union. The latter powers became de facto the two new main reorganizers of post–World War II order, as previous European powers had either been defeated (such as Germany and Italy) or severely weakened by the war efforts (such as Britain and France). Second, each of the emerging superpowers had its own agenda on how to reorganize the world. This inexorably made it impossible to continue playing international politics according to the pre–World War II rules of world politics. Nor was it possible to continue the short-lived wartime spirit of cooperation. The two superpowers began to initiate new patterns of practices, with each of them attempting to justify its choices, contest the other's choices, and persuade the other side to abandon its self-styled vision of a new world order.

The Cold War slowly but almost ineluctably developed a constitutive rule of international bloc politics that bounded the practice of politics throughout the international system (Koslowski and Kratochwil 1994, 232–33). This constitutive rule was rooted in the practice of communist conquest by subversion and in the United States' practice of communism containment initially embodied in the Truman Doctrine and the Marshall Plan in 1947–50

**Table 4.1. Summary of Theoretical Expectations**
DCSG: Degree of Consolidation of State Governance

External Variable:
International environment: emergence and consolidation of the Cold War defined by the constitutive rule of international bloc politics in post-1947.

| *Observed Outcome: State Governance* | *Intercommunal Vulnerability* | *Intercommunal Trust* | *Reliance on Institutional Power* |
| --- | --- | --- | --- |
| Consolidating: | | | |
| DCSG increasing after the 1948–49 Tito-Stalin split and more so after the 1953 Constitutional Law. | Low during the period 1948–53 due to low to moderate information complexity, moderate to high intercommunal predictability, and heightened sense of intercommunal interdependence. | Moderate, increased significantly with the formulation of the 1953 Constitutional Law—i.e., as the scope of collective intentionality increased during the post-1948 debates (hypothesis 5). | Low—the Tito regime was able to maintain a more or less even distribution of institutional power among constituent nations, thereby not allowing institutional power to become a device through which communal groups might attempt to address any concern about intercommunal vulnerability. |
| | A heightened sense of strategic interdependence among major communal groups greatly strengthened incentives for communal groups to transform state governance in dealing with fundamental changes occurring in international environment (hypothesis 1). | | Somewhat stagnated as national question began to reemerge (hypothesis 9). |
| | As Yugoslav communists increasingly succeeded in surpassing the 1948 crisis, intercommunal vulnerability decreased with increases in the scope of collective intentionality—i.e., as communal groups increasingly took for granted emerging rules and practices of state governance encapsulated eventually in the 1953 Constitutional Law (hypothesis 3). | | |

(Leffler 1984; Gaddis 1987; Cohen 1993). The relations between the two superpowers developed, as described by Kenneth Waltz (1979, 171), through successive action-reaction processes—"communist guerrillas operating in Greece prompted the Truman Doctrine. The tightening of the Soviet Union's control over the states of Eastern Europe led to the Marshall Plan and the Atlantic Defense Treaty, and these in turn gave rise to the Cominform and the Warsaw Pact. The plan to form a Western German government produced the Berlin blockade. And so on through the 1950's, 60's, and 70's. Our responses are geared to the Soviet Union's actions, and theirs to ours." This process consolidated into a set of intersubjective expectations and practices that defined the relations between the two superpowers as a rivalry. Each superpower perceived the other as its rival and in time expected it to behave accordingly, thereby seizing every opportunity to contain, deter, or defeat it. Nevertheless, the superpowers came also to expect, especially under the conditions of MAD (mutually assured destruction) and Cold War penetration of various regions of the globe, that each would endeavor to sustain the rivalry at tolerable levels and avoid a catastrophic nuclear war that neither party wanted. The rivalry became institutionalized in a set of tacit rules that both superpowers either unilaterally or bilaterally enacted, such as to respect each other's spheres of influence, avoid direct military confrontation, use nuclear weapons only as an ultimate resort, prefer predictable anomaly over unpredictable rationality, and not seek to undermine the other side's leadership (Gaddis 1987, 238–43).

These new rules and practices of international politics had two effects on Yugoslavia. First, the Tito regime had its own agenda for constructing a new international role for Yugoslavia that clearly clashed with the emerging international constitutive rules and practices. This eventually culminated in a split between the Soviet Union and Yugoslavia. The split simultaneously challenged and reinforced the emerging Cold War system of international bloc politics in Europe, even if the split was initially a challenge to the self-chosen role of the Soviet Union as the guiding leader of the communist bloc in Europe. The split allowed the United States and its Western allies an opportunity to attempt to divide the communist bloc, thereby reinforcing the competition between the superpowers for spheres of influence. Second, the new international context induced domestic political debates about the system of state governance in socialist Yugoslavia. Domestic legitimacy of the Tito regime immediately after the war partly depended on the legitimacy of international communism and the Soviet Union. Splitting with Moscow threatened to undermine the revolutionary legitimacy of the Yugoslav communists. Although Tito was ultimately able to prevail in implementing his own vision of a socialist Yugoslavia, the country, and particularly the ruling class, was the theater of political debates that had multiple possible outcomes. Soviet external tactics could have succeeded in reining the Tito regime. Internal opposition supported by the Soviets and their East European clients could also have succeeded in toppling the Tito regime. That the Tito regime was ultimately able to reconsolidate itself and rebuilt state governance under the new international conditions was far from being the only plausible outcome of the crisis. To explicate this argument, I begin by process-tracing how the new international role of Yugoslavia emerged and then examine how this process of constructing a new international role for Yugoslavia shaped the reconstitution of its form of state governance.

In the immediate aftermath of World War II, Yugoslavia not only was on excellent terms with the Soviet Union, but also looked forward to closely emulating the Soviet Union. On May 21, 1945, Tito, visiting Zagreb, described the Soviet-Yugoslav friendship as "a brotherhood affirmed and hardened through all the common battles in which we fought side by side with our great Slav brothers, our great and mighty ally the Soviet Union under the leadership and genius of Stalin."[1] However, only a few days later, Tito stated his vision of an independent role for Yugoslavia in the emerging Cold War rivalry: "we demand also a just termination of this war, we demand that everyone be master in his own house . . . we will not be mixed up in the politics of spheres of interests."[2] Such a challenge to the Soviet agenda for East and Central Europe and hence the emerging constitutive rule of international blocs politics did not please Moscow (Dedijer 1953, 271–72; Djilas 1962, 82). Molotov responded on the behalf of the Soviet Union that "we regard Comrade Tito's speech as an unfriendly attack on the Soviet Union . . . if he should once again permit such an attack on the Soviet Union, we shall be forced to reply with open criticism in the press, and disavow him" (Clissold 1975, 166). These exchanges were only a precursor to the beginning of a struggle for the fate of Yugoslavia, leading eventually to the 1948 Tito-Stalin split (Dedijer 1972, 74–96; Kardelj 1982, 90–114).

Tito persisted in seeking an independent foreign policy agenda, as the issues of creating a Yugoslav-Bulgarian federation and Yugoslavia's support for the revolutionary Greek communists illustrate. In November 1947, the Yugoslav and Bulgarian governments jointly declared that Yugoslavia and Bulgaria share a common goal of eventual unification of the two countries in a single federation. Stalin was very angry because they agreed without consulting him, or even informing him. Stalin also advised both Tito and Dimitrov to discontinue their support to the communist guerrilla movement in Greece. Tito did not heed Stalin's advice and continued to support the guerrillas (Dedjier 1953, 322–33; Djilas 1962, 164–65). To the surprise of the Soviets and the reluctant amazement of the West, the Tito regime was hence slowly following a communist path independently of Stalin. This was a serious challenge to Stalin's approach, rooted in the practice of communist conquest by subversion to create a sphere of domination and influence. An independent Yugoslavia would in effect mean in Stalin's eyes a victory for the Western camp of the Cold War. Communist neutrality was not yet part of the grand strategy luggage of the Soviet regime. Stalin sought to rein in "rebellious" Tito on two fronts.

First, Stalin applied overt political, economic, and military pressures against the Tito regime. On March 18, 1948, the Soviet Union withdrew all Soviet military experts and civilian technicians who had been working in Yugoslavia. All Soviet economic advisers would then also follow suit. On March 27, Stalin and Molotov sent a letter to Tito and the leaders of the Communist Party of Yugoslavia (CPY), accusing the Yugoslav secret police of spying on Soviet intelligence officers and other Soviet citizens in Yugoslavia. The letter also charged that the Yugoslav communists were not pursuing a genuinely communist policy of class struggle.[3] Tito and Kardelj rebutted all these accusations and stressed their loyalty to the Soviet Union.[4] They also invited the CPSU to send one of its leading members to Belgrade to resolve the mutual disagreements with the CPY. The Soviets decided instead that the whole dispute should be discussed at the next meeting of the Cominform in Bucharest.[5] The CPY did not attend the meeting, and Cominform members decided to expel the CPY on June 28. In spring 1949, Cominformist radios and presses became much more violently critical of the Tito regime. The Soviet Union and the communist countries of Eastern Europe eventually imposed economic sanctions against Yugoslavia in summer 1949. The Red Army High Command also began drawing up plans for invading Yugoslavia either in the spring or summer of 1951. Although a number of Soviet divisions carried out maneuvers on the Yugoslav-Hungarian and Yugoslav-Romanian borders, Stalin rescinded the order in fall 1950 (Ridley 1994, 307).

Second, confronted with the Soviet/Cominform threat and with a fear of sedition within Yugoslavia, the Tito regime could not easily appeal to the West for help and protection. Not surprisingly, the Tito communist regime was not friendly to the United States and its allies for a number of reasons. In August 1946 Yugoslav fighters had shot down two U.S. military jets flying between Vienna and Udine in Italy.[6] Moreover, Tito had sent two divisions of Yugoslav troops into Albania to protect the country against the danger of an invasion from Greece. Tito feared that the Greek government might decide to retaliate against Albanian assistance to the communist forces (Dedijer 1953, 310–13, 318, 320, 329–39). Tito was also still at odds with the United States and its allies on the future of Trieste. Belgrade wanted to annex most of Trieste's population to Yugoslavia. The United States and its allies preferred to divide it into two zones (A and B), with only zone B annexed to Yugoslavia. The American government, together with the British and French, had also proposed to place the entire Free Territory of Trieste under Italian sovereignty on March 20, 1948.

Not surprisingly, Western governments initially did not know what to make of the emerging split between Stalin and Tito.[7] The West eventually decided to help the Tito regime with the U.S. National Security Council, arguing that "as much as we dislike him, Tito is presently performing brilliantly in our interests in leading successfully and effectively the attack from within the communist family on Soviet imperialism" (Heuser 1988, 63). Britain and the United States, however, required that Tito stop supporting the communist guerrillas in Greece before they would make any serious commitment toward Yugoslavia, a move that Tito had already been considering (Heuser 1988, 91–92). The escalation of the Cold War in East Asia worked to the benefit of the Tito regime. Within a fortnight of the outbreak of the Korean War, the U.S. military authorities began discussing whether and how Yugoslavia could become part of Western defense plans. Yet neither Tito nor Western foreign ministers wanted Yugoslavia to join NATO. In January 1951, Stalin summoned the defense ministers of Eastern Europe to a conference in the Kremlin to inform them that he was again considering launching an attack on Yugoslavia in the spring.[8] This time the United States was ready to help Tito, granting Yugoslavia's request for arms without even consulting any of its allies (Heuser 1988, 160–62). Tito also took the initiative and promised on February 22 that if the Red Army attacked Greece, West Germany, or Italy through Austria, Yugoslavia would enter the war on the side of NATO (Heuser 1988, 156).

Therefore, Tito's goal of making Yugoslavia a communist state independent of the Soviet Union was increasingly achieved through the combined effects of his regime's strategies and positions, the Soviet Union's policies and actions, and the actions (and reactions) and positions taken by the United States and its allies. The split with Stalin consolidated only through Western economic assistance and limited military aid from the United States as well as continuous Soviet alienation of the Tito regime. To further consolidate its international role independent of the Cold War rivalry, while channeling benefits from the two rivals, Belgrade sought to strengthen its emerging buffer state role in two ways. Tito sought effective participation in the United Nations and formulated Yugoslav's foreign policies independently on issues such as the French war in Indochina and the Korean War.

In 1949 the Tito regime sought to compete for a seat on the UN Security Council. Yugoslavia hoped to make of it a gesture of world support for itself, thereby not only contributing to deter the Soviet Union and its satellites from invading it, but also avoiding falling prey to the Western bloc of the Cold War (Heuser 1988, 109–10). The Soviet Union reacted angrily, for the election of Yugoslavia would constitute a breach of the informal agreement among the Great Powers about the distribution of seats in the Security Council. Yugoslavia won the seat thanks to Washington's help and lobbying (Heuser 1988, 109–12). Yet Belgrade remained committed to entrenching its international role as a communist state that is neutral in the Cold War rivalry. Yugoslavia's position on the North Vietnam issue is indicative of this. The revolutionary movement in French Indochina, under the leadership of communist Ho Chi Minh, had gained control of the northern part of the country and established a government in Hanoi. On January 31, 1950, the Soviet Union recognized Ho Chi Minh's regime as the government of the independent state of Vietnam. So, too, did Tito. The United States did not like Tito's move and threatened to cut its economic assistance to Yugoslavia.[9] Tito responded that no one could buy Yugoslavia's independence with economic aid. Likewise, Yugoslavia held an independent position on the Korean War. On June 25, 1950, the North Korean army crossed the 38th Parallel and invaded South Korea. When the United States asked for a UN Security Council resolution on sending UN troops to repel North Korean aggression, the proposal passed with nine votes, with Yugoslavia abstaining. The United States informed Tito that Washington was disappointed with Belgrade's policy. Tito responded that he feared that had he voted for the resolution, the Soviet Union would have interpreted it as a sign that Yugoslavia had joined the Western alliance, which might have provoked a Soviet invasion of Yugoslavia (Heuser 1988, 193–94). When the UN Security Council voted to invade North Korea, Yugoslavia again abstained. When the Chinese troops crossed the Yalu and drove the American and UN forces back to the 38th Parallel, the UN General Assembly passed a resolution condemning communist China as the aggressor. The Soviet Union and its allies voted against the resolution, but Yugoslavia abstained (Wilson 1979, 123).

In sum, the 1948 Stalin-Tito split was a milestone toward a radical transformation of Yugoslavia's international role and foreign policy (Rubinstein 1989; Zimmerman 1987, 18–21). The West initiated a flow of economic aid that saved Yugoslavia from hunger in 1950. The United States also began shipping weapons to Yugoslavia in 1951, and a military security arrangement was concluded in 1953 (Heuser 1988; Greene 1988; Johnson 1972; Lampe, Prickett, and Adamovic 1990). Through these actions and policies, the West became strongly involved in the construction of the new international role of the socialist Yugoslav state. Thus, Tito consolidated a buffer role for Yugoslavia by first maintaining Yugoslavia's independent path and then increasingly usefully channeling the Cold War rivalry to strengthen Yugoslavia's international role. Preserving independence from Moscow while not being a member of the Western bloc meant that Yugoslavia counted as a buffer state in an international context underpinned by a constitutive rule of international bloc politics. Yugoslavia could not have become a buffer state without the constitutive rule of international bloc politics. Nor would Yugoslavia have become a buffer state had Belgrade not insisted on remaining a communist state independent of Moscow. However, absent the constitutive rule of international bloc politics, neither the Soviet Union nor the United States and its Western allies would have been that much interested in Yugoslavia's position or fate. Because Yugoslavia had strongly tied itself to the communist bloc in the immediate aftermath of World War II, the split with Stalin and the Cominform sanctions against Yugoslavia as well as the need to sustain the new international role of Yugoslavia induced much debate about transforming the system of state governance in post-1948 Yugoslavia.

## Transforming State Governance, the Yugoslav Way

The legitimacy of the pre-1948 system of state governance in Yugoslavia was tightly linked to the Soviet form of communism. The collective intentionality that underpinned the form of state governance strongly depended on this linkage. The system was anchored in the 1946 Constitution, which was closely modeled after the 1936 Soviet Constitution and dominated by a Soviet-style Communist Party. In the wake of World War II the Communist Party of Yugoslavia (CPY) had a vision of a new and better (Soviet-inspired) society to be realized by transforming not only the political and economic systems of the country but also its citizens—their values, morals, goals, aesthetics, and social behavior. The CPY actively manipulated the popular culture for political and ideological purposes, prescribing what it termed its appropriate form and content and severely restricting and proscribing the production and distribution of any work not deemed as serving these purposes. However, these policies were already failing by 1947. Most producers of popular and media culture would not precisely follow the government's dictates. Nor would the consumers of culture modify their tastes and interests in accordance with party wishes. The Tito regime also formulated a five-year economic plan with very ambitious goals, which soon became a disaster. The regime planners overestimated existing industrial capacity as well as the number of trained personnel by at least some 50 percent. Only the developed industrial sectors of Slovenia, Croatia, and Serbia came close to realizing their targets for 1947 (Horvat 1976, 42–44).

These early difficulties were not peculiar to Yugoslavia per se and were somewhat to be expected given the revolutionary character of the communists' agenda as well as the level of destruction that the country had suffered during the war. Had the Tito-Stalin break not occurred in 1948, Yugoslavia might have perhaps been able to solve some, if not all, of these problems, much like other Central and East European states did. However, the split with Stalin in 1948 and numerous Soviet attempts to subdue, if not topple, the Tito regime did not allow for such a scenario to become reality. The Soviet-led campaigns and Tito's resilience to them in effect conspired to raise a much more serious and threatening problem. The collective intentionality that the communist leadership had endeavored to build by very closely emulating the Stalinist model was in jeopardy. A collapsing collective intentionality would mean the end of the regime, if not Tito himself. The leaders had no other alternative but to prevent a complete collapse of collective intentionality, or at least rebuild it given the new international context.

The Yugoslav leaders slowly developed a new spirit of experimentation that became a mark of the whole period of post-1948 reforms, after having become convinced that the Stalin regime and its Eastern European clients wanted to circumscribe, if not abort, Yugoslavia's independence. The Tito regime decided to transform the constitutive rules and practices of state governance in Yugoslavia. However, doing so meant reconstructing the collective intentionality underpinning state governance, away from the Soviet-linked communist legitimation. The transformation had to be a comprehensive redefinition of most dimensions of domestic political, economic, social, and cultural life in the federation. The reforms were termed "democratic socialism," as opposed to Soviet "bureaucratic socialism" (Neal 1958, 40).

The debates that surrounded these reforms played a key role in the construction of collective intentionality in the polity. Yet because there was a Soviet-encouraged opposition to the break away from the communist bloc, the Tito regime feared potential rebellion, and did indeed have to confront actual dissent, in the polity. Hence, in an effort to enhance the likelihood of success of the reforms and therewith the new form of state governance, the regime launched a manhunt for supporters of the Cominform within Yugoslavia. This manhunt ultimately eliminated any serious challenge to the new form of state governance and was an integral part of the process of building collective intentionality.

In the following, I discuss how a new scope of collective intentionality developed through reforms in the state ideological doctrine, the Communist Party, the constitutional framework, and the state political- and economic-institutional makeup. I then discuss how the manhunt of Cominformists within Yugoslavia helped to entrench the new collective intentionality.

### *State Ideology*

Simultaneously challenging the Soviet ideological hegemony in Eastern Europe and seeking to present a Yugoslav alternative led the theoreticians of the Communist Party of Yugoslavia to formulate a new set of ideological guidelines, a mixture of Marxist dogmatism and political pragmatism. The ideological transformation and debate effectively began with Edvard Kardelj going back in May 1949 to the "fundamental axiom" of Marx, Engels, and Lenin that the socialist state would whither by drawing the masses into the tasks of running state affairs. Through a critical assessment of Soviet evolution and experience with socialism the Yugoslav leaders concluded that the despotism of state bureaucracy and state management of the economy were at the root of all evil (Hoffman and Neal 1962; Hondius 1968, 194–209, 337–38).[10] Henceforth, the Yugoslav theoreticians formulated the doctrine of "the withering away of the state," which stands for an "ever less state intervention in specific areas of social life and ever greater mass participation in exercising the state functions which remain."[11] The meaning and content of the new doctrine were the subjects of lengthy intra-party debates. A variety of viewpoints emerged, ranging from "dogmatic" Stalinist conceptions to "utopian" ideas that proposed a large-scale surrender of state functions to public bodies. The debates on the new doctrine ended only in 1951 when Edvard Kardelj finalized the essential elements of a new orthodox CPY position. The new doctrine placed emphasis on the powers and authority of the local state organs and the people's committees.[12] It ultimately took the form of a new law on the people's committees of 1952 and in the Constitutional Law of 1953 (McVicker 1957, 145–75; Neal 1958, 89–117, 160–84).

The withering process meant a qualitative, gradual "democratization" of the state organs themselves through a process of drawing the masses into their operations. The withering process did not imply a complete elimination of all centralized state functions and organs. The latter would cease to exhibit "state" attributes when they would ultimately function to represent the interests of the whole society and involve all the citizens in their affairs.[13] More pointedly, the doctrine upheld the necessity of a continued existence of central representative state bodies and hence excluded from the withering process certain categories of state functions. At lower levels of the government, the doctrine foresaw a qualitative change in the essence of state bodies as ordinary citizens would increasingly participate in state affairs.

Ideological consensus at the higher ranks of the party facilitated the process of rebuilding collective intentionality. The Yugoslav leadership was able to construct an ideological framework through which it could express as well as legitimize the need for reforms in state governance without any linkage to Soviet-sponsored or inspired legitimation. This in effect provided a ready-to-use discourse that the communists could channel to create and sustain collective intentionality, that is, to "naturalize" or turn the emerging form of state governance into a taken-for-granted way of governing. However, to effect the construction of a new collective intentionality, the new ideological discourse had to be "actualized" in practical reforms, such as a corresponding reformulation of the nature, role, and mission of the core institutions of the state.

### *Role of the Communist Party*

For more than a year after the break with Stalin, the Yugoslav communists continued to adhere closely to the Leninist-Stalinist doctrine on the role of the party. The party had an absolute directive role both in mass organizations—the purely proletarian trade union as well as the broader People's Front—and in the state apparatus. Pursuing an ideology of "the withering of the state" necessarily entailed a reassessment of the role of the party. If the formulation of a new ideological doctrine was for the most part dependent on the higher ranks of the party theoreticians, the design of a corresponding role for the Communist Party depended in addition on the local leaders as well as the party membership at large. Hence, constructing a collective intentionality on this aspect of reforms was potentially more vulnerable to dissent or a lack of cohesiveness at least.

The process of rethinking the role of the party effectively began in 1949 with Tito characterizing the total identification of party and state in the Soviet Union as one of the factors responsible for exploitation of the working class by the bureaucratized state.[14] Tito concluded that the new Yugoslav party should instead maintain a certain distance from the state apparatus and act as its socialist critic.[15] This entailed an overhaul reevaluation of the party. To this effect, the Federal Council of the People's Front adopted a resolution in January 1950, which made raising the political consciousness of the masses the most important task of the party.[16] A Central Committee directive of June 22, 1950, further prescribed organizational changes that would prevent excessive party interference in state matters, including separating the positions of party secretary and president of the people's committee at the district level. The practice of entrusting the executive committee members of individual local party with responsibility for state organs was replaced (or was supposed to be replaced) with "collective leadership."[17] The directive ordered local party organizations to focus "all their work to mobilizing the masses, attracting the masses to the business of managing economic affairs, raising the socialist consciousness of the masses."[18] The withering of the state effectively required a strengthening of the party mobilizing role within the population at large.[19] While the party would continue to oppose and subdue the enemies of socialism, it had to act primarily as a factor of consciousness, "educating" the working class with its ideals. The Tito regime also understood that constructing collective intentionality required not just the continued loyalty of the CPY but also the support, even if passive, of the predominantly noncommunist Yugoslav population. Tito thereby initiated a series of popular concessions to increase popular support, such as the abolition of special shops, houses, and other privileges enjoyed by the members of the Communist Party.

The process of reformulating the role of the party in the system of socialist democracy and clarifying its principles of internal organization were the major concerns of the Sixth CPY Congress held in November 1952. The final resolution stated that "as a result of the development of social relations in the direction of ever more democratic forms of rule, the basic duty and role of communists is political and ideological work in educating the masses. . . . The League of Communists is not and cannot be the direct operative manager and commander in economic, state, or social life."[20] The CPY changed its name to the League of Communists of Yugoslavia (LCY, Savez komunista

Jogoslavije) to symbolically mark its new role and distinguish it from the Soviet-dominated Communist Parties of Eastern Europe. The new statute of the LCY henceforth relaxed the rigid organizational centralism of the 1948 statute. Republican congresses now had the right to determine the political line of the republican communist organizations, if within the framework of the general LCY political line. The new statute also expressed the desirability of greater autonomy for the basic party organizations and gave them the power to accept and expel party members without reference to higher organs.[21]

In sum, after the Sixth Congress the party became committed to self-management and self-government, that is, decentralization and democratization of all decision-making bodies in the party. In practice, the main organizational changes in the party revolved on a decentralization of functions and a reduction of the party apparatus at various levels, in large by curtailing party functions. For example, the Socialist Alliance was now responsible for all formal agitation-propaganda work and supervision of women's and youth groups. However, by 1953 many communists still had no clear understanding of the new role of the party. The communists knew that they must emphasize democracy and tolerate dissenting opinions, that the party no longer had a monopoly on setting the political line, and that the party was to "wither away." Yet they also learned that the party must maintain and even strengthen its leading position throughout the society and that they must fight all bourgeois tendencies and anti-state activities. The criticisms leveled toward the Soviet Union notwithstanding, the Communist Party retained its leading role in manufacturing collective intentionality through indoctrination and coercion, as it did during the war and its immediate aftermath. The Tito regime then relied both on its historical legitimacy of resistance to the Nazis and on a set of Soviet-inspired institutions to reinforce and strengthen its communist strategy of building collective intentionality. Likewise, the split with Stalin and consequent formulation of a new ideological doctrine and recasting of the nature and role of the Communist Party also called for appropriate constitutional and institutional arrangements, which I discuss next.

*The New Constitutional and Institutional Arrangements*

As the ideological doctrine and the role of the Communist Party were recast in the aftermath of Stalin-Tito split to rebuild collective intentionality away from the Soviet-linked legitimation, so were the political arrangements of the Yugoslav state transformed, too (Woodward 1995a, 64–163; Bicanic 1973; Burg 1983; Zimmerman 1987, 13–73; Lampe 1996, 229–325). By the end of 1952, the process of constitutional and institutional reorganization of the federation took the form of a new act, the Constitutional Law on the Bases of the Social and Political Structure of the FNRJ and on the Federal Organs of

Power[22] (Johnson 1972, 143–58; Djilas 1991, 176–79). These transformations made the construction of collective intentionality an integral part of the routines of institutional practice.

First, the republics lost the rights of secession and sovereignty granted to them by article 49 of the 1946 Constitution. Sovereignty now reposed with the people, defined as the unified Yugoslav working class. Article 3 of the Constitutional Law declared the People's Committees to be the "basic organs of power of the working people" and that "to the federation belong only those rights confirmed by the federal constitution, and to the People's Republics only those rights confirmed by the republican constitution" (Hondius 1968, 199–206).

Second, a reconfiguration of the bicameral Federal Assembly weakened the representation of the republics in the Federal People's Assembly. The Federal Chamber now included the previous Chamber of Nationalities and a Chamber of Producers, with new representatives from the republic and provincial assemblies. The new chamber favored industry over agriculture by 135 delegates to 67 so that it would represent the workers' councils better and hence would be a reflection of their socialist Yugoslav "consciousness." The two chambers met in separate sessions, and their consensus was needed for the enactment of laws, decrees, international agreements, and so forth (Hondius 1968, 202).

Third, the Constitutional Law made two important changes in the executive system. The president of the federation and a Federal Executive Council replaced the Presidium and the government. The Executive Council as a whole was responsible for the entire executive sphere, with no sharp division of work among or delegation of power to any of its members. The Constitutional Law stressed the idea of cooperative federalism by stipulating that the Federal Executive Council should include members from all people's republics (article 82, paragraph 4) (Hondius 1968, 204). These new measures effectively amounted to the creation of dual authority at the federal level, however.

Fourth, the new institutional arrangement for enacting laws and other decisions had two effects: (a) the execution became the prerogative of the lower organs; (b) execution by the higher organs became more of an exception than the rule. Article 9 stated, for example, that "federal organs carry out federal acts directly and deal with other executive matters only in the field of constitutionally defined exclusive rights and duties of the federation, as well as when such application is brought under the competence of the federation by a law, in keeping with its rights and duties" (as quoted in Hondius 1968, 198). Hence, the Constitutional Law abrogated the principle of dual responsibility. The federal organs did nonetheless retain a limited right of intervention in case of breach of federal acts by a republican executive. In such cases, the republic had the right of appeal to the Federal People's Assembly.

In sum, collective intentionality was the product of ideological indoctrination and propaganda and party coercion, control, and mobilization. Constitutional and institutional reforms made the process of constructing collective intentionality—that is, making the new rules and practices of the political game taken for granted—a decentralized "daily routine." As the republics and federal organs of state carried out their normal functions, they by the same token increased the sense of collective intentionality in practice. Collective intentionality emerged through a process of normalizing new political rights, obligations, and practices. Transforming economic institutions and practices also reinforced this process, as is discussed next.

*Reforming the Economic Institutions*

The 1953 Constitutional Law stipulated a number of important institutional reforms for the economy. The reforms started when in 1949 a number of prominent Yugoslav communists led by Kardelj introduced the doctrine of "workers' self-management" as an alternative to Soviet-style bureaucratic management of the economy (Djilas 1980, 45, 73, 75; Wilson 1979, 142; Lang 1975; Lampe 1996, 229–92). The new doctrine sought to replace state ownership of the means of production with social ownership and entrust management responsibilities to the workers of each enterprise. In December 1949, the Politburo had launched a public critique of Soviet bureaucratism and almost simultaneously ordered the establishment on an experimental basis of workers' councils as advisory bodies in 215 large industrial enterprises. The performance of these initial workers' councils turned out to be quite satisfactory. In spring 1950, Tito accepted a proposal by Djilas, Kardelj, and Kidric to endow the workers' councils with ultimate legal control of the enterprises,[23] thereby making them a key institution distinguishing the Yugoslav political-economic system from the Soviet one (Djilas 1969, 220–23). Actual implementation of the doctrine occurred through two major institutional steps.

The first step consisted of reducing the size and scope of the federal administration over the economy, as well as reinforcing interdepartmental coordination and decision making. For example, between February and June 1950, the Federal Ministry of Electrical Power and Federal-Republican Ministry of Mining were abolished. A new Energy and Extractive Industry Board was set up to coordinate the remaining federal agencies in this field. Some months later, overseeing of energy policy was fully delegated to the republics (Hondius 1968, 187). Similar changes in the republican administration followed the changes at the federal level of administration. Economic councils were founded in all republics while the republican ministries of electricity, industry, mining, timber, and communal affairs were all abolished and replaced by boards between March and July 1950 (Hondius 1968, 188).

The second step in the process of institutional reform of the economy began when, on July 2, 1950, the People's Assembly of the Federation passed a new law transferring the entire management of economic enterprises and associations from state organs to the workers' councils of these enterprises. Each enterprise henceforth became responsible for its own operations, while the state remained responsible for overall direction and control (Hondius 1968, 188). A reform of the planning and budgeting process followed this decentralization, bringing the practice of the common "general budget" to an end. A new federal Act on the Budgets instead stipulated that the budgets of the people's republics were to be independent from the federal budget.[24]

Although the Yugoslav leaders portrayed the doctrine of workers' self-management as socialist economic rationality, there was more to it. First, the doctrine allowed the Yugoslav system to demarcate itself even more from the Stalin model of communism. The Tito regime needed this to enhance its domestic legitimacy without relying on ideological and political linkages with Soviet communism. Second, the doctrine also contributed to the process of collective intentionality that the Tito regime needed to sustain its rule in the face of Soviet pressures and potential internal dissent. The regime endeavored to strengthen the process of constructing collective intentionality by involving the workers more closely in the economic decision and planning, that is, through a decentralization of economic management.

In sum, formulating a new ideological doctrine that clearly demarcated the Yugoslav path from the Stalin road provided a new discourse through which the Yugoslav leaders could reconstruct the collective intentionality without a need for Soviet legitimation of their form of communism. Likewise, recasting the role of the CPY as a mechanism for the creation and maintenance of collective consciousness effectively allowed the Yugoslav leaders to turn the party into an agent of constructing collective intentionality. Launching a process of decentralizing the political institutions and establishing in practice the doctrine of workers' self-management made the very process of reconstructing the collective intentionality a daily routine inherently intertwined within "normal" politics, both at the federal and republican levels. These were no easy tasks, since they amounted to an overhaul of the Yugoslav system of state governance. Not surprisingly, there was internal resistance not only to the split with Stalin but also to the radical reform of state governance. The Soviet Union and its clients in Eastern Europe helped to foment as well as reinforce this internal resistance and dissent. Protecting the new Yugoslav path hence was a crucial element of Tito's construction of a new Yugoslav collective intentionality.

## Cominformist Manhunt: Protecting the Yugoslav Path

That constructing a collective intentionality not legitimated by Soviet-style communism was not an easy task quickly became transparent in Soviet-inspired Cominformist dissent in Yugoslavia. The June 28, 1948, Cominform

Resolution called upon the Yugoslav communists to "compel their present leaders to recognize their mistakes. . . . Should the present leaders of the KPJ prove incapable of doing this, their job is to replace them and advance a new internationalist leader of the Party."[25] This helped to create a siege mentality within the top Yugoslav leadership, as illustrated in Tito's statement in January 1949, "do not permit anyone to wreck the ranks of our party, no matter who he is. Be aware that this is enemy activity, not only toward our party but also toward our peoples. Be vigilant and merciless toward anyone who would attempt such a thing."[26] Not only the Soviets attempted to destabilize the Yugoslav state in this way, but also the Yugoslav leaders themselves strongly believed that they must eradicate the possibility of such a dissent. This was important for constructing and preserving a high scope of collective intentionality of the new form of state governance.

Cominformists varied in function, territory, and nationality. No party or state institution was immune to penetration by Cominformist sentiments. The police and the army received special attention, since these institutions were in charge of defending the political system. The CPY depended on their reliability and loyalty for preventive measures against the Cominformists and any other type of dissent (Banac 1988, 157). For example, the security apparatus in Bosnia-Hercegovina was thoroughly purged after all state security personnel in the second district of Sarajevo openly expressed their adherence to the Resolution.[27] Pro-Resolution sentiments also spread among the UDB (Uprava Drzavne Bezbednosti) chiefs in Mostar and Banja Luka. In Serbia, too, there were *ibeovci* (conformists) in the security forces (Banac 1988, 157). Several officers of the UDB at the Belgrade headquarters and in Vojvodina escaped to Romania (Pauljevic 1982, 10–21, 78, 193). Cominformism also reached epidemic proportions in the Yugoslav army (Djilas 1980, 80). Soviet intelligence agencies were able to enlist many of the Partisan officers who had attended Soviet military academies for training (Banac 1988, 161). These links became crucial for the development of Cominformism within the ranks of the Yugoslav army.

The Cominformists came from all republics and national groups but were not evenly distributed in them. Their concentrations in Montenegro and Serbia were well above those among the Slovenes, Hungarians, Albanians, and Croats (Banac 1988, 151). Montenegro, the smallest of Yugoslavia's republics both in population and in area, had proportionally the largest number of Cominformists, almost four times the Yugoslav average (Banac 1988, 164). Bosnian Muslims had the smallest incidence of Cominformism. Slovenia had the smallest number of *ibeovci*. No prominent Slovene party leader defected, although some old cadres and occasionally a number of high-level officials did side with the Cominformist Resolution (Banac 1988, 186–87).

The purge of Cominformists played a dual role in the process of reconstructing state governance. First, it eliminated real as well as potential Soviet-linked fifth columns in Yugoslavia. Between 1949 and 1952, the secret police rounded up more than twelve thousand people, who were held in an internment camp (Ridley 1994, 296–97). Most of the internees were members of the Communist Party, and some had even fought with the Partisans during World War II.[28] Second, the leaders used these "new enemies" as scapegoats to solidify popular support for the Tito regime, thereby reinforcing the process of collective intentionality. In a Rijeka factory, for example, the regime portrayed party members who complained of low wages as Cominform sympathizers. In the same plant in 1952, "directives were given to report anybody who spoke against US military aid, because [such opposition] would indicate that the speaker was a Cominformist" (Banac 1988, 154). In the army, "if somebody complained about something, he was immediately looked upon as an *ibeovac* or an enemy of the regime" (Banac 1988, 155). The university party organization purged a fifth of its members between 1948 and 1950, even if of all those purged only a quarter agreed with all points of the Cominform Resolution (Banac 1988, 155).

In sum, during the period 1948–53, the emerging Cold war environment induced a series of domestic debates that resulted in a major transformation and reconsolidation of state governance. The scope of collective intentionality slowly increased after the reforms were launched in 1949, and more so after the formulation of the 1953 Constitutional Law. That the Tito regime was able to reconsolidate itself in the period 1948–53 is not a matter of dispute. That the new arrangement was based on a moderate scope of collective intentionality is perhaps more disputable. The ruling class of Yugoslavia used a mixture of coercion and institutional incentives as well as ideological propaganda to build such a scope of collective intentionality. As discussed in chapter 2, it is difficult to precisely identify the scope of collective intentionality of the Tito regime in the period 1948–53. Yet it is possible to argue with a good degree of confidence that the regime had succeeded in launching a process of reconsolidating state governance after 1949, and more so after the reforms were encapsulated in the 1953 Constitutional Law. After the elimination of the Cominformist challenge inside Yugoslavia, the scope of collective intentionality was, one can argue, not low but rather significantly increasing. However, as the national question began to reemerge in the late 1950s, one cannot ascertain that the scope of collective intentionality continued to increase beyond a moderate level. Explaining why the Yugoslav leaders were able to build a moderate scope of collective intentionality is the question to which I now turn.

## Intercommunal Vulnerability

The game of transforming state governance in multi-communal polities depends on intercommunal vulnerability, which in turn depends on intercommunal interdependence. The higher the sense of interdependence among the politicized communal groups in the polity, the more likely it is that they will seek to debate state governance to deal with the fundamental changes occurring in the international environment. The sense of intercommunal interdependence in Yugoslavia greatly strengthened the incentives for the Yugoslav polity as a whole to transform state governance in dealing with the fundamental changes occurring in the international environment. Yet transforming state governance had the potential to create intercommunal vulnerability. In the period 1948–53, the major communal groups had no serious fear of intercommunal abandonment or exploitation. Nor did they fear exclusion from participating in the processes that transformed state governance. Rather, as the communists increasingly succeeded in surpassing the 1948 crisis, intercommunal vulnerability in the Yugoslav polity decreased even further, with increases in the scope of collective intentionality underpinning the emerging rules and practices of state governance encapsulated eventually in the 1953 Constitutional Law. As discussed in chapter 3, vulnerability arises from three mutually reinforcing sources: intercommunal information complexity, predictability, and interdependence. I estimate these variables in the following.

*Intercommunal Information Complexity*

In Yugoslavia, information complexity was low to moderate because, as primary participants in the Communist Party and other state organs, the major communal groups had enough reliable information on each other's intentions and capabilities during the period 1948–53. The low information complexity was a direct result of the solution to the national question that the communists had devised in the immediate aftermath of the war. In its original form, the 1946 Yugoslav Constitution had recognized the ethnic particularity and full equality of most national groups and embodied the right of cultural-linguistic self-determination. The communists organized the state as a federation with extensive decentralization and a right of political self-determination, including in principle the right of secession. The 1946 Constitution recognized five nationalities: Serbs, Croats, Slovenes, Macedonians, and Montenegrins. Federalism was a de facto acceptable solution to a nationality problem that most Yugoslavs preferred to pass over silently. This implied that their intentions toward one another were at least not against the general expectations that the communist solution to the national question assumed. Likewise, the major communal groups had no incentive to misrepresent (private) information regarding their organizational capabilities, since they had accepted the new rules of intercommunal relations. Four factors reinforced the low information complexity among the major communal groups that the institutional incentives helped to anchor. First, many Yugoslav welcomed the opportunity to escape from the nationalistic mood of the preceding bloody years. Second, the communist takeover encouraged "collective amnesia" about the national question by posing new challenges and hardships to all classes and nationalities in the society. Third, prewar nationalistic parties and their spokespersons were scattered or suppressed, leaving most nationalistic forces without leadership or links to the populace. Fourth, although the party made some concessions on the issue of cultural specificities and sensitivities, cultural freedom was still by and large circumscribed.

That the issue of information complexity was more or less resolved among the major national groups did not extend to a number of important minorities, however. Albanians, Serbs in Croatia, and Macedonians threatened to raise the level of information complexity in the polity. Albanians were the most hostile to the postwar arrangement, and their uprising turned into an armed rebellion against the government.[29] The party sought to appease the Albanians and hence made considerable efforts to undo a number of past injustices committed against this community. The Serbs in Croatia, who had suffered at the hands of the Ustasha while contributing much to the Partisan cause, also posed a serious problem for the communists, thereby prompting the party to take a number of steps hoping to mollify the Serbian population in Croatia. For example, the regime allowed the Serbs who returned to Croatia after the war to claim their land and resettle there without difficulty (Shoup 1968, 112–13).

The party followed a number of strategies in trying to stabilize the intercommunal status quo and thereby reduce intercommunal information complexity between the major and minor groups, as well as among the latter themselves. First, the party used its control of the press and ceaseless propaganda to create the impression that prewar national attitudes had few supporters among the Yugoslav population and that the national question had permanently vanished. Second, the communists passed legislation aimed at severely punishing as a criminal offense any act inciting national, racial, or religious antagonisms (Shoup 1968, 110). The law was vigorously enforced and helped to limit nationalistic outbursts, especially in areas with mixed nationalities. Third, the communists attempted, although not without risks, to appease some national groups. The policies adopted toward the Serbs in both Croatia and Macedonia illustrate well the reluctance with which the party granted special concessions to any one national group. The communists faced the potential that such appeasements might lead to negative reactions among the other nationalities. Fourth, the Communist Party emphasized the need to equalize economic conditions throughout the federal units and equally recognized the claims by all nationalities to economic resources and higher standards of living. The Yugoslav communists employed two methods in seeking to ease the plight of economically underdeveloped regions: the allocation of investment funds to the poorer areas for the development of industry and the practice of providing grants-in-aid to the republics to meet immediate financial needs. The policy was that regardless of how wealthy a republic might be, it should be able to provide the same educational facilities, public services, and amount of pensions and other benefits to its constituents.

Information complexity threatened to increase when the Yugoslav solution to the national problem became an issue as the Soviet bloc sought to mobilize the minority populations against Tito. The Hungarian and Albanian governments, in particular, strongly attacked the treatment of minorities by the Yugoslav communist regime.[30] The Cominformist regimes also sent agitators across the Yugoslav border into the minority regions. These anti-Tito efforts were partially successful.[31] Yet these incidents did not build up to create a major crisis within the CPY. As discussed earlier, the Tito regime was able to subdue all signs of Cominformist mobilization and dissent in Yugoslavia. This allowed the rulers to maintain low information complexity among the major national groups. It also helped to at least reduce the potential for increased intercommunal information complexity between the major and minor groups of Yugoslavia.

### *Intercommunal Predictability*

Intercommunal predictability was moderate to high because there was enough intercommunal commitment to the communist arrangement. This also was a consequence of the communist solution to the national question in the aftermath of the war. The intercommunal arrangement as stipulated in the 1946 Constitution and enforced by the Communist Party framed the balance of political power among the communal groups and their beliefs about mutual intentions and likely behavior. This thereby ensured enough intercommunal predictability.

As discussed in chapter 3, two sorts of change can undermine intercommunal predictability. First, problems of predictability could arise whenever the balance of intercommunal power shifts. As the influence of one (or more) group declines, previously held expectations increasingly become an unreliable source of predicting intergroup behavior. Second, uncertainty over previously shared understandings about intercommunal relations can generate problems of predictability. Both sorts of change occurred during the 1948–53 period. The regime, however, did not leave it up to the communal groups to address the problem of predictability. Rather, the regime carefully managed the issue through the new institutionalization of the state, the new role of the Communist Party, and its strategy in dealing with the nationalist aspect of the Cominformist manhunt. The choices that the regime made reinforced the pre-1948 level of intercommunal predictability, particularly among the major communal groups.

The transformation of state institutions entailed a re-institutionalization of intercommunal predictability. To this end, the regime followed two mutually supportive strategies. First, the regime rolled back the republics' rights of secession and sovereignty granted to them in 1946. Article 9 of the 1946 Constitution made the republics sovereign except for those rights expressly granted to the federation. The regime now lodged that sovereignty to the unified but diffuse Yugoslav working class. This implied that the major communal groups could no longer use their right to sovereignty as a means of influencing the intercommunal balance of power at the federal level. Nor could the right to sovereignty be used at the republican level, where dominant communal groups might be tempted to use it against the minorities within their republics. It also meant that intercommunal relations depended more on the peoples than on the constituent nations and republics.

Second, a reconfiguration of the bicameral Federal Assembly weakened representation of the republican interests and rights in the Federal People's Assembly. The latter now contained seventy newly added representatives from the republican and provincial assemblies as members of a Chamber of Producers. The Chamber of Nationalities had the right to meet separately whenever there was a bill touching upon the legal equality of the peoples of Yugoslavia or the constitutionally fixed relations between the federation and the republics (Hondius 1968, 202). This hence became a framework to institutionalize and protect intercommunal predictability against unilateral changes from the status quo. The bicameral character of the Federal Assembly also circumscribed the relevance of communal identity by making a nonidentity-based body—the Chamber of Producers—an important actor in the economy. The regime was hence able simultaneously to protect and restrain the constituent nations by institutionally circumscribing any potential drive for communally based interests and policies. The new role of the Communist Party as a socialist critic was another tool used to maintain intercommunal predictability. As discussed earlier, the June 1950 Central Committee directive ordered local party organizations to act primarily as a factor of consciousness, imbuing the working class with its ideals. Although the main outcome of Sixth Congress was a party commitment to self-management and self-government, the party remained an important mechanism of creating intercommunal predictability through either indoctrination or coercion. Likewise, the manhunt for Cominformists played an important role in maintaining intercommunal predictability, even increasing it. The anti-Cominformist purge was a unique opportunity for the CPY leadership to cleanse the land of all potential troublemakers, given the fact that the Cominformists came from all republics and national groups. This elimination de facto helped to strengthen the internal cohesiveness of the Communist Party and, by the same token, intercommunal predictability both within the party and in the polity at large.

*Intercommunal Interdependence*

Communal groups become strategically interdependent when they share control over the outcome of their mutual interactions. The debating communal groups are strategically interdependent because the outcome of the debate depends on all, and the fates of all depend, in turn, on the outcome of the debate. The sense of interdependence among the major communal groups in the Yugoslav polity during 1948–53 was high enough to make any one of them avoid the exit strategy and unilateral moves, such as attempting to side with the Soviet Union against the Tito regime. This sense of intercommunal interdependence was the result of the very structure of ethnic cleavages in Yugoslavia, the regime goal and efforts to solve the national question in the immediate aftermath of the war, and the combined external and internal threats posed by the Cominformist challenge to the Tito regime and Yugoslavia at large. The section below on intercommunal trust explains in detail how both the structure of ethnic cleavages and Tito's solution to the national question inherently built a sense of intercommunal interdependence among the major communal groups. Briefly, the regime efforts to maintain a de facto widely accepted respite to the national question by the major communal groups created more intercommunal interdependence and preserved intercommunal trust.

The external and internal Cominformist threats to the Tito regime reinforced its efforts to build and preserve a strong sense of intercommunal interdependence in the polity. As discussed earlier, Stalin's pressures posed a serious threat to the Tito regime, which was in effect the guarantor of the intercommunal status quo. Yet the regime also relied strongly on the sense of interdependence among the major communal groups in the polity. Had the major communal groups forfeited the Tito regime and sided with the Soviets, Tito would have had serious difficulties maintaining his regime. That the ethnically diversified entourage around Tito remained firmly behind him helped to contain the subversive maneuvers launched by the Cominform against the regime. The Cominform Resolution of June 28, 1948, contributed to the creation of a siege mentality within the top leadership of Yugoslavia, which in turn played an important role in preserving the sense of common fate among the leaders. Cominformist defections from within the minority groups also reinforced the sense of interdependence among the leading groups. The sense of intercommunal interdependence thus became "normal" in the Communist Party as well as in all other major federal institutional arrangements that emerged during the period of experimentation.

To summarize this discussion, the sense of intercommunal interdependence under the Soviet threats of domestic subversion and military invasion induced the various national groups to close ranks and seek a common strategy on how to adapt to the new international conditions. Intercommunal vulnerability was somewhat low and did not show signs of serious increase except at the margins, due to the disruptive effect of Cominformists within the various national groups. Such low vulnerability made it more likely that the Tito regime would be able to reconsolidate state governance despite Soviet best efforts to the contrary. However, as the theory in chapter 3 suggests, low vulnerability is a necessary but insufficient condition for a reconsolidation of state governance in time of change. The transformation of state governance also depends upon intercommunal trust and distribution of institutional power, to which I turn now.

## Intercommunal Trust

When the period of transformation began after the 1948 split with Stalin, the constituent nations were mutually vulnerable enough to realize that it was their common interest to remain united against the Soviets' threats of invasion and subversive maneuvers. The latter also demonstrated to the Yugoslav leaders that the intercommunal trust that had been emerging since the end of the war was an important device that they should use to preempt or contain and address any increase in intercommunal vulnerability. In fact, as the debates unfolded, intercommunal trust increased with the emerging form of state governance, that is, as the scope of collective intentionality increased during the post-1948 debates. However, intercommunal trust remained somewhat moderate and increased significantly only after the formulation of the 1953 Constitutional Law.

Trust emerged and developed after the end of the war through a process of intercommunal construction strongly shaped by then-existing structural lock-in. The latter was a symbiotic relationship between the state institutions and domestic social structures within the opportunities and constraints provided by the 1946 Constitution. Two types of social structure were particularly important in the case of Yugoslavia: salient historical memories and the structure of communal cleavages. Each of the major ethnic groups (Serbs, Croats, Slovenes, and Muslims) justified its aspirations and goals with self-proclaimed historical rights and grievances. Persistent ethnic cleavages of the Yugoslav polity since its inception in 1918 reinforced these memories. The combination of divergent communal memories and the structure of ethnic cleavages was the source material of a national question that remained a characteristic feature of Yugoslavia until its disintegration in 1991. The national question and Tito's constitutional and institutional solutions to it combined to create a structural lock-in, the effects of which characteristically shaped the Yugoslav politics during the period 1948–53. In the following, I briefly discuss the role of communal history in the Yugoslav polity by examining its importance for the major communal groups. I then introduce the structure of ethnic cleavages to show how Tito's solution to the national question in the immediate aftermath of the war created a structural lock-in, the effects of which shaped the transformation of state governance in the 1948–53 period.

*Historical Memories*

Serb historical memory has played a determining role in preserving a strong Serb identity and in rallying Serbs' support for the idea of Greater Serbia, either as an independent state or within Yugoslavia. Three major historical events have particularly shaped Serbs' historical memory: the collapse of the fourteenth-century Serbian Kingdom (Petrovich 1976; Clissold 1966; Singleton 1985), the defeat in the Battle of Kosovo against the Ottomans in 1389 (Emmert 1990; Banac 1995), and Ustasha and Nazi crimes against Serbs during World War II (Denitch 1994). These memories have created within the Serb community both a sense of insecurity and a messianic goal of revenge vis-à-vis Muslims and Croats.

Orthodox Serbs everywhere share an idealized memory of their medieval empire, which allegedly comprised all their ancestors in the fourteenth century under Tsar Dusan the Mighty (Petrovich 1976). They also share the pain of the defeat on the plain of Kosovo in 1389, by which the already crumbling medieval Serbian Empire fell to the Ottoman.[32] The medieval state continued to live in the Serb memory through the ages. The Orthodox Church sanctified it, and folk poetry idealized it. Every Serb is nurtured in the epic tales of past glory and learns the sacred commandment to "avenge Kosovo." Most of these folk poems center around two themes: "the destruction of the Serbian empire" at Kosovo and "the avenging of Kosovo" (Petrovich 1976). Kosovo is sacred to Serbs; they perceive it as the cradle of their culture, church, and statehood and like to call it "our Jerusalem" (Rusinow 1995). After the end of World War II and the establishment of socialist Yugoslavia under Tito, there was a marked decline in public comments on the meaning of Kosovo, even on the anniversary of the battle. The commemorations of the Battle of Kosovo then consisted of services in the Serb Orthodox Church, which compounded the role that the church had historically played in preserving the Kosovo legend (Emmert 1990). The list of complaints in the contemporary discourse of Serb clerics is long and reflects the Serbian Church's construed history as an experience of pain and suffering. The Serbian Orthodox people "remember" that their original church, the Patriarchate of Pec, was suppressed in 1459, at a time when many Serbian monasteries had been razed to ground level during the Ottoman conquest. They also "remember" that upon completing their military conquest of medieval Serbia, the Ottomans gradually converted all large and beautiful churches and monasteries around the cities into mosques or alternatively dismantled them and used their stones to build bridges (Ramet 1995).

The massacres committed during World War II by the Nazis and the Ustasha became engraved in the Serb collective memory as an integral part of the political discourse of communal struggle (Denitch 1994). Systematic destruction of hundreds of monasteries and church buildings, the liquidation of hundreds of Serbian Orthodox clergy, and the wartime deaths of at least six of the church's top hierarchy during the Ustasha campaign of brutal "Croatianization" had a lasting traumatic effect on the Serbian clergy. The fact that this plan of forced exile and liquidation was supplemented by the coercive conversion to Catholicism of part of the Orthodox population under the fascist Independent State of Croatia deepened the identification of Serbdom with Orthodoxy in the consciousness of the Serbian Church. Therefore, the Orthodox Church construed the resistance against the Axis powers occupation as a nationalist cause of the Serb people against two evil forces: Croats and Nazis (Ramet 1992a).

A legendary longing for statehood and preservation of national identity, a continuous struggle against Serb domination during the first Yugoslavia (1919–41), and the images of large numbers of Croats whom the Serb Chetniks killed during World War II dominate the Croats' collective memory (Djilas 1991). The Croats' eagerness and relentless demands for more autonomy and recognition of their national aspirations and self-proclaimed historic rights have been rationalized by a belief in a Serb conspiracy to establish hegemony over Yugoslavia (Ramet 1992b). The Croat question was a most serious and unyielding political issue during both the Kingdom of Yugoslavia and socialist Yugoslavia (Avakumovic 1964; Banac 1984; Ramet 1992b). The Croatian national aspirations for statehood remained the most serious and constant issue for Croatians, before and after the creation of the first Yugoslavia. The debates and conflicts concerning the character of both the interwar and post-1945 Yugoslav state have been in part rooted in Croats' yearning for statehood. Hence, when the Axis powers invaded Yugoslavia in 1941, an important segment of the Croat political elite seized the opportunity and established the Independent State of Croatia under the leadership of the Croat fascist organization, Ustasha. The latter intended to solve the Croat question—the creation of an independent Croatian nation-state—permanently, through all possible means. Thus, the Ustasha endeavored to exterminate and deport the Serb population living within the borders of a purportedly new Croatia. This brutal campaign led to fierce fighting between the Croats, Serbs, and Muslims, which neither the Communist Party nor the old Yugoslav political elite could stop.

More generally, the sense of a Croat question shaped Croatian participation in the war of national liberation. The communists appealed to the nationalist sentiments of the diverse communal groups, both against the occupying powers and in their efforts to rebuild Yugoslavia. The Serbs joined the Partisan movement in large numbers, but the Croats did not, at least not at the beginning of the Resistance. Even after they had joined the Resistance, a large segment of the Croats continued to look mainly to the Croat Peasant Party to achieve their national goals (Irvine 1993). These aspirations thus interfered with the CPY's goal to build a highly centralized state under a strong, monolithic Communist Party. By the last year of the war, the Communist Party was, however, able to achieve a more powerful political and military position, and thus was able to suppress both the Croat Peasant Party and the Catholic Church, which the Croats considered a serious setback to their national sentiments (Avakumovic 1964).[33]

A quest for national, cultural, and linguistic recognition, denied by the Habsburgs and both the first and second Yugoslavia, has dominated the Slovenes' historical memory. Early in the seventh century, the Slovenes established a polity, Karantania. Historically, Karantania remained the only state that the Slovenes could claim as their own before 1991 (Banac 1984; Vodopivec 1994). The Slovene question, primarily a cultural-linguistic question (Rogel 1971; 1994), remained unsolved at the end of World War I, to the disappointment of a majority of the Slovenes. This fundamental question remained an issue of dispute between the Slovenes and the two consecutive Yugoslav states (Dolenc 1994). In the years before World War I, all major Slovene political parties espoused the Yugoslav idea. Common to all was the view that the Slovenes were pressed into a corner between the Germans and Italians. The centrist Constitution of Yugoslavia, which divided the state into thirty-three provinces with no regard for ethnic composition, was, however, a great disappointment for the Slovenes. Thus, in the 1920s, the Slovene political leaders had to resist Belgrade's centralizing tendencies and instead attempted to achieve some degree of Slovene national unity and autonomy. In the 1930s, the question of a national future remained a central theme in the Slovene political debates. The introduction of the Royal Dictatorship in 1929 and the ideology of Yugoslav unitarism accompanied by a suppression of nationalist symbols led many Slovenes, particularly the Slovene intellectuals, to believe that their national existence was in jeopardy (Vodopivec 1994). Yet the Slovenes did not seek outright territorial secession until 1941. Rather, most Slovenes believed in a federal Yugoslavia as an effective solution to their national question. Only in 1944 did the Slovene leadership proclaim as its goal the liberation of all Slovenes and their inclusion in a Slovene state that would still be part of a federal Yugoslavia, if with a guaranteed right of secession. When World War II ended, Slovenia gained a substantial part of territory at Italy's expense (Novak 1990).

The memory of having been part of a major power—the Ottoman Empire—and sharp religious differentiation between the various religious communities in the Balkans have prompted the Muslims to continuously seek a distinct national identity.[34] This quest constantly ran counter to the Serb and Croat nationalistic aspirations. Both the Serb and Croat nationalists often asserted identical, if diametrically conflicting, claims on the Muslims; each insisted that the Bosnian Muslims were part of its nation.[35] For example, during World War II, Bosnia-Herzegovina became an integral part of the Ustasha-led Independent State of Croatia. The Ustasha regarded the Muslims as Croats who converted to Islam and attempted to implicate them in the Ustasha anti-Serb violence. Several Muslim *ulamah* (religious scholars) and notables protested to the German authorities, denying the implication of Muslims in the Ustasha crimes. Ignoring Muslims' claims to the contrary, the Serb Chetniks accused the Muslims of being allied with the Ustasha and accordingly took revenge against the Muslim population by terrorizing and then killing some 86,000 Muslims—6.8 percent of the Muslim population of Bosnia. This genocide so shocked the Muslim community that it became a defining element of its relationship with the Serbs (Banac 1984).

To sum up, historical memory divergences were a salient feature of Yugoslavia's domestic politics. Even Tito's iron fist could not erase the impact of historical memory on the people of Yugoslavia. Yet divergences in historical memory did not necessarily lead to conflicts. They rather were "raw material" that the communal elites and other political entrepreneurs channeled to achieve their agendas. The divergences were reinforced by and, in turn, sustained the role that the structure of ethnic cleavages played in the evolution of the federation.

### *Structure of Ethnic Cleavages*

Yugoslavia was a multinational country, with no clearly dominant ethnic group. Out of a total population of 22.4 million in 1981, for example, the Serbs represented 36.3 percent and the Croats 19.7 percent (Ramet 1992b; Woodward 1995a, 21–46). Significant similarities in terms of language, ethnic origin, and customs exist among the Yugoslav national groups. The country's overall ethnic makeup did not change drastically in the seventy years after the creation of the country in 1918, although the population has grown by more than 70 percent. Exceptions to this pattern of stability were a marked increase of the Albanian population and a steep decline in the numbers of Jews, ethnic Germans, and Hungarians after World War II. Most nationalities were not confined within the borders of the country's republics or provinces, thereby complicating the ethnic landscape. For example, in 1981 about 98 percent of all Yugoslavia's ethnic Slovenes lived in Slovenia, and about 96 percent of its ethnic Macedonians lived in Macedonia. In comparison, only 60 percent of ethnic Serbs lived in Serbia, and only 70 percent of ethnic Montenegrins lived in Montenegro. Croatia had a substantial Serb minority of about 12 percent (Woodward 1995a, 21–46; Djilas 1995, 85–106).

The structure of ethnic cleavages combined with persistent and divergent communal memories to become the source material of a national question that remained a characteristic feature of Yugoslavia from 1918 until 1991. That the national question shaped Yugoslav politics in important ways is evident in the evolution of the Communist Party before, during, and after World War II. First, the Communist Party, like every other communist party, initially based its analysis of the Yugoslav history and formulated its project of an eventual communist Yugoslav polity and society on the premise that class struggle was the determining factor of the unfolding historical process in Yugoslavia. However, the national question slowly suffused the Communist Party as its members increasingly debated the issue during the interwar period. Second, the national question shaped the resistance struggle during World War II from beginning to end, thereby creating a legacy that the communists had to put up with until the collapse of the federation in 1991. Third, the close relationship between the partisan struggle during the war and the national question was passed on to the federal system established in the aftermath of the war.

### *National Question and Prewar Communist Party of Yugoslavia*

The Communist movement played a major role in the struggle for the unity of the Yugoslav peoples but remained itself internally divided on the national question prior to World War II. During the period 1919–41, the communists debated the national question among themselves almost as fiercely as the non-communist parties did, even though the communists were not particularly interested in being defenders of local peoples' interests or the national honor. They were instead pursuing their own revolutionary aims. For example, neither the First nor the Second Congress of the Yugoslav Communist Party passed a resolution on the national question. Nor was this question an issue in any of the intra-party factional struggles of this period. The communists then vigorously supported the principle of state centralism and advocated the formation of a unitary state. They hence did not even attempt to exploit the national question for their own revolutionary ends (Shoup 1968, 19). Before 1922, the communists were blind to the real meaning of the national question, refusing to recognize that the movements of non-Serb nationalities had a popular base and expressed the interests of the lower classes. The communists perceived the nationalist struggle as a creature of native capitalists. For example, *Borba* (struggle), the organ of the left faction in Zagreb, portrayed the national radicalism of the Croat Peasant Party and the Croat Party of Right as nothing but a bogey invented by Croat capitalists to put pressure on the Serbian bourgeoisie.[36] Beginning in 1922, however, a debate over the national question began to develop within the Communist Party between the Markovic faction,[37] on the one hand, and a left faction supporting the Communist International (Comintern), on the other. In general, the Yugoslav communists saw an analogy between the nationality problems of Russia and

Yugoslavia and hence took guidance from the way in which the Soviet Union treated multinational relationships (Pipes 1980, 144; Williams 1955, 32–35, 59; Shoup 1968, 24; Hondius 1968, 120).

Intra-party debates on the national question brought two main benefits to the Yugoslav Communist Party. First, thanks to internal chronic disputes on the question, the party gained an important experience in dealing with the Yugoslav nationalities. The party slowly evolved to identify with the demands of the exploited nationalities, thereby gaining a vital appreciation of the national differences that existed among the Yugoslav peoples. Second, the party's association with the struggle for national rights slowly built up its strength in many different national regions. Yet the party was fully committed to finding an all-Yugoslav solution to the national question. The emergence of this attitude and the appearance of a party leadership (Tito and his chosen men)[38] capable of carrying it out benefited the party immensely when it could not escape addressing the national question in the course of the resistance struggle.

*National Question and Partisan Resistance*

During the Second World War, the Communist Party formulated a successful nationalities policy, which became instrumental to the victory of the Partisans over the occupation authorities and rival anticommunist Yugoslav groups. The success of the CPY depended on the restoration of Yugoslavia, for which the communists espoused a qualitatively new type of state. This inevitably brought them into conflict with the supporters of the old regime—the government in exile and its supporting Chetnik guerrillas at home (Banac 1988, 78–79). After Germany attacked the Soviet Union, Tito genuinely sought to change the party ideological-programmatic line from one driven by a communist class struggle to a war for national liberation against the occupiers and their domestic accomplices. Ustasha terror against the Serbs in Croatia and Bosnia-Herzegovina, the harsh German measures in Slovenia and Serbia, the unpopularity of the Italians in Dalmatia and Montenegro, and the Chetnik terror against Muslims and Croats all combined to create an insurgent popular base, which the militarized CPY successfully co-opted. Using its well-organized structure, the CPY in time absorbed the amorphous mass movement in most areas of Yugoslavia, infusing it with a dual ideology of communist revolution and national liberation. Two factors contributed to the success of the communist agenda at the expense of all other parties and movements in Yugoslavia. First, anticommunist national forces failed to understand the long-range implications of deserting Yugoslavia in its hour of need. They made a fatal mistake in underestimating the national appeal of the resistance struggle to the Slav nationalities. In contrast, the communists capitalized on the national "chord" and channeled it in organizing the resistance.[39] Second, the communist Partisans were able to build a strong base of popular support within certain national groups, especially the Serbs outside Serbia, the Montenegrins, the Dalmatians, the Slovenes, and, in the closing years of the war, the Macedonians.[40]

There is no doubt that the communists succeeded in rallying behind their party most of the Yugoslav ethnic groups for the cause of fighting the war of national liberation. The communists nevertheless avoided committing themselves to any one general solution to the national question in the first year and a half of the resistance. They instead concentrated their efforts on attempting to strengthen the military discipline and establish party control over widely scattered partisan units. To this end, they formed on November 26 and 27 two governing boards: the Antifascist Council for the National Liberation of Yugoslavia (AVNOJ) and its executive board, the National Liberation Committee (NOO). Delegates sent by the Partisan movements of the various regions of Yugoslavia proclaimed AVNOJ to be the sole representative of the resistance in Yugoslavia (Bokovoy 1998, 18). To keep up this momentum of success, Tito refrained from directly addressing any potentially divisive solution to the national question, at least not before holding the first meeting of AVNOJ. Only afterward did Tito begin drawing the general contours for a discussion on the rights of the national regions, which consisted of following the Bolshevik principle of self-determination and secession.[41] As a result, in November 1943 AVNOJ issued a resolution that Yugoslavia will be a federation guaranteeing the right to self-determination and secession for the constituent nationalities, which was eventually formalized in the 1946 Constitution. The Partisan way of dealing with the national question—the combined effects of divergent communal memories and the structure of ethnic cleavages—during the resistance struggle hence strongly shaped the communists' approach to the national question after the war.

*Structural Lock-In: National Question Immediately after the War*

The Tito regime decided to adapt to the Yugoslav context the 1936 Soviet solution to the nationalities problem by designing the new political system as a federation that would reconcile the communist ideal with the realities of the national question.[42] The combination of the realities of the national question and the constitutional and institutional solutions to it became a structural lock-in that shaped the evolution of state governance in socialist Yugoslavia.

The structural lock-in is evident in how the 1946 Yugoslav Constitution addressed important issues such as defining "the Yugoslav people," deciding on which nations to officially recognize, and formulating how the federation should put these principles into practice. The Constitution did not introduce a new definition of the Yugoslav peoples, for the Third AVNOJ Resolution of November 29, 1943, had already done so. Article 2 of the resolution stipulated that as "Yugoslavia develops and will continue to develop according to the federative principle which will guarantee full legal equality to the Serbs, Croats, Slovenes, Macedonians and Montenegrins, respectively the peoples of Serbia, Croatia, Slovenia, Macedonia, Montenegro and Bosnia and Hercegovina" (Hondius 1968, 138). The Constitution recognized five nationalities: Serbs, Croats, Slovenes, Macedonians, and Montenegrins. The members of a nation were restricted to the republic in which the nationality was demographically predominant, but also included all those with the same ethnic or national background, irrespective of their geographical location within Yugoslavia. At the same time, each republic became the homeland of the dominant nationality within its boundaries. In deference to national feelings, the communists established republican parties in Serbia in 1945 and in Montenegro and Bosnia-Herzegovina in the period 1948–49. The 1946 Constitution also defined the inter-nation relations according to the principles of national equality, respect for national differences, and an end to the exploitation of any one nationality. These three principles became basic rights that the Yugoslav Party sought to introduce into postwar politics (Shoup 1968, 120). In terms of implementation, the structural lock-in also shaped the party's strategy. This transpires from a set of continuing practices developed during the war. For example, the party deployed politically reliable and nationally acceptable personnel among the minorities to overcome hostility to the communists. The party also used national cadres to spread Yugoslav influence into neighboring republics. Likewise, the party staffed government and political posts with indigenous officials who were representatives of the national composition of the respective regions.

This structural lock-in between the national question and the regime solution to it had three important effects on domestic politics. First, the lock-in reinforced the importance of nationalities below the federal level in the day-to-day political practice both within and outside the Communist Party. Even though in the Politburo proportionality of national representation did not play a decisive role, Yugoslav federalism was severely constrained with the centralism that characterized the structure of the Communist Party itself. The party leadership, making its decisions in the Politburo, had to rely on a large bureaucracy that reached down to the republic and local levels. Yet the local party members were still largely provincial in their habits and approach to the national question, in spite of being loyal to the party leadership and to the larger aims of the Communist movement as a whole. The dichotomy created many distortions in regions of mixed nationality, reflecting local prejudices, the strong resistance of certain groups to participating in the system, or both. For example, in Croatia, the Serbs outnumbered the Croats in government and party positions, even though the Serbs were only a minority in Croatia (Shoup 1968, 121–22).

Second, the structural lock-in shaped the *ex ante* agency (that is, what counts as a political agent and its degree of freedom of action) and *ex post* agency (that is, the potential to go beyond the expected limits of political behavior and action). This is evident both in the official policies and practices and in the challenges to them from different quarters of the population. Defining and delimiting as well as enforcing *ex ante* and *ex post* agency were at the core of the 1946 Constitution, the development of the national question in the aftermath of the war, and the evolution of the manhunt for Yugoslav Cominformists after 1948. Nationalist federalism clearly became an official framework that defined the *ex ante* agency of the major communal groups. The number of officially recognized nationalities was set at five (Serbs, Croats, Slovenes, Macedonians, and Montenegrins). The members of a nation were not restricted to the republic in which the nationality predominated, for they also included all those with the same ethnic or national background, whatever part of Yugoslavia they inhabited. At the same time, each republic was considered the homeland of the dominant nationality within its boundaries. This way of circumscribing the *ex ante* agency of national groups was challenged in different areas of Yugoslavia. For example, nationalistic disputes emerged within the party between the Serbs and Croats over the allocation of the autonomous area of Vojvodina and the Srem. The Croats had much interest in the Srem, for it had traditionally been part of Croatian Slavonia, and the Croatian main command had exercised jurisdiction over most of the area during the war. The Serbs tended to view Vojvodina as part of Serbia and the Srem as part of Vojvodina because of the large number of Serbs in both regions.[43] There also were debates over the autonomous status of the Sandzak region. The convening of the Anti-Fascist Assembly for the Sandzak in November 1943 had created the impression that the area was being prepared for autonomous status after the war. The Yugoslav leadership had to send a special commission to the region to explain and rally support for its decision of dividing it between Serbia and Montenegro after the war (Shoup 1968, 118). Moreover, as discussed earlier, most national groups de facto accepted the communist solution to the national question after the World War II massacres, thereby creating a sort of self-imposed limitation on *ex ante* agency.

The centralism that characterized the structure of the Communist Party itself strongly circumscribed the *ex post* agency of the communal groups. The party leadership used a large bureaucracy, with main sections that reached down to the republic and local levels to limit and control the freedom of the national groups. The party also used its propaganda machine to minimize the nationalist threat. Through control of the press and other mass media outlets, the party created the impression that prewar national attitudes had only few supporters within the population at large. In addition, the communists passed legislation that severely punished as a criminal offense any act inciting national, racial, or religious antagonisms (Shoup 1968, 110). There were challenges to the limitations imposed by the party on the *ex post* agency of the communal groups, however. Most of these challenges came from the minorities. The Albanians were the most hostile element among the minorities, advocating the idea of a "Greater Albania" that would include Kosovo-Metohija in Albania.[44] The Serbs in Croatia also posed a serious problem for the communists. The party took a number of steps to mollify the Serbian population in Croatia and the Serbs who returned to Croatia after the war to claim their land (Shoup 1968, 112–13).

Hence, the structural lock-in that emerged from a symbiotic combination of communal histories, the structure of ethnic cleavages, and Tito's postwar state institutionalization defined as well as delimited the *ex ante* and *ex post* agency of communal groups. The latter conditions in turn shaped the process of preserving the intercommunal trust that existed at the beginning of the period, 1948–53.

### *Preserving Intercommunal Trust*

Preserving intercommunal trust during the 1948–53 period of radical transformation of state governance was necessarily linked to the national question. In contrast with the interethnic massacres that occurred during the war, a respite on the national question by and large characterized the immediate aftermath of the war. The major communal groups were willing to trust one another enough and consequently accept the new framework of intercommunal relations. Yet the process of preserving this intercommunal trust did not evolve without serious challenges. As discussed earlier, the Cominformist dissent and Soviet subversive attempts threatened to reignite the issue. As a countermeasure, the regime used a number of strategies in its continuous attempt to preserve the level of intercommunal trust that existed in the immediate postwar years.

First, the regime endeavored to create and propagate two major myths via ideological manipulation of history and a sense of dual identity (Siber 1994, 371–99). The first myth was that the communists had succeeded in solving the national question. Tito epitomized this strategy when he declared, "the reason that I don't say anything about the national question is not because with us, it is posed in this or that form. No, the national question with us has been solved and to be precise, solved very well, to the general satisfaction of all our nationalities. It has been solved in the way Lenin and Stalin have taught us."[45] The party propaganda machine also sought to create the myth that the Partisan wartime victory was due to the communist success in solving the national question during the war (Djilas 1991, 150–74; Banac 1988, 98–111; Shoup 1968, 101–42). To drive the point home, the official Yugoslav party journal called in 1950 for a reassessment of the history of Yugoslavia in order to demonstrate that the Yugoslav state was no "accident," but a long-standing aspiration of the Yugoslav people.[46]

In addition, the Communist Party endeavored to construct a sense of dual identity—a superposition of national identity (Serb, Croat, Slovene, etc.) with an overall Yugoslav identity—through a process of widespread political socialization. The party hence emphasized the "all-Yugoslav" historical experience of a joint struggle for freedom, independence, and a common state during the War of National Liberation, symbolized in the famous slogan of "*bratstvo i jedinstvo*" (brotherhood and unity). In textbooks and various educational materials for the lower grades, the ideological values were often linked with Tito himself, identifying the system strongly with the leader. The texts intentionally sought to exaggerate the share of the so-called history of the workers' movement. For instance, the role of the Communist Party in chapters dealing with interwar Yugoslavia usually occupied nine to ten pages or more. The share of party and partisan politics and military events in the chapter on World War II covered usually more than half of the entire war period in the textbooks and almost four-fifths of the description of the war on Yugoslav territory (Höpken 1997, 88).

Second, the communist leaders purposively tailored the educational curricula to downplay the historical as well as social role of the national question. All textbooks described the national conflicts within interwar Yugoslavia as being the result of the Serbian bourgeoisie's desire for hegemony and of quarrels, bargaining, and unclean arrangements among all three south Slav bourgeoisies (Höpken 1997, 91). Croatian and Serbian textbooks presented very little information on this topic and were reluctant to bring up the history of the Serbian-Croatian conflict too frankly in class. For instance, only about two to three pages in Serbian and Croatian textbooks dealt with this crucial issue in interwar history. Slovenian and Macedonian textbooks gave more room to the national question, dedicating most of that space, however, to the fate of "co-nationals" abroad in Austria, Bulgaria, and Greece (Höpken 1997, 91). Nor were the textbooks dealing with the bloodiest conflicts of World War II differently organized. The Ustasha, the Chetniks, the question of terror and ethnic violence, World War II as a civil war, that is, most of the hot topics that could potentially serve as materials for nationalistic manipulation in the dawn of the second Yugoslav state were practically absent from the teaching curricula. Overall, the textbooks referred to these topics by means of a superficially balanced view of reciprocity, arguing that all nations had their traitors, all committed cruelties, and no nation had more or less guilt (Höpken 1997, 92).

In parallel, the party used coercive measures to deal with those who might undermine the sense of intercommunal coexistence and mutual trust in the polity. The confrontation between the Communist Party and religious organizations is illustrative. In Zagreb, in May 1945, Tito proposed a truce to the Catholic Church if the Yugoslav Catholics would form a "national" church and cut their ties with the papacy.[47] The Catholics rejected the offer and a struggle between the church and the party ensued. The communists were interested in discrediting the Catholic Church and driving a wedge between the Croats and the church. The attempt failed, however, and the Church of Croatia remained a symbol of noncommunist nationalism (Pattee 1953, 417). The Serbian Orthodox Church, despite its patriarch's reputation as a vehement foe of the communists, reached an understanding with the new regime.[48] In return, the communists decided to ignore the fact that the Serbian Orthodox Church had favored the Chetniks during the war and allowed the Orthodox religion to survive as a symbol of Serbian national traditions. The Muslims posed a special challenge for the communists. The party at first tried to avoid a clash with the Muslim Religious Community (IVZ). The communist tactics of appeasing the Muslims were not successful, however. Not only were anticommunist Muslim leaders able to win official posts in the IVZ in fall 1945 elections, but the following year saw even more rapid growth of anticommunist feeling throughout the Muslim community.[49] The communists thus decided to use more coercive means against the IVZ in 1947 by cutting off its financial support to the community and by making it impossible for the Muslims to raise their own funds for schools and other activities from private benefactors.[50] Furthermore, the regime formulated a new constitution for the IVZ, making it an autonomous organization representing all Yugoslav Muslims. By enlarging the organization membership so much while at the same time keeping tight control over its financial sources and a close eye on most of its activities, the regime succeeded in severely circumscribing the IVZ, if not making it completely ineffective and irrelevant to the cause of the Muslims. This was compounded by other far-reaching measures that sought to impose many changes on the traditionally distinctive Muslim way of life. For example, the *Shariah* (Islamic) courts were dissolved and wearing the *hijab* (a women's Islamic veil) was prohibited in the period 1950–51.

Official rhetoric on having solved the national question notwithstanding, the task of preserving intercommunal trust as a solution the national question was not without challenges. The nationalities question reemerged in the late 1950s, slowly taking the form of a cultural problem and an economic national question. That the regime worked to preempt an effective separation of the polity into isolated "cultural" republics is an indication of the challenges that confronted the process of constructing a higher level of intercommunal trust. The regime sought to deal with this issue by organizing a campaign against any move to isolate the republics from one another. To this end, the regime encouraged inter-republican exchanges of delegations made up of artists, writers, performers, and other culture producers, as well as active participation in multi-republican performances. The regime also launched a broad attack against the reappearance of romantic national works on the public stage and criticized those cultural associations, particularly among the minorities, that exclusively focused their concerns on narrow national themes.[51] Likewise, the authorities criticized the major newspapers for not devoting enough space to events taking place in republics other than their own. The regime also made a great effort in pointing out the waste involved in the duplication in such fields as scientific research and publishing.[52] A favorite object of attack was the practice of publishing school textbooks separately, and at great expense, in each of the six republics.[53]

The national question was also evident in the economic realm. In the postwar period, the communists had persistently linked the national question to economic issues by asserting that the national question would remain a problem as long as inequalities in levels of economic development persisted in Yugoslavia. The Yugoslav communists self-servingly placed the blame for economic nationalism on narrow-minded bureaucrats, or so-called remnants of bourgeois nationalism. These ideological and self-serving claims notwithstanding, inter-republican economic rivalry became very visible in the post-1953 era as each republic or region sought to pursue its narrow economic interests without much regard for the welfare of the country as a whole. This occurred in two ways: first, in efforts to deal with the great contrast between the developed and underdeveloped regions of Yugoslavia; second, in a competition between local or regional units, known as *particularism* and often taking the form of national rivalries. The existence of great contrasts in levels of economic development across different regions (and often among the districts within the same region) had been a fundamental problem of Yugoslavia since the time of the country's formation. The communists tried to ease the plight of the economically underdeveloped regions in two ways. A first approach, which became the center of a controversy among the republics, was to allocate investment funds to the poorer areas for industrial development. The other approach was the practice of providing grants-in-aid, or their equivalent, to the republics to meet immediate financial needs. The regime largely overlooked shortcomings in the program of federal aid until the 1950s, that is, only when it became apparent that the poorer republics would not reach the level of economic development of the more advanced regions any time soon. At the end of the adjustment period, that is, in 1956, the poorer republics had not appreciably improved their position relative to the more advanced ones. The developed republics argued that it was a waste of their resources and that the failure of new industries to prove their profitability raised doubts about the very policy of aiding underdeveloped regions. The federal government had thus to address the very delicate problem of reconciling diverging republican economic interests. Attempts to limit the dispute were unsuccessful because not only were the economic problems insoluble, but also because of the new trend of particularism. The party had serious difficulties deciding where economics ended and nationalism began, as Tito himself admitted.[54] Frequent party declarations that referred to the role of nationalism in these economic controversies clearly evidence the rise and persistence of a national economic question. For example, one letter of the Executive Committee of the League of Communists of February 1958 spoke of "powerful particularistic tendencies which are appearing . . . frequently assuming a nationalistic, even chauvinistic, form."[55] The emergence of self-reinforcing debate on the national economic question was also visible in the split between the conservative group led by Alexander Rankovic (a Serb leader) and the liberal wing of the party in the late 1950s (Shoup 1968, 248).

In chapter 3, I discussed three indicators of the level of trust, namely, (1) intercommunal policies and actions that tie together the fates of the groups, (2) the discursive explanations of the group positions toward each other and their mutual descriptions, and (3) the safeguard mechanisms designed to address the issues of *ex ante* and *ex post* agency. Because of the nature of the Tito regime during the period 1948–53, it is somewhat hard to use the first two indicators to measure directly the level of intercommunal trust.[56] As discussed earlier, in its efforts to contain and eliminate the Cominformist challenge the Tito regime used a variety of strategies, spanning a spectrum extending from ideological indoctrination to camp internment and jail. One effect of these strategies was to suppress almost all avenues of expressing intercommunal positions and policies independently of the regime. In other words, the regime attempted and succeeded in homogenizing the communal groups' responses and actions during the Cominformist challenge. It is plausible to argue that the regime did so by preventing any intercommunal "coloration" of the federation policies in its dealing with the Soviet threats and challenges. Hence, although it is not easy to measure the extent to which the major communal groups behaved both trustworthily and trustingly toward one another, one can argue that they did not show signs of acting untrustworthily or untrustingly toward one another. Likewise, the major communal groups did not have much leeway in designing safeguard mechanisms to monitor compliance with mutual intercommunal commitments. The regime, as also discussed earlier, designed a number of safeguard mechanisms and strategies to ensure a shift from being *ex ante* preemption to *ex post* detection of "breach of trust." The regime homogenized these safeguard mechanisms in the federation, thereby preventing an intercommunal coloration, even during the challenges posed by certain minorities during the Cominformist challenges.

In conclusion, intercommunal trust during 1948–53, while not high, was clearly not decreasing. This enabled the Tito regime to reconsolidate state governance despite the external Soviet threat, the Cominformist "fifth-column" inside Yugoslavia, and the challenges entailed by a transformation of the state ideological doctrine, the role of the Communist Party, and the constitutional, political, and economic institutional arrangements of the state. Intercommunal trust did, however, stagnate and begin to decline somewhat as the national question slowly reemerged in the late 1950s. Understanding the role of this evolution of intercommunal trust in the debates following the Stalin-Tito split is necessary for a comprehensive understanding of how the regime succeeded in transforming the system of state governance. However, as expected from the theory explicated in chapter 3, the effects of this evolution of intercommunal trust on the construction of a new form of state governance did not occur in isolation from another important factor, namely, the intercommunal distribution of institutional power.

## Institutional Power Leverage

As argued in chapter 3, for a given level of vulnerability, reliance on institutional power increases as intercommunal trust decreases, and vice versa. For a given level of vulnerability, the more rapidly the reliance on institutional power increases (decreases), the more rapidly intercommunal trust will decrease (increase), and the more rapidly the scope of collective intentionality will decrease (increase). Testing these two hypotheses in the case of 1948–53, Yugoslavia can be done only indirectly because the fear as well as the facts of Soviet subversive maneuvers induced the Tito regime to rely on coercion to preempt any serious threats of dissent. This preempted de facto an emergence of intercommunal competition for institutional power. Even during the Cominformist manhunt, Tito and his close (multi-communal) entourage strongly controlled the distribution of institutional power. None of the major communal groups thus had used, or even tried to use, its share of institutional power to shape the debates on the transformation of state governance.

Broadly speaking, the evolution of the intercommunal distribution of institutional power can be traced in the move from the framework of the 1946 Constitution to the one encapsulated in the 1953 Constitutional Law. The transformation amounted to abandoning a Soviet solution to the nationality problem. The Yugoslav leaders opted for a system that did not perpetuate the national divisions in the polity by rescinding the republics' rights of secession and sovereignty granted to them in 1946. The regime also weakened the representation of the republics in the Federal People's Assembly through a reconfiguration of the bicameral Federal Assembly, with part of its delegates elected directly while the other part was composed of indirectly elected representatives of the republics and autonomous units. The Constitutional Law also concentrated more powers in the hands of Tito and his close entourage by abolishing the Presidium and the government and replacing it with the president of the federation. A Federal Executive Council (FEC) replaced the Council of Ministers, which as a whole was responsible for the entire executive sphere, with no sharp division of work among or delegation of power to any of its members. The Constitutional Law emphasized the idea of cooperative federalism by stipulating that the Federal Executive Council should include members from all people's republics (article 82, paragraph 4).[57] The net effect of these transformations was that the Tito regime acquired tighter control of the federal institutions. This effectively preempted the emergence of any effective asymmetry of institutional power among the major communal groups, particularly at the federal level. The situation inside the republics was different, however. The republics differed in terms of who dominated the republican institutions, with minorities usually playing only a subordinate role in the republics' institutions.

The Tito regime, as noted earlier, combined coercive and manipulative policies and means in instituting the various transformations as well as in subduing and eradicating any serious challenge from the Cominformists and other would-be pretenders. However, as the Soviet threat receded, the Yugoslav leaders slowly opted for a greater devolution of institutional power across the intercommunal landscape, as the new 1963 federal and republican Constitutions indicate. Self-management and self-government brought fundamental changes to the political scene, especially on the role of the republics, which now assumed the role of mediators, or transmission wheels, between the self-governing communities and the federation.[58]

That intercommunal reliance on institutional power was rather low and somewhat stagnated as the national question began to reemerge in the late 1950s is indicated (if indirectly) in the three ways discussed near the end of chapter 3. The Tito regime had a tight grip on institutional power, which implies that no communal group could muster more institutional power than the other groups. That, for example, the Serbs were better represented in certain institutions than other groups did not grant them more influence than these other communal groups simply because the leaders themselves were committed to the communist path. Consequently, the debates among the major communal groups (or, more exactly, their leaders) did not become intercommunally colored, the challenge posed by some minority groups notwithstanding. Nor did the division of rights and obligations among the dominant and subordinate groups play an important role during the debates process. In short, the Tito regime did rely much on institutional power to transform the system of state governance; however, for the most part this reliance on institutional power was not intercommunally "colored"—intercommunal reliance on institutional power remained quite low during the whole episode of debating state governance.

## Conclusion

The transformation of state governance during 1948–53 in Yugoslavia was rooted in the fundamental transformation of the international environment with the emergence of the Cold War and in the dual Cominformist internal and external threats that the Stalin-Tito split created for the Tito regime. Adapting to the new constitutive rule of international bloc politics while preserving independence from the Soviets, remaining a communist state, and eliminating domestic challenges led the Yugoslav leaders to seek a radical transformation of state governance.

The transformation of state governance into a reconsolidated form was possible because intercommunal vulnerability remained quite low during the period 1948–53, if somewhat increasing as the divisive national question began to reemerge in the late 1950s. Under these conditions, the major communal groups had no serious fear of intercommunal abandonment, exploitation, or exclusion from participating in the debates that transformed state governance. This was expected, as information complexity was low to moderate since the major communal groups had reliable information on each other's intentions and capabilities. In addition, intercommunal predictability was moderate to high since there was enough mutual intercommunal commitment to the communist arrangement. The dual Cominformist threats from the Soviet Union (and its allies) and domestic Cominformists created a sense of intercommunal interdependence among the major communal groups in Yugoslavia. This greatly strengthened the incentives for the communal groups to transform state governance in dealing with the fundamental changes occurring in the international environment. Also, as the communists increasingly succeeded in surpassing the 1948 crisis and the emerging rules and practices of state governance were enacted and encapsulated eventually in the 1953 Constitutional Law, intercommunal vulnerability decreased.

However, the outcome of transforming state governance was not solely determined by the somewhat low intercommunal vulnerability. As outlined in the theory, and shown in this case, intercommunal vulnerability and trust are interactive. Although intercommunal trust was not yet high, it nonetheless was enough to contain the fear of intercommunal vulnerability. The Yugoslav leaders understood that the intercommunal trust that had been developing since the end of the war of liberation was an important asset that they should strengthen and use to preempt or contain any increase in intercommunal vulnerability. In fact, as the debates unfolded, intercommunal trust increased with the emerging form of state governance. Hence, intercommunal trust increased as the scope of collective intentionality increased during the post-1948 debates. Moreover, had intercommunal trust been much lower, the transformation of state governance under the dual external-internal Cominformist threats might have ended in a failing form of state governance. A reconsolidated form of state governance was likely but not inevitable during the period 1948–53.

The outcome of the debates over transforming state governance, in turn, depended on the interaction of intercommunal trust and reliance on institutional power. Yet, as noted above, because Tito and his entourage had retreated from the more decentralized 1946 institutional arrangement to a more centralized institutional design, the major communal groups could not rely on institutional power as a means to shape the debates on state governance. Instead, the Tito regime concentrated most of the institutional powers in its hand and used them as a means to carry on the transformation agenda as well as eliminate the domestic Cominformist challenge. The regime effectively used its control over institutional power to maintain intercommunal trust as the 1953 Constitutional Law was being formulated.

By transforming the rules and practices of state governance, the Tito regime created a new set of constitutional-institutional incentives toward which domestic actors responded by making new commitments on a perennially sensitive issue—the national question. These commitments slowly became self-reinforcing and led to a process of increasing returns. In other words, the incentive sets that emerged with the transformed rules and practices of state governance consolidated into a new structural lock-in on the national question that would ultimately shape the evolution of the federation toward adopting a new constitution in 1974 and would outlive the Tito regime itself.

# Five

# Yugoslavia and the Waning Cold War, 1987–91

After Tito's death in 1980, and especially after the emergence of an new style of republican leadership that did not hesitate to revive and utilize intercommunal fears and threats in pursuit of political goals as epitomized by Slobodan Milosevic of Serbia, the Yugoslav polity was confronted with a waning Cold War within difficult global economic conditions. The federation was consequently losing its buffer role between the two sides of the Cold War. Absent the Cold War, privileges such as economic assistance were lost. More important, the Yugoslav state found itself immersed in new international conditions that it was not prepared to deal with. The dire political and economic conditions within the federation compounded such difficulties and generated divisive and heated debates on the future of the state. The outcome of the debates was a collapse of the federal state and a territorial dismemberment of Yugoslavia. State governance completely collapsed because of three elements. First, intercommunal vulnerability was high and rapidly increased as the republican leaders relied increasingly more on ultranationalistic agendas and rhetoric. Second, intercommunal trust was low and quickly decreased as the debates raised more doubts on the existing form of state governance. Third, reliance on institutional power increased quickly (for the Serbs) as the debates became more virulent.

## Theoretical Expectations

The end of the Cold War in the late 1980s fundamentally redefined the constitutive rules and practices of international politics (Koslowski and Kratochwil 1994). The 1989 revolutions in Europe changed the rules governing superpower relations and, therewith, the practices underpinning the international system. The collapse of communism in Eastern Europe hollowed the Warsaw Pact and resulted in the collapse of the Soviet Empire and state. This had far-reaching consequences for Yugoslavia because various constitutive rules and practices such as the U.S. strategy of containment and Soviet Brezhnev doctrine of the Cold War system had become defining elements of the Yugoslav state. These international rules and practices produced and sustained the buffer role that Yugoslavia held between the two camps of the Cold War. As discussed in the previous chapter, the post-1948 Yugoslav state was as much the product of the constitutive rules and practices of the Cold War rivalry as Tito's efforts to construct and consolidate a fully independent Yugoslav state with its own brand of communism. The Tito regime, the United States and its Western allies, and the Soviet Union and its East European informal empire all helped to legitimize the constitutive rules and practices of the Yugoslav political system. State governance of the federation remained dependent on this two-level dynamic legitimation until the waning of the Cold War context in the late 1980s.

Tito played the role of an arbiter between the various Yugoslav ideological and national divisions. His death thus deprived the political system of an important stabilizing element. Before his death, however, Tito had built an important set of federal institutions (such as the Collective Presidency), which, if not yet completely successful, had the potential to maintain stability in the federal state. The global economic recession of the late 1970s had an impact on the evolution of the Yugoslav polity in the 1980s by depriving Yugoslavia of much-needed external financial and economic support to continue subsidizing its socioeconomic self-management establishment. However, Yugoslavia was not the only state affected by the worldwide economic recession. These two factors—the global economic recession and Tito's death—cannot satisfactorily explain the collapse of the Yugoslav state, since the federation lasted under these conditions for another eleven years. The state was undoubtedly weak and faced various socioeconomic and political problems but nonetheless was able to maintain itself, despite ethnic upheavals such as those of the Albanian population in Kosovo in 1980. Rather, the end of the Cold War, which fundamentally redefined international politics, problematized the constitutive rules and practices of the Yugoslav state. The theory outlined in chapter 3 suggests that in this case the outcome of the debates on state governance in the period 1987–91 was most likely to be a collapse of state governance of the Yugoslav federation.

Three primary factors mutually reinforced one another and combined to produce this outcome. First, the level of intercommunal vulnerability reached a high level in the period 1987–91 as the republican leaders began to seek unilateral moves that would protect and promote their communal interests. Under these conditions, the major communal groups increasingly became fearful of intercommunal abandonment, exploitation, or exclusion from participating in the debates on the fate of the Yugoslav state. The high and rapidly increasing level of intercommunal vulnerability was the result of a very high level of information complexity, a low level of intercommunal predictability, and a high level of intercommunal interdependence. Information complexity became very high as communal leaders increasingly faced a lack as well as misrepresentation of information on each other' intentions and actions. The level of intercommunal predictability was low since there increasingly was no commitment to the status quo arrangement and the leaders and political entrepreneurs were increasingly sidestepping the federal institutions. At the same time, the major communal groups remained strongly interdependent due to a mismatch of the structure of ethnic cleavages and the republics. This situation was more acute for the Serbian leaders as the Serbs were dispersed in almost all the republics, with particularly strong concentrations in Croatia and Bosnia-Herzegovina. These leaders rose to, and remained in, power positions due largely to their ultranationalistic leadership style. They hence would not downplay the role of intercommunal vulnerability for themselves as well as for their respective communal groups. Strong interdependence among the major communal groups in the Yugoslav polity greatly strengthened the incentives for the Yugoslav communal groups to debate state governance in seeking a way out of the crisis (hypothesis 1). How to address this vulnerability was not an easy matter, however. As communal leaders increasingly debated how to transform state governance, intercommunal vulnerability increased with decreases in the scope of collective intentionality in the polity, that is, as the different leaders and their followers were increasingly less willing to accept the existing rules and practices of state governance as a framework for playing the game of politics (hypothesis 3).

Second, intercommunal trust that the federal institutions and policies had managed to secure under Tito and his aftermath was quickly eroding, particularly after the rise of the new style of ultranationalistic leadership under dire socioeconomic conditions. As the debates on state governance unfolded in the late 1980s, intercommunal trust eroded even more rapidly as the republican leaders not only began to talk past one another but also engaged each other in rhetorical wars of incriminations and blame for the problems that one's communal group was facing or could face. Hence, intercommunal trust rapidly decreased as the scope of collective intentionality decreased in the debates of 1988–91 (hypothesis 5).

Third, as intercommunal trust was quickly eroding, the leaders began to resort to whatever institutional power they believed they had or could muster. However, not every republican leader had access to the federal institutional power in the same way. There indeed was much asymmetry in this respect, with the Serbian leadership reserving for itself the lion's share. Hence, the Serbs began to rely increasingly more on their institutional power to impose their choices on the other republics (hypotheses 6 and 7). Yet the latter, most prominently the Slovenes and Croats, opposed such moves and began to act outside the political boundaries set by the existing rules and practices of state governance. The more the Serbian leadership resorted to its power advantage in the federal institutions, the more the Slovenes and Croats defected, and the more the various competing actors were less willing to continue abiding by the existing rules and practices of state governance. This in turn eroded further an already weak intercommunal trust. This cycle continued until fighting between the Slovenes and the Yugoslav National Army (YNA) troops erupted in June 1990. Hence, the level of reliance on institutional power increased with rapidly decreasing scope of collective intentionality (hypothesis 8). Therefore, overall the reliance on institutional power increased as intercommunal trust decreased (hypothesis 9).

These values of the three variables—intercommunal vulnerability, trust, and distribution of institutional power—are close to the "most likely conditions" for collapsed governance with a zero scope of collective intentionality, as explicated in table 3.1 (chapter 3). Hence, that the Yugoslav polity failed to preserve its state confirms the expectations of the theory outlined in chapters 2 and 3. These theoretical expectations are summarized in table 5.1.

## Changes in the Constitutive Rules of the International Environment

The end of the Cold War in the late 1980s fundamentally redefined the constitutive rules and practices of international politics. This had far-reaching consequences for Yugoslavia because various constitutive rules and practices of the Cold War system, such as the U.S. strategy of containment and Soviet Brezhnev doctrine, had become defining elements of the Yugoslav state. Before the waning of the Cold War system, the worldwide economic recession of the late 1970s and early 1980s created serious socioeconomic difficulties for Yugoslavia. A growing global economy had allowed the West to use its economic power to assist Yugoslavia in consolidating its buffer role between the two blocs of the Cold War system. This economic advantage began, however, to wane due to the Western economic recession, which started in 1975 and intensified into a worldwide economic depression in the 1980s.

Like many countries in the developing world, Yugoslavia had fueled its economic growth during the 1970s with foreign borrowing, which made it highly vulnerable to global economic fluctuations and recessions. For example, the oil price rise in 1978–79 and the jump to double digits of the interest rates for U.S. dollars, in which the Yugoslav debt was denominated, had strong, negative effects on Yugoslavia's economic growth. By the end of 1979, that is, still during Tito's rule, the government had to introduce many austerity measures in order to cut domestic consumption of imported goods and increase exports. In 1982, the government sought a compensatory loan from the

**Table 5.1. Summary of Theoretical Expectations**
DCSG: Degree of Consolidation of State Governance

External Variable:
International environment: waning and end of the Cold War in 1989–91.

| *Observed Outcome: State Governance* | *Intercommunal Vulnerability* | *Intercommunal Trust* | *Reliance on Institutional Power* |
|---|---|---|---|
| Collapsed: | | | |
| DCSG low, rapidly vanishing, particularly after Slovenia and Croatia initiated unilateral moves toward independence in June 1990. | High in the period 1987–91 as the republican leaders began to seek unilateral moves to protect and promote their communal interests due to very high level of information complexity, low level of intercommunal predictability, and high level of intercommunal interdependence because of a mismatch of the structure of ethnic cleavages and the republics.<br><br>Strong interdependence among major communal groups greatly strengthened incentives for communal groups to debate state governance in seeking a way out of the crisis (hypothesis 1).<br><br>As communal leaders increasingly debated how to transform state governance, intercommunal vulnerability increased with decreases in the scope of collective intentionality in the polityi.e., as different leaders and followers were less and less accepting of existing rules and practices of state governance as a framework for playing the game of politics (hypothesis 3). | Low--intercommunal trust that federal institutions and policies had managed to secure under Tito and his aftermath was quickly eroding, particularly after the rise of the new style of ultranationalistic leadership under dire socioeconomic conditions.<br><br>Decreased more rapidly with the stalemate within the Collective Presidency and the polarization of the YNA in the debates of 1988–91 (hypothesis 5). | High, increased rapidly with the stalemate within the Collective Presidency and the polarization of the YNA; leaders began to have recourse to whatever institutional power they believed they had or could muster (hypotheses 6 and 7).<br><br>Increased with the rapidly decreasing scope of collective intentionality (hypothesis 8).<br><br>Overall increased as intercommunal trust decreased (hypothesis 9). |

International Monetary Fund (IMF). The latter proposed in return an anti-inflationary macroeconomic stabilization policy of radical austerity, trade and price liberalization, and institutional reforms to impose on firms and governments monetary discipline and real price incentives (Woodward 1995a, 47–81; Cohen 1995, 45–77). This was problematic, however, because there were strong linkages between domestic producers and economic regions and Yugoslavia's international position. More specifically, Yugoslavia's foreign economic relations operated in three distinct markets. First, Yugoslavia borrowed capital and imported advanced technology and spare parts from the West. Second, Yugoslavia imported natural resources and most specifically oil from Third World countries such as Iraq and Libya. Third, Yugoslavia struck bilateral contracts with the Eastern bloc countries to secure access to fuel and other strategic resources in exchange for armaments, construction projects, and manufactured goods (Woodward 1995a, 21–46). This trilateral division of Yugoslavia's economic exchanges shaped the domestic regional division of labor by creating regional economic disparities. Slovenia and Croatia were part of West European economic networks because of geographic proximity and industrial policy favoring export production. Producers and traders from Macedonia and Bosnia-Herzegovina were inclined toward the Middle East and Greece. Serbia had relatively more business with Eastern bloc markets because of its substantial metal industry and heavy manufacturing and the economic importance of the Danube River. In 1985–86 foreign investment began to flow into Slovenia and Croatia. The two republics also became intensely involved in a new tourist and cultural organization of regions around the border of Italy, Austria, and Yugoslavia. Conversely, the demand in Yugoslavia's traditional Eastern and Middle Eastern markets was declining due to Soviet attempts to find Western partners and the consequences of the Iran-Iraq War.

New policies of international financial institutions compounded these difficulties. For example, the IMF and World Bank began in 1987 conditioning new credits on constitutional change. IMF advisers and economic liberals attributed the lack of monetary discipline in Yugoslavia to excessive decentralization of the banking and foreign exchange systems. The dispersed authority over money, credit, and foreign exchange made it impossible to have any effective monetary and exchange rate policy. Integration in the global economy required a unified domestic financial and trade market. This meant a reintegration of the segmented economies of the republics and the free movement of labor, capital, and goods across local and republican borders according to price signals and opportunities for profit. The IMF pressed the Yugoslav authorities to return monetary authority to the National Bank and to strengthen the independence of the bank to enable the government to implement a true macroeconomic policy (Woodward 1995a, 47–81).

The end of the Cold War radically enhanced these difficulties by removing the ideological interests that the Cold War protagonists had shown in the country's fate and by heralding a new era of cooperation in international security (Gow 1997, 1–45; Woodward 1995a, 22–29). This had four critical implications for the Yugoslav state. First, after Mikhail Gorbachev abolished the Brezhnev doctrine, the constitutive practices of international security began changing, thereby raising questions about the role of the Yugoslav state. Gorbachev's visit to Belgrade in 1988, rapid political changes in Eastern Europe, possible Soviet troop withdrawal from Eastern Europe, and the declining military relevance of the Warsaw Pact all combined to change the international security environment around Yugoslavia. Preserving Yugoslavia's buffer-state role in the early stages of the Cold War had led Belgrade to restructure not only its constitutional and institutional makeup and economic organization and doctrine (as discussed in the previous chapter), but also its military doctrine and organization (Woodward 1995a, 21–42; Gow 1992).

The military doctrine of the federation was for the most part a direct response to the constitutive rule of international bloc politics (Neal 1958, 101). Between 1948 and 1955, the possibility of a Soviet invasion remained the most serious external threat to Yugoslavia under the expectation that the Western bloc would remain passive, as during the 1956 Hungarian revolt. Joint Soviet-Yugoslav declarations in 1955 and 1956 prohibited the threat or use of force between the two countries. However, the Soviet invasion of Hungary in 1956 had undermined the credibility of those declarations. The Soviet-led Warsaw Pact invasion of Czechoslovakia in 1968 further heightened Yugoslavia's conception of a continuously threatening external environment, resulting in a dramatic shift in Yugoslavia's military doctrine. Yugoslavia hence formulated a new military doctrine—Total National Defense (TND), which sought to reconcile the country's domestic policies with international realities. The invasion of Czechoslovakia had shown that the standing conventional forces of a small country could not successfully oppose a surprise attack by the Soviet and Warsaw Pact troops. The invasion also showed that the Western policy of containment effectively accepted the division of Europe, and the West was not willing to risk a major confrontation with the Soviet Union for the sake of defending East or Central European states. The TND doctrine was designed as the only reliable way to allow Yugoslavia to maintain or eventually reestablish its independent and nonaligned status, should a Soviet invasion occur. Specifically, the most likely scenario in the TND doctrine was a general war between the Warsaw Pact and NATO in Europe. The Territorial Defense Forces (TDF) would mobilize the Yugoslav population for this purpose, thereby supplementing the YNA by giving it greater defensive depth and an armed local population ready to support combat actions. At the end of the Cold War, a unilateral Soviet invasion had become a virtual impossibility, thereby raising serious questions about Yugoslavia's TND military doctrine and organization. As a result, the YNA lost its historic rationale for claiming itself to be the guarantor of Yugoslavia's constitutional and territorial integrity and for enjoying the lion's share of the federal budget.

Second, external support evaporated because Yugoslavia lost its strategic role. This meant that great powers were not sufficiently interested in the fate of the Yugoslav state to act resolutely in response to trouble there. U.S.–Soviet strategic parity, the progress of arms and force reduction talks between the two blocs, and Gorbachev's reforms made Yugoslavia's role in NATO policy superfluous (Woodward 1995a, 104). Third, although there was awareness of an imminent clash between the south Slavs, other issues absorbed the time of international diplomats and major powers.[1] Fourth, the spread of a new wave of national self-determination and the demise of communist parties in Eastern Europe fundamentally redefined the fate of communism and one-party rule in Europe, including the Yugoslav Communist Party.

Therefore, not only did Yugoslavia lose its strategic buffer role between the East and the West and suffer a serious economic crisis. The fall of communism and the eruption of national self-determination movements in the former Soviet Union and Eastern Europe also set precedents for Yugoslavia and hence helped to undermine a precarious and already trembling balance of satisfaction among the Yugoslav ethnic communities. The very rationale for creating both interwar and socialist Yugoslavia—that is, the risk that neighboring European powers might subordinate would-be weak nation-states within the Balkans—disappeared, engulfing in its thrall an ideal Yugoslavia based on "brotherhood and unity." The events in Eastern Europe and the Soviet Union encouraged the relatively well-off republics, Slovenia and Croatia, to seek sovereignty and establish independent foreign relations with their old "brethren" in Western Europe, Germany and Austria. Moreover, the wave of democratization sweeping through Eastern Europe set examples to the republican leaders of how to establish their republic sovereignty in a way that is self-legitimating before both domestic and foreign arenas: democratic elections in which ultranationalistic discourse and propaganda is used to mobilize the electorate. The democratic process in Yugoslavia provided a means through which communal mobilization, especially in Slovenia and Croatia, succeeded while being legitimated by the international euphoria for democratization that erupted earlier in Eastern Europe. The elections legitimized the republics as objects of political loyalty for their respective dominant ethnic communities. The combination of communal self-determination and democratic elections de facto delegitimized the federal institutions and shattered an already weakening Yugoslav identity.

In sum, absent the constitutive rule of international bloc politics, neither the Soviet Union and its informal empire in Eastern Europe nor the United States and its Western allies had any serious interest in Yugoslavia's position or fate. Yet because Yugoslavia had strongly tied its state to its international buffer-state role, the end of the Cold War had major implications for state governance. As a result, the new international environment induced major debates on how to transform the state as the Cold War was winding down.

## Debating State Governance via Ultranationalism

The changes in the international environment that faced Yugoslavia in the early 1980s prompted a series of debates not only on how to improve the economy, but also more fundamentally on how to transform the existing form of state governance (Cohen 1995, 45–77; Woodward 1995a, 82–145; Sekelj 1993, 227–63). Economic and political issues were inseparable because socialist self-management, which was the foundation of the economic system, shaped the political institutions. The two were also inextricably related to the multinational character of the federation. As discussed in the previous chapter, Yugoslavia had continuously faced a national question—how to reconcile demands for national recognition by its constituent nations while building and preserving a strongly integrated Yugoslav state. Despite Tito's multifaceted assault on the roots of this dilemma, the national question was still one of the country's most problematic issues after his death, as illustrated by the recurrent intercommunal debates on the idea of Yugoslavism and corresponding form of state governance.

Each of the three major communities had its interpretation of Yugoslavism (Ramet 1992a; Cohen 1995, 1–44). For many Serbs, Yugoslavism was tantamount to preserving a unified Serb nation within a single state. For Croats and Slovenes, Yugoslavism was a means to protect themselves against foreign powers. Not surprisingly, these interpretations implied different forms for the Yugoslav state. For the Serbs, a strong unitary Yugoslav state was the best provisional safeguard against any future dispersion of their nation. The Croats and Slovenes preferred a loose federation within which they would be secure from Serbian hegemony and escape a fate similar to that of interwar Yugoslavia. The international conditions surrounding the waning of the Cold War system strongly enhanced these debates, with the latter increasingly dominating the core state institutions and leading to institutional crises in the late 1980s. The debates divided the republican elites into conservatives and revisionists. The conservatives, led mainly by the Serbian leadership, wanted to strengthen the federation as a unitary state. In contrast, the revisionists, led by the Slovene leadership and subsequently joined by the Croatian leadership, wanted to transform the state into a more "confederal" type of federation. The evolution of the Collective Presidency after Tito's death best illustrates these crises (Cohen 1995, 45–77).

The Collective Presidency was the theater of three consecutive debates, which ultimately paralyzed it. The first debate revolved around different proposals on how to deal with the impending socioeconomic crisis. The most controversial proposal came from the Serbian Party in October 1984. The Serbs pushed for a strengthening of the role and autonomy of economic enterprises, a strengthening of the federal government, a democratization of the electoral system, and a rollback of the prerogatives and overall autonomy of the two autonomous provinces, Vojvodina and Kosovo. The party organizations of Kosovo, Vojvodina, Slovenia, and Croatia firmly opposed such reforms. These reforms would threaten the autonomy not only of Kosovo and Vojvodina, but potentially also of Croatia and Slovenia. Notwithstanding this strong opposition, the Constitutional Court of Serbia decided to annul a number of decrees that had guaranteed proportional ethnic representation in the leadership in Kosovo, thereby disempowering its Albanian majority (Ramet 1992a; Silber and Little 1997). This unilateral action strained the relations between Serbia and Slovenia, as the latter saw the Serbian action as a bad precedent that might encourage more Serbian hegemonic adventures against the rest of the federation.

In a second debate, three different strategies emerged—the Serbian strategy inspired by Milosevic, the Slovene strategy representing the views expressed by the republican elites and the Communist Party leadership in Slovenia, and the strategy of the federal government (Cohen 1995, 45–77). The Serbian reform strategy criticized the state as a regulator of economic development and the Constitution for having opened the door to autarkic republican economies. The Serbian proposal promoted an integrated Yugoslav market with major political reforms. The proposal recommended that the decision-making process in the Federal Assembly be rooted in a principle of interregional unanimity and limited only to the narrowest circle of constitutional questions. The proposal also suggested that the voting process follow the principle of qualified majorities and rejected political pluralism as a solution to the legitimacy crisis allegedly created by the Titoist legacy (Woodward 1995a, 82–145; Cohen 1995, 45–77; Silber and Little 1997). Slovenia's communist leaders shared Milosevic's view that the federal authorities must be adequately empowered to deal with major issues of economic policy (Benderly and Kraft 1994, 93–182). The Slovenes, however, rejected the majoritarian scheme that the Serbs proposed, fearing that such a scheme would outvote them due to the demographic predominance of the Serbs in Yugoslavia. Therefore, throughout the late 1980s the Slovene communist leadership categorically opposed its Serbian counterpart, adhering to the idea of a federation based on unanimity and equally weighted constituent units. Later, the Slovene leadership advanced the idea of an asymmetric federation scheme, wherein each republic would negotiate its own terms of power sharing and distribution with the federal government (Cohen 1995, 59–66). The strategy of the federal government revolved around reforms toward a market economy. The Yugoslav Federal Assembly promulgated in 1988 a series of constitutional amendments as a basis for economic and political reforms. Most of the amendments laid the ground for market principles and pro-growth economic policies. These and similar efforts won early on a large popularity throughout Yugoslavia. However, various republican leaders opposed the reforms, perceiving them either as too limited or, conversely, as too austere. Hence the federal government had to delay macroeconomic reforms, resorting instead to incremental economic renovation (Cohen 1995, 66–73).

In a third debate, the Collective Presidency effectively became a zero-sum arena, wherein the republican leaders were in effect not listening to one another (Woodward 1995a, 82–145). By 1990, the effective number of delegates in the Collective Presidency was only five—Serbian, Slovene, Croatian, Macedonian, and Bosnian representatives. Milosevic had transformed Montenegro, Vojvodina, and Kosovo into satellites of Serbia, assuring himself the support of their delegates. He thus was able to control four votes in the Collective Presidency. The latter convened a series of meetings on four divisive issues dealing with the future of the federal state: the value of maintaining the federation, the rights of the republics to secede, the character of the republican borders, and future political arrangements among the republics. The Slovene and Croat leaders proposed a confederation of sovereign republics, based on the principle that preserved republican sovereignty and existing republican borders. For Serbia and Montenegro, the federation not only remained a political reality but also needed to be stronger. They both rejected the notion that a republic could unilaterally turn its administrative borders into state borders. The Serbian leadership believed that Serbia and Yugoslavia had inextricably linked fates. The Muslim leadership of Bosnia simultaneously advocated the principles of republican sovereignty and the inviolability of borders within a unified Yugoslav state. Macedonia agreed with Slovenia, Croatia, and Bosnia on the issues of sovereignty and borders but wanted to maintain strong economic and security relations among the republics. The result of these increasingly more irreconcilable positions was a protracted paralysis of the Collective Presidency.

In addition, debates at the republican level, especially in Serbia, Croatia, and Slovenia, helped to shape the fate of the federation. Federal and republican debates fed on and mutually reinforced one another (Benderly and Kraft 1994, 93–182; Cohen 1995, 79–114). Beginning in April 1987, the Serbian Party adopted an increasingly more nationalistic orientation as a by-product of a factional struggle within the Serbian Party. The struggle reached an apex at the eighth party plenum (September 23–24) when Slobodan Milosevic successfully ousted Ivan Stambolic, the incumbent president of Serbia, and engineered a coup against its Belgrade Party organization. Milosevic accused Stambolic's supporters of being too compromising with the Albanians in Kosovo and of failing to protect Serbia's national and territorial integrity. Milosevic and his faction used their power in the party executive and Belgrade Party organizations to purge large sections of the Serbian political class from the government, party, and mass media, accusing them of being too harsh on Serb nationalists (Gagnon 1994–95; Banac 1992; Woodward 1995a, 90–93).

The Slovene leaders sought sovereignty status for their republic by opposing all federal decisions that interfered with republican rights or were not rooted in parliamentary and republican supremacy. This strategy cohered with a campaign of radical young Slovene people and intellectuals to attack the YNA. Slovene nationalist intellectuals and radical youth had already begun criticizing the YNA as early as 1986. The Slovene government supported the young people who campaigned for conscientious objectors' right to alternative civilian service. The Slovene government also adopted a policy calling for devolution of military power to the republics (Woodward 1995a, 89–90; Gow 1992).

Following the development in Central and East Europe in the late 1980s, the Croatian leadership fractured into reform and conservative factions. The reform faction maneuvered a shift from a strategy of slow social mobilization by suppressing liberal intellectuals and potential leaders to an approach designed to manage the pace of change by opening a dialogue. The debate over the constitutional revisions within Croatia rendered another division within the party leadership more salient in 1988–89—that between confederalists in sympathy with Slovenia and committed federalists. Ultimately, explicitly anti-federal positions of the Croatian Parliament throughout the 1980s and the tilt within the party leadership toward the reformers prevailed by early 1989. The party slowly allowed a transformation of the political landscape toward multiparty politics (Woodward 1995a, 103).

That the Yugoslav state collapsed in the period 1987–91 is not a matter of dispute. More disputable is perhaps the assertion that the collective debates at the federal and republican levels resulted in an erosion of the moderate scope of collective intentionality that existed in the late 1980s. As pointed out in chapter 2, it is not easy to identify precisely the scope of collective intentionality that existed before the rise of ultranationalism in the late 1980s. Yet it is nonetheless possible to argue that the post-Tito regime failed to reconsolidate state governance after 1987, and more so after the end of the Cold War. It is also possible to ascertain with enough confidence that after the rise of ultranationalism the scope of collective intentionality began to decrease quite rapidly. The evolution of a "perpetual" disagreement within the Collective Presidency on any of the thorny issues dividing the various leaders produced a steady trend of increasingly ignoring existing rules and practices of state governance, especially at the federal level. The more the lack of consensus lasted, the more divided and intransigent the republics' leaders became, and the more this eroded whatever collective intentionality sustained the existing form of federal governance. Explaining this outcome is the topic of the remainder of this chapter. I explore the extent to which the theory outlined in chapter 3 can explain the rapid decrease in the scope of collective intentionality as it evolved through the debates. I show how the debates at the republican and federal levels resulted in a climate of uncertainty wherein the major communities became convinced that the federation will—should—not continue to exist.

## Intercommunal Vulnerability

Intercommunal vulnerability reached a high and rapidly increasing level in the period 1987–91 as the republican leaders unilaterally moved to protect and promote their communal (and personal) interests during the debates on federal governance. Under these conditions, the major communal groups increasingly became fearful of intercommunal abandonment, exploitation, or exclusion from participating in the debates. As discussed in chapter 3, vulnerability arises from three mutually reinforcing sources: intercommunal information complexity, predictability, and interdependence. I estimate these variables in the following.

### *Intercommunal Information Complexity*

In the period 1987–91, information complexity became very high as the communal leaders became increasingly confronted with a lack, as well as problems of misrepresentation, of information on each other' intentions and actions. Within the crisis that the waning of the Cold War created in Yugoslavia, a new leadership style, drawing on and legitimizing itself via nationalistic myths, emerged around the mid-1980s in Serbia and Slovenia, and later in Croatia (Banac 1992; Rusinow 1995). The elites were able to propagate and maintain the perception that their views, rooted in nationalistic myths, were the only viable solutions to Yugoslavia's dire socioeconomic and political conditions. As a result, the nationalistic myths became collective lenses through which the Serb, Croat, and Slovene communities framed their future relations with one another, as well as with the federal government (Banac 1992; Rusinow 1995; Denitch 1994; Snyder and Ballentine 1996; Silber and Little 1997, 25–153). As a by-product, this helped to legitimize the new leadership style, establish a new political discourse anchored in ultranationalism, and thereby defeat challenging strategies that did not advocate ultranationalistic discourses (Gagnon 1994–95; Arfi 1998).

Not surprisingly, ultranationalistic discourses clashed with one another. The Serb and Croat ultranationalistic leaders increasingly engaged one another in rhetorical wars, incriminating one another while self-justifying their respective actions and positions in historical grievances and self-acclaimed rights. Demonizing the "Other" became an intercommunal routine (Banac 1992; Thompson, 1994). Sharply opposed, self-proclaimed national historical rights and grievances and irreconcilably construed nationalistic myths framed the intercommunal relations as zero-sums. The more assertive each group became in its ultranationalistic project, the more it intruded on politics in the other republics, and the fewer prospects there were to reach any compromise on divisive issues. As Woodward put it, "Other republics or the federal government were increasingly identified as external enemies to be defeated" (1995a, 113). Under such conditions, the level of information complexity became very high because the major communal groups became highly uncertain about each other's intentions, and the emerging zero-sum relations became a strong incentive for misrepresenting (private) information on intentions and goals. That the level of information complexity became very high is clear in three ways at least.

First, political loyalty to the federation eroded, and nationality-defined political loyalties gradually replaced it. A public opinion survey conducted in 1990 reveals that only 26 percent of the Slovenes and 48 percent of the Croats gave more allegiance to Yugoslavia than to their respective republics. At the same time, 71 percent of the Serbs still had strong political loyalty to Yugoslavia. This high percentage of Serb support for Yugoslavia came from a belief that the fate of the Serb nation and Yugoslavia's integrity are inseparable. The same data also showed that most Slovenes (83 percent) and Croats (62 percent) did not support the notion that federal constitutional provisions should have precedence over republican ones, in contrast to most Serbs (83 percent) who did (Cohen 1995, 172–73). Hence, the political loyalties of large segments of the Serb, Croat, and Slovene communities were cast in such a way as to conflate individual citizenship rights and communal rights. This implies that the intentions of these sections of the populations as far as maintaining the federation and the preexisting intercommunal arrangements were to say the least doubtful and ambiguous. Did this imply, for example, that the Serbs would attempt to reestablish their domination over the federation as they had done during the interwar period? Likewise, did this imply that even if the Serbs were not intent on imposing themselves on the federation, the Croats would not trust them? Would the Muslims be afraid to lose the rights granted to them after the 1974 constitutional amendments? The extent to which these and similar questions were on the minds of these sections of the population cannot be easily probed. However, the ultranationalistic leaders of the Serbs, Croats, and to some extent the Slovenes were already espousing such claims and were questioning each other's motives and agendas accordingly. The high level of information complexity thus became a self-fulfilling prophecy under the influence of these leaders—the more they questioned each other's motives and agendas, the more they shaped their respective agendas accordingly to confirm the claims made therewith.

Second, the evolution of the electoral process in Yugoslavia also indicates that the relations between the Slovene, Croat, and Serb communities enhanced the level of information complexity among these and the other smaller groups. The democratization process began within the republics before the federal level (which never took place). This sequencing of elections is an indication that the Slovene, Croat, and Serb communities were viewing Yugoslavia's future through communal lenses. The election campaigns were part of the process of shifting the political loyalties toward the republics at the expense of the federal state. This reconstruction of political loyalty was then "institutionalized" through the ballot boxes (Linz and Stepan 1992).

In Slovenia, three major political parties competed in the 1990 elections: DEMOS, a coalition of opposition parties opposed to communist rule; ZKM-LS, which advocated democratic principles and Slovenian control of its military affairs; and ZKS-SDP, led by the former communist leader Milan Kucan. All three parties advocated political autonomy for Slovenia. In addition, DEMOS generally advocated an independent and sovereign Slovenia. The elections resulted in a tricameral legislature with 47 seats for DEMOS, 12 seats for ZKM-LS, and 14 seats for ZKS-SDP. Milan Kucan became the president of the republic because of his personal reputation, rather than the strength or popularity of his party. The winning party, DEMOS, was the most nationalistic party, as evidenced in its calls for abolishing the special laws protecting the republic's ethnic minorities (Cohen 1995, 89–94). In Croatia, Franjo Tudjman, leader of the Croatian Democratic Alliance (HDZ), launched his electoral campaign by promising to assert the priority of Croatia's national interests. The HDZ won 205 out of 356 seats in Croatia's legislature, including a majority in each of its three chambers. Most Serbs residing in Croatia voted heavily against the HDZ, supporting instead either the communists or the nationalistic Serbian Democratic Party (SDP) (Cohen 1995, 88–107). In Serbia, the three main parties—Milosevic's SPS (Socialist Party of Serbia), SMR (Serbia Movement for Renewal), and DP (Democratic Party)—shared a strong commitment to Serbian national interests, opposed the establishment of a Yugoslav confederation, and supported continued Serbian political control over Kosovo. In the December 1990 elections, Milosevic was able to garner the two-thirds of the votes needed to win the presidency, as his party won 194 out of 250 seats. The SMR won the largest opposition share with 19 seats (Cohen 1995, 151–59).

Therefore, by July 1990, political pluralism was legal in all republics as well as on the federal level. In the first half of 1991, the number of registered parties reached 290. Most of these parties were registered in one republic only. Almost a third of these parties were committed to some nationalist or regionalist agenda. Moreover, "a large number of new parties, though not explicitly nationalistic in their platforms or ideological labels, nevertheless were emphatically anti-federalist, or linked to the achievement of their particular goals within a single ethnic constituency" (Cohen 1995, 106). In sum, the sequencing of the elections and their outcomes reinforced the atmosphere of uncertainty and doubt about the existing intercommunal modus vivendi. The republican elections helped to increase the level of information complexity that equally confronted the major and minor communal groups.

Third, the dismal record of core federal institutions enhanced the level of information complexity. The various communal groups and their leaders could not rely on these and other federal institutions as a means to check—and reduce uncertainty on—each other's intentions and actions. As discussed earlier, the Collective Presidency effectively fell into paralysis. Opposed elites created internal divisions within the Collective Presidency, thereby transforming it into an arena of discord and conflict. Persistent discords and conflicts froze the institution, thereby curtailing its ability to play a proactive role in alleviating the information complexity.

The YNA lost its historical neutrality and eventually sided with the Serbs. Under the 1974 Constitution, the army had the right and duty to use all necessary means to protect the country and its system of socialist self-management (Gow 1992; Cohen 1995, 181–92). At first, the army was staunchly opposed to political pluralism because the military leaders perceived it as a direct attack on the Constitution. Eventually the military, if reluctantly, however, accepted a de facto political liberalization. The army changed its position when it saw the federal government and a majority of regional political authorities belatedly accepting the principle of party pluralism in the wake of the East European wave of democratic revolution (Woodward 1995a, 101–11; Stokes 1993). However, when the new Slovene leadership asserted Slovenia's sovereignty and began groundwork toward independence, the YNA strongly opposed such goals. This ultimately led to a confrontation between newly proclaimed Slovene forces and the YNA in June 1991 (Cohen 1995, 197–217; Woodward 1995a, 114–45). Thereafter, the Slovenes, Croats, and subsequently Muslims increasingly perceived the YNA as a tool in the hands of Serb ultranationalists and left its ranks in large numbers.

The LCY increasingly became politically marginal, particularly after the onset of democratic elections in most of the republics in 1990. Already fragmented, the LCY lost its leading role and had to enter into a dialogue with the opposition in almost every region of the country.[2] The LCY hence failed to provide an authoritative forum that the leaders could use to gather information on their mutual intentions. Moreover, the LCY could not play the role of information regulator, a role that the CPY played in the period 1947–53 (see the previous chapter).

In sum, the emergence of ultranationalistic republican leaderships, the shifting of political loyalties away from the federation, the holding of democratic elections in the republics that reinforced the ultranationalistic rhetoric and agenda, and a rapid weakening and marginalization of key federal institutions all helped to create a high and increasing information complexity. The major communal groups were not sure anymore about each other's intentions, and the period 1987–91 became an era of high uncertainty. That the ultranationalistic leaderships benefited from such an atmosphere of suspicion and high intercommunal information complexity is without any dispute. However, this was not enough to create a high intercommunal vulnerability. The system of federal governance was at stake, and the major groups had to be able to strategize for future intercommunal relations. Doing so necessarily confronted the groups with the issue of intercommunal predictability.

### *Intercommunal Predictability*

Intercommunal predictability was low because the commitment to intercommunal and institutional arrangements inherited from the Tito era was quickly eroding. Low intercommunal predictability was the combined product of major shifts in intercommunal relations and the institutional arrangements that underpinned and preserved these relations.

First, ultranationalistic leaders and entrepreneurs increasingly attacked and subsequently undermined or annulled the institutional and constitutional arrangements inherited from the Tito period, particularly at the federal level and in Serbia following Milosevic's rise to power in 1987. Yugoslavia's array of federal institutions (e.g., the Collective Presidency, the LCY, and the Yugoslav National Army) failed to effectively stall or reverse the erosion of intercommunal predictability. The federal institutions in fact became arenas where aggressive nationalistic politics flourished, thereby contributing even more to the weakening and eventual complete marginalization of the institutions themselves. The more the communal leaders asserted their ultranationalistic strategies within the federal state institutions, the more the latter became incapable of resolving the divisive issues among the major groups (namely, the Serbs, Croats, and Slovenes), and the more intransigent the political entrepreneurs and ethnic activists became in pursuing their zero-sum strategies. The resonance between the elites' strategies and the weakening of the institutions reinforced the belief that the federation was unable to protect the rights and security of any community. Each communal group increasingly believed that it had to take matters into its hands.

Second, as noted above, the rise of ultranationalism and the shift of political loyalties away from the federation as well as the democratic electoral process at the level of the republics helped to undermine the intercommunal understandings that had existed since Tito's time. Tito's multifaceted nationalities policy notwithstanding, the nationalities question became one of the country's thorniest issues, as illustrated by the recurrent intercommunal debates on the idea of Yugoslavism (Ramet 1992a; Cohen 1995, 1–44).

In sum, that intercommunal predictability was quite low as the debates were reaching a stalemate in late 1989 and early 1990 transpired clearly in the behavior of the main leaders of the Serbs and Croats. All major players in the debates developed bad faith in each other in the months preceding the civil war. For example, the Slovene leadership agreed to a series of negotiations on the future of the federation in December 1990. Yet the Slovenian Parliament declared independence on the very day that the negotiations began, which of course preempted any serious negotiations.[3] Nor did Milosevic enjoy a better record. He in effect became a master of breaching commitments and in the art of deception.[4] For example, in March 1990 Milosevic met with Tudjman, and both agreed to stop the war in the Krajina region.[5] Yet only one week later, Milosevic allowed Krajina to declare itself part of Serbia. Neither Milosevic nor Tudjman was negotiating in good faith (Silber and Little 1997, 141–42). Although low and decreasing intercommunal predictability is bad enough for maintaining intercommunal cohabitation, the issue was made more relevant by the high intercommunal interdependence that tightly linked together the fates of major groups, as discussed next.

*Intercommunal Strategic Interdependence*

Strategic interdependence among the major communal groups in the Yugoslav polity during 1987–91 remained high due to, first, the mismatch created by the structure of ethnic cleavages between the constituent nations and the republics bearing their names and, second, the interwoven nature of economic and communal relations of the Tito legacy. This situation was the more acute for the Serbian leaders, as the Serbs were located in almost every republic, particularly in Croatia and Bosnia-Herzegovina. The Serbs were the plurality in the federation, and yet they constituted many potentially vulnerable minorities outside of Serbia proper (Levinshohn 1994, 15). The Serb plurality in turn created another type of interdependence between the other communal groups, particularly the Croats and the Slovenes. The latter have continuously felt a sense of linguistic vulnerability due to the dominance of the Serb-Croat language in the federation. Nonetheless, the Slovenes have overall played the role of a pivotal group whose presence within the federation has provided the Croats with an ally with whom to balance the Serbian efforts to dominate the federation. When the Slovenes decided to secede in 1990, the Croats soon followed suit. Remaining with the Serbs inside a federation that did not include the balancing Slovenes would have left the Croats a prey to Serb domination. Hence, protecting the Serb minorities outside Serbia meant keeping the federation together, including not only Croatia, where there was a sizeable Serb minority, but also Slovenia, without which Croatia would not agree to remain part of the federation. The fates of the Serbs, Croats, and Slovenes as well as that of the federation were inseparable.[6]

The nature of the economic system that survived Tito reinforced this interdependence. As argued in the previous chapter, the post-1953 era witnessed a sharp reemergence of the national question under the form of economic nationalism. The tendency for each republic or region to pursue its narrow economic interests without regard for the welfare of the federation became almost a trademark of the system until 1991. As noted above, in the debates that unfolded within the Collective Presidency in the 1980s, the Serbian reform strategy criticized the state as a regulator of economic development and the Constitution for having opened the door to autarkic republican economies. The Serbian proposal emphasized the importance of an integrated Yugoslav market (Woodward 1995a, 82–145; Cohen 1995, 45–77; Silber and Little 1997). Slovenia's communist leaders shared Milosevic's view that the federal authorities must be adequately empowered to deal with major issues of economic policy (Cohen 1995, 66–73). Most of these and other economic debates had inexorable implications for intercommunal relations, thereby reinforcing the sense of interdependence that the ethnic cleavages already created.

Thus, during the 1989–91 debates, not only could no communal group unilaterally determine the outcome of the debates, but they also all depended on each other's decisions and actions. Neither the geographic distribution of the various ethnic groups throughout Yugoslavia (except for Slovenia) nor the economic system allowed for the possibility of a "clean" separation of the republics. That intercommunal interdependence was quite high, particularly as the debates on the form of state governance lingered well into 1990, is visible in the fact that the issues determining the fate of Yugoslavia became closely interwoven. The drive for secession by Slovenia is illustrative of this dynamic. Although Slovenia had originally played the role of a dominant actor in the debates on state governance (compared to Serbia and Croatia), its absence from the debates would have fundamentally changed the outcomes by giving Serbia (and its allies Montenegro, Kosovo, and Vojvodina) an absolute majority of votes (4 to 3) in the Collective Presidency. Absent Slovenia, Croatia quickly followed suit, since it could no more prevent Serbia from dominating the federal institutions. Absent both Slovenia and Croatia, Bosnia-Herzegovina could not avoid seeking secession. The majority of Bosnia's population was composed of Croats and Muslims who feared Serbian domination, that is, if Bosnia were to remain in a reduced federation. Yet the Serbs residing in Bosnia (as well as the Croats) were opposed to Bosnia's secession and did not identify with a would-be Bosnian state (Djilas 1992, 25–31). On top of it all, Serbia was opposed to Croatia and Bosnia seceding from the federation even after Milosevic and the Slovenian leadership agreed on Slovenia's secession.

To summarize, a high interdependence, a high information complexity, and a very low intercommunal predictability during the 1989–90 debates all conspired to engender a high and increasing intercommunal vulnerability. This made it more likely that Yugoslavia would find it extremely hard to avoid falling into the thrall of state collapse. However, as the theory in chapter 3 suggests, a high intercommunal vulnerability is a necessary but insufficient condition for state collapse, even in a time of crisis. A collapse of state governance also depends on how the relevant actors rely on intercommunal trust and institutional power to address their mutual vulnerabilities.

## Intercommunal Trust

The level of trust that the federal institutions and policies had managed to secure under Tito and his aftermath quickly eroded after the rise of ultranationalistic leaders under dire economic conditions in the mid-1980s. As the debates on state governance began in the late 1980s, intercommunal trust eroded even more rapidly; the republican leaders not only began to talk past one another, they also engaged each other in rhetorical wars of incriminations and blame for the problems that their respective communal groups were facing or could face. Ethnic fear took hold when this dynamic destroyed whatever intercommunal trust remained in early 1990. Ethnic fear thenceforth dominated the Serb-Croat relations and eventually led to an eruption of intercommunal violence, thereby eroding whatever was left of the collective intentionality that had underpinned the constitutive rules and practices of Yugoslav politics.

This section analyzes the processes through which intercommunal trust between the Serbs and Croats (and Slovenes) was deconstructed in the 1987–91 period. I begin by analyzing the structural lock-in that emerged between the national question and the state's institutional arrangements. I then explicate the most important effects that this lock-in had on intercommunal politics. This is followed next by an exploration of how these structural effects resulted in a set of important conditions that facilitated the erosion of intercommunal trust. The remaining section explicates the actual processes of deconstructing intercommunal trust; these are the construction of political myths, the masses' internalization of these myths, and the use of these popularly internalized myths to routinize new intercommunal practices and discourses into a new framework for intercommunal relations.

### *Emergence and Consolidation of Structural Lock-In*

The emergence of a structural lock-in between the national question and the institutional arrangements of the state effectively started with the formulation of a new constitution in 1963. The lock-in was reinforced in the debates and events that led to a new constitution in 1974 and its aftermath and ultimately solidified in the immediate aftermath of Tito's death. As discussed below, the new structural lock-in, although somewhat similar to and dependent on the structural lock-in that emerged in the immediate aftermath of the war period, is not simply its continuation. New political-economic and ideological contexts as well as new solutions to new challenges combined with the legacy of the previous structural lock-in to lead to a new structural lock-in. More important, the two types of structural lock-in differ in their effects on intercommunal as well as state-group relations.

The formulation of a new constitution in 1963 was a turning point in this process of structural lock-in development. This is so because most of the political-economic and ideological debates that followed the formulation of the 1953 Constitutional Law were largely encapsulated as well as developed even further in the 1963 Constitution. The republics acquired new rights or expanded old ones at the expense of the federation. For example, the federation and republics were now communities with an independent though mutually associate existence.[7] Both entities had the power of "self-organization" and could independently adopt their own constitutions, since it was no longer up to the federation to regulate the internal organization of the republics. The statement of general principles prefacing the federal Constitution introduced a broad statement of rights of the republics, the two most prominent of which were self-determination and secession. The new importance given to the republics was also evident in the statute adopted by the LCY at its Eighth Congress in 1964. Not only should republican congresses now convene immediately before the congress of the entire Yugoslav Party. The republican congresses now enjoyed the right to "determine the policies, positions, and tasks of the League of Communists of the socialist republic in harmony with the policy of the League of Communists of Yugoslavia."[8] In addition, while the 1963 Constitution preserved the Federal Chamber, it abolished the Producers' Council and instituted four new chambers, representing the working people in the working communities (article 165). These are the Economic Chamber, the Chamber of Education and Culture, the Chamber of Social Welfare and Health, and the Organizational-Political Chamber. All delegates to these various chambers emanated either from the Municipalities or from the Republics and Autonomous Provinces.

The new institutional framework became a context that encouraged a reemergence of the national question in many parts of the country. In Croatia, there were manifestations of Croatian nationalism such as the performance of previously banned nationalistic theatrical works as well as the appearance of nationalistic-minded student groups at the University of Zagreb.[9] In 1967, Croatian intellectuals, including Miroslav Krleza, who was the most respected literary figure in Croatia, signed a statement disputing the validity of Serbo-Croatian as a historical language, instead promoting Croatian as a distinct language. The Croats' repudiation of the Novi Sad agreement on the Serbo-Croatian language proved to be only a precursor to a strong reemergence of nationalism among the Croatian intellectuals. In 1970, a popular movement emerged to openly debate many grievances and claims that the communist regime had been repressing since 1945. More generally, the Croats began reexamining their history, "searching" for lost Croat heroes whom the communist regime had intentionally ignored. For example, Stjepan Radic (d. 1928), the founder of the Croatian Peasant Party, became a legendary figure. In August 1971, the cultural committee of the League of Students of Croatia erected a commemorative plaque in his honor. Similarly, the coastal town of Sibenik canceled plans to erect a monument to the victims of fascism and erected instead a statue of a Croatian king, Petar Kresimir IV. There also were efforts to rehabilitate and restore to the Valhalla of Croatian gods and heroes a nineteenth-century Croatian military governor, Josip Jelacic (Ramet 1992b). The high nationalistic mood spread widely to day-to-day life in Croatia, to the point where many of Croatia's restaurants were entertaining their customers with traditional patriotic songs of the Croatian homeland, something unheard of in previous years.

Likewise, there was a strong reemergence of Serbian nationalism, as Serb intellectuals seized the opportunity and responded to the Croats by insisting that the Serbs residing in Croatia must be educated in their own language, too. They also demanded that Radio-Television Belgrade "have Cyrillic in local programs" and "that common emissions to all Yugoslavia use both scripts."[10] The struggle of the Rankovic faction against the party leadership in Serbia was another occasion for boosting the nationalistic feelings during the period between the Eighth Congress of the League of Communists (fall 1964) and the Fourth Plenum of the Central Committee (July 1966).[11] Old national military hymns and patriotic songs that had been banned since the war reappeared in Serbia, as did the habit of discussing and settling issues in the informal and often emotional atmosphere of the local café.[12]

A simultaneous development of a national economic question helped to reinforce these nationalistic revivals. In the postwar period, the communists had persistently linked the national question to economic issues, asserting that the national question would remain a problem as long as inequalities in the level of economic development persisted in Yugoslavia.[13] That the economic and nationalist aspects of inter-republican relations were slowly merging is evident, for example, in the period 1962–66. During these years, the Serbian Party began to look for allies among the underdeveloped republics that had economically suffered from cutbacks in investments. For example, the central committees of Serbia and Montenegro announced in December 1963 a bilateral agreement for cooperation in the fields of culture, education, and economics.[14] The economic dimension was quite comprehensive, for it encompassed the integration of many industries in the two republics and entailed cooperation in the development of communications, foreign trade, marketing, and long-term joint planning. The central committees of the two republics justified this venture on the premise that the 1963 Constitution provided for the possibility of agreements between the republics for the sake of furthering collaboration in the cultural sphere and in other related activities.

However, the agreement was in reality a political act dictated not only by economic considerations but also by the traditional ties of nationalistic sentiment between the two republics.

That the linkages between economic reforms and the national question were increasingly shaping the debates within and across the republics is also evident from the several meetings that the Executive Committee of the League of Communists held in November 1965–February 1966. The goal of these meetings was to examine the problem of implementing the economic reforms and dealing with rising national feelings.[15] As subsequently revealed in the press, the center of resistance to economic reforms was in Serbia, where nationalistic manifestations had been brewing for some time.[16] That there was a strong conflation of the economic reforms and the national question is also evident in the events of summer 1966. These events soon marked a climax in the struggle over the future course of Yugoslavia's economic development. Nationalism and rivalries between the various republics had become almost inseparable in this struggle.

The reemergence of the Croat national question is illustrative of this dynamic. Reform advocates in Croatia used the proposed doctrine of economic self-management to justify their demands for greater political autonomy. They argued that economic self-management could occur and succeed only through a decentralization of the economy and a simultaneous devolution of decision-making power to the republics (Irvine 1993). The League of Communists of Croatia (LCC) thus sought to increase the autonomy of Croatia's party organizations as well as other institutions. LCC reformers emphasized the primacy of Croatian statehood and the importance of placing the Croatian political interests above those of the Yugoslav state as a whole. Croatian economists complained of disproportionate levies on Croatia for the federal budget and development fund. Croatia's oldest cultural society, Matica Hrvatska, began calling for constitutional changes that would give the republic a virtual independence. These and other increasingly more vocal manifestations of Croatian nationalism resulted in a crisis (1971–72), which the Tito regime eventually tamed in a heavy-handed way. The federal authorities disbanded Matica Hrvatska and purged nationalists and liberals from all Croatian organizations and institutions. The prolonged Croatian nationalist assertiveness (1967–72) in effect gave Tito and Kardelj an opportunity to eliminate the new liberal leadership of the Serbian Party and to purge any reformist party leader in Slovenia, Macedonia, and Vojvodina (Lampe 1996, 303). Tito replaced these reformist-liberal leaders in most instances with anti-reform party veterans who were more politically reliable and loyal to Tito, notwithstanding that many among the newly appointed officials had less political talent than the purged ones.

The Tito regime also decided to amend the 1963 Constitution as a solution to the various political-economic and nationalist problems that faced the federation. Overall, the constitutional drafting process was an attempt to overcome inter-regional deadlocks over the federal policies by developing new institutions and procedures for decision making that would smooth out inter-republican debates. By 1970, the 1963 Constitution had already been amended nineteen times. A further package of twenty-one amendments was later proposed in March 1971. The latter would reduce the power of the federal government by allowing individual republics to control their earnings of foreign currencies. The republics were also allowed to rule on their respective social plans before the federation could group them together in a federal package (Lampe 1996, 304–05). Further amendments in 1971 created five new inter-republican committees that would coexist with the Federal Assembly. The amendments that were finally adopted in 1971 focused on the division of authority between the federation and its constituent units, the formulation of general principles and formulas for federal decision making, and the creation of specific institutional arrangements for putting these principles and formulas into practice. These changes, however, failed to resolve or even reduce the conflict. One problem was that adopting these changes necessitated separate amendments to each of the republican and provincial constitutions. This in turn led to heated public debates on highly sensitive and conflict-arousing issues in the fall. The result was that the legislative institutions of the federation became superfluous due to the continuing political conflict between the regions (Burg 1983, 214–17). Ultimately, the process culminated in the 1974 Constitution, which ratified and adjusted preceding changes and attempted to construct a system that would survive Tito. In the final analysis, the 1974 Constitution tried to refine the balance between economic and ethnic diversity, on the one hand, and the communist ideal of social unity, on the other. The new framework reduced the number of federal chambers from five to two (Lampe 1996, 306–07). In addition, the new Constitution contained elaborate language designed to protect the self-management system from too much state interference. The new constitutional setup expanded the representation of the republics and provinces in all electoral and policy forums, while it reduced the State Presidency from twenty-three to only nine members, thereby creating equal representation for each republic and province as well as an ex-officio position for the president of the League of Communists.

In practice, however, despite a nominal dispersal of federal power, the structure of power rested entirely on the personal leadership of Tito and his chief theoretician, Edvard Kardelj. Not only was Tito elected as president of the LCY for life in 1974, but the new Constitution also increased his powers as president of the federation. Thinking about an eventual post-Tito Yugoslavia, Kardelj began in 1977 to lay down the ideological groundwork for a more pluralistic political system. He readily recognized in his manuscript "The Directions of Development of the Political System of Self-Management" that political pluralism was an inevitable fact of Yugoslav political life. Yet he insisted that Yugoslav pluralism had nothing in common with the pluralism of the bourgeois democracies of the West. He claimed that in Yugoslavia the scope of the LCY can accommodate conflicting interests, an area where, according to him, bourgeois democracy had failed. Pluralism in the Yugoslav context, he argued, had a stronger chance for success because it was a manifestation of the principles of economic and political self-management. The trend of preparing for a post-Tito Yugoslavia was continued in 1976 with the promulgation of the Law on Associated Labor (LAL). The latter introduced the Basic Organization of Associated Labor (BOALs) as a basis for reorganizing the Yugoslav labor force. It also formulated a set of self-management agreements that would define the relationship between the economic enterprises and the government. The 1974 Constitution and the 1976 LAL not only provided new building blocks for the Yugoslav economy, they also reinforced the trend of political devolution by reducing the role of centralized political control and stimulating the growth of nonparty interest groups. Hence, "all-Yugoslav" interests, already endangered by persistent regional differences, suffered a further fragmentation with the political reforms of the mid-1970s and onward. In 1979, the chief executive body of the LCY—the Presidium—established a system of annual rotation of its chairmanship. After Tito died, his power to choose the Presidium members devolved to a special Presidium commission that included among its members a number of regional party leaders. The rotation of the Presidium chairmanship continued throughout the 1980s on a regular schedule according to a "nationality key" rule that divided the position equally among the eight federal jurisdictions, that is, six republics and two autonomous provinces.

Although Tito's death began a new era in Yugoslav politics, many of the trends of the 1970s continued unchanged. There were eight amendments to the Constitution in 1981, the purpose of which was to consolidate the elements of the system of rotational government developed at various times in preceding years. The Twelfth Party Congress of 1982, which was expected to lay new political ground and provide a sense of a strong direction for the polity, failed to achieve any major progress on any front. The failure was due to the by then familiar regional stalemate between centralizers and decentralizers within the party. As it soon became clear, the Twelfth Congress was only the first of what proved to be a long series of stages marred with strident, fruitless debates within the LCY.

### *Effects of the Structural Lock-In*

The structural lock-in between the national question and the institutional arrangements of post-1974 federal state had three important effects which strongly shaped the changes that occurred in intercommunal relations throughout the 1980s and 1990–91.

First, the structural lock-in defined the criteria of success for political entrepreneurship and leadership. It also delimited the realm of feasible political agendas that these entrepreneurs could opt for, if they wanted to retain their entrepreneurial roles and retain their popular legitimacy. The entrepreneurs in turn used the post-1974 institutional political arrangements and the national question as resources to pursue their agendas. Hence, a new leadership style based on ultranationalistic strategies and communal mobilization emerged by the mid-1980s. The difficult socioeconomic conditions in the federation bolstered the new leadership style even further. The new leaders endeavored to revive and politicize selected historical memories that they then used to create nationalistic political myths. Simultaneously revived historical memories and associated reified political myths clashed with each other across intercommunal fault lines. The clashing became an overriding condition, strongly shaping intercommunal as well as community-federal relations. The elites were able to reach topmost leadership positions in Serbia and Croatia and carry out their respective agendas. In this pursuit, the elites propagated and maintained the perception that their views, rooted in ultranationalistic political myths, were the only viable solution to Yugoslavia's dire socioeconomic and political conditions. Framing the problems in this way also helped to legitimize the new leadership style and thereby defeat challenging strategies. As a result, the political myths became lenses through which the Serb and Croat (and Slovene) communities envisioned their future relations with one another, as well as with the federal government.

Second, post-1974 institutional arrangements became a liability to state stability and efficacy. The Serbs and Albanians attacked the constitutional arrangements implemented in 1974. A segment of the Serb elite began questioning the status quo immediately after Tito's death and increasingly challenged Tito's legacy of "quasi-confederal federalism." It portrayed Tito's federalism as a plot, based on the principle that a weak Serbia is tantamount to a strong Yugoslavia. The conspiracy was thus to keep the Serbs divided and powerless in a state they believed they had done the most to create and defend (Rusinow 1995, 13–37). In addition, many party members and increasingly larger numbers of citizens began losing confidence in the LCY's capacity to resolve the country's difficulties. Republican and provincial party organizations and elites became more autonomous, unwilling to implement the decisions that their respective representatives had worked out at the federal level (Ramet 1992a). Moreover, from Tito's death until Milosevic's rise in 1987, the regional party organizations were increasingly fragmented. The Collective Presidency also became entangled in the same divisive issue that faced the south Slavs in 1918 when they created the first Yugoslavia—the nature of the political system (Ramet 1995; Woodward 1995a, 82–145; Cohen 1995, 79–225).

Third, the structural lock-in provided facilitating conditions for a deconstruction of intercommunal trust. As explained in chapter 3, three conditions —intercommunal interdependence, *ex ante* agency, and *ex post* agency—shape the evolution of intercommunal trust. As seen in the previous chapter, intercommunal interdependence and the structural lock-in reinforced intercommunal trust that had emerged immediately after the end of the war of national liberation. In the case of this chapter, the high level of interdependence and the new structural lock-in facilitated the deconstruction of whatever level of intercommunal trust remained from the Tito era. As argued earlier, during the 1989–91 debates intercommunal interdependence was quite high, particularly as the debates on the form of state governance lingered well into 1990–91.

Defining and delimiting as well as enforcing *ex ante* agency and *ex post* agency were at the core of the 1974 Constitution and subsequent developments under Tito's rule. The structural lock-in resulting both from the 1974 Constitution and subsequent institutional changes enhanced the *ex ante* agency of national groups well beyond the level that the 1946–53 era had witnessed. As noted earlier, the Constitution of 1974 (particularly preamble 8) anchored the LCY's leading role. However, after Tito's death a vacuum of authority developed in the central party apparatus. Political life in the federal League of Communists shifted to the republics and provinces and consisted almost entirely of infighting between party representatives of the republics and provinces. Moreover, the 1974 Constitution defined the republics explicitly as states (article 3) and made them into independent agents of ultimate political decision making. Both houses of the Yugoslav Federal Assembly—the Federal Chamber and the Chamber of Republics and Provinces—were in fact bodies representing and speaking for the republics and provinces. The parliaments of the republics or provinces or other republic organs appointed the members of both houses of the Federal Assembly. Because legislative procedure revolved around the principle of consensus among the republics and provinces, this signified that every republic or province enjoyed a veto right in practically all affairs. As long as Tito was the president, the republics were more or less kept under control. However, absent Tito's arbitrating role, the constituent units of the federation began to increase their *ex ante* agency in any way they could. The federal institutions thus became theaters wherein the republican leaders not only exercised but also de facto, and sometimes de jure, enhanced *ex ante* agency.[17]

That the structural lock-in provided a framework for seeking more *ex post* agency is evident in the debates on state governance that evolved in the 1980s. Whereas Slovenia and Croatia sought to increase their respective levels of *ex post* agency, Serbia instead sought to reduce further the *ex post* agency of the constituent republics. More specifically, as discussed earlier in the chapter, in the second phase of the debates within the Collective Presidency, the Serbian reform strategy recommended that the decision-making process in the Federal Assembly abide by the principle of interregional unanimity and be limited only to the narrowest circle of constitutional questions. The proposal also suggested that most voting follow the principle of qualified majorities and rejected political pluralism as a solution to the legitimacy crisis. The Slovene reform strategy rejected this majoritarian scheme, fearing that supporters of such a scheme would outvote them due to the demographic predominance of the Serbs in Yugoslavia. The Slovene leadership instead advanced the idea of an asymmetric federation scheme, wherein each republic would negotiate its own terms of power sharing and distribution with the federal government (Cohen 1995, 59–66). In the third phase, the Slovene and Croat leaders proposed a confederation of sovereign republics, based on the principle that the organization of the country must preserve both the sovereignty of all republics and the existing borders between the republics. Serbia and Montenegro saw the federation not only as a political reality, but also as more likely to become stronger. They hence rejected the notion that a republic could unilaterally proclaim its administrative borders as state borders. In short, concerns about defining and exercising *ex post* agency were the driving force underlying these debates.

Therefore, as Yugoslavia entered the 1990 decade, the main constituent units of the federation, namely, Serbia, Slovenia, and Croatia (and increasingly more Bosnia-Herzegovina), faced a high level of intercommunal interdependence. Yet they simultaneously were increasingly acquiring more *ex ante* agency and seeking more *ex post* agency as republics. The blend of a new style of leadership based on ultranationalistic rhetoric and strategies and the increase in *ex ante* and *ex post* agency of the republics under a condition of very high interdependence ultimately resulted in a deconstruction of intercommunal trust. Arguably, without the increase in both *ex ante* and *ex post* agency of the republics, ultranationalistic leaders would have had a hard time selling their rhetoric to their respective constituencies. Yet what became strongly, but not solely, determinative of the process of deconstructing intercommunal trust were the intra- and intercommunal strategies that the respective ultranationalistic leaders opted for. The latter, as discussed earlier, in combination with a high and increasing level of information complexity and a low and rapidly decreasing level of intercommunal predictability, created a high and rapidly increasing level of vulnerability. Put differently, a blend of mutually reinforcing, ultranationalistic elite strategies and a high and rapidly increasing level intercommunal vulnerability could not but end up in a rapid deconstruction of intercommunal trust. Next, I discuss how the process of deconstructing intercommunal trust unfolded.

*Deconstructing Intercommunal Trust*

The process of deconstructing trust developed as the Serb and Croat political entrepreneurs and activists began politicizing ethnic historical memories, manipulating the structure of ethnic cleavages, and using the opportunities offered by the structural lock-in to implement their respective agendas. However, these leaders were not in complete control of the process of deconstructing trust, even if their strategies ignited it. As the discussion below shows, the structure of ethnic cleavages in Yugoslavia provided the Serb and Croat political entrepreneurs and activists with "raw materials" through which they enacted their strategies. The mutual feedback between the reciprocated strategic practices of the elites, the response of the Serb and Croat communities at large, and the simultaneous weakening of key federal institutions all combined to sustain the process of trust deconstruction.

THE SERB ELITE: CONSTRUCTION OF POLITICAL MYTHS

The Serb political entrepreneurs and activists politicized the memories of major historical events that are widely shared among the Serbs. They particularly focused their efforts on the collapse of the fourteenth-century Serbian kingdom (Petrovich 1976; Clissold 1966; Singleton 1985), the Serb defeat in the Battle of Kosovo against the Ottomans in 1389 (Emmert 1990; Banac 1995, 39–65), and Ustasha (Croatian fascist party) and Nazi crimes against the Serbs during World War II (Emmert 1990; Banac 1995; Denitch 1994). Many Serb politicians and intellectuals freely drew analogies between their struggle against the political decentralization trend then occurring in Yugoslavia in the late 1980s and the disintegration of the Serbian medieval kingdom. The historic meaning of Kosovo regained tremendous value after Tito's death. The turning point came in April 1981, when Albanian riots in the province of Kosovo stirred up much resentment and bitterness among the Serbs. The Serb backlash was summarized in 1982 by several Serb orthodox priests in a document titled "appeal for the protection of the Serb inhabitants and their holy places in Kosovo." This momentum was reinforced by the publication on May 15, 1982, of a lengthy "Appeal for the Protection of the Serbian Inhabitants and Their Holy Places in Kosovo" by the patriarchate's organ, *Pravoslavlje.* The article asserted that "the question of Kosovo is a question of the spiritual, cultural, and historical identity of the Serbian people. . . . Kosovo is our memory, our hearth, the focus of our being."[18] The collective memory on Kosovo received another strong impetus in a 1986 memorandum of the Serbian Academy of Sciences (Banac 1995, 39–65). A variety of people and groups, including the Serbian Writers' Association, many news media and cultural figures, key figures in the Serbian Orthodox Church, and most significantly, the older generation of the Serbian countryside, all sanctified the memorandum into a matter of creed.

Three years later, in spring 1989, Patriarch German gave an interview to the journal *Politika* in which he claimed that in the 1389 Battle of Kosovo, the Serbian army fought not only to protect the sovereignty of Tsar Lazar's kingdom, but also to protect Christianity, human freedom, culture, and all of Christian Europe.[19] To arouse the Serbs' emotions and reinforce their attachments to Kosovo even more, the Orthodox Church commemorated the Battle of Kosovo in Bosnia in August 1989 as an outdoor service. The commemoration was rife with many ultranationalistic symbols drawn from the Serb historical memory. Some 150,000 Orthodox Serbs attended the gathering, many holding banners with pictures of various Orthodox saints (Ramet 1992a). The legend of Kosovo thus recaptured the hearts of Serbs throughout the Serbian community. "Liberating" Kosovo became a daytime dream, with, for example, bookstores filling their shelves with numerous books about Kosovo and artists dedicating their works to Kosovo. There also was much revived interest and nostalgia for past and still living monarchs. For example, the Serbian patriarchate invited Princess Jelena Karadjordjevic (who was living between Paris and Peru) to attend the 600th anniversary celebrations of the Battle of Kosovo. On September 10, 1989, the remains of Tsar Lazar were ceremoniously reburied at the Monastery of Ravanica. There was even talk of transporting the last remains of King Peter II back to Yugoslavia, for burial in Oplenac (Ramet 1995, 102–22).

Likewise, the massacres committed during World War II by the Nazis and the Ustasha became part of the rhetoric of intercommunal struggles between Serbs and Croats in the late 1980s (Banac 1992, 168–87). The Serb political entrepreneurs and activists portrayed past and present Croats' persistent quest for national autonomy and statehood as a continuous conspiracy to divide the Serbian nation and eradicate its political unity (Denitch 1994). Not surprisingly, these historical memories became a source for wild charges and countercharges of past attempts at ethnic genocide between the Serbs and Croats. For example, many Serb elements in the Yugoslav army and Serbia's government often cited the wartime massacres as a justification for their recent war against Croatia and Bosnia in the 1990s. Many Serbs also interpreted the fact that Germany and Austria were active defenders of an independent Croatia in the late 1980s and early 1990s as a confirmation of their suspicion that the Germans and Croats are in fact targeting the Serb people, as they did during World War II (Denitch 1994).

The Serb political entrepreneurs and activists transformed these historical memories into political myths, especially after Slobodan Milosevic seized power in 1987. The political myths created a sense of a besieged Serb nation, not only in Kosovo but also in Croatia and elsewhere in Yugoslavia. Milosevic quickly became the most visible advocate of Serbian grievances and a self-appointed spokesperson for the survival of Serbs as a unified nation within a strong unitary Yugoslav state. He willingly conflated Yugoslavia's integrity with the national security and survival of the Serbs as a people (Ramet 1995)—any threat to Yugoslavia's integrity was a threat to the security and survival of the Serb nation.

### THE SERB ELITE: INTERNALIZATION OF POLITICAL MYTHS

Slobodan Milosevic (and like-minded Serb leaders) used ritualization as well as both coercive inducements and incentives to propagate and entrench his self-styled political myths within the Serb population. The approach was multidimensional. Milosevic skillfully channeled the yearning of the Orthodox Church for its past status as a defender of the Serb nation. Before 1987, the communists had suppressed the church press, confiscated church land, harassed the clergy, and relegated the Orthodox Church itself to second-class status. The Serbian Church was conscious of its weakness under Tito's regime. Nevertheless, it did not allow the regime to co-opt it by occasionally assuming an opposition posture openly, at least until 1987. Milosevic pronounced the church the spiritual component of the Serb national identity and extended and deepened his rapprochement with it by granting permits to build new churches and to restore old ones (Ramet 1992a). The church returned his favors and assumed an active role in promoting Serbian ultranationalism.

Milosevic also focused his attention on Serbian concerns about the rise of Albanian nationalism in Kosovo. In a visit to Kosovo in April 1987, Milosevic assured the Serb population living there that "No one will be allowed to beat you. No one will be allowed to beat you" (Cohen 1995, 52). By November 1988, Milosevic's message was rapidly spreading in Serbia. He soon called for new constitutional amendments that would restore Serbian authority over Kosovo and Vojvodina, and indeed reduced the autonomy of Kosovo and Vojvodina by de facto annexing them to Serbia. In 1989 he modified the Serbian Constitution to reduce de jure autonomy status of the two provinces. The Orthodox Church encouraged Milosevic and published a Saint Vitus Day message in its newspaper, *Glas Crkve,* proclaiming that the proffered changes in the Serbian Constitution are but a restoration of state sovereignty to Serbia over its natural territory.[20]

Milosevic and his coalition also used education as a medium to propagate their ultranationalistic political myths. They introduced the Cyrillic alphabet, simply brushing away years of increasingly shifting toward the Latin alphabet. The church sent a letter of support to the Ministry of Education of Serbia, demanding the introduction of Orthodox religious education as a mandatory subject in all elementary and secondary schools (Ramet 1995). Jumping on the occasion and as a gesture of goodwill toward the Orthodox Church, the Serbian government removed Marxism from school curricula and replaced it with religious instruction in June 1990 (Ramet 1992a).

Milosevic disposed of many prominent political figures in Serbia (such as his predecessor, Ivo Stambolic) to further consolidate his power within the Serb community. He accused them of becoming either too assertive or too compromised. However, to win their continuous support, he appointed them to important and lucrative positions in business as well as other nonpolitical occupations (Djilas 1991; Gagnon 1994–95). He also skillfully channeled the congruence of interests between his political goals and those of the Yugoslav army to reinforce his power base in the military institution, at least among the Serbs (Gagnon 1994–95).

At the top of his strategy, Milosevic domesticated the news media and co-opted them to promote his political myths. For example, in September 1990, the Serbian daily *Politika* published an article calling for a lift of the Titoist proscription of a nationalist role for the church. The article praised the Serbian Church for its service to the Serb nation and declared Orthodoxy the spiritual basis and most essential component of the Serb national identity.[21] In general, "nationalist media manipulation was the centerpiece of Milosevic's successful strategy for defeating liberal reformers in the scramble for both mass and elite support" (Snyder and Ballentine 1996, 26). Although Milosevic never fully controlled all media outlets, he had under his direct supervision the state television station and Belgrade's three major newspapers (Thompson 1994). In addition, he indirectly coerced the members, as well as constrained the scope, of more independent and opposition media (Gagnon 1994–95; Woodward 1995a; Thompson 1994).

### THE CROAT ELITE: CONSTRUCTION OF POLITICAL MYTHS

Much like their Serbian counterparts, the Croat political entrepreneurs and activists also revived key Croatian historical memories. They thus highlighted the memories of a legendary longing for statehood, the images of Croatian struggles against the Serb domination during the first Yugoslavia (1919–41), and the images of large numbers of Croats who were killed by the Serb Chetniks during World War II (Djilas 1991). To legitimize the Croats' continuous demands for political autonomy and recognition of their nationalist aspirations and self-proclaimed historic rights, the leaders and entrepreneurs promoted the idea of a Serb conspiracy to reestablish hegemony over Yugoslavia (Irvine 1993). The threat allegedly assumed three forms: a demographic displacement of the Croats by the Serbs, an effort to split Croatia in two, and a "Serbianization" of the Croatian language (Ramet 1992a). Transforming these concerns into political myths became the approach that the Croat leaders used to mobilize their fellow nationals against the Serbian nationalists. As in the case of Serbia, the Croat political entrepreneurs and ethnic activists of the 1980s and 1990s did not create the Croats' historical memories. Nor did they need to distort them to fit their self-serving goals. Indeed, the Croat national question has remained a persistent issue during both the kingdom and socialist Yugoslavia (Irvine 1993; Ramet 1992b).

Therefore, when the new style of leadership emerged in the 1980s in Yugoslavia, the Croat leaders had within their reach a set of historical memories that could easily be used as raw materials for nationalist mythmaking. As their counterpart in Serbia used ritualization, coercive inducements, and various incentives to rally support for ultranationalistic political myths, so did the Croat leaders. The process of democratization also played an important role in the Croatian elites' bid to win popular support. The electorate was "sold" and hence internalized the ultranationalistic political myths through the processes of electoral campaigns and ballot boxes (Cohen 1995). Holding democratic elections opened up the space of political contestation and became an entry into ultranationalistic politics (Linz and Stepan 1992). Franjo Tudjman, the leader of the Croatian Democratic Alliance (HDZ), built his campaign around promises to reassert the priority of Croatia's national interests. The HDZ appealed directly to the voters' nationalist sentiments and to their dissatisfaction with the communist regime. Its core program was the affirmation of Croatian national identity and sovereignty, though without calling for outright secession from Yugoslavia. In addition, Tudjman called for the Croats and Muslims living in Bosnia-Herzegovina to be included in the new Croatia, echoing a widely held Croatian view to enhance his popular appeal among the Croats' nationalists even more. The elections held in late April and May gave Tudjman's alliance an impressive victory.[22] A by-product of the election campaign was a mobilization of the Croatian community around their long-time aspiration to national sovereignty and autonomy.

### ROUTINIZATION OF NEW INTERCOMMUNAL RELATIONS

The intercommunal strategies promoted by the various communal elites reinforced their respective intra-communal strategies, thereby strengthening the process of mobilization of the Serb and Croat communities. Milosevic-controlled media in Belgrade launched a propaganda campaign against the Croats, accusing them of nurturing a conspiracy against the Serbs because they were opposing the annexation of Kosovo to Croatia. Although the nationalists in Croatia had persistently warned of an impending "Serbianization," the leaders of the LCC nevertheless avoided any major clash with the Serb leadership throughout the late 1980s. The delicate relationship of Croatia's ethnic majority with the Serb minority in Croatia itself heightened the Croatian elite's prudence regarding the Croatian question. The Croatian leaders nonetheless accused Milosevic of "Stalinist" and "unitarist" tendencies after Milosevic reduced the autonomy of Kosovo and began calling for more political centralization at the federal level. The Croat leaders alleged that the Serbian politicians were aiming at destabilizing Croatia. The Serb and Croat ultranationalistic leaders henceforth increasingly engaged one another in rhetorical battles, incriminating each other while self-justifying their respective actions and positions on the basis of historical grievances. Demonizing the

"Other" became an intercommunal routine. By 1990, the relations between Serbia and Croatia (and between Serbia and Slovenia) became increasingly a zero-sum game. Aggressive rhetoric and practices incited aggressive responses. The more assertive each group became in its ultranationalistic project, the more it intruded on politics in the other republic, and the fewer prospects there were to reach any compromise on an increasing number of divisive issues. As stated by Woodward, "Other republics or the federal government were increasingly identified as external enemies to be defeated" (1995a, 113).

The Serb and Croat relations henceforth increasingly became sharply mutually opposed and based on self-proclaimed national historical rights, grievances, and irreconcilably construed political myths. The loyalties of large segments of these communities changed in such a way that there was a conflation of individual citizenship rights and communal rights. Political loyalty to the federation eroded, and nationality-defined political loyalties gradually replaced it. A public opinion survey conducted in mid-1990 reveals, for example, that only 48 percent of the Croats gave more allegiance to Yugoslavia than to their republic. At the same time, 71 percent of the Serbs still showed strong political loyalty to Yugoslavia. The high percentage of Serb support for Yugoslavia came from a belief that the fate of the Serbian nation and Yugoslavia's integrity were inseparable. The same data also showed that most Croats (72 percent) did not support the notion that the federal constitutional provisions should have precedence over the republican ones, in contrast to most Serbs (83 percent) who did (Cohen 1995, 172–73).

That the level of reliance on intercommunal trust was rapidly vanishing is evident in three ways. First, the evolution of the intercommunal policies and actions that tied together the fates of the groups clearly demonstrates that the groups were far from behaving either trustworthily or trustingly toward one another. The major communal groups were increasingly resorting to unilateral moves and policies, the purpose of which was to de-link their fates from one another as much as possible. The more the groups formulated policies and actions that sought to de-link their respective fates from one another, the more rapidly decreasing was the reliance on intercommunal trust.

Second, because mutual trust is based on creating and communicating as well as sustaining shared meanings, an exploration of the discursive explanations of the group positions toward each other as well as their mutual descriptions provides another set of indicators on the level of mutual trust among the groups. The more the groups would explain and justify their mutual relations in terms of mutual trust, the more this would indicate mutual trust between them. In addition, the more the groups identify one another as trustworthy and trusting, the more this would indicate the relevance of trust for their mutual relations. As discussed earlier, intercommunal relations became increasingly zero-sum games, and the "Other" became increasingly the enemy to vanquish and not trust.

Third, the type of safeguard mechanisms that the groups use to monitor compliance with mutual commitments are a third set of indicators of the level of mutual trust. The more these safeguard mechanisms shift from being *ex ante* preemption to *ex post* detection of "breach of trust," the higher should be the level of mutual trust. In the present case, the Serbs, Croats, and Slovenes, as discussed earlier, increasingly sought to enhance their *ex ante* agency. The communal leaders recurrently used unilateralist moves and preemptive strategies whether, for example, in the debates within the Collective Presidency or on the news media and ballot boxes.

In sum, the level of intercommunal trust that the federal institutions and policies had managed to secure under Tito and his aftermath quickly eroded after the rise of the new style of ultranationalistic leadership. As the debates on state governance began in the late 1980s, intercommunal trust eroded even more rapidly because the republics' leaders began to engage each other in rhetorical wars of incriminations and blame and use these inter-leaders' "wars" to enhance their respective intra-communal postures. Hence, the level of reliance on trust rapidly decreased as the scope of collective intentionality decreased in the debates of 1990–91, that is, as the antagonists increasingly challenged the intercommunal status quo and acted more in the "I" mode than in the "we" mode. The evolution of the distribution of institutional power accentuated even more this erosion of whatever remained from the scope of collective intentionality, as I explain next.

## Institutional Power Leverage

For a given intercommunal vulnerability, the reliance on institutional power increases as intercommunal trust decreases, and vice versa. For a given vulnerability, the more rapidly the reliance on institutional power increases, the more rapidly intercommunal trust would decrease, and the more rapidly the scope of collective intentionality would decrease. The 1987–91 case provides a better test of these hypotheses than the 1948–53 case. In the latter case, the Tito regime played an essential role in preventing any one republic or communal group from acquiring any institutional advantage at the expense of the others. This effectively preempted any one group from attempting to use institutional power to address any perception of intercommunal vulnerability. In contrast, in the late 1980s no Yugoslav leader occupied Tito's role. The system of the Collective Presidency inherited from the Tito era was potentially susceptible to become an arena for an intercommunal race for domination, as it indeed turned out to be. As the discussion below shows, the Serbian leadership precisely attempted to dominate key federal institutions and use any ensuing institutional power to pursue its own Serbian agenda.

Yugoslavia's core federal institutions—the Collective Presidency, the LCY, and the Yugoslav National Army—rapidly became dueling arenas wherein aggressive intercommunal politics and fear flourished. With each communal group believing that it had to take matters into its hands, the two key federal institutions—the Collective Presidency and the YNA—inexorably became highly coveted due to their central political roles in the polity.[23] Milosevic aggressively sought to dominate the Collective Presidency. By 1990, the effective number of delegates in the Collective Presidency became five—Serbian, Slovene, Croatian, Macedonian, and Bosnian representatives. Milosevic had transformed Montenegro, Vojvodina, and Kosovo into satellites of Serbia, assuring himself the unequivocal support of their delegates. Milosevic's was thus able to control a majority of votes (four) in the Collective Presidency, thereby effectively paralyzing the institution. The debates within the Collective Presidency revolved around four divisive issues: the status and value of maintaining the Yugoslav federation, the rights of the republics to secede from the existing federal arrangement, the character of the republican borders, and the most desirable type of future political arrangements among the republics. As discussed earlier in the chapter, the republican leaders held irreconcilable positions on these issues, thereby leading the Collective Presidency into paralysis.

The Serbian leadership fared much better with the YNA, however. The latter became polarized, and what remained of it increasingly took sides with the Serbs. Under the 1974 Constitution, the army could in principle use all necessary means to protect the country and its system of socialist self-management (Gow 1992). Not surprisingly, the YNA hence opposed the new Slovene leadership's assertion of Slovenia's political sovereignty in 1990. The standoff ultimately led to a confrontation between newly proclaimed Slovene forces and the YNA in June 1991. As a consequence, the YNA lost its reputation as an impartial federal institution because it had acted without being authorized to do so by the federal prime minister. The Slovenes, Croats, and subsequently Muslims henceforth came to perceive the YNA as but a tool in the hands of the Serb ultranationalists.

Therefore, in a bid to use its institutional power, the Serbian leadership ended up stalling two key federal institutions and thereby reinforcing the deconstruction of trust among the Serb, Croat, and Slovene communities. The stalling of key federal institutions and the deconstruction of intercommunal trust mutually reinforced one another. Had the federal institutions not reached such a dismal state, the ultranationalistic leaders would not have been able to portray their strategies as the only routes of salvation for their respective communities. However, the federal institutions did not weaken independently of the elites' strategies. Rather, the federal institutions were part of the "resources" that facilitated the leaders' strategies. The simultaneous weakening of state institutions and the elites' reciprocating strategies were inseparable from one another.

In sum, as intercommunal trust was quickly eroding, the leaders began to have recourse to whatever institutional power they believed they had or could muster. However, not every republican leader had access to the federal institutional powers in the same way, since the Serbian leadership reserved for itself the lion's share of institutional power. Hence the Serbian leadership led by Milosevic began to rely increasingly more on its institutional power in trying to impose its choices on the other republics. Yet the Slovenes and Croats were far from resigning themselves to this "Milosevic fact" and endeavored to act outside the existing rules and practices of state governance. The more the Serbian leadership resorted to its power in the federal institutions, the more the Slovenes and Croats "exited" from the system of "normal politics," and the more the authority and legitimacy of the federal state eroded. This in turn eroded further an already rapidly vanishing intercommunal trust and caused a more-rapid erosion of collective intentionality.

## Conclusion

The transformation of state governance during 1987–91 in Yugoslavia was rooted in the fundamental transformation of the international environment as the Cold War between the United States and the Soviet Union was coming to an end and in the post-1979 unfavorable global economic conditions. Adapting to the new international milieu and preserving the integrity of the federation led the Yugoslav leaders to debate whether and how to transform the form of state governance.

The collapse of state governance and subsequent territorial disintegration of the federation occurred because the level of intercommunal vulnerability became high and rapidly increased in 1987–91. Under these conditions, the major communal groups represented by the leaders of the constituent republics began to fear intercommunal abandonment, exploitation, or exclusion from participating in the debates that would decide the future form of the state.[24] This was expected to occur because the level of information complexity was quite high. The major communal groups had little reliable information on each other's intentions. In addition, intercommunal predictability was quite low and significantly decreased as the debates on state governance unfolded. There was little shared intercommunal commitment to the Tito institutional legacy anymore. The more the republic leaders debated the issues dividing them, the less intercommunal commitment ensued. The structure of ethnic cleavages and much-enhanced *ex ante* and *ex post* republics' agency (much beyond what 1974 institutional arrangements allowed for) combined to create a strong sense of intercommunal interdependence among the major communal groups. This greatly strengthened the incentives for the communal leaders to seek a transformation of state governance in dealing with the fundamental changes occurring in the international environment. However, as the republics' leaders debated the form of state governance, intercommunal vulnerability rapidly increased, undermining the legitimacy of the post-1974 constitutional and institutional arrangements even more.

Yet the outcome of debating state governance was not solely determined by the high vulnerability among the major communal groups. As outlined in the theory and shown in this case, intercommunal vulnerability and trust mutually fed into one another. Intercommunal trust was low and rapidly decreasing. This henceforth helped to enhance the fear of intercommunal vulnerability. The republics' leaders understood that the intercommunal trust that had existed previously had seriously eroded and thus was no longer an effective or reliable device that they could use to reduce or at least preempt any further increase in intercommunal vulnerability. Hence, intercommunal trust decreased as the scope of collective intentionality decreased during the post-1987 debates, and more so in the 1990–91 debates. Had intercommunal trust been higher, the collapse of state governance might have been avoided or at least delayed for some time. A collapse of state governance was very likely but not inevitable in 1987–91.

The outcome of the debates over transforming the state, in turn, depended on the interaction of a low intercommunal trust and the Serb leaders' attempt to rely on institutional power, initially within the Collective Presidency and then through the YNA. The Tito regime concentrated most of the institutional powers in its hand and used them as a means to carry on the transformation agenda as well as eliminate the domestic challenge to the legitimacy of the reforms. In contrast, in 1987–91 the regime was divided against itself, with no dominant actor to play Tito's role in preserving regime integrity. Hence, in contrast with the 1948–53 case, the major communal groups and republics (more specifically the Serbs) sought to use their leverage of institutional power to shape the debates on governance transformation, which undermined intercommunal trust even more.

By seeking to transform the rules and practices of state governance, the divided regime of 1990–91 ended up undermining itself. It failed to create a new set of constitutional-institutional incentives that would have encouraged domestic actors to make new commitments on a perennially sensitive issue—the national question. The lack of any such commitment slowly became self-sustaining and ultimately a process of increasing returns. The collapse of the federation became a self-fulfilling prophecy as the republics' leaders prevented the consolidation of a new structural lock-in on the national question, which might have stabilized the evolution of the federation toward adopting a new form of state governance, as it did in 1963 and 1974.

# Six

# Lebanon, the Cold War Penetration, and the Rise of Nasserism, 1957–58

In the years 1955–58, President Camille Chamoun opted for a number of foreign policy choices that breached Lebanon's international neutrality. He supported the conclusion of the Baghdad Pact in 1955. He disapproved of Gamel Abdul Nasser's move to nationalize the British-owned Suez Canal. He resisted Arab pressures to break off diplomatic relations with Britain and France during the 1956 Suez Canal crisis. He adhered to the Eisenhower Doctrine in 1957. These policies antagonized most opposition groups in Lebanon. Chamoun set the stage for a domestic confrontation when he manipulated the parliamentary elections in June 1957 in a bid to secure a Chamber of Deputies. The latter was expected to amend the Constitution and hence allow him to run for a second presidential term in a year's time. The domestic situation quickly deteriorated, however, and a crisis of state governance erupted, eventually ending in violent street confrontations in May 1958. Chamoun ordered the army to intervene against his opponents. The army disobeyed the order, deciding instead to remain neutral in the conflict. Its commander, Fuad Shihab, subsequently became president in September 1958. He was able to restore "normal politics," the Lebanese way. State governance was reconsolidated with a significantly rising scope of collective intentionality due to a combination of three elements. First, the level of intercommunal vulnerability was moderate and decreased significantly under Shihab's rule. Second, the level of intercommunal trust was low but significantly increased with Shihab's emergence. Third, the level of reliance on institutional power was moderate and decreased with Shihab's emergence.

## Theoretical Expectations

The successful, bloodless coup organized by the Free Officers against the Egyptian monarchy on July 23, 1952, ushered in a new era in regional politics.

The subsequent rise of Arab nationalism and the superpower penetration in the region signified the beginning of major changes in regional order. The withdrawal of Britain and France and their replacement by the United States as the major Western power in the region, the Soviets' reluctant attempts to gain a foothold in the region, and the rise of Nasser's Egypt as the dominant Arab state all combined to initiate a competition over regional order. The competition took the form of a struggle between Arab nationalism promoted by Nasser and his camp and the Cold War logic driving the United States and a reluctant Soviet Union. These entailed fundamental changes in regional constitutive rules and practices. This transformation of regional order in turn pressured Lebanon to seek for itself a new international role by abandoning its previously held neutralist doctrine of foreign policy. The new environment also induced domestic political debates about the very system of state governance in Lebanon that had existed since the end of the French mandate. The collective intentionality that had underpinned the form of state governance established in the aftermath of the French mandate system was at stake, facing the threat of being undermined.

More specifically, in order to maintain itself the Chamoun regime sought to modify the rules of the political game in Lebanon through constitutional amendments. Changing the Lebanese Constitution, however, threatened to jeopardize a core element of the Lebanese polity, the so-called 1943 National Pact. Jeopardizing the latter in turn implied a destruction of the political fabric of the confessional system, that is, the backbone of the Lebanese society since the mandate system. Yet because the constituent sectarian communities of Lebanon felt so interdependent, they realized that it was in their common interest to preserve the integrity of the National Pact, and hence the confessional polity. The theory outlined in chapter 3 suggests that under these conditions the outcome of the debates on state governance in the period 1957–58 was most likely to be a reconsolidation of state governance of Lebanon.

Three primary factors combined to bring about a reconsolidation of state governance in the period 1957–58. First, after the Maronite president manipulated the 1957 legislative elections, the level of intercommunal vulnerability began to rise steadily as the communal groups (first the Druzes and subsequently the Maronites) feared exclusion. Yet after Fuad Shihab emerged as the candidate who would most likely become the next president of Lebanon, intercommunal vulnerability began to decrease significantly. Under these new conditions, the major communal groups had no serious fear of intercommunal abandonment, exploitation, or exclusion. The low level of vulnerability was the result of a low to moderate information complexity, a moderate to high intercommunal predictability, and an important sense of intercommunal interdependence. Information complexity was low to moderate because, under Shihab's rule, the major communal groups had reliable information on each other's intentions and capabilities. Intercommunal predictability was moderate to high since there was enough intercommunal commitment to the Shihab regime. The sense of interdependence among the major communal groups in the Lebanese polity greatly strengthened the incentives for the communal groups to reconsolidate state governance in dealing with the fundamental changes occurring in the international environment (hypothesis 1). Also, as the Shihab regime increasingly succeeded in putting behind it the 1958 crisis, vulnerability decreased with increases in the scope of collective intentionality in the polity, that is, as the emerging rules and practices of state governance were more and more accepted as the framework for playing "normal politics" (hypothesis 3).

Second, from 1957 to 1958 (that is, before Shihab became the president), the level of intercommunal trust began to decrease as the Maronite president, Camille Chamoun, and his supporters raised serious challenges to the status quo and began pushing for a transformation of the rules of state governance. However, after Shihab's emergence and Chamoun's stepping down, intercommunal trust increased significantly to reach moderate (if not higher) levels, particularly during Shihab's presidential tenure. Hence, intercommunal trust increased as the scope of collective intentionality increased during the post-1958 Shihab era (hypothesis 5).

Third, under Chamoun's presidency, the level of reliance on institutional power by the Maronites began to rise, particularly after the 1957 parliamentary elections. The Chamoun regime and supporters were, for all practical purposes, dominant in the Parliament, and Chamoun was willing to use that control to seek another presidential term. However, Shihab's tenure restored a more "normal" distribution of institutional power among, at least, the dominant communal groups. The Shihab regime thereby reduced significantly the reliance on institutional power in the debates over state governance. The level of reliance on institutional power hence decreased with the scope of collective intentionality (hypothesis 8). Therefore, overall the reliance on institutional power decreased as intercommunal trust increased (hypothesis 9).

These values of the three variables—vulnerability, trust, and reliance on institutional power—are close to the "most likely conditions" for a consolidating form of state governance with an increasing scope of collective intentionality, as explicated in table 3.1 (chapter 3). Hence, that the Lebanese polity was able to reconsolidate its state governance conforms to the expectations of the theory outlined in chapters 2 and 3. These theoretical expectations are summarized in table 6.1.

## Changes in the Constitutive Rules of Regional Environment

The creation of the modern Lebanese state under the French mandate in 1920 came after the end of World War I, the collapse of the Ottoman Empire and the division of its spoils among Britain, France, and Russia, the rise of

**Table 6.1. Summary of Theoretical Expectations**
DCSG: Degree of Consolidation of State Governance

External Variable:
Regional environment: the Rise of Nasserism, the 1957 Eisenhower Doctrine, and the formation of the United Arab Republic (UAR) in 1958.

| *Observed Outcome State Governance* | *Intercommunal Vulnerability* | *Intercommunal Trust* | *Reliance on Institutional Power* |
|---|---|---|---|
| Consolidating: | | | |
| DCSG moderate, significantly rising, particularly after the emergence of Shihab as president. | Moderate, increased significantly in summer 1958 as the communal groups (first the Druzes and then the Maronites) feared exclusion. | Moderate, decreased rapidly in summer 1958 but then increased significantly with the emergence of Shihab as president--i.e., as the scope of collective intentionality increased during the post-1958 era (hypothesis 5). | Moderate, increased somewhat with Chamoun's attempt to rely on state institutions. |
| | Decreased significantly with the emergence of Shihab as president due to low to moderate information complexity, moderate to high intercommunal predictability, and the important sense of intercommunal interdependence. | | Decreased with the emergence of Shihab as president—i.e., with the increase in the scope of collective intentionality (hypothesis 8). |
| | Sense of interdependence among major communal groups greatly strengthened the incentives for communal groups to reconsolidate state governance in dealing with fundamental changes occurring in the regional environment (hypothesis 1). | | Overall, decreased as intercommunal increased (hypothesis 9). |
| | Vulnerability decreased with increases in the scope of collective intentionality in the polity—i.e., as the Shihab regime increasingly succeeded in putting behind it the 1958 crisis and the emerging rules and practices of state governance were more and more taken for granted (hypothesis 3). | | |

Arab nationalism, and the beginning of Arab rivalries (Fromkin 1989). Lebanon was by and large able to maintain a foreign policy of neutrality in the region since its complete independence in 1946 until the 1955 Baghdad episode. Such a regional role became an integral element of state legitimacy as part of the system of state governance initiated through the 1943 National Pact and reinforced thereafter. The National Pact—al Mithaq al Watani—defined the foreign policy neutrality of Lebanon through three important principles. First, Lebanon is a completely independent state. The Christian communities were not to identify with the West whereas the Muslim communities were to protect the independence of Lebanon and prevent its merger with any Arab state. Second, although Lebanon is an Arab country with Arabic as its official language, it cannot and should not cut off its spiritual and intellectual ties with the West. Third, Lebanon should cooperate with all Arab states, without siding with any one state against any other.

As a result, Lebanon was spared most of the tremors that ensued from the 1948 Arab-Israeli War and subsequent developments within inter-Arab politics, even though Lebanon was a founding member of the League of Arab States and became host to large numbers of Palestinian refugees who fled Palestine. In the 1948 war, the Lebanese army deployed four battalions along the border with Israel but quickly withdrew them from combat. The Israeli army captured a strip of eastern Lebanon in October 1948 but returned it after Israel and Lebanon signed an armistice on March 23, 1949. Lebanon and Israel then exchanged mutual assurances that neither would embark on military offensives against the other and that both would respect each other's territorial sovereignty. From 1943 to 1952, President Bishara al-Khuri never contracted a military or political treaty with any state that might abridge Lebanon's sovereignty or contravene its neutrality policy. Within the Arab League Lebanon participated willingly in mutually beneficial economic and social programs and effectively mediated quarrels and misunderstandings between rival Arab states.

However, Lebanon's neutrality option and territorial integrity was not completely without threats from potentially explosive issues such as the never-achieved aspiration of Arab political unity (Meo 1965, 93–94). Two such plans for unification were proposed and debated among the Arab states during the al-Khuri regime (1943–52). A "Greater Syria" plan put forward by King Abdallah of Transjordan sought the unification of his kingdom with Arab Palestine, Syria, Lebanon, and possibly Iraq under the king's leadership. Alternatively, the "Fertile Crescent" plan proposed by Nuri al-Said of Iraq called for a similar arrangement, if under Iraqi leadership. The realization of either plan depended for the most part on the initial unification of the proposing country—Transjordan or Iraq—with Syria. However, Syria was far from adhering to either proposal; it was not willing to substitute its republican regime for a monarchical one that either union would have created. Syria's position further consolidated when Egypt led a strong movement against either unification, proposing instead a collective security pact among the Arab states. After many rounds of debates and much "arm twisting," the Egyptian leadership was able to convince enough Arab states to sign the Treaty of Joint Defense and Economic Cooperation on April 13, 1950 (Barnett 1998, 99–103; Seale 1987, 90–91). Through this pact, the Arab states pledged to settle their mutual conflicts through nonviolent means, to engage in collective defense, and to integrate their military and foreign policies. Although the pact never became an effective tool of Arab collective security, it not only offered Syria an alternative to unification but also spared the other states such as Lebanon from making difficult foreign policy choices (Barnett 1998, 103; Podeh 1995, 153–55).

The international conditions (to a large extent shaped by the emerging Cold War) also allowed states such as Lebanon to maintain a norm of neutrality in dealing both with Arab and non-Arab states. Neutrality was part of the constitutive rules of Middle Eastern regional politics. The Cold War rivalry between the United States and the Soviet Union had yet to become part of the regional dynamic in the Middle East. Before the 1955 Baghdad Pact episode, the Middle East was still part of Western sphere of influence. The Soviet Union had yet to become a major player in the region. Lebanon and the other Arab states had yet to face a choice between the Western alliance and the communist bloc. Nor was the Arab world strongly polarized into opposed Arab camps, the rivalries between the Iraqi and Egyptian leaderships and between the Hijaz Saudis and the Hashemite notwithstanding. In contrast, major new international developments during the period 1955–58 would ultimately challenge the constitutive rule of neutrality, thereby inexorably polarizing domestic politics in Lebanon. The transformation of the regional context both induced and reinforced a debate on state governance within Lebanon that eventually resulted in a short civil war in the summer of 1958, that Lebanon was not much involved in the international processes that were reconstructing the regional order notwithstanding. First, the Cold War emerged in Europe in 1947, consolidated through the Korean War in 1950, and then spread to the Middle East. Second, the Free Officers rose to power in Egypt in 1952 and began to advocate a radical form of Arab nationalism by nationalizing the Suez Canal Company in 1956. Third, the British, French, Israeli military alliance and campaign against Egypt failed to either stop the nationalization of Suez Canal or weaken the Nasser regime. Fourth, the enunciation of the 1957 Eisenhower Doctrine polarized inter-Arab politics.

Under Nasser's leadership and because of his aspirations for unity and nonalignment, Egypt was able to stir up the Arab passions using a variety of anti-imperialist slogans based on ideas of popular nationalism and unity, political independence, and Third World solidarity and neutralism. Nasser's ability to manipulate these symbols allowed him to strongly shape the agenda of Arab relations both within and beyond the region in the 1950s. To this end, he used a strategy of standing up to Britain, France, and the United States and challenging their hegemony in the region. Henceforth, the whole region was in flux from the beginning of the 1955 Baghdad episode onward. Although many states were involved in these regional developments, the events and outcomes were mostly the result of a combination of the foreign policy goals of and interactions between two global powers, the United States and the Soviet Union, and two regional actors, Egypt and Iraq.

Despite the nascent Cold War in 1947 in Europe, both superpowers supported the termination of the British and French mandates as well as the United Nations plan to partition Palestine. The Soviets were looking for an opportunity to reduce the British presence in the Middle East and lay, they hoped, the ground for positive relations with the Arabs. The Soviets initially favored a solution short of partition, in the form of a binational state that they thought might be more acceptable to the Arabs. Regional conditions, however, were not favorable for Soviet penetration. On the one hand, the pro-British orientation of the Arab regimes at the time led Moscow to support the Jews, if temporarily only. On the other hand, the British sought to enlist American opposition to partition, arguing that supporting the Zionist project of a Jewish homeland would mean a zero-sum gain for the Soviets in the form of a new socialist state in the region. The United States nonetheless opted for a tacit cooperation with the Soviet Union, against its ally Britain. Washington's decision was responsive to a strong public sentiment within the United States in favor of the Jews. It was also seeking potential strategic and political advantages in supporting what it hoped would be a Western-style democracy with strong links to the American Jewry and the United States as a whole. Yet the United States opposed the dispatch of a United Nations force to impose peace. Such a UN mission would have included the Soviet Union, and the United States was intent in reducing the likelihood of a Soviet role in the Middle East. This early setback for the Soviet Union in the region effectively lasted for a decade (Freedman 1975, 10; Talbot 1971, 431–32).

Nor did the United States become a major player in the region before the mid-1950s. After World War II, the imperial order established by England and France was rapidly eroding as the colonial powers relinquished their control over areas they had inherited from the collapsed Ottoman Empire. Their withdrawal was also due to the resurgence of Arab nationalism throughout the Middle East. By the 1950s, this nationalism translated into a variety of radical political movements in Egypt (e.g., the Muslim Brotherhood and the Young Egypt movement), Syria (e.g., the Ba'ath Party and the Syrian National Party), and Iraq (e.g., the Ba'ath Party and the Iraqi Communist Party). Yet Britain and France remained the predominant global powers in the Middle East until the debacle of the 1956 Suez War.

Despite consenting to the British and French roles prior to the 1956 war, the United States policy in the Middle East had five main objectives. First, Washington actively sought to deny any regional role for the Soviets as part of its policy of communist containment (Badeau 1958, 232). The Truman Doctrine (1947) and Eisenhower Doctrine (1957) sought to contain Soviet expansion to the area. The United States construed any alliance or even rapprochement between any Arab state and the Soviet Union as a threat to Western interests.[1] Second, the United States sought to deny a neutrality policy to the states in the Middle East. Washington would become increasingly more determined after the 1956 war when it became the major power in the region, of course as long as its national interests were at stake (Brands and Henry 1986). The United States was hence ready to react to any sign that a third country might seek to play off the United States against the Soviet Union for its own advantages (Hoopes 1973, 317). Third, the United States was committed to continue its support for the state of Israel during both the Truman and Eisenhower administrations (Badeau 1958, 235). Fourth, the United States was determined to ensure the continued availability of Middle Eastern oil to itself and its Western allies.[2] The United States was also committed to ensure free and equal access for U.S. oil companies. Fifth, the United States was determined to protect a continued availability of existing strategic positions such as military bases and communications and transit rights for commercial and military purposes.[3]

These U.S. policy goals were opposed to those of the key Arab states in general, and Egypt in particular. Neutralism in the Cold War and pan-Arabism were the cornerstones of Nasser's policies at both home and abroad (Kerr 1972a; 1972b; Nasser 1954). The Arab nationalists also sought to establish a monopoly over Arab oil. Likewise, the Arab states were opposed to the creation of the state of Israel and did not recognize its sovereignty, viewing it as a direct challenge to the Arab leadership in the region (Walt 1987, 52–102). Yet not every Arab state shared all these goals. Most members of the Arab ruling elite who owed their positions to their former colonial rulers—so-called conservatives—preferred to continue to collaborate with the West, as a preventive measure against the rise to power of nationalist, independent-minded leaders (Ismael 1986). This led to a race between Egypt, representing the radical nationalist camp, and Iraq, representing the conservative states. Thus, until July 1958, at which date the Iraqi conservative monarchy collapsed, Egypt's leading challenger for Arab leadership was the Iraqi monarchy.

Different conceptions of regional order lied at the heart of the Egyptian-Iraqi rivalry. Nasser, who was able to obtain Britain's agreement to evacuate the Suez Canal in 1954, saw this as the end of Britain's role as well as any other great power's interest in the area. The Iraqis attempted to challenge Egypt's self-proclaimed leadership role by joining the Baghdad Pact (1955). This would have provided Iraq with enough counterweight to Egypt, but only if Jordan, Syria, and Lebanon were to join ranks with Iraq (Kerr 1972b, 43–44). Nasser viewed the Baghdad Pact as a threat to Egyptian independence and leadership over Arab politics, since the pact would perpetuate Britain's strategic position in Iraq and the Middle East.[4] Ultimately, the Baghdad Pact episode proved to be a transformative period of Arab politics (Barnett 1998, 119). The pact set off an intense Egyptian-Iraqi rivalry for influence in three key states: Syria, Lebanon, and Jordan (Kerr 1972b, 44). The Arab world hence became split between those who saw the region's progress and destiny in close alliance with the West and those who preferred to follow an independent, nonaligned policy between the Western and Eastern blocs of the Cold War. Eventually Nasser prevailed, and the Iraqi leadership had to forgo joining the Baghdad Pact.

No sooner had the crisis of the Baghdad Pact elapsed than another major transformative episode began in the region. Nasser surprised the West on July 26, 1956, by nationalizing the Suez Canal. Egypt needed its revenues to build the Aswan Dam (Heikal 1978, 68). The nationalization of the Suez Canal placed the United States in a position of tacit cooperation with the Soviet Union at the expense of Britain, France, and Israel (Smolanski 1965). Whereas Washington opposed Nasser's decision to evict the British, Moscow clearly welcomed the anticolonial step as a possible door through which the Soviets might gain some recognition of their interests in the region. Yet both superpowers sought a negotiated solution to the crisis, thereby opposing the British, French, and Israeli jointly led military intervention against Egypt. Overall, the Suez crisis was the beginning of a radical shift in the regional constitutive rules and practices. Washington and Moscow now replaced London and Paris as the dominant global players in the Middle East, and Nasser's Egypt emerged as the dominant state in the Arab world. Nasser became an icon and spokesperson for Arab nationalism, neutrality, and independence from the great powers.

Egypt's increasing inclination toward the Soviets and Eisenhower's impatience with Nasser soon culminated in the promulgation of the Eisenhower Doctrine. The latter was construed as a means through which to mobilize the Middle East against a perceived Soviet threat that had emerged after the withdrawal of the British and French following the 1956 Suez crisis. The doctrine promised the nations of the region protection of their independence and integrity against overt armed aggression from any communist or communist-dominated country. Specifically, the doctrine sought to achieve four main goals: preventing the expansion of Soviet influence in the region, securing allies without reverting to a pact scheme, aiding friendly Middle Eastern states with economic and military assistance without micromanagement by the U.S. Congress, and formulating a policy that favored neither Israel nor the Arab states. The promulgation of the Eisenhower Doctrine had two consequences. First, in the next two years the Eisenhower administration would find itself locked in a confrontation with the forces of radical Arab nationalism. Second, the Cold war would fully expand its logic into the Arab theater.

The Arab nationalists believed that the Suez War had demolished the myth of the Soviet threat to regional security. Hence they saw the Eisenhower Doctrine's emphasis on the danger of international communism as misplaced. Egypt and Syria also rejected the premise behind the doctrine that there was a vacuum of power in the Middle East. They instead believed that the United States had inherited the imperial mantle of Britain and France. The Eisenhower Doctrine reinforced a two-camp split among the Arab governments. A first pro-Iraqi camp viewed Nasserism as a set of reckless policies that would pave the way for communist penetration and eventual Soviet domination. Libya and Lebanon were the only Arab states to endorse publicly the Eisenhower Doctrine and the military and economic aid it offered.[5] A second Egyptian-led camp recognized no such Soviet threat and saw the various Western defense plans for the area (the 1955 Baghdad Pact and the 1957 Eisenhower Doctrine) as attempts to embroil the Arab world into a Cold War in which they had no interest (Qubain 1961, 44–46; Badeau 1958, 237). The regional environment imposed certain limitations that the Arab rulers could ignore only at their peril—Nasser's ability to incite the crowds and to mobilize Arab public opinion deterred pro-Western Iraq, Saudi Arabia, and Jordan from supporting the doctrine.

Before the dust of the tornado created by the Eisenhower Doctrine was to settle down, another episode of regional transformation soon began when Syria decided to unite with Egypt in the new United Arab Republic (UAR) (Odeh 1985, 95). The merger of Egypt and Syria sent a profound shock both to the inter-Arab state system as well as to the whole Middle East region. The establishment of the UAR became the focal point of inter-Arab rivalries, notwithstanding that it failed to usher in a broad Arab unity. The Arab nationalists saw the Egyptian-Syrian union as a watershed in the history of their movement, a true first step on the road to total unification. In contrast, the Arab conservatives believed that their political survival was at stake and hence were determined to resist Nasser's revolutionary ideas and strategies by all means, including issuing requests for foreign military intervention to rescue their respective regimes. Thus, on February 14, 1958, Iraq and Jordan formed the Arab Federal Union as a counterbalance to the UAR. Saudi Arabia and Lebanon secretly informed U.S. officials of their anxiety about potential spillover effects on their societies (Noble 1984, 48).

In Lebanon, the government was against Nasser's positive neutralism and preferred to maintain closer relations with the West. However, Nasser and the UAR galvanized the popular imagination in Lebanon, thereby threatening to destabilize the Lebanese political system. The Lebanese Constitution had already been in dire need of reforms for some time because of hard-to-ignore economic, political, and demographic changes. Although domestic forces were largely responsible for propelling an emerging political crisis in Lebanon, Nasser's fingerprints were also present to make the issues more complicated. The Lebanese president, Camille Chamoun, though confessing that Lebanon was "going through a difficult ordeal," decided to put the blame for Lebanon's impending political crisis on the UAR, arguing that the latter was "interfering in our internal affairs with the aim of affecting a radical change in our basic political policy."[6]

In sum, as the region evolved in the 1950s, the Cold War penetration and the rise of Nasserism forced Lebanon to increasingly give up neutrality as its preferred foreign policy and seek a new role for itself in regional politics and security. However, the imperatives of the Cold War logic and those of Nasserism and the ensuing polarization of the Arab states system conflicted with one another. This divided and divisive regional environment created difficult-to-resolve dilemmas for Lebanon given its domestic political fabric. The 1955 Baghdad Pact episode, the 1956 Suez War and its aftermath, the 1957 Eisenhower Doctrine, the 1958 formation of the UAR, and the 1958 Iraqi revolution all combined to stretch the fabric of the Lebanese society beyond the limits of "normal" politics and in opposite directions.

First, during the 1955 Baghdad Pact episode, Syria suspected Lebanon of planning to join the pact and accordingly increased its efforts to bring down Lebanese president Chamoun. Lebanon did not eventually join the Baghdad Pact and remained neutral on the issue. Notwithstanding this final position, the whole episode did not please Nasser, who hence launched a propaganda campaign against Chamoun. Nasser's campaign escalated during the episode of the 1956 Suez War when the Lebanese government refused to break off diplomatic relations with Britain and France as a gesture of solidarity with Egypt. As a result, Lebanon was thrown into a major political crisis. The Lebanese premier Abdullah Yafi resigned, asserting that Lebanon should adopt the same responses to the crisis as the other Arab states and that a failure to do so would only arouse further suspicion of Lebanon's role in the Arab world.[7] Many Lebanese were sympathetic to Nasser's message before 1956. The Suez War only swelled and intensified their numbers and further weakened the credentials of the conservative politicians (Khalidi 1989, 385). The Egyptian-Lebanese relations deteriorated even further during the Lebanese parliamentary elections when Nasser openly sided with those opposed to Chamoun.

Second, adhering to the 1957 Eisenhower Doctrine violated the Lebanese National Pact, thereby threatening to upset the rules of normal domestic politics (Odeh 1985). There was a mixed feeling in Lebanon regarding the Eisenhower Doctrine. Chamoun's opponents considered the adoption of the doctrine as a political act against pan-Arabism. Chamoun's allies, however, saw it as a guarantee of Lebanon's independence and sovereignty against any attack from neighboring states. Chamoun and the Christian Maronite community as a whole began to feel increasingly more isolated within the wave of pan-Arab and Nasserist ideologies among Lebanese Muslims.

Third, the Free Officers' overthrow of the Iraqi monarchy on July 14, 1958, magnified the polarization within Lebanon (Dann 1969). The Iraqi revolution destroyed the government of the only Arab country that had originally accepted to become a member of the Baghdad Pact, threatened Western strategic positions in the Middle East, and terminated the Iraq-Jordan federation. Chamoun appealed to the United States and Britain to intervene within forty-eight hours to help protect Lebanon from what he claimed to be rampant communism in the Arab world. Yet doing so meant unequivocally foregoing Lebanon's foreign policy of neutrality (McClintock 1967; Gerges 1994, 10).

The assassination of the editor of *The Telegraph* newspaper who was a staunch critic of the Chamoun administration sparked a civil war. Concerned about his political future, Chamoun supplemented his public appeals to the Arab League and the UN Security Council with a private request to the United States for armed intervention and protection. The U.S. initial reaction was to wait and hope for an internally formulated compromise solution. However, the overthrow of the Iraqi monarchy in July prompted the United States to send military troops to Lebanon. The official U.S. motivation was to protect American lives and property and to preserve Lebanon's territorial sovereignty while influencing the Soviet and Egyptian images of the United States and enhancing the credibility of U.S. commitments around the world (George and Smoke 1974, 353).[8] The United States deployed fourteen thousand troops to Beirut but nevertheless maintained a neutral position in the civil war. U.S. envoy Richard Murphy quickly became convinced that communism was not a factor in the insurrection in Lebanon and that the internal war was largely due to a combination of domestic problems and the effects of inter-Arab politics.

Therefore, competition and friction between Arab nationalism and Cold War logic caused a series of fundamental changes in regional constitutive rules and practices. The latter in turn pressured Lebanon not only to abandon its neutralist doctrine of foreign policy but also induced domestic political debates about the existing system of state governance in Lebanon. The collective intentionality that had underpinned state governance was seriously undermined, with the Chamoun regime seeking to reconstruct the system of state governance through manipulated constitutional changes. Yet transforming state governance threatened to jeopardize a core element of the Lebanese polity, the 1943 National Pact. Jeopardizing the National Pact and changing the Constitution in turn entailed a destruction of the political fabric of the confessional system upon which the governance system was built and around which Lebanese politics had revolved since independence.

## Debating State Governance, the Lebanese Way

The legitimacy of the pre-1957 state governance in Lebanon presumed the continuous observance of the 1943 National Pact and state Constitution. The collective intentionality that underpinned state governance strongly depended on and was reinforced by the confessional balance of political power as defined in both covenants. The debates about the confessional system in the period 1957–58 initially undermined but ultimately reinforced the collective intentionality underpinning the confessional system.

I next discuss how the scope of collective intentionality of the new form of state governance evolved through a series of domestic debates around three key issues: the foreign policy orientation of Lebanon, President Chamoun's bid for a consecutive second term, and finding a way out of the crisis. The debates struck at the heart of the Lebanese polity, as defined by the 1943 National Pact and the Constitution. Moreover, the three issues somewhat overlapped with one another, thereby making the debates feed back into one another, compounding the difficulty of resolving any one issue to the satisfaction of any one major political group in Lebanon.

In effect, debating state governance meant debating the provisions of the 1943 National Pact and the Constitution. Both covenants had been the guarantors of political stability and confessional coexistence in Lebanon. The debates created a strong likelihood of failing to reach a consensus on any one of the above three key issues. The prospect of such a failure in turn threatened to undermine the two guarantors of coexistence and the integrity of the polity as a whole. Under the conditions that prevailed between May and August 1958, the scope of collective intentionality reached dangerously low levels, to a point where the outcome of the confrontation became quite unpredictable. Yet by the end of summer 1958, the conflicting sides were able to agree on a successful resolution of the three key issues, thereby making it possible to preserve the integrity of the polity and reinstate peaceful and accommodative intercommunal coexistence and cooperation. When it became clear that General Shihab was the ideal presidential candidate best fitted for saving the country and improving a rapidly worsening situation, the scope of collective intentionality began to recover steadfastly from a very low level. It eventually reached a "normal" level in the immediate aftermath of the 1960 parliamentary elections and the inauguration of a new prime minister and his cabinet, who were agreeable to all sides of the conflict.

To explicate how the scope of collective intentionality evolved through the debates, I organize the discussion around a series of important events that shaped the course of the overall process of transforming state governance. Specifically, I focus the discussion on Lebanon's adherence to the 1957 Eisenhower Doctrine, Chamoun's manipulation of the 1957 parliamentary elections, the 1958 formation of the United Arab Republic, the assassination of the publisher of *The Telegraph* on May 8, 1958, the 1958 Iraqi revolution against the monarchy, and the rise of Shihabism.

*Debating Foreign Policy Orientation*

Debating the foreign policy orientation of Lebanon became a major issue separating the opposition and regime supporters, both within the Chamber of Deputies dominated by Chamoun's supporters and the polity at large. The more the debate lingered, the more irreconcilable and hardened the views of the two sides became. This in turn led the opposition to close its ranks tighter and more effectively reorganize its forces to challenge the regime outside the Chamber of Deputies, including going outside the boundaries of "normal" politics. The more hardened the position of the regime became, the further beyond "politics as usual" the opposition's challenges became. This in turn eroded even further the scope of collective intentionality.

That the two sides hardened their respective positions was in part a reflection of regional upheavals. During the period 1956–58, there was a general unrest in the Arab world following the 1956 Suez Canal crisis and the doomed attacks on Egypt by Britain, France, and Israel. President Nasser of Egypt, who became a living symbol of pan-Arabism after the 1956 Suez crisis, had great influence on Lebanese Muslims, thereby scaring the Lebanese Christians, in particular the Maronites. President Chamoun's refusal to respond favorably to pan-Arab pressures antagonized several prominent Sunni leaders who believed in Nasser and the pan-Arab cause. Between November 1956 and March 1957, the opposition and the government gradually drifted into diametrically opposed positions. Chamoun and the Maronite community began to feel increasingly more isolated from the rising tide of Nasserist ideology among the Lebanese Muslims. The more the allegiance of the Lebanese Muslims appeared to be drifting toward Egypt and Syria, the more the Maronites feared for their survival as a politically dominant minority. The result was a polarization of Lebanon into two camps: first, an anti-Western, pro-Nasser side among the Lebanese Muslims (primarily Sunnis), and second, a pro-Western, anti-Nasser and anti-Syrian side among the Maronites. The gap between the two sides widened even more when President Chamoun officially adhered to the Eisenhower Doctrine on March 16, 1957.[9]

Chamoun's allies saw the doctrine as a guarantor of Lebanon's independence and sovereignty against potential attacks from neighboring states. In contrast, the opposition believed that by aligning Lebanon with the West, therewith against Egypt and Syria, the president not only violated Beirut's traditional neutrality but also upset the delicate balance among the various

Lebanese factions.[10] First, the government initiative was contrary to the National Pact of 1943, which required Lebanon's neutrality in inter-Arab relations. Second, this was a deviation from the traditional Lebanese foreign policy of maintaining a common front with the Arab world. Third, the government policy made Lebanon party to an effort to isolate Egypt from the Arab world. Lebanon should not adhere to the Eisenhower Doctrine as it did not adhere to the Baghdad Pact because both pacts extend Western domination over the Arab world. Fourth, the government policy would bring the Cold War to Lebanon by putting the country in the Western camp against the Soviet Union, with which Lebanon had good relations. Fifth, the arrangement ignored the Israeli and Zionist threat and instead forced Lebanon to accept the status quo created by Israel (Meo 1965, 126).

Prime Minister al-Sulh attempted to resolve the issue by agreeing to hold a parliamentary debate on foreign policy and then submitting to a vote of confidence from the Chamber of Deputies on April 4 and 5. A majority of deputies supported the government initiative. The opposition deputies attempted but failed to delay the resolution of the issue until after the upcoming June parliamentary elections, rationalizing that only then would the vote effectively represent the whole nation. A number of opposition deputies resigned from the Chamber and thereafter launched a campaign against the Eisenhower Doctrine in preparation for the forthcoming elections (Meo 1965, 129). This is had no noticeable impact on the Chamber. To the contrary, the government received an overwhelming vote of confidence of thirty to one.[11]

Having failed in their efforts to unseat the incumbent cabinet or achieve a change in foreign policy orientation, the opposition deputies sought the masses' support for continuing their fight for a return to Lebanon's traditional neutralist foreign policy. They formed early in April the United National Front, bringing together a variety of groups who were dissatisfied with the regime. The Front was predominantly Muslim, three members of whom were important Lebanese personalities, namely Sa'ib Salam and Abdallah al-Yafi (both Sunni Muslims) and Kamal Jumblatt (Druze). Many prominent Christian political leaders such as Hamid Franjiyah and Bishara al-Khuri also joined the Front. Politically, the Front had a general "Nasserist" orientation, but it also included almost every shade of political trend from Right to Left, except for communism.[12] The political scene was also enriched with another organization calling itself Third Force and claiming to have more moderate demands than the Front. The Third Force described itself as primarily interested in playing the role of a neutral mediator between the Front and the government. However, as the fault line between the regime and the opposition became more rigid, the views of the United National Force and the Third Front slowly converged. In an effort to further consolidate its popular and political representation, the opposition formed the Congress of Parties, Organizations, and Personalities in Lebanon, which included political parties and individuals belonging to the Front and the Third Force as well as all other opposition organizations and personalities.[13]

The membership size of the Chamber of Deputies was one of the first issues on the political agenda of the reorganized opposition. The president's plan, which a majority of the deputies supported, had proposed an increase from 44 to 66 members. The opposition proposed instead an 88-member Chamber. The opposition charged that the government wanted to limit the size of the Chamber to 66 members so that it would continue to control it and thus be able to perpetuate political discrimination in the Chamber and preserve its deviationist foreign policy agenda.[14] The parliamentary debate on the various proposals began on March 28 and ended on April 3, with an adoption of the 66-member plan (Meo 1965, 132). Far from conceding defeat, the United National Front responded by organizing on May 12 a mass rally in Beirut. The rally called for a strict re-adherence to the 1943 National Pact and a return to a policy of real cooperation with the Arab states. The opposition called for maintaining Lebanese neutrality in any political or military conflict between foreign nations, denying foreign powers any military bases on Lebanese territory, and rejecting the Baghdad Pact and all similar foreign military pacts. The opposition also called on the government to refuse any kind of conditional aid that might constrain Lebanon's free conduct of its foreign policy or might impinge on its independence and sovereignty (Odeh 1985, 100). The government and loyalist candidates reacted by accusing the opposition of wanting to make Lebanon subservient to Cairo.[15]

Therefore, as the June 1957 parliamentary elections approached, two major issues sharply divided Lebanon. First, the protagonists sharply differed on the issue of foreign policy orientation, symbolized in the debates on the Eisenhower Doctrine. Second, the two sides sharply differed on whether to amend the Constitution, thereby enabling President Chamoun to run for reelection. The opposition, which for the most part was Muslim, saw such a move as a threat to the very balance of intercommunal power and satisfaction that the 1943 National Pact had created and helped to perpetuate. In contrast, the Christians, particularly the Maronites, believed that President Chamoun was the best safeguard for Lebanon's sovereignty and against any foreign attempts to subvert it. Hence, as the polity was preparing itself for elections, the existing collective intentionality underpinning the confessional state was inexorably at stake and seemed to depend crucially on how legitimating (or delegitimating) the process and results of elections would turn out to be.

Pro-government candidates won more than two-thirds of the seats in the Chamber, leaving eight seats only to the opposition. Prominent leaders of the opposition such as Ahmed al-Asaad, Kamal Jumblatt, Abdallah al-Yafi, and Saeb Salam lost their seats. The opposition firmly believed that the government had orchestrated these losses. For example, Kamal Jumblatt lost because the government gerrymandered his traditional district to include pro-government Christians who would not and did not vote for him. Likewise, Charles Malik (the foreign affairs minister) was elected only after Chamoun pressured his opposing candidate, Fuʿad al-Ghusn, to withdraw his candidacy.[16] The opposition felt vindicated in its accusations when, on June 17th, two "neutral" ministers—Yusuf Hitti and Muhammed Bayhum—whose job was to supervise and ensure the honesty of the elections, resigned. The two men declared that they could no longer bear "the general atmosphere" wherein "pressure of various kinds had been brought to bear on the voters."[17] The United National Front hence rejected the election results, and the battle between the regime and the opposition shifted over to the issue of Chamoun's bid for reelection. The Lebanese Constitution specifically prohibited an incumbent president from seeking reelection while being in office. Amending the Constitution through a two-thirds vote in the Chamber of Deputies was, however, the only way for Chamoun to seek a successive second presidential term. After the May–June 1957 elections, Chamoun's supporters in- and outside the Chamber of Deputies began setting the climate for such a prospect by openly advocating for his reelection.

### *Debating the United Arab Republic*

While the various Lebanese groups were busy arguing with one another, a major event sent shock waves into both regional and domestic politics. Presidents Nasser of Egypt and al-Quwwatli of Syria announced on February 1, 1958, the merger of Syria and Egypt into the United Arab Republic (UAR). The news had an impact on all strata of the Lebanese society, driving even wider an already existing divide between the Christians and government, on the one hand, and the Muslim communities and opposition, on the other. Not only did the event tilt ongoing debates on the foreign policy orientation in the Chamber of Deputies seemingly in favor of the opposition; it also meant that the challenge to the existing form of state governance was much more serious, with both sides unilaterally seeking foreign support for their irreconcilably construed positions. The scope of collective intentionality was henceforth very rapidly decreasing.

The opposition leadership seized the opportunity to ride a new wave of pan-Arabist feelings in Lebanon. A delegation representing the United National Front visited Damascus on February 9 to congratulate President al-Quwwatli on the birth of the UAR and express its full support. President al-Quwwatli responded that the new republic was the best guarantee of Lebanon's existence and that Lebanon was welcome to join in whenever its people may so desire. Sabri Hamadah, the former speaker of the Lebanese Chamber of Deputies, declared that the great majority of the Lebanese people and members of the United National Front wanted a union with the United Arab

Republic.[18] Thousands of Lebanese citizens from Beirut, Tripoli, Sidon, Tyre, and other Lebanese towns traveled to Damascus to join the cheering crowds and pay their respects to President Nasser when he visited Damascus, much to the dismay of the Lebanese Christian communities.[19]

Most Lebanese Christians feared such a growing admiration for Nasser among their Muslim compatriots and the threat that this might pose to the viability and sovereignty of the Lebanese state.[20] Thus, counteracting such a potential threat, Chamoun declared on February 8 that Lebanon's independence was and had to remain perpetual. Charles Malik told the Chamber of Deputies on February 11, "Lebanon is and always will be a country with her own flag, sovereignty and mission in life. She will play her part internationally: she will take part in every good action which might affect her friends."[21] Father Antoine Qurtbawi wrote in a Maronite publication, "Lebanon is not Arab, but is the Lebanon—a Mediterranean country whose language is Arabic."[22] Moreover, Chamoun and his government began to portray the increasing tension as a struggle between pro-Western Lebanon and radical Arab nationalism, with the latter allegedly allied with international communism. In three separate statements in May, Chamoun, Solh, and Malik accused the United Arab Republic of intending to overthrow Lebanon's democratically elected government (Agwani 1965, 58, 85). Chamoun and Malik actually hoped to internationalize the dispute and hence involve the United States on their side. In contrast, the opposition was adamantly against any internationalization of the crisis, asserting instead that the roots of the conflict were domestic with no connection to the UAR. The opposition stressed its dedication to a continued existence of Lebanon as an independent state and to the 1943 National Pact, blamed the Chamoun administration for the deterioration of law and order in the country, and accused the president of spreading anxiety concerning the independence of Lebanon in order to serve his own political goals. To this effect, some three hundred Muslim leaders, including former prime ministers, speakers of the Chamber, opposition deputies, and religious leaders, warned Chamoun that amending the Constitution would give the people the legitimate right to oppose his regime using all means at their disposal (Qubain 1961, 66–67).

### *Pursuing the Debate through Other Means: Street Clashes*

The situation quickly deteriorated after the opposition became convinced that the incumbent regime was bound to seek Chamoun's reelection for a second term, ignoring the opposition's repeated warnings not to do so. The assassination on May 8, 1958, of Nasib al-Matni, a Maronite Christian, publisher and owner of the Beirut Arabic daily *The Telegraph,* was the spark that transformed the debate from a rhetorical war to violent clashes and armed conflicts on the streets. Most opposition groups and organizations, including the Third

Force, the National Organization, the Progressive Socialist Party, the Constitutional Bloc, al-Najjadah, the Popular Front, the Free Press, the Arab Liberation Part, and the Grand Mufti of Lebanon Shaykh Muhammad ᶜAlaya, collectively called for a general three-day strike from May 10 to 13 throughout the country to force Chamoun's resignation. The president responded instead that the UAR was behind the troubles at home and accused the opposition leaders of acting as its agents (Meo 1965, 165–66).

Politics in the Chamber of Deputies was also rapidly becoming more polarized and confrontational. The new 66-man Chamber of Deputies was able to hold only four sessions—two extraordinary and two ordinary sessions between August 12, 1957, and May 8, 1958, that is, before the outbreak of the civil war. These meetings were lengthy debates over the government domestic, regional, and foreign policies, inexorably moving the Chamber toward a deadlock. The debates were but a reflection of the widening split between the Christian and Muslim communities within Lebanon as well as a precursor to domestic political disturbances and the growing diplomatic and political gap between Lebanon and Syria-Egypt. Premier al-Sulh blamed bomb explosions, riots, and other disturbances on "foreign agents," hinting that these were the agents of Syria and Egypt. In contrast, the opposition deputies charged that Lebanon had become a center of foreign intrigues against Syria and Egypt. Loyalist deputies countercharged that Syria and Egypt were in fact conspiring against Lebanon and claimed that arms were being smuggled into Lebanon. The opposition replied that the government was arming its partisans against the people and curtailing the rights and freedom of the public (Meo 1965, 157–58). As the two sides of the debate became deaf to each other's arguments and complaints and the conflict temperature kept on rising very quickly on the streets, the authority and legitimacy of the government began to erode rapidly. The 1943 National Pact and the state Constitution were increasingly either fiercely defended or seriously challenged, and henceforth, the scope of collective intentionality rapidly decreased.

The opposition increased its level of challenge to the government even further by taking its cause to the streets and calling for general strikes. On May 9, about 1,000 worshipers at the Mansuri Mosque who were attempting to organize a demonstration after prayers clashed with security forces. The clash resulted in 40 injured persons. On the following day the clashes continued, with some 10 persons killed and 60 wounded.[23] Fighting resumed on May 11, putting the official toll of three days of violence at 13 dead and 110 injured. The wave of violence reached Beirut on the following day (Qubain 1961, 72). The United National Front had already opted for armed revolt on May 9 (Jumblatt 1959, 83–89). Collective intentionality was collapsing very rapidly as the opposed sides seriously prepared for and indeed began fighting one another.

In the midst of all this, the fall of the Iraqi monarchy on July 14, 1958, created a sense of panic within the Chamoun regime and the Christian population. In contrast, the opposition and the Muslim population entered a state of jubilation, with radio stations announcing that the Chamoun regime would be next. Chamoun requested immediate assistance from the United States, Britain, and France, insisting that the independence of Lebanon was in jeopardy. The United States responded by landing some fourteen thousand U.S. marines in Beirut on July 15, 1958. However, the Chamoun regime soon realized that there was no serious threat of a coup d'état or an invasion from Syria. Likewise, the opposition understood that the United States had not come in to impose a puppet government on them. Both sides henceforth became ready to talk to each other and agreed that the first important point of negotiation to be resolved was the next presidency.[24]

### *Debating a Way out of the Crisis*

A necessary condition for a successful resolution of the crisis was the election of a new president and the appointment of a new cabinet acceptable to all belligerents. Chamoun and his supporters favored the election of a pro-government deputy from Parliament; the opposition was against the nomination of any deputy and favored among others either former president Bishara al-Khuri or General Shihab. The Third Force believed that only General Shihab could solve the crisis and restore peace in the country. Shihab accepted the candidacy, and the opposition endorsed him on July 30, 1958. Although Shihab was not due to assume power until September 23, his election brought a slow but clearly discernible sense of widespread relief. Rashid Karami, the opposition leader in Tripoli, ordered a cease-fire among his followers on August 4, and the city began gradually to return to normal life. Security forces began confiscating all arms carried by any individual in the center of Beirut. Four opposition clandestine radio stations were closed down on September 5. On the same day, the Phalanges Party ordered its members to surrender their arms. On September 8, the chiefs of fifteen leading clans in the Baᶜlbak and Hirmil areas declared their allegiance to the new government, asked that the army be sent to their areas, and promised their full cooperation and support.

The overall political climate continued to improve, if somewhat reservedly, as all sides adopted a "wait and see" attitude.[25] General Shihab immediately decreed the formation of a new cabinet under Rashid Karami. The new eight-man cabinet consisted of four members from the United National Front, three from the Third Force, and one neutral, provoking a negative reaction from Chamoun's faction and the Phalanges. The situation was already facing a serious risk of deterioration due to the kidnapping of Fu'ad Haddad, assistant editor of *al-ᶜAmal* newspaper, organ of the Phalanges Party, on September 19. The following day the Phalanges Party called for a general strike to start on the 22d and began erecting barricades in their Beirut quarters. A period of extreme tension followed (September 20–October 4), with antigovernment demonstrations erupting in Beirut, Zahlah, and other towns as well as armed clashes between the government security forces and the Phalanges.

In an effort to deflate the mounting crisis, President Shihab received the leaders of most embattled parties between September 27 and October 13 and held numerous meetings with his prime minister, Rashid Karami. These consultations eventually bore their fruits. The Phalanges announced on October 10 that they were entrusting President Shihab to find a solution to the crisis with "no victor, no vanquished." Likewise, Jumblatt began to disband his private army on October 27. Karami's government received a unanimous vote of confidence from the Chamber on October 17. After reestablishing domestic equilibrium, the government proceeded to resume the country's traditional policy of neutrality among its Arab neighbors, thereby reassuring both the Muslim and Christian communities about the future of Lebanon and the 1943 National Pact. The government also forthwith declared the Eisenhower Doctrine no longer applicable to Lebanon and requested that the United States withdraw its troops from the Lebanese territory. Normalizing "politics" even further, the Chamber of Deputies increased the number of deputies from 66 to 99 and introduced the secret ballot procedure of voting in the Chamber on April 20, 1960. The 1960 elections turned out to be the most honest elections in Lebanon since 1943 and thus marked the true end of the 1958 Lebanese crisis. The new Chamber was a mosaic of parties and groups representing almost every political current—none of which had a commanding majority (Qubain 1961, 165–66). President Shihab showed a strong determination to observe the terms of the 1943 National Pact and to serve the Christian and Muslim groups equally. He also worked to improve Lebanon's infrastructure, develop an extensive road system, provide running water and electricity to remote villages, and build new hospitals and dispensaries in many rural areas. In sum, the winding down of the crisis had two important consequences for state governance in Lebanon. First, the Lebanese groups returned to the spirit as well as the form of the 1943 National Pact. Second, Lebanon returned to a neutralist foreign policy.

Therefore, one cannot dispute that the Lebanese polity underwent during the period 1957–58 a major crisis of state governance. Nor can one dispute the fact that Lebanon was able to reestablish peaceful and accommodative relations between the various communities and political actors. That a moderate and increasing scope of collective intentionality underpinned the new arrangement of state governance is also evident. The regime combined Shihab's personal charisma and generalized trust in him with institutional incentives and constraints to build such a scope of collective intentionality. One can argue with a good degree of confidence that the regime had succeeded in launching a process of reconsolidating state governance after 1958, and even more so after the 1960 parliamentary elections. Explaining this evolution from a very low scope of collective intentionality in summer 1958 to subsequently moderate and increasing scope of collective intentionality by 1960 is the focus of the remainder of the chapter.

## Intercommunal Vulnerability

When the president sought to manipulate the 1957 legislative elections, intercommunal vulnerability began to rise to moderate levels as other groups (especially the Druzes) feared exploitation and exclusion. However, after Fuad Shihab assumed the presidency, intercommunal vulnerability began to decrease significantly. Under these new conditions, fears of intercommunal abandonment, exploitation, or exclusion decreased quite significantly. In the following, I discuss the three mutually reinforcing sources of vulnerability: intercommunal information complexity, predictability, and interdependence.

### *Intercommunal Information Complexity*

Information complexity began and continued to rise from March 16, 1957, the date at which the Chamoun regime adhered to the Eisenhower Doctrine, until it reached a very high level during the fighting of summer 1958. This is evident in the debates that unfolded between the opposition and the regime (and its supporters). Information complexity increased as the intentions of both the opposition and the regime increasingly became more opaque and their respective capabilities increasingly harder to estimate reliably. Thus, as domestic and regional events unfolded, both the opposition and the regime faced hard-to-resolve questions on their mutual intentions and relative capabilities. Each side increasingly feared that the other side was misrepresenting its intentions as well as not faithfully displaying its relative capabilities. Both the nature and level of information complexity changed as the confrontation developed in four successive stages.

The first stage extended from March 16, 1957, to the June 1957 elections. The adoption of the Eisenhower Doctrine in March divided Lebanon against itself. One important question confronted the opposition: why did the Chamoun regime seek and then accept to take part in the Eisenhower Doctrine? Rhetoric and propaganda notwithstanding, President Chamoun did not adhere to the Eisenhower Doctrine due to a fear of domestic communism. He did indeed state, when asked how serious he felt about the threat of domestic communism, that "no doubt communism has made some progress here. But with appropriate measures its advance can be halted."[26] Nor was Lebanon under any sort of threat from international communism, either. The opposition saw the Eisenhower Doctrine as contrary to the 1943 National Pact, which required Lebanon to remain neutral in regional as well as West versus Arab politics. The opposition hence concluded that the regime was misrepresenting its true intentions of seeking to make Lebanon party to a West-led effort to isolate Egypt from the Arab world. The opposition also believed that Chamoun was attempting to internationalize his problems with domestic opposition to create a climate within which he might secure himself a second presidential term in contravention with the Lebanese Constitution.

Two additional questions confronted the opposition before the elections; both questions cast more doubts on the true intentions of the regime. First, why was the regime seeking to increase the membership size of the Chamber of Deputies from 44 to 66, and not to 88 as demanded by the opposition? Second, why was the regime seeking to manipulate the 1957 parliamentary elections? For the opposition, the regime was increasing the membership size to 66 instead of 88 and manipulating the elections to guarantee itself an absolute majority in the Chamber of Deputies. This would then allow the regime to continue its adventurous foreign policy aimed at isolating Lebanon in the Arab world and joining the Western camp of the Cold War, even if it is at the expense of Lebanon's independence, freedom of action, and historic neutrality (as dictated by the 1943 National Pact). Furthermore, President Chamoun was trying to create propitious conditions for amending the Constitution, which would enable him to run for presidential reelection in 1958. Both moves, argued the opposition, not only are against the content and spirit of the 1943 National Pact, but also are a threat to the viability and continuity of the Lebanese system of governance. Hence, for the opposition the regime's intentions were clear: Chamoun and his supporters were engaged in a process of destroying the Lebanese form of state governance, alienating the opposition and a large portion of the population, and turning Lebanon into a pariah state in the Arab world.

The regime and its supporters did not agree with these readings of their intentions. They counterattacked by raising their own set of related questions that cast doubts on the intentions of the opposition. First, why was the opposition against adhering to the Eisenhower Doctrine? Second, what relationship did the opposition have with the regional Nasserist movement? The regime believed that the opposition was against the doctrine because it was becoming increasingly more like a fifth column for the Nasserists. Chamoun and the Maronites in general were opposed to Nasserism. They perceived it as a threat to the viability of Lebanon and the privileged role of the Maronite community in the Lebanese system. Too close an association with the Nasserist movement was anathema to a majority of the Maronites.

These charges and countercharges between the opposition and regime notwithstanding, the information complexity that was emerging did not have yet an intercommunal "coloration." Although the situation was deteriorating between the opposition and the regime, events had yet to assume an intercommunal character. Only at such a moment would intercommunal information complexity become an important factor for the relations between the major communal groups, namely the Sunnis, Shiites, Maronites, and Druzes. That the United National Front, which was predominantly a Muslim-populated organization, did dominate most of the events and debates with the regime was not enough to make the debates "intercommunal." The Front and other organizations as well as many former government officials and religious figures from the Christian population made a conscientious effort not to let the issues become "intercommunal," even if in fact most of the regime supporters were Christians. Moreover, the level of information complexity was quite low anyway at this stage as the polity moved into the 1957 June parliamentary elections.

The situation began to change rapidly following the parliamentary elections. This was the beginning of a second stage, which lasted until the birth of the United Arab Republic on February 1, 1958. As discussed earlier, the regime manipulated the parliamentary elections through a variety of strategies such as gerrymandering and presidential pressures on certain opposition candidates to ensure a landslide victory for the regime supporters. This led to the defeat of many prominent opposition deputies, most of whom were Muslims. The issue of a second term for Chamoun became now a much more pressing matter, since the president had gathered enough support in the Chamber of Deputies to amend the Constitution and hence run for reelection. This fact confronted the opposition with an important question about the regime's intentions and agenda: Why was the president seeking a second consecutive term, knowing very well that this might jeopardize the balance of confessional satisfaction without which the Lebanese system cannot persist? For the opposition, the president was seeking reelection to be able to continue his previous foreign policies of trying to isolate Lebanon within the Arab world as well as help to weaken Egypt and Syria in their struggle against Western domination of the region. As the organized opposition and the regime continued to clash on the answer to this question, information complexity increased much beyond that of the previous stage. More important, the character of the confrontation was increasingly more intercommunally colored. The Maronites began to close ranks more tightly around President Chamoun to preserve the momentum that the regime and its supporters had gained at the parliamentary elections. The Maronites began to perceive Chamoun's reelection as a guarantee of their status in Lebanon, given the rising tide of Nasserism in the Arab world and the strong domestic support for it. Yet the (Muslim-dominated) organized opposition did not let the intercommunal "coloration" drift away its strategy from its original goal of countering the Chamoun regime as a deviationist regime, not as a guarantor of the Maronites' fate.

This soon would change, however, with the birth of the United Arab Republic on February 1, 1958. This event marked a qualitative shift to a third stage that extended to Nasib al-Matni's assassination on May 8, 1958. As the

Muslim opposition became jubilant and showed no restraint in displaying its support for the UAR and Nasser, the regime and its Maronite supporters started to worry seriously about their future in Lebanon as well as the future of Lebanon itself as an independent and sovereign multi-confessional state. Three important questions on the intentions of the Muslim opposition confronted Chamoun and his supporters. First, what was the relationship of the opposition with the UAR? Second, was the opposition still truly committed to the sovereignty and independence of Lebanon? Third, was the opposition trying to abolish the stipulations of the 1943 National Pact that protected the Christian population, particularly the Maronites? For the president and many Maronites, the answers to these questions were clear.[27] Father Antoine Qurtbawi clarified this position when he stated, "Lebanon is not Arab, but is the Lebanon—a Mediterranean country whose language is Arabic."[28] Although a number of influential Christian personalities—such as former president Bishara al-Khuri and the Maronite patriarch Monsignor Paul Meouchy—sided with the opposition, overall the formation of the UAR and the widespread support that it received from the Lebanese opposition and Muslim population helped to create a sense of fear in the Maronite community.

To summarize, the birth of the UAR increasingly tainted the problem of information complexity with an intercommunal "coloration." That the Maronites began to perceive the problem as intercommunal is evident in two ways at least. First, their support for the president's policies and his plan to seek reelection became much stronger. The president in turn did not hesitate to capitalize on such unqualified support, even if it meant jeopardizing the 1943 National Pact. Chamoun did so particularly after he lost the support of the armed forces following General Shihab's refusal to take sides in the emerging conflict. Second, the Phalanges began arming themselves and preparing for any eventual show of force with the Muslim opposition, a process encouraged by the government itself. At the time of al-Matni's assassination on May 8, 1958, intercommunal information complexity was rapidly increasing as the intercommunal "coloration" became more visible in the confrontation between regime supporters and Muslim-dominated opposition. The president's strategy in forging an alliance with the Maronite Phalanges and the (Syrian opposition) party PPS confused the issue even further, especially for the opposition. To the Maronites, the confrontation was undoubtedly becoming one of Christians versus Muslims, based on the way they read and interpreted the Muslim opposition's intentions. However, the opposition had yet to read the president's intentions along the same lines. That former president al-Khuri and the Maronite patriarch remained with the opposition reinforced such an attitude of the opposition. Yet this added more complexity to the intercommunal information on mutual intentions and actions, as the Maronites did not believe that such an attitude of a number of prominent Maronite figures would have an impact on the "true" intentions of the Muslim-dominated opposition. That statements made by the patriarch were vociferously condemned in the Maronite community is an indication that the latter was determined to read the attitudes and intentions of the Muslim-dominated opposition with an intercommunal subtext.

This dynamic continued (in a fourth stage) from al-Matni's assassination on May 8 to Shihab's election as president on September 23. After al-Matni's assassination, the opposition increased the level of its challenge to the regime by taking its case to the streets and calling for general strikes. The situation deteriorated very quickly and clashes flared up in various parts of the country, with the toll of casualties increasing by the day. The United National Front finally decided to take up arms against the regime. A characteristic feature of the ensuing armed clashes is that Muslims such as Jumblatt's forces did most of the fighting on the opposition's behalf. This in itself reinforced the Maronites' reading of the intentions and goals of the Muslim opposition. In fact, as the fighting developed in various parts of the country, the fault lines increasingly became intercommunal, that is, Sunnis and Druzes against Maronites. Yet the opposition leadership still maintained that its goal was to remove Chamoun from power, not to abrogate the stipulations of the Constitution or 1943 National Pact, or to de-confessionalize the system of governance. On the Maronite side, though, the fact that most opposition fighters came from the Muslim population was enough of an indication that the opposition was intent on annulling the privileges and rights of the Maronites, a feeling that the regime fostered very much. Put differently, the de facto disconnect between the official positions of the opposition leadership and the battlegrounds put the level of intercommunal information complexity very high during summer 1958.

The fall of the Iraqi monarchy on July 14, 1958, and the fact that the Muslim opposition began to openly advocate a removal of Chamoun reinforced the sense of panic in the Christian population at large. The regime and the Maronites confronted a difficult-to-resolve question: Was the Muslim opposition trying to organize a revolution reminiscent of the Iraqi revolution on July 14, 1958, which would inescapably jeopardize the Maronites' future in Lebanon? Riding on this wave of panic, Chamoun answered this question in his own self-serving way by requesting immediate military assistance from the United States, Britain, and France, insisting that the independence and integrity of Lebanon was at stake. The United States responded by landing about fourteen thousand marines in Beirut on July 15, 1958. This in turn confronted the opposition with two pressing questions: Why did the regime request the landing of U.S. troops? What were the regime's true intentions? Now the level of information complexity became very high. All parties in the confrontation were highly confused about each other's intentions and agendas.

In sum, information complexity began to increase as the opposition and the regime (and its supporters) steadily moved toward more confrontational strategies in the aftermath of the 1957 June parliamentary elections. However, the complexity of *intercommunal* information began to increase significantly only after the formation of the United Arab Republic on February 1, 1958, and the Muslim population and elites became jubilant about it. From then onward, intercommunal information complexity kept on increasing even more rapidly to reach a very high level during the short civil war (May 1958–September 1958). The divide increasingly assumed a Muslim versus Christian character. Conversely, the regime supporters were for the most part from the Maronite community. By the end of summer, though, information complexity began to stagnate and then decrease. The U.S. policy to remain neutral in the confrontation in spite of landing troops in Lebanon had two positive effects in this respect. First, it reassured the opposition that the United States was not attempting to impose a puppet government on them. Second, it convinced the Chamoun regime that the United States was not prepared to fight the domestic political battles for the regime. Hence, Undersecretary of State Robert Murphy was able to win the confidence of the opposition, which in turn facilitated a return to "normal politics," the Lebanese way. Under the Shihab regime installed on September 23, 1958, intercommunal information complexity decreased even further. The Sunni, Druze, and Maronite communities now believed that they had enough reliable information on each other's intentions and capabilities. The system ultimately stabilized during and immediately after the 1960 parliamentary elections. This is transparent in a number of ways.

First, the regime clearly proclaimed that there would be no second presidential term for Chamoun. Prime Minister Sami al-Sulh declared to the nation on May 27 that neither the president nor the Chamber of Deputies had officially requested such an amendment. Chamoun in person rejected such an eventuality in interviews with the correspondents of *Newsweek* and the United Press during the first week of July and affirmed that he would step down at the end of his term.[29] Second, all sides slowly resumed the process of "normal politics" by beginning to clash over the composition of the next cabinet. Third, Shihab's election brought a gradual but clearly discernible improvement in intercommunal as well as government-opposition relations. Although the various parties were still much inclined to disagree on many political issues, enough momentum was building toward resuming a normal political life. Fourth, that the so-called counterrevolution that the Phalanges launched after the kidnapping of an assistant editor of *al-ᶜAmal* newspaper, an organ of the Phalanges Party, on September 19 was peacefully resolved also shows that normal politics was becoming slowly the practice. Presidential consultations with various political forces eventually appeased the Phalanges, who eventually announced on October 10 that they trusted Shihab to finalize the solution based on a "no victor, no vanquished" principle.

*Intercommunal Predictability*

Prior to the period 1957–58, intercommunal predictability depended on a close adherence to the stipulations of the 1943 National Pact and the state Constitution. The confessional arrangement was quite precarious, and hence any change to the National Pact or the Constitution would immediately threaten to create havoc and much uncertainty concerning the future of intercommunal relations and the integrity of the Lebanese state. As argued in chapter 3, two sorts of change can shape intercommunal predictability, namely, first, a major shift in intercommunal relations or the institutional arrangements that underpin and preserve these relations and, second, uncertainty over previously shared understandings regarding intercommunal relations. Both sorts of change occurred during the period June 1957–September 1958 in Lebanon. This happened through the unfolding of five major events, namely, the results of the June 1957 elections; the formation of the UAR on February 1, 1958; al-Matni's assassination on May 8, 1958; the fall of the Iraqi monarchy on July 14, 1958; and the election of General Shihab as president on September 23, 1958. Yet predictability became a serious issue for different communal groups at different times and for different reasons. Thus, intercommunal predictability was a concern mainly for the Muslim-dominated opposition prior to the formation of the UAR. Only after the latter became a reality did the Maronite-dominated support base of the regime become concerned about intercommunal predictability. As the hostilities started after May 8, 1958, intercommunal predictability became an overriding concern for all parties.

The results of the June 1957 elections provided President Chamoun and his supporters with more than two-thirds of the seats in the Chamber of Deputies. This meant that the "rumor" concerning his "idea" to change the Constitution to secure a bid for a second consecutive presidential term became a realistic option, much to the dismay of the opposition. The June elections also produced, as discussed above, a major loss for the opposition, with many prominent opposition leaders losing their seats and with the opposition now holding eight seats only. Together, the opposition losses and the "rumor" about Chamoun's bid for reelection meant that the predictability that the Constitution had provided so far in terms of defining and dividing intercommunal power was at stake. The issue was ambiguous, since not only was the opposition not ready to give free reign to Chamoun, but also the regime still refrained from openly seeking to change the Constitution. As matters stood in January 1958, intercommunal predictability was yet to become a major driving issue of the political game. The Maronite supporters of the regime saw no imminent problem of intercommunal predictability. The opposition was concerned about Chamoun's potential bid for reelection but was not too alarmed about the issue. The issue of changing the Constitution had yet to assume an intercommunal coloration. The situation was not unprecedented in the history of independent Lebanon, for Chamoun was not the first president to make such a bid.[30]

The formation of the UAR changed the whole picture, though. The confidence that the regime and its supporters had shown in the system of governance in the aftermath of the June 1957 elections was shattered overnight, leaving room for a sense of threat and panic for the future of the Maronites as a community and the integrity and independence of Lebanon as a whole. The stake for the Maronites was the intercommunal understandings of the 1943 National Pact, particularly those guaranteeing the independence and sovereignty of Lebanon. The Maronites and their leaders read the overwhelming show of support of the Lebanese Muslim population for the UAR as a signal that those understandings were unraveling. This thereby reinforced the Maronites' determination to support Chamoun in his bid for changing the Constitution to seek a second term to protect their future. Yet doing precisely that, or at least promoting it, induced the Muslims and their various leaderships to believe that the institutional arrangement of Lebanon could be at stake.

Thus, in the immediate aftermath of the formation of the UAR two sorts of changes—a change in intercommunal understandings and a change in intercommunal power arrangements—were expected (or feared) to occur, should the events continue unfolding the way they started. Although the Maronites and the majority of the Muslim population expected different changes, this did not lessen the gravity of the moment. Intercommunal predictability was rapidly decreasing as the confrontation began to linger and take on more of an intercommunal coloration. The formation on March 27, 1958, of a Congress, which issued a manifesto affirming its members' dedication to the continued existence of Lebanon as an independent state and to the 1943 National Pact, fell short of reassuring the Maronites about their future. The situation worsened even more when George ᶜAql announced his intention to propose an amendment to the Constitution (Qubain 1961, 66–67). The opposed groups increasingly faced a lack of intercommunal predictability. Al-Matni's assassination made this issue even more problematic. Most groups and organizations in the opposition seized the opportunity and declared a general three-day strike from May 10 to 13 throughout the country in a bid to force the resignation of President Chamoun. The president saw the unfolding events as an instance of massive external interference in the affairs of Lebanon to destroy its independence and sovereignty. A similar debate was also unfolding in the Chamber of Deputies, which ended up being strongly polarized and ultimately paralyzed. The regime supporters and opposition deputies became completely deaf to each other's complaints or explanations.

As strikes and street confrontations were becoming daily routines, the fall of the Iraqi monarchy created a sense of panic in the Chamoun regime and the Christian population. Under these conditions of extreme unpredictability, the Chamoun regime requested immediate assistance from the United States, Britain, and France. This in turn heightened the sense of unpredictability for the opposition as to the future of Lebanon as an independent, sovereign country.[31] Partly due to the U.S. envoy's efforts and partly due to Chamnoun's realization that his strategy was failing as well as to the Muslim opposition's realization that confrontation was not the best strategy, General Shihab was chosen as the main candidate for presidency. Shihab's emergence as the "savior" of Lebanon and his wide acceptance by the main belligerent parties helped strongly to increase intercommunal predictability. He became a focal point of trust. Expectations of intercommunal predictability converged on his approach to resolve the conflict. As discussed earlier, his neutral approach to the dividing issues and his readiness to abide to the letter by the 1943 National Pact and the Constitution both preserved and reinforced the central role of these two constitutive elements of the Lebanese system of state governance. This in turn increased intercommunal predictability—the various opposed parties were now much more confident about their mutual relations. This rising level of intercommunal predictability quickly consolidated as the various fighting groups not only gave up their willingness to resort to arms but also surrendered their weapons to the new government authority. As politics was slowly resuming to a "normal" Lebanese mode, with clashes over the membership of the new cabinet and other related "normal politics" issues, intercommunal predictability steadily increased, eventually reaching a pre-1957 "normal" level during the 1960 parliamentary election.

In sum, the changes in intercommunal predictability and the changes in the nature and level of information complexity during the period 1957–58 mutually reinforced one another. Intercommunal predictability began and continued to decrease after February 1, 1958, until it reached a very low level during the fighting of summer 1958. Likewise, the complexity of *intercommunal* information began to increase significantly only after the formation of the United Arab Republic on February 1, 1958. Intercommunal information complexity increased even more rapidly to reach a very high level during the short civil war (May 1958–September 1958). Intercommunal predictability began to increase only after it became clear that Shihab would be the next president and Maronite, Sunni, and Druze communities clearly expressed their commitment to a Shihabist solution to the crisis. Likewise, information complexity began to stagnate by the end of the summer and then decrease under the Shihab regime installed on September 23, 1958. It decreased even further as the Sunni, Druze, and Maronite communities trusted available information on each other's intentions and capabilities. The system ultimately stabilized during and immediately after the 1960 parliamentary elections. Yet the dynamics of information complexity and predictability cannot explain why the various opposed groups remained so susceptible to one another's beliefs and strategic actions. Indeed, the intercommunal debates were also shaped by intercommunal interdependence.

### *Intercommunal Interdependence*

The sense of interdependence between the opposition and the Maronites-regime alliance remained high between February 1, 1958, and September 23, 1958, due to the interwoven nature of the confessional system of governance in Lebanon, the fact that opposed sides of the conflict attempted to rid themselves of intercommunal interdependence notwithstanding. Eventually, intercommunal interdependence made them more likely to seek a collective debate on whether and, if yes, how to reconsolidate state governance.

That a high level of intercommunal interdependence remained a characteristic feature of the Lebanese state has its origins in the very creation of the state. The 1943 National Pact and constitutional solutions to the confessional nature of Lebanese polity created much intercommunal interdependence among the major groups—Maronites, Sunnis, Shiites, and Druzes. In the period June 1957–September 1958, the level of intercommunal interdependence wavered during the debates on the three key issues: foreign policy orientation, Chamoun's bid for reelection, and finding a way out of summer 1958 crisis. As the polity was debating these issues, major events such as Lebanon's adherence to the Eisenhower Doctrine, Chamoun's manipulation of the 1957 parliamentary elections, the 1958 proclamation of the UAR, the clashes of summer 1958 following al-Matni's assassination, the July Iraqi revolution, and the emergence and rise of Fuad Shihab as the country's savior all helped to shape the level of intercommunal interdependence. In general, both the regime and the opposition took turns in attempting to undermine the high level of interdependence inherently built in the system of state governance by seeking to determine unilaterally the outcome of the ongoing debates.

The Chamoun regime took the "first turn" when it adhered to the Eisenhower Doctrine in March 1957 and then manipulated the June 1957 parliamentary elections to ensure itself a compliant Chamber of Deputies. Although, as argued earlier, the conflict between the regime and the opposition was yet to acquire an intercommunal "coloration," the events entailed a serious threat to intercommunal interdependence as defined by the National Pact and Constitution. As explained earlier, the regime and opposition interpreted in starkly opposed ways Lebanon's adherence to the Eisenhower Doctrine. That the regime was trying to reorient the foreign policy of the country was not in doubt. Although that was a major issue for the opposition, upcoming parliamentary elections made it less intrinsically important. Whether the regime would opt for a foreign policy orientation tilted more toward the West than the Arab world effectively depended on the outcome of the parliamentary elections. Should the Chamoun regime win more than two-thirds of the seats, the regime would be able to ensure itself dominance over all policies, including foreign policy. The regime manipulated the June elections and won a landslide victory. Although the victory empowered the regime and its supporters, it had yet to undermine effectively intercommunal interdependence as defined in the National Pact and Constitution. Neither the opposition nor the regime framed the outcome of elections in intercommunal terms. Nonetheless, the fact that the regime and its supporters were able to amend the Constitution unilaterally if they wanted to had the potential to undermine the intercommunal interdependence provided by the National Pact and the Constitution.

Although this "first turn" did not actually undermine intercommunal interdependence as defined by the National Pact, it did nonetheless raise the "temperature" over two issues: foreign policy orientation and presidential reelection. There was now a strong potential that the regime and its supporters, particularly the Maronites, would seek to marginalize the role of the Muslim-dominated opposition in shaping the system of state governance. This threat regarding reducing intercommunal interdependence—that is, intercommunally shared control over the fate of state governance—soon became more serious. The regime and its supporters now feared that the Muslim-dominated opposition might put Lebanon on a course that would marginalize the role of Maronites in shaping state governance.

The Muslim-dominated opposition took "the second turn" as it became jubilant about the formation of the UAR in February 1958, seized on the assassination of al-Matni to begin playing politics by other means, and embraced the Iraqi revolution in July 1958. The formation of the UAR and starkly opposed responses to it by the Muslim-dominated opposition and the regime (and its Maronite supporters) changed the regime-opposition conflict into an intercommunal one. The Maronites were now afraid to loose their privileged position in the state based on the belief that UAR influence would contravene Lebanon's sovereignty and independence. They also feared that the stipulations of the National Pact, which simultaneously created strong intercommunal interdependence and put the Maronites in a special position, would become practically obsolete. On the other hand, the Muslim-dominated opposition viewed the opportunity of clearly aligning Lebanon with the Arab world more important than seeking to preserve the stipulations of the National Pact. This intercommunal coloration of the conflict became stronger after al-Matni's assassination in May and the Iraqi revolution in July. As noted earlier, in the aftermath of al-Matni's assassination, the war moved from being rhetorical to clashes and violence on the streets. At this point, each of the belligerents did not believe in the possibility or feasibility of sharing control over the situation with the others and hence sought unilateral solutions, including radical ones. The strong intercommunal interdependence provided for in the National Pact and Constitution was at stake during summer 1958. The demise of the Iraqi monarchy in July 1958 magnified the stakes even more as the Chamoun regime became paranoid about spillover effects from Iraq to Lebanon and the Muslim-dominated opposition openly advocated a similar revolution in Lebanon.

Yet as the crisis lingered during the months of July and August 1958, the belligerents began to realize that none of them could unilaterally impose a "realistic" solution. Both the regime (and supporters) and the Muslim-dominated opposition hence took the "third turn" during summer 1958 after street clashes became the way of debating the issues, and more so after it became clear that Shihab was the country's savior. The more confidence the opposed parties put in the Shihab candidacy, the more they reversed back to the 1943 National Pact and its generated system of intercommunal interdependence. Eventually, reversing back to the high level of intercommunal interdependence among the major communal groups built in the confessional system greatly strengthened the incentives for the communal groups to reconsolidate state governance as the only way out of the lingering crisis.

In sum, the confessional system of governance had inherently built in it a high sense of intercommunal interdependence. The latter had thus created a potential, if not always actual, sense of intercommunal vulnerability. Yet the strong sense of intercommunal interdependence did not always translate to high intercommunal vulnerability. The latter varied with the changes in intercommunal predictability and the changes in the level and nature of information complexity during the period 1957–58. As discussed earlier, *intercommunal* predictability began and continued to decrease after the birth of the UAR, until it reached a very low level during the fighting of summer 1958. Likewise, the complexity of *intercommunal* information began to increase significantly after the formation of the United Arab Republic and the Muslim population and elites became jubilant about it. Information complexity increased even more rapidly to reach a very high level during the short civil war (May 1958–September 1958). Nevertheless, intercommunal predictability reversed course and began to increase after the Maronite, Sunni, and Druze leaders clearly expressed their commitment to the Shihab regime. Likewise, information complexity began to stagnate by the end of the summer and then decrease under the Shihab regime. Therefore, a low intercommunal vulnerability made it more likely that the Shihab regime would be able to reconsolidate state governance. However, as the theory in chapter 3 suggests, intercommunal vulnerability is a necessary but insufficient explanation for how state governance evolves in times of crisis. The fate of state governance depends on intercommunal trust and on how the relevant actors actually rely on the distribution of institutional power to address intercommunal vulnerability.

## Intercommunal Trust

Intercommunal trust emerged and somewhat consolidated after the end of the mandate system through a process of intercommunal construction that started before the French left and culminated in the 1943 National Pact. The latter became a structural lock-in, a symbiotic relationship between the constitutional arrangements designed during the French mandate and domestic structural organizations. Two types of social-structural organization were particularly important: salient sectarian memories and the structure of sectarian cleavages. These two elements mutually reinforced one another to constitute the basis of the National Pact. In the following, I first discuss a few important aspects of communal memories for the three most politically active communities—the Maronites, Sunnis, and Druzes—and, second, the structure of sectarian cleavages. This discussion allows me next to trace the evolution of a structural lock-in.

### *The Maronite Community*

The Maronites' historical memory has four major dimensions: the historic role of the Maronite religion, the ethnic and civilizational origin of the Maronites, the memory of the 1860s massacres between Muslims and Christians on Mount Lebanon, and the historic relations between the Maronites and the West.[32] The Maronite leadership and avant-garde movement (the Kataeb or Phalanges) draw heavily on these historical memories in designing their communal strategies and policies on various matters of importance to the Maronite community.

Historical symbolism plays a vital role in the Maronites' sense of a community. The Lebanese national anthem, written by a Maronite poet, Rashid Nakhleh, portrays old and young men of Lebanon in the mountains and the plains responding to the call of the historical fatherland and rallying around the "eternal" cedar flag to defend "Lebanon forever." Two of the community's most enduring traditional institutions have been the patriarch, with the priestly structure under his control, and the network of Maronite monasteries. Throughout the centuries, the church hierarchies played crucial roles in the evolution of the Maronite community. In the 1958 civil war, the Maronite patriarch played a key role in the denouement of the crisis. He maintained a careful distance from the Maronite president Chamoun. This allowed him to preserve the allegiance of a large segment of the Maronite community, which helped in tipping the balance of Maronite opinion against Chamoun's bid to renew his presidential term and in ensuring a smooth succession for Fuad Shihab (Cobban 1985).

The Maronites take much pride in their non-Arab origin. The Maronite intellectuals use Phoenicianism—an ideology that links their community to the Phoenician civilization of five thousand years ago—to differentiate themselves from the Arabs. Prominent Maronite figures such as Michel Chiha (one of the writers of the Lebanese Constitution) strongly promoted the idea that Lebanon belonged to an older and more superior civilization than that of the Arabs (Gilmour 1987). Hence, the rationale goes, the idea of a "Lebanon" had its origin in the distant past when Phoenicians introduced their alphabet to the Greeks and so helped to bring civilization to the West (Cobban 1985). Political leaders such as Pierre Gemayyel, founder and leader of the Kataeb (Phalanges) Party, believed that a Maronite Lebanon had a continuing *"mission civilisatrice."* According to the Kataeb Party Manifesto, "Lebanon is a soul, a spiritual principle" and has a mission "incompatible with that which the Arabs aspire generally to realize" (Yamak 1966, 48). Lebanon should thus remain independent indefinitely. Moreover, to the Maronites (and Greek Catholics), Lebanon is the only place in the Arab world where Christians can be genuinely free (Gordon 1980). The Kataeb Party has been the unequivocal representative and defender of this idea. Personalities such as Camille Chamoun, Charles Malik, and Pierre Gemayyel have been among the fiercest defenders of Lebanism. These and similarly minded leaders became thence objects of virtual idolatry among the Maronite masses. Mountains carry pictures showing, for example, Chamoun's face within a heart on the bosom of Christ, who points one finger to Chamoun as a sign of approval (Gordon 1980). Lebanism, as an ideology, rejects Islam and the Arab world, identifies with the West and adheres to Western values, insists on Lebanon's survival as a Christian and democratic country in the Middle East, and advocates individualism and self-sufficiency (Gilmour 1987).

For the Maronites, preserving a strong and positive relationship with the West is also an historical imperative and part of their identity as Christians. The good relationship between France (and Europe in general) and the Maronites is a product of a long historical legacy of friendship that began around the twelfth century when Catholic France initiated a relationship with the Maronite patriarch. Relations with Catholic Europe became stronger after the Vatican recognized the sect's doctrinal "orthodoxy." The Vatican also established lasting institutional links with the Maronite Church hierarchies (Cobban 1985). The Maronites interpret the European intervention on their behalf with the Ottoman sultanate to favor the Christian sects over other religious sects in the aftermath of the 1860 massacres as a sign that they share a common destiny with the Christian West rather than with the Arab world. Because of their collusion with the French authorities during the mandate, the Maronites acquired a position of permanent political supremacy in the 1943 National Pact.

The Maronite sense of common fate with Western Europe was a determining factor during the Sykes-Picot Agreement in spring 1919, during which

Iraq and Palestine were placed under British rule and Lebanon and western (later all of) Syria under French rule. A Maronite delegation attended the peace conference at Versailles to press their case for a French mandate over Lebanon because they believed that the Christians had a right to control Lebanon. The Maronites pressed for the extension of their small Lebanese territory—Mount Lebanon—to what they argued were its natural and historical boundaries. These included the coastal towns of Tripoli, Beirut, Sidon, and Tyre and their respective hinterlands and the fertile valley of the Bekaa. After World War I, the Maronite leaders succeeded in convincing the French to yield to the Maronite belief that such a "Greater Lebanon" had always had a special social and historical character, different from that of its surroundings. This self-styled necessity to dominate Lebanese politics remained a strong imperative for the Maronite community.

These Maronite memories and beliefs have helped to create in the minds of many Maronites a sense of siege within the Arab world. This sense of siege has, most importantly, been transparent in the ideology and organization of the radical Maronite organization, the Phalanges (Kataeb), and is a "raw material" that the Maronite leaders (e.g., Camille Chamoun) draw on in promoting their visions for Lebanon. For example, Pierre Gemayyel formed the Phalange (Kataeb) on November 21, 1936, as a paramilitary youth organization to preserve and promote the Maronite sense of community and interests. The Kataeb sought to defend Lebanon against the challenge of a pan-Syrian movement. They also believed that they should defend Lebanon against the Muslim leaders who, at the "Conference of the Coast" on March 10, 1936, had issued a demand that parts of Lebanon be reintegrated into Syria (Gordon 1980). After the French left Lebanon, Gemayel's (and the Kataeb's) general policy was to insulate Lebanon from the affairs of other Arab states (Gordon 1980). The Kataeb's policies have been uniformly anti-Palestinian and have allowed no place for competing ideologies such as pan-Arabism. The 1958 civil war was a turning point for the Phalanges Party. Whereas in 1936, the party had a following of some three hundred Maronites, by 1958 its membership had swelled to something around forty thousand.

### *The Druze Community*

Much like the Maronites, the Druzes of Lebanon also have a strong sense of historical memory and rootedness. The very character of the Druze religion as a secret order, with its books accessible only to a minority of *uqqals* (persons with a certain type of knowledge) even within the circle of believing Druzes themselves, makes the historical evolution of the community a defining element of their identity and of their relations with both the Muslims and the Christians (Alamuddin 1993). Three main elements of the Druze historical memory structure the community's identity and its relations with other Lebanese sects and factions, especially the Maronites. The Druzes still "remember" having been a persecuted religious minority in the Arab world, their uncontested political and economic power on Mount Lebanon before the 1860 massacres, and the 1860 massacres themselves as well as their denouement following the intervention of Western powers on the Maronites' behalf.

The Druze emerged as a near-mystic branch of Shiism in Cairo around AD 1017. The main difference between the Druzes and other Shiite sects is that the Druzes believe in reincarnation, do not believe in the obligatory character of the five daily prayers, reject the Hajj (pilgrimage) to Mecca, and do not fast during Ramadan. These religious differences set the Druzes on a collision course with most other Islamic communities and orders. The Druze sect closed its doors to further conversion in 1043 as a defensive strategy against mounting attacks by mainstream Shiites. Prolonged persecution and weakness have prompted the Druzes to assume peaceful and accommodationist relations toward other Muslim sects and powerful groups in general.

In early sixteenth century, the Druze lords helped the Ottoman Turks to seize control of the region from the Egyptian Mamlukes. The Ottomans in return appointed a Druze as prince of Mount Lebanon in 1516. From then on and up to the 1860 massacres, the Druzes thus enjoyed both economic supremacy and political power in Mount Lebanon and its surroundings. In the aftermath of the massacres, the new *Mutassarriffiyya* system established by the Ottomans on Mount Lebanon and the eradication of feudalism hurt the Druzes both politically and economically. The Ottoman decision to appoint a Christian governor over Mount Lebanon removed whatever political power they still controlled. The new status quo was further entrenched during the French mandate and in independent Lebanon (Haddad 1985).

Persistent suspicion between the Maronites and the Druzes is rooted to a large degree in the 1860 bloody conflict between the two communities. The Druzes see the Maronites as having been the aggressors in that conflict. The Druzes found it unacceptable that not only did the aggressing Maronites come out victorious with the help of the European powers, but they also won the acquiescence of the Ottoman sultanate. The Druzes could not resign themselves to a "new fact on the ground" wherein the Maronites dominated Mount Lebanon. The French plans for a Greater Lebanon heightened even further the Druzes' sense of being an alienated community as well as their grievances against the Maronites. They thus revolted against the French decision to create a "Greater Lebanon" and refused to accept the French policy of arbitrarily separating the Arab populations (including the Druze community) living around Mount Lebanon and Syria. Notwithstanding the French success in quelling the Arab revolts against the mandate divisions of Lebanon and Syria, the sentiments of Arab unity among the Druzes have since then crystallized more, and the Lebanese Druzes have never accepted as final the partition of Greater Syria into Syria and Lebanon.

Two major events determined the Druzes' political status in Lebanon. First, the 1860 massacres and the subsequent establishment of a new political system in Mount Lebanon—the *Mutassarifiyya*—removed the Druzes from a position of leadership to that of a minority, subordinated to the Maronites. Second, during the French mandate the National Pact in 1943 between the Maronites and Sunni Muslims put the Druzes in a very unfavorable posture that remained constant from then onward.[33] Changing the status quo became a defining element of the Druze identity and a major concern of most Druze leaders.

These historical grievances give the Druzes a strong sense of communal dissatisfaction in spite of their division into partisans of the two historic rivals since the early eighteenth century, the Arslan and Jumblatt families. For example, many of Kamal Jumblatt's followers supported him not because they agree with his socialist program, but because he was their traditional Druze leader. The Druzes might quarrel among themselves and take different sides in civil crises, but they always avoid open strife among themselves. In the final analysis, the Druzes' loyalty to their community takes priority over allegiance to either Syrianism or Arabism, however ideologically important and politically useful these might be (Gordon 1980).

### *The Sunni Community*

Two main dimensions define the historical memory of the Lebanese Sunnis. First, most Sunnis are of an Arab origin. Second, the Sunnis have always constituted a majority in the region, with all the privileges that this entails. These two dimensions shape the dynamics of the relations between the Sunnis and other religious sects and communal groups. The creation of Lebanon and Syria in the aftermath of World War I was the first major instance during which the Sunni historical memory manifested itself strongly. The evolution of the Sunni community since then illustrates more or less the waxing and waning impacts of these two dimensions of historical memory.

The Sunnis have always viewed themselves part of the community—Islamic Ummah—in whose interest succeeding empires had existed since Islam spread to the area in the seventh century. They have continued to relate primarily to the politics of that broader group, even after the Druzes and, then, the Maronites succeeded in creating new, local forms of polity on Mount Lebanon. The Sunni Muslims became for the first time subordinated to the Christians in 1860 with the creation of the *Mutassarrifiyya* system. Their communal status weakened further after the collapse of the Ottoman Empire and the collusion between the Maronites and the French interests, right before and during the establishment of the French mandate in 1920.

The French policies and preferential treatment of the Maronites were determining factors in crystallizing the Sunnis' historical memory. To achieve their own agenda in the region and exercise more influence over local political movements in the Middle East at the expense of the Ottoman Empire, France helped to create the Central Syrian Committee in Paris in 1917. The committee called for a Syrian state extending over much of "Natural Syria under French Mandate." In October 1918, Ottoman Ismail Bey reacted and proclaimed the establishment of an Arab government. What France did not expect or at least discounted was that the Arabs were aspiring to establish a unified state for the Arab nation, a goal that France's friends, the Maronites, strongly rejected. France thus supported the Maronite clergy, who was already opposing the Arab nationalists' call for a unification of Syria and Lebanon. The Sunnis, who saw their community becoming once more subordinate to the Christians in Lebanon, strongly opposed the French policy of separating the local population into Syrians and Lebanese (Gilmour 1987).

Not satisfied with the French-imposed status quo, the Sunni community moved on the offensive. In March 1936, a group of Sunnis calling themselves the Conference of the Coast convened in Beirut to revive, if without much success, the call for a reintegration of Lebanon's Muslim districts with Syria. In contrast, the Maronite president Edde and the French authorities agreed in November 1936 that France would recognize Lebanon's independence, and in return, the French would enjoy military privileges in an eventually independent Lebanon. The Muslim public was outraged, even though the treaty called for a guarantee that all Lebanese sects would have fair representation in the government and administration and that all Christian and Muslim members of the Lebanese Chamber of Deputies approve it. To clear up the atmosphere, President Edde appointed in January 1937 a Sunni as prime minister and requested him to form a government (Cobban 1985). The matter was provisionally resolved in 1943 with the promulgation of the 1943 National Pact between the Maronites, Sunnis, Shiites, and Druzes.

To sum up, sectarian memory divergence was a salient feature of Lebanon's domestic politics. The divergence depended on, and in turn sustained, the role that the structure of sectarian cleavages played in the evolution of the polity since the end of the French mandate system.

### *Structure of Sectarian Cleavages*

Ethnic Arabs constitute more than 90 percent of the Lebanese population. The Muslim and Christian Lebanese speak Arabic. The ethnic map also includes other smaller minorities such as the Armenians, Kurds, and Jews. Confessionalism is the dominant social, economic, and political reality. The religious sects are not monolithic blocs, however. Strife within confessional groups is as common as conflict across sects. Sectarianism preceded the creation of modern Lebanon in 1920. The Druzes and the Maronites, who inhabited Mount Lebanon, differed in their religious beliefs, had separate cultural outlooks, and did not always coexist in peace and harmony. They often engaged in fierce battles over issues such as land ownership, the distribution of political power, foreign allegiances, and family feuds.

The French created modern Lebanon with a constitutional arrangement that perpetuated the structure of sectarian cleavages. On September 1, 1920, French General Gouraud proclaimed the establishment of Greater Lebanon with its present boundaries. On May 24, 1926, the Lebanese Republic was born, with Charles Dabbas as its first president. The French amended the Lebanese Constitution in 1927 and 1929 to guarantee proportional representation for all religious sects. Modeled after that of the French Third Republic, the Constitution provided for a unicameral parliament called the Chamber of Deputies, a president, and a cabinet. The Chamber of Deputies elects the president for one six-year term. An incumbent president can run for reelection only after having been out of the office of the president for six years at least. The first complete census ever held in Lebanon took place in 1932 and resulted in the custom of selecting major political officers according to the proportion of the principal sects in the population. Thus, the president was to be a Maronite, the prime minister a Sunni, and the speaker of the Chamber of Deputies a Shiite. These institutional arrangements became enshrined in an intercommunal arrangement worked out among the leaders of the two major communities, the Maronites and the Sunnis—the 1943 National Pact.

The structure of sectarian cleavages was the source material for a national identity question that remained a characteristic feature of Lebanon until its collapse in 1975. The evolution of the Lebanese polity during the French mandate and afterward clearly shows the important role of the national identity question. Since the creation of the republic, the Lebanese have disagreed over the identity of the state. The Muslims, particularly the Sunnis, were more inclined toward a close association with Greater Syria and the Arab world. The Christians, particularly the Maronites, preferred linking Lebanon culturally and politically to the Western world. The Christians were not opposed to economic cooperation with the Arab countries, to which Lebanon exported most of its products, but insisted on distinguishing Lebanon's foreign policy from that of its Arab neighbors. After independence, the national identity question revolved not on whether Lebanon should be Arab, but rather on "how Arab" Lebanon should be. There thus were two broad orientations in Lebanon on the national identity question. One orientation saw Lebanon as a provisionally separate state with temporary legitimacy that would someday become part of a Greater Syria or a member of a united Arab world. This orientation became more visible in the post-mandate era. A manifesto issued by a group of eminent Sunni and Shiite leaders in 1954 (translated into English as "Muslim Lebanon Today") stated that Greater Lebanon was an artificial creation of the French who, seeking to divide and rule, went against the desire of the great majority of people who wanted the creation of a United Arab Nation (Gordon 1980). The second orientation saw Lebanon as a fully sovereign state with a unique identity and close ties to the West. Most adherents to this view were Christians, particularly the Maronites and Greek Orthodox. They saw Lebanon as the only place in the Arab world where the Christians can be genuinely free. Hence, for these people, although the Muslims in Lebanon were citizens, the reins of power must remain in the hands of the Christians. This orientation was encapsulated in the notion of a "Lebanese idea"—that is, Lebanon has a special destiny to represent both West and East to one another. This mission, the argument goes, had its origin in the distant past when Phoenicians introduced the alphabet to the Greeks and hence helped to bring civilization to the West. The Maronites promoted this idea and the Phalanges most unequivocally espoused it.

In sum, the structure of sectarian cleavages, the fabric of sectarian memories, and the constitutional arrangements of the mandate period combined to produce a structural lock-in that became encapsulated in the 1943 National Pact (al Mithaq al Watani), the effects of which shaped the Lebanese polity for decades. The actual process leading to the agreement on the National Pact consisted of numerous meetings between the then Maronite president, Bishara al-Khuri, and then Sunni prime minister, Riyad al-Sulh. At the heart of the negotiations were, on the one hand, the Christians' fears of Muslim domination of Lebanon and the surrounding Arab countries and, on the other hand, Muslims' fears of Western hegemony. In return for the Christian promise not to seek foreign (mainly French) protection and to accept Lebanon's "Arab face," the Muslim side agreed to recognize the independence and legitimacy of the Lebanese state with its 1920 boundaries and to renounce aspirations for union with Syria. The National Pact revolved around four principles. First, Lebanon was to be a completely independent state. The Christian communities should primarily identify with Lebanon and not with the West. The Muslim communities, in return, were to protect the independence of Lebanon and prevent its merger with any Arab state. Second, although Lebanon is an Arab country with Arabic as its official language, it should not cut off its spiritual and intellectual ties with the West. Third, Lebanon, as a member of the family of Arab states, should cooperate with the other Arab states, and in case of conflict among them, it should not side with one state against another. Fourth, public offices should be distributed proportionally among the recognized religious groups, but preference should be given to competence without regard to confessional considerations in technical positions. More specifically, the president of the republic should always be a Maronite, the prime minister a Sunni, and the speaker of the Chamber of

Deputies a Shiite. This confessional distribution of high-level posts in the government was based on the 1932 census' six-to-five ratio favoring the Christians over the Muslims.

*Effects of the Structural Lock-In*

The structural lock-in had two main effects that became a trademark of the Lebanese body politic: first, the emergence of a dominant role for the sociopolitical institution of *za'im* in Lebanese politics and, second, the post-mandate institutional arrangements of the state.

First, the National Pact helped to guarantee the maintenance of the status quo and the continuation of privileges for the sectarian elites—the *zu'ama*. The *za'im* occupies immensely powerful social and political positions both in the cities and in rural areas. He does not necessarily have to be a minister or even a deputy. Yet he can have effective authority of entire groups of deputies as well as government ministers. In his particular constituency, the *za'im* would exercise greater power than the government itself. A *za'im* generally owed his position to his ancestry, and politics was often a family business. A *za'im's* main task is to please his clients and constituents by finding jobs for them, settling communal disputes, or persuading the government to provide a village with a mosque or a church, drinking water, or other needed public services. Not surprisingly, a *za'im* who becomes a minister or a deputy is expected to favor his clients with new projects and other special services (Hottinger 1966).

Second, the National Pact strongly shaped the dynamic of the political game within and outside the state institutions. The forms and dynamics of the office of the president, the prime minister, the Chamber of Deputies, and political parties are illustrative. Lebanon is a presidential system, with the Constitution consigning vast authority to the president. In theory, anyone who meets certain eligibility requirements for election to the Chamber of Deputies can be the president of Lebanon; in reality, though, before the 1975 civil war powerful Maronite *zu'ama* usually held the post. The necessity of obtaining cooperation from at least a majority of the *zu'ama* of the various confessional communities constrains the presidential power and effective authority. Moreover, the Maronite president must try to work in harmony with the Sunni prime minister. The cabinets are the products of intricate accommodations of diverse sectarian interests. Consequently, the cabinets have sometimes degenerated into arenas for political sniping and backroom machinations, with ever-changing coalitions and factions. Intra-cabinet antipathies would often paralyze the business of government. Influential *zu'ama* have most often held the cabinet positions.

A strong presidency and powerful *zu'ama* have often fragmented the Chamber of Deputies, relegating it to an insignificant role in Lebanese politics. Nor are party politics "politics of parties" per se. The *za'im* institution heavily manipulated the electoral system. Political parties usually consisted of the followers of a particular *za'im* and tended to be de facto organizations representing confessional groupings, whatever the ideology might be. For example, most of Jumblatt's followers were with him because he was a Druze leader, not because of his socialist ideology. Most members of the Phalanges were Maronite. Conversely, most sectarian groupings tended to act as if they were political parties. At every election since independence, some 60 percent of the deputies have not belonged to political parties. In most cases, these deputies succeeded because of the family's position or their relationship with the local *za'im*. Once elected, a new deputy would remain under the *za'im's* influence, for the latter can withdraw his support at any time and ensure the deputy's defeat at the next election (Hottinger 1966). Candidates would campaign as part of a "list" sponsored by a local *za'im*, and competition within districts was intra-sectarian. For example, a Greek Catholic from one list would campaign against Greek Catholics from other lists. To ensure success for his list, a *za'im* often entered into complex alliances with *zu'ama* supporting other lists in other districts. One *za'im* might support another *za'im* in a neighboring district but oppose him in another district. Regardless of confessional association, candidates have tended to be men of wealth, often property owners, lawyers, or businesspersons with family connections to the local *za'im*.

These two effects of the structural lock-in defined what counted both as "normal" and as "beyond-the-normal" Lebanese politics until the collapse of the state in 1975. "Normal" politics has consisted of rivalries among various *zu'ama*.[34] Given their pivotal positions between their respective communities and the state, the *za'ims* could usually quite easily mobilize their followers if they wanted to, especially if the community feels its interests or status threatened. Rivalries or collusions among the Maronite, Druze, and Ṣunni *za'ims* and government officials usually strongly shaped the dynamics of Lebanon's body politic. Most of this dynamic revolved around a core issue—the balance of power among the major sects and factions as stipulated in the National Pact. Changing the stipulations of the 1943 National Pact was the overriding issue of "beyond-the-normal" politics.

### *Deconstructing Intercommunal Trust*

Trust, as explained in chapter 3, arises and changes with three facilitating conditions: intercommunal interdependence, *ex ante* agency, and *ex post* agency. As discussed earlier, the post-mandate arrangements created much interdependence among the major sectarian groups of Lebanon. This high level of intercommunal interdependence constituted "normal" politics in Lebanon. Defining and delimiting as well as enforcing *ex ante* agency and *ex post* agency was at the core of the 1943 National Pact, state Constitution, and state institutional arrangements. The stipulations of the National Pact were to alleviate fears of the Christians and Muslims—that the Christians promise not to seek foreign protection and to accept Lebanon's "Arab face" and that the Muslims recognize the independence and legitimacy of the Lebanese state in its 1920 boundaries and renounce aspirations for a union with Syria. In other words, the two sides wanted to circumscribe each other's *ex ante* agency in deciding the fate of Lebanon. This is precisely what abiding by the first three principles of the National Pact, mentioned earlier, should do. The Christian communities were to identify primarily with Lebanon and not with the West. Muslim communities, in return, were to protect the independence of Lebanon and prevent its merger with any Arab state. The fourth principle of the National Pact and the institutional arrangements of the state combined to define and delimit the *ex post* agency of the major sectarian communities. The principle thus stipulated that public offices should be distributed proportionally among the recognized religious groups. This principle, as discussed above, defined the division of institutional power among the Maronite, Sunni, Shiite, and Druze communities. At a practical level, though, the *zaʾim* institution effectively became the mechanism through which both *ex ante* agency and *ex post* agency were exercised, as well as restrained. Not only did the *zuʾama* play an important role in upholding the delimitations imposed on *ex ante* and *ex post* agency as part of playing "normal" politics, they also on one occasion at least before 1958 joined efforts to enforce these delimitations. Most *zuʾama* collectively revolted against President al-Khuri when he threatened to destroy the arrangements in 1951, eventually forcing him to resign.

In sum, at the time of the June 1957 elections the Lebanese polity faced a situation in which the major sectarian communities shared a high sense of intercommunal interdependence as encapsulated in the state institutional arrangements and the stipulations of the National Pact and as practiced by the *zuʾama*. The state institutional arrangements and the *zaʾim* institution together helped to delimit the *ex ante* agency and *ex post* agency of the sectarian groups. As long as these conditions were fulfilled there was enough intercommunal trust among the major sectarian groups. Conversely, any changes that would undermine these conditions had the potential to negate or at least reduce intercommunal trust. This occurred in 1958 following Chamoun's success in manipulating the 1957 June elections to ensure himself a compliant Chamber of Deputies. By manipulating the elections and reducing the power of the opposition in the Chamber, the regime set in motion a dynamic that eventually led to an erosion of intercommunal trust after the formation of the UAR in February 1958. Yet intercommunal trust did not erode spontaneously, but rather was the result of a process of deconstruction to which both the regime (and its Maronite supporters) and the Muslim-dominated opposition contributed. As events unfolded in the period 1957–58, the regime and its Maronite supporters sought to increase their level of *ex post* agency, whereas the Muslim-dominated opposition sought to prevent that. Therefore, as summer 1958 began, the Muslim-dominated opposition and the regime (and its supporters) were under a high level of interdependence while they simultaneously were increasingly achieving more *ex ante* agency and seeking more *ex post* agency. The mix of an intransigent opposition and a paranoid regime and the increase in *ex ante* and *ex post* agency under a condition of very high interdependence ultimately produced a process of deconstructing intercommunal trust. Arguably, what really became strongly, but not solely, determinative of the level of intercommunal trust were the intra- and intercommunal strategies that the respective leaders opted for. The latter, as discussed earlier, in combination with a high and increasing level of information complexity and a low and rapidly decreasing level of intercommunal predictability, created a high and increasing level of intercommunal vulnerability.

Next, I discuss how the process of deconstructing intercommunal trust evolved in the period February 1957–August 1958. The discussion shows how the structural lock-in of the National Pact with the institutional arrangements of a post-mandate state strongly shaped this process of deconstructing intercommunal trust. The latter unfolded largely through a reenactment of old political myths and the routinization of new practices and discourses that redefined the intercommunal relations in terms of antagonistic and irreconcilable goals. The mutual feedback between the reciprocated strategic practices of the elites and the responses of the sectarian communities at large helped to sustain the process of trust deconstruction.

### THE MUSLIM ELITE: REVIVING OLD POLITICAL MYTHS

Two mutually reinforcing political myths, Western imperialism and pan-Arabism, quickly dominated and framed the political discourses of the Muslim-dominated opposition. Both myths had a long pedigree within the Arab masses and resonated well with concurrently changing regional context. Lebanon's acceptance of the Eisenhower Doctrine had revived fears of Western imperialism, or at least the opposition elites portrayed it as such. Likewise, the birth of the UAR in February 1958 also strongly revived the political myth of pan-Arabism. The opposition used these myths to challenge the regime and its supporters not only before and after the June 1957 parliamentary elections, but also during the fighting of summer 1958. The message framed with these two myths resonated widely in the Muslim populace of Lebanon. This increased the political influence of the Muslim-dominated opposition in the Lebanese populace and in return reinforced the pivotal role that the *zaʾim* institution played in Lebanese politics.

That the Muslim-dominated opposition used these two political myths to frame its various challenges to the regime and its supporters is evident, as discussed earlier, in a series of domestic and international events. Lebanon's adherence to the Eisenhower Doctrine in March 1957, the debates preceding the June 1957 parliamentary elections, the debates surrounding Chamoun's bid for reelection, the birth of the UAR in February 1958, the fall of the Iraqi monarchy in July 1958, and the intervention of U.S. marines in July 1958 are all illustrative. The two political myths resonated widely in the Muslim populace because both myths corresponded strongly with the historical memories of the Muslim populace, particularly the Sunni, Shiite, and Druze communities. The Muslim *zu'ama* did not have to engage their respective communities into processes of myth internalization since these myths were already part of the "historical memory" background and the supportive regional conditions that Lebanon was enthralled in, as discussed earlier in the chapter. Not only did most Muslims believe in the ideology of pan-Arabism, but also the formation of the UAR became a vindication of this belief. In the immediate aftermath of the formation of the UAR it looked as if both the opposition leadership and the masses were competing with one another to show their respective support to the UAR and Nasser. The resonance between the leaders' self-serving strategies in countering Chamoun's plans for seeking a second presidential term and the masses' jubilant support for pan-Arabism had never been stronger in the life of independent Lebanon. Moreover, the formation of the UAR and the eruption of fighting provided the *zu'ama* within the opposition as well as within the Maronite community an opportunity to strengthen their pivotal roles in Lebanese politics. If the Chamoun regime had tried to exclude many prominent opposition *zu'ama* from the Chamber of Deputies by manipulating the 1957 elections, these *zu'ama* came back forcefully to the political front stage and helped to set the agenda for the whole country. Yet if the opposition *zu'ama* and their respective followers were able to resonate with one another to the tune of pan-Arabism and anti-imperialism, this in turn prompted the regime supporters, especially the Phalanges, to also revive their own self-styled political myths. The latter also resonated with large sections of the Maronite population.

### THE MARONITE ELITE: REVIVING OLD POLITICAL MYTHS

Although the regime and its Maronite supporters had gained enough institutional power through the June elections, the unfolding events contrived such a momentum. The birth of the UAR and the jubilant support that the Lebanese Muslims showed for it and the strong reemergence of pan-Arabist discourse on the political scene created a strong sense of fear in the Maronite community, and more so in the regime and its main ally, the Phalanges Party. Both the regime and the Phalanges leaders seized the opportunity to revive the long-held Maronite, and more generally Christian, fears of Muslim domination of Lebanon and of seeing Lebanon absorbed into the Arab world, losing its sovereignty and unique identity. The events of the first half of 1958 resuscitated the old schisms concerning the national identity of Lebanon and threatened to undermine the intercommunal understanding that the National Pact encapsulated.

Notwithstanding the fact that all sides claimed their allegiance to the National Pact while accusing the other side of violating its stipulations, the polity as a whole was drifting away from the National Pact. The Maronite leadership and the regime did not need to do much convincing in the ranks of their followers, for the latter were witnessing the pan-Arabist fervor within the opposition with great concern and fear. Yet the Christian community was somewhat divided, forcing Chamoun to compete for its loyalty with other Christian leaders who joined the opposition such as the Maronite patriarch, former president al-Khuri, the Franjiyyahs, and the Ammuns. Nevertheless, appealing to the old myth of Christian Lebanon in danger from Muslims contributed to the regime's success, if partial, in convincing many Christians about an impending Arab danger. The regime had no problem in mobilizing the militant Phalange, who already believed that the Christians faced the imminent danger of being drowned in a "sea of Muslims."[35] This in return reinforced even more the Muslim-dominated alliance resolve in opposing the Chamoun regime. Belligerent actions and reactions on both sides quickly became the routine in dealing with one another.

### ROUTINIZATION OF NEW INTERCOMMUNAL RELATIONS

The process of routinizing new intercommunal relations effectively began at the beginning of the fighting that erupted in summer 1958. The result was a vanishing level of intercommunal trust, at least between the Muslims within the opposition and the Maronites in the regime camp, most prominently the Phalanges. After the regime officially adhered to the Eisenhower Doctrine, the opposition and the regime began to drift rapidly toward opposed extremes. The regime busied itself with preparatory manipulations in a bid to secure an overwhelming victory in upcoming parliamentary elections, whereas the opposition began to organize itself more effectively and more broadly, as discussed earlier, through the formation of the United National Front, the Third Force, and the Congress of Parties, Organizations, and Personalities in Lebanon. Although much of the rhetorical war had already been going on between the deputies, as evidenced in the debates over the size of the Chamber itself in April 1957, the fault lines of discourse were not for the most part intercommunally drawn. As noted above, the formation of the UAR and the strong Muslim support for it both at the level of leadership and with the masses pushed the confrontation between the regime and the opposition increasingly toward intercommunally framed discourses and practices. After the fighting and clashes erupted on the streets, the fault lines clearly became intercommunal. The fighting became exclusively a Muslim matter on the opposition side and mostly a Maronite issue on the regime side. Henceforth, the mutual feedback between the reciprocated strategic practices of the Muslim and Maronite elites and the response of their respective communities at large helped to strengthen the process of trust deconstruction.

The opposition relied on a number of strategies that built on the popular momentum induced by the formation of the UAR. Conversely, the regime and its supporters within the Christian communities, particularly the Maronites, capitalized also on that momentum to reinforce their prior positions and strategies. The opposition versus regime strategic interaction inexorably turned into a down-spiraling game that ultimately resulted in violent clashes and armed confrontations. The assassination of al-Matni was the spark that unalterably transformed the debate from a war of words and preparations to a war of armies on the streets. Concurrently, politics in the Chamber of Deputies were rapidly becoming even more polarized and confrontational. Finally, when Chamoun requested immediate military assistance from the United States, Britain, and France, intercommunal trust completely vanished.

Thus, what started as a battle over constitutional amendments between the opposition and Chamoun turned into an intercommunal conflict. Three main factors combined to produce this outcome: (1) the formation of the UAR and the overwhelming show of Muslim support for it, (2) the regime and its supporters' intransigent postures on foreign policy and control over the Chamber of Deputies, and (3) the strategic feedback between the Muslim-dominated opposition and the Maronite-dominated alliance of the regime. Yet these factors are insufficient to explain why intercommunal trust eroded the way it did. That the predisposing conditions of the structural lock-in shaped the responses of the Maronites (and more generally Christians) and the Muslim masses to the formation of the UAR and each other's stand on this issue can be affirmed with a large degree of confidence. In addition, a propitious blend of two conditions made the formation of the UAR a favorable context for turning the opposition-regime conflict into an intercommunal clash, henceforth completely deconstructing intercommunal trust built and maintained from independence until the formation of the UAR. First, the Maronites were suffering from a siege mentality inherited from the past. Second, the ideology of pan-Arabism under Nasser's leadership reinforced the continuous grievances of the Muslim masses against the French and British mandate systems.

The regime and the opposition soon realized that they needed to talk to each other as General Fuad Shihab agreed to run for and won the presidency. As discussed earlier, the overall political climate continued to improve, if somewhat reservedly, as all sides adopted a "wait and see" attitude.[36] President Shihab worked to normalize the situation even more by showing a strong determination to observe the terms of the 1943 National Pact and to have the government serve both Christian and Muslim groups equally. In brief, enough intercommunal trust was restored and politics had gone back to its "normal" Lebanese way by the time of the 1960 parliamentary elections.

To recap, in Lebanon the construction of intercommunal trust started under the French mandate and culminated in the 1943 National Pact. However, from 1957 until Shihab's election in summer 1958, the level of intercommunal trust inexorably decreased as the Chamoun regime (and its Maronite supporters) and the Muslim-dominated opposition began clashing about whether to change the rules of state governance after the formation of the UAR in February. The level of trust reached a vanishing level during the fighting that broke out in summer 1958. Intercommunal trust, however, increased significantly to reach moderate (if not higher) levels during Shihab's presidential tenure. Henceforth, the level of reliance on intercommunal trust increased as the scope of collective intentionality increased during the post-1958 Shihab era. The erosion of the scope of collective intentionality during the first half of 1958 and then its subsequent increase under Shihab's rule was not solely due to changes in intercommunal trust, but also crucially depended on the level of institutional power, as explained next.

## Institutional Power Leverage

As discussed in chapter 3, for a given level of intercommunal vulnerability, the level of reliance on institutional power increases as intercommunal trust decreases, and vice versa. For a given level of vulnerability, the more rapidly the reliance on institutional power increases, the more rapidly intercommunal trust would decrease, and the more rapidly the scope of collective intentionality would decrease. These two hypotheses can be easily tested in this case because much debate and conflict between the opposition and the Chamoun regime revolved around Chamoun's bid to control the Chamber of Deputies and by extension the process of creating constitutional amendments. Therefore, three key institutions were at stake in the crisis of 1957–58: the presidency, the Chamber of Deputies, and the army. Chamoun and his supporters were able to control the presidency and the Chamber of Deputies (the latter after the June 1957 elections) but failed to control or manipulate the army. The army chief, General Shihab, refused to take sides in the opposition-regime conflict and instead opted for a largely neutral position.

There undoubtedly was a clear asymmetry in the distribution of institutional power between the antagonists. Lebanon is a presidential system, with the Constitution consigning vast authority to the president. The president is normally constrained by the practical necessity of obtaining cooperation from at least a majority of the *zu'ama* of the various communities. Yet Chamoun did not abide by this "golden" practice of Lebanese politics. In fact, many earlier grievances against Chamoun were rooted in his departure from "politics as normal." Moreover, the president is constitutionally empowered to appoint the prime minister and the cabinet. As the highest Muslim political official, the prime minister can bring a significant amount of authority to his community. In practice, however, the power of the prime minister has varied according to his personality, his base of support, and the preferences of the president he served. Chamoun was able to appoint a compliant Sunni *za'im* as prime minister who tended to follow all of Chamoun's moves and policies, irrespective of their negative implications for the opposition leaders, including the Sunni community at large.

The asymmetry in the distribution of institutional power became stronger after the landslide victory of the regime supporters in the June elections. The president and his entourage did not hesitate to use manipulative strategies, such as during the June 1957 parliamentary elections, as noted earlier. As a result, Chamoun was able to prevent many prominent *zu'ama* from being reelected to the Chamber of Deputies. This made it easier for the regime and its supporters to have total control over the Chamber. Because of the strength of the presidency and the power of the *zu'ama*, the Chamber generally has been a fragmented, inefficient body, playing an insignificant role in Lebanese politics. The Chamber became important for the president during the period 1957–58 only because it alone could amend the Constitution and elect the president. Since Chamoun was seeking a second presidential term, he had first to amend the Constitution. Only then would the Chamber be able to reelect him for a second consecutive term. Controlling more than a two-thirds majority in the Chamber was the guarantee that Chamoun needed to achieve both results.

Because Chamoun failed to convince the army chief to take his side in the conflict, the president could not muster enough coercive state power to pursue his self-serving policies. The army maintained a detached attitude, never committed its entire strength to the government, restricted itself to maintaining basic elements of law and order, and tried to remain neutral in the clashes between the opposition and the regime. Whenever the opposition forces became too aggressive or too successful, the army would intervene to limit their power in undermining regime stability, such as when Jumblatt's forces threatened Beirut airport. At other times, the army acted against the government loyalists, particularly the PPS. Chamoun thus could not depend on the army to suppress the opposition.[37]

In sum, that the regime attempted to and did rely on its institutional power is not a matter of dispute. Not only did the opposition try hard to prevent that from occurring through "normal politics," but the opposition also resorted to politics by other means, as the events of summer 1958 show. However, as the regime began accumulating institutional power during the June elections and more after them, the level of reliance on trust, as discussed earlier, began to decrease. The more the regime relied on its institutional power in debating the various dividing issues such as foreign policy or a new constitutional amendment, the less the antagonists would trust one another. Thus, as intercommunal trust was quickly eroding after the formation of the UAR in February 1958, the regime leaders began to have recourse to whatever institutional power they believed they had or could acquire. The more the Chamoun regime resorted to its leverage over the key state institutions, the more the opposition leaders resorted to extralegal means, and the more state authority and legitimacy eroded. This in turn eroded further an already rapidly vanishing intercommunal trust. This cycle continued during the summer fighting. Overall, the level of reliance on institutional power increased as intercommunal trust decreased. Only when Chamoun accepted to abide by the stipulations of the Constitution and hence not seek a second presidential term was General Shihab able to restore a distribution of institutional power much more acceptable to the major communal groups, including the Maronites themselves. This thereby significantly reduced the reliance on institutional power in the debates over state governance.

## Conclusion

The debates over state governance during 1957–58 in Lebanon were in part induced by a competition between Arab nationalism promoted by Nasser and Cold War logic. These entailed fundamental changes in the regional constitutive rules and practices. These changes not only pressured Lebanon to abandon its neutralist doctrine of foreign policy but also induced domestic political debates about the Lebanese system of state. State governance was eventually reconsolidated after a short civil war in summer 1958. That state governance was reconsolidated with a significantly rising scope of collective intentionality was the result of a combination of a moderate intercommunal vulnerability that eventually decreased significantly, a low intercommunal trust that significantly increased, and a moderate reliance on institutional power that decreased.

The crisis effectively began when President Chamoun sought to manipulate the 1957 legislative elections. Intercommunal vulnerability hence began to rise to moderate levels for other groups (especially their respective *zu'ama*), who feared exploitation and exclusion from effectively participating in state governance. Yet after Fuad Shihab assumed the presidency, intercommunal vulnerability began to decrease significantly. Under these new conditions, fears of intercommunal abandonment, exploitation, or exclusion from participating in the debates decreased quite significantly. The change in vulnerability from somewhat rapidly increasing during the June 1957–September 1958 period to reversing course and significantly decreasing during the October 1958–60 period was the result of changing information complexity from high to moderate and intercommunal predictability from low to moderate, under conditions of high intercommunal interdependence. As the Shihab regime increasingly succeeded in putting behind it the 1958 crisis, intercommunal vulnerability decreased, with increases in the scope of collective intentionality in the polity, that is, with increases in the legitimacy of the emerging rules and practices of state governance.

However, the outcome of debating state governance was not solely determined by intercommunal vulnerability. As outlined in the theory and shown in this case, intercommunal vulnerability and trust are interactive. From 1957 to 1958 (that is, before Shihab's rise to the office of the president), intercommunal trust began to decrease as the Chamoun regime (and its Maronite supporters) and the Muslim-dominated opposition began clashing after the formation of the UAR in February 1958. Intercommunal trust reached a vanishing level during the fighting that broke out in summer 1958. Nevertheless, after Shihab's emergence as the country's savior and Chamoun's stepping down, intercommunal trust increased significantly to reach moderate (if not higher) levels, particularly under Shihab's presidential tenure. Henceforth, intercommunal trust increased as the scope of collective intentionality increased during the post-1958 Shihab era.

The outcome of the debates, in turn, depended on the interaction of intercommunal trust and the regime's attempt to rely on institutional power in the presidency and the Chamber of Deputies. As intercommunal trust was quickly eroding after the formation of the UAR in February 1958, the regime began to have recourse to whatever institutional power it mustered or could acquire. The more the Chamoun regime resorted to its leverage over the key state institutions, the more the opposition leaders resorted to extralegal means, and the more the legitimacy of state governance eroded. This in turn eroded further an already rapidly decreasing intercommunal trust. This cycle continued during the fighting of the summer months. Hence, the level of reliance on institutional power increased with the rapidly decreasing scope of collective intentionality. Overall, the reliance on institutional power increased as intercommunal trust decreased. However, after Chamoun's departure, General Shihab was able to restore a distribution of institutional power more acceptable to the dominant communal groups, thereby reducing significantly the reliance on institutional power in the debates over state governance. The level of reliance on institutional power decreased with the scope of collective intentionality.

By seeking to transform the form of state governance through a domination of the Chamber of Deputies and an amendment to the Constitution, the regime threatened to undermine the 1943 National Pact, without which the integrity of the Lebanese polity would not persist. Having failed to "domesticate" an intransigent Muslim-dominated opposition, the regime ended up provoking a short civil war in summer 1958. Not surprisingly, the denouement of the crisis hinged on Chamoun's resignation. Only when the latter became a reality did it become possible to preserve the integrity of the Lebanese polity and reconsolidate state governance. This occurred after the neutralist chief of the army, General Fuad Shihab, became the accepted "savior" of the country. That the army remained neutral in the conflict and that the U.S. intervention did not "buy into" Chamoun's game of self-preservation at any cost facilitated the transition from the civil war to a "normal" Lebanese politics dominated by the powerful sociopolitical institution of *zaʾim*.

# Seven

# Lebanon and the Metamorphosis of Arab-Israeli Relations, 1973–75

The Lebanese polity endured another major crisis of state governance from May 1973 to April 1975. A number of factors defined the conditions for this second major crisis of governance. These are changing socio-demographic structures in the 1960s, the exodus to Lebanon of large numbers of Palestinians after the 1967 Arab-Israeli War, the expulsion of thousands of armed Palestinians from Jordan to Lebanon after the 1970–71 Black September episode, and the socioeconomic, political, and security ramifications of the 1973 Arab-Israeli Ramadan War. Efforts by a coalition of leftist organizations to redefine the rules of the political game of governance and the Maronites' intransigent opposition to any such changes resulted in a crisis and eventually civil war in 1975. By November 1976, the toll was fifty to sixty thousand human lives and more than $5 billion in material destruction. State governance collapsed, and a protracted civil war began. Three mutually reinforcing elements combined to produce this result. First, the level of intercommunal vulnerability was high and increased after the 1969 Cairo Agreement between the PLO and the Lebanese army. Vulnerability increased much more significantly after the 1971 exodus of the Palestinians from Jordan to Lebanon following the Black September confrontation in Jordan, subsequent paralyses of the army, the Parliament, and the government, and the polarization of the presidency in the aftermath of the May 1973 crisis. Second, the level of intercommunal trust was low and significantly decreased rapidly after the May 1973 crisis, subsequent paralyses of the army, the Parliament, and the government, and the polarization of the presidency. Third, the level of reliance on institutional power was high and increased rapidly after the May 1973 crisis, and subsequent paralyses of the army, the Parliament, and the government, and the polarization of the presidency.

## Theoretical Expectations

In the period 1967–75, three major events that had far-reaching consequences for the region, and Lebanon in particular, occurred in the region. The outcome of the 1967 Six-Day Arab-Israeli War, the expulsion of PLO's troops and thousands of Palestinians from Jordan to Lebanon after the 1970–71 Black September episode in Jordan, and the socioeconomic, political, and security consequences of the 1973 Arab-Israeli War all combined to provoke fundamental changes in the regional constitutive rules and practices. This in turn pressured Lebanon to seek a new regional role for itself by abandoning its neutralist doctrine of foreign policy. The new regional context also induced domestic political debates about the very system of governance in Lebanon that had consolidated after the 1958 crisis. The collective intentionality underpinning the post-1958 form of state governance was strongly undermined. In contrast to 1958, efforts by a coalition of leftist organizations to redefine the rules of the political game of governance and the Maronites' intransigent opposition to any such fundamental changes jeopardized state integrity. The Lebanese polity as a whole failed to preserve even a low scope of collective intentionality, which is necessary to sustain the state's continuous existence, even if it is a weakened one.

The strategic goals of the leftist organizations threatened to jeopardize the 1943 National Pact. Jeopardizing the latter in turn implied a destruction of the political fabric of the confessional system that defined and sustained Lebanon. Yet when the period of radical political debates began after the 1967 war, the constituent communities of the Lebanese polity were interdependent enough to realize that it was in their common interest not to seek the exit option out of the political system. The various parties to the conflict did not intend to abolish the Lebanese state, but only to either radically transform it (e.g., the Sunnis, Druzes, and Shiites) or preserve it as is (e.g., the Maronites). The theory outlined in chapter 3 suggests that under the conditions that prevailed in Lebanon in 1973–75, the outcome of the debates on state governance was "most likely" to be a collapse of state governance.

Three primary factors led to the collapse of state governance in the period 1973–75. First, intercommunal vulnerability reached a high and rapidly increasing level in the period 1973–75 as the communal leaders began taking unilateral moves to protect their communal interests. Under these conditions, the major communal groups increasingly became fearful of abandonment, exploitation, or exclusion from participating in the debates over state governance, debates that were triggered by the changes occurring in the regional environment. This level of vulnerability was the result of very high information complexity, low intercommunal predictability, and high intercommunal interdependence. The level of information complexity became high as the communal leaders increasingly faced a lack of reliable information on each other's intentions and actions. The level of intercommunal predictability was low since there increasingly was no commitment to the status quo arrangement and the communal leaders were increasingly ignoring the stipulations of the 1943 National Pact as the debates were unfolding. At the same time, the major communal groups remained interdependent, and none sought the exit option from Lebanese politics. Hence, strong interdependence among the major sectarian groups enhanced the incentives for debating state governance (hypothesis 1). How to address this vulnerability was not an easy matter, however. As the sectarian leaders increasingly debated whether and, if yes, how to transform state governance, intercommunal vulnerability increased with decreases in the scope of collective intentionality, that is, as commitments to the existing rules and practices of state governance waned (hypothesis 3).

Second, the intercommunal trust that the state institutions and policies had managed to secure under the Shihab regime was quickly eroding, particularly after the emergence of the Palestinians as an independent actor in Lebanese politics and the rise of the aggrieved Shiites in South Lebanon as a force to reckon with. As the debates on state governance evolved in the aftermath of the May 1973 crisis, intercommunal trust eroded rapidly. The sectarian leaders began not only to talk past one another but also to engage each other in rhetorical wars of incriminations and blame for each other's problems. Hence, the level of intercommunal trust rapidly decreased as the scope of collective intentionality decreased during the debates of 1973–75 (hypothesis 5).

Third, as intercommunal trust was quickly eroding, the communal leaders began to have recourse to whatever institutional power they believed they had or could muster. However, not every sectarian leader had access to the state institutional powers in the same way. There indeed was much asymmetry in this respect, with the Maronite leadership reserving for itself the lion's share of institutional power. Hence, the Maronites began to rely increasingly more on their institutional power in attempting to force their policy choices on the other groups. Yet the latter, most prominently the Druzes and the Shiites, opposed such moves and began to act outside the existing rules and practices of state governance. The more the Maronite leadership resorted to its leverage over state institutions, the more the leftist alliance grouping the Druzes, the Sunnis, and the Shiites (and Palestinians) defected from "normal politics," and the more state authority and legitimacy eroded. This in turn eroded further an already weak level of intercommunal trust. This cycle continued until serious fighting erupted in April 1975. Hence the reliance on institutional power increased with rapidly decreasing scope of collective intentionality (hypothesis 8), and with decreasing intercommunal trust (hypothesis 9).

These values of the three variables—vulnerability, trust, and reliance on institutional power—are close to the "most likely conditions" for a collapse of state governance with a vanished scope of collective intentionality, as explicated in table 3.1 (chapter 3). Hence, that the Lebanese polity was not able to preserve its system of state governance confirms the expectations of the theory outlined in chapters 2 and 3. These theoretical expectations are summarized in table 7.1.

## Changes in the Constitutive Rules of Regional Order

As argued in the previous chapter, up until the 1955 Baghdad Pact episode Lebanon was able to maintain a foreign policy of neutrality, which was compatible with the constitutive practices and rules of existing regional order. A neutral foreign policy was inherent in the 1943 National Pact. As also discussed in the previous chapter, major developments during the period 1955–58 challenged this Lebanese foreign policy. The resolution of the 1958 crisis nonetheless reestablished domestic politics as usual and a neutralist international role for Lebanon.

Soon thereafter, however, Lebanon found itself once again enthralled in new heated debates over regional order and domestic state governance. The devastating defeat of the Arab states during the 1967 Six-Day War ushered in an era of profound reconstruction of the constitutive rules and practices of inter-Arab politics and Arab-Israeli relations and a reframing of the Palestinian cause. Lebanon now harbored hundreds of thousands of newly arrived Palestinian refugees, including thousands of Palestinian guerrillas who fled from Jordan following the Black September civil war. These new conditions conspired to challenge both Lebanon's foreign policy doctrine of neutrality and the confessional core of the Lebanese system of state governance. The challenge went much beyond the level of the 1958 crisis, eventually destroying the very sociopolitical fabric of the Lebanese polity as defined in the 1943 National Pact. The new challenge was rooted in part in the radical transformation of the constitutive rules and practices of regional order that evolved from a combination of the outcomes of two regional wars—the 1967 Six-Day War and the 1973 October War—and in part in the radicalization and diversification of the Palestinian Resistance in the post-1967 era. The challenge was also rooted to some extent in the domestic demographic and sociopolitical pressures that the Lebanese system faced in late 1960s. As external and domestic pressures resonated with and mutually reinforced one another, a transformation of state governance became imperative. The polity did not succeed in coping with these simultaneous and mutually reinforcing external and internal challenges. Nor was Lebanon able to preserve its preexisting form of state governance; the country fell into a bloody civil war in 1975–76. I next

**Table 7.1. Summary of Theoretical Expectations**
DCSG: Degree of Consolidation of State Governance

**External Variable:**
International environment: 1967 Six-Day Arab-Israeli War, 1970–71 Black September episode in Jordan, 1973 Ramadan/October War.

| *Observed Outcome: State Governance* | *Intercommunal Vulnerability* | *Intercommunal Trust* | *Reliance on Institutional Power* |
|---|---|---|---|
| Collapsed: | | | |
| DCSG low, rapidly vanishing, particularly after the Maronites and other groups began to form strong paramilitary units in the post–May 1973 crisis. | High, increased rapidly after the 1971 exodus of the Palestinians to Lebanon from Jordan and the subsequent paralysis of the army, Parliament, and government, and the polarization of the presidency in the post–May 1973 crisis due to very high information complexity, low intercommunal predictability, and high intercommunal interdependence.<br><br>Strong interdependence among major sectarian groups enhanced incentives for debating state governance (hypothesis 1).<br><br>Intercommunal vulnerability increased with decreases in the scope of collective intentionality as commitments to existing rules and practices of state governance decreased (hypothesis 3). | Low, decreased rapidly after 1971 exodus of Palestinians to Lebanon from Jordan and subsequent paralysis of army, Parliament, and government, and polarization of presidency in post–May 1973 crisis—i.e., as scope of collective intentionality decreased in debates of 1973–1975 (hypothesis 5). | High—communal leaders had recourse to whatever institutional power they believed they had or could muster, with Maronite leadership enjoying lion's share of institutional power.<br><br>Increased rapidly after 1971 exodus of Palestinians to Lebanon from Jordan and subsequent paralysis of army, Parliament, and government, and polarization of presidency in post–May 1973 crisis—i.e., with rapidly decreasing scope of collective intentionality (hypothesis 8).<br><br>Increased as intercommunal trust decreased (hypothesis 9). |

analyze how the regional changes in 1967–73 helped to induce a heated debate on the form of state governance in Lebanon in the early 1970s.

*Post-1967 Demise of Nasserism and Egyptian Regional Leadership Role*

The 1967 war inaugurated a new chapter in the debate about regional order marked by a decline in pan-Arabism and an increasingly stronger adherence to the principle of state territorial sovereignty (Barnett 1998,162). Pan-Arabism lost most of its appeal by the mid-1960s after the UAR project had failed, the unification talks between Syria, Iraq, and Egypt had faded away, and the various military and political agreements between these and other Arab states had produced no results. The Six-Day War had devastating effects on Egypt. The Sinai desert was under Israeli control, and the Suez Canal was closed to shipping.[1] An exhausted and isolated Egypt abandoned its pan-Arabist mission and refocused its attention and energies on bettering its domestic socioeconomic conditions (Kerr 1971, 129). Yet pan-Arabism did not completely disappear from regional politics. It instead became expressed in terms of the Arab-Israeli conflict. Prior to the 1967 war, a state's stance toward the 1916 Sykes-Picot Agreement and the West in general defined it as either a radical or conservative Arab state. Beginning in the mid-1960s, those labels increasingly depended on where a state stood toward Israel (Barnett 1998, 163–64). Ultimately, at the September 1967 Khartoum summit, adhering to Arabism meant opposing Israel in what became known as "the three no's": no peace, no negotiations, no recognition.

Summitry rhetoric notwithstanding, many plans for Arab-Israeli peace were formulated, only to be quickly rejected. Convinced that diplomacy alone would never recover the Sinai desert and skeptical of American intentions, Nasser launched a major overhaul and expansion of Egypt's armed forces and engaged in a war of attrition (1969–70) to challenge Israel's hold on the Sinai Peninsula. However, a confluence of factors convinced a growing portion of the Egyptian political elite that the United States effectively held the keys to a solution, which meant that Cairo would have to come to terms with Washington first. The crushing defeat in the 1967 war shattered much of Egypt's self-confidence. This was compounded by a growing belief that the Soviet Union would not supply offensive weapons that Egypt needed to militarily recover the Sinai land. The Egyptian elite also became convinced that the United States would keep Israel strong enough to repulse any such recovery efforts. Seizing the opportunity of the moment, William Rogers, the U.S. secretary of state, put forward the so-called Rogers Plan on June 25, 1970, and immediately launched a dialogue. This effort eventually led to a long-awaited cease-fire in the war of attrition along the Suez Canal.[2] In accepting the Rogers Plan, Nasser signaled Egypt's readiness for an eventual peaceful settlement of the Arab-Israeli conflict. This meant the acceptance of Israel and acknowledged the role of the United States as a dominant power broker in the region. Jordan followed Egypt's lead and accepted the plan. Likewise, Israel accepted the plan in August.[3]

Egypt's abandonment of its leadership role in the Arab world and its peace overtures toward Israel had three important effects on the regional order, and on the domestic politics and foreign policy of Lebanon in particular. First, the torch of Arab leadership shifted from the radical to the conservative camp. This waning of Arab radicalism led to a rise of conservative regional politics, most importantly manifested in the regional shift in power from ideology to oil and economic capital (Dawisha 1983, 69). The dramatic shift was clearly noticeable at the Khartoum meeting in September 1967. Egyptian president Nasser and Saudi king Faisal reached an agreement to the effect that Nasser would stop his attempts to destabilize the Saudi regime, and the latter in return would provide Egypt with the financial aid needed to rebuild its army and hopefully retake the territory lost to Israel. More generally, Nasser renounced his irredentist claims by accepting the existing Arab territorial order and pledged to abandon all forms of subversive tactics against other Arab leaders (Hamroush 1984, 244, 254). Second, the Palestinian cause became a stand-alone dimension of inter-Arab and Arab-Israeli politics. The Palestinian Resistance acquired an increasingly independent and more autonomous role in the regional politics as well as the domestic politics in many Arab countries, particularly in Lebanon and Jordan. The Palestinian Resistance in effect became a radical challenge to the established Arab order, even if the Palestinian guerrillas were no match for the organized military power and resources of the Arab conservatives (Gerges 1994, 235). Third, Syria became the principal pretender for Arab leadership in the subregion of the Fertile Crescent. This had far-reaching consequences for the Lebanese polity, as discussed next.

### *Syria's Bid for Subregional Leadership in the Fertile Crescent*

Although Syria's bid for leadership is rooted in the ideology of the Syrian Ba<sup>c</sup>ath Party, which champions pan-Arab nationalism and unification of all Arab countries into one Arab nation, many Syrian leaders sought to focus their efforts on restoring a Greater Syria that would include Lebanon, Jordan, and the land of Palestine.[4] Syria's goal of enhanced regional role would become a realistic one only with the fulfillment of two conditions. On the regional level, Syria's rivals for power had to be contained, at least in the immediate subregional arena of the Fertile Crescent. Syria also needed sufficient internal stability such that it could seek a coalition with other Arab states from a position of domestic strength. This actually became possible after the radical faction of the Ba<sup>c</sup>ath Party assumed control in February 1966. Syria's leader, Salah Jadid, hence rejected the Egyptian leadership of the Arab world and even sought to "outdistance Nasser in militancy on nationalist and revolutionary issues," including the Palestinian cause (Kerr 1971, 42–43; 1972b, 47–48). Likewise, his successor, Hafiz al-Asad, continued to build a firm base of subregional power in the Fertile Crescent that would eventually enable Syria to supersede Egypt's regional stature (Jureidini and McLaurin 1979, 149–53; Dishon 1977, 28). This approach had three crucial dimensions: Syria's relationship with Lebanon, Syria's connections with the Palestinian issue, and the Syrian-Israeli conflict.

First, Syria's attitude toward Lebanon was ambivalent. Although Syria officially recognized Lebanon's de jure existence, it had refused to establish formal diplomatic relations with Lebanon. Syria gradually replaced Egypt as the external center—demanding allegiance and extending support—for both the Sunni and Shiite Lebanese politicians (Rabinovich 1979, 58). Second, the operations of the Palestinian guerrillas in Lebanon created new opportunities and imperatives for inter-Arab entanglement. At the Khartoum summit of August 1967, Arab governments had agreed that the Palestinian guerrillas could initiate activities against Israel from Egypt, Syria, or Jordan only, not Lebanon. However, the Arab consensus on Lebanon's right to neutrality had vanished by the time the Lebanese government and the Palestinian Resistance negotiated the Cairo Agreement of November 1969. One provision of the Cairo Agreement went so far as to emphasize that "the Palestinian armed struggle is in the interest of Lebanon as well as of the Palestinian revolution and all Arabs" (Snider 1979, 180). Syria thence continued to intervene in Lebanese politics on the ground that it could uphold the interests of the Palestinians in Lebanon better than their own leaders (Rabinovich 1979, 69). The Palestinians returned the favor and tended to regard the Syrians as their most important mentors in the Arab world, at least until Syria militarily intervened in Lebanon.[5] Third, the Egyptian strategies in part conditioned Syria's perceptions for the prospects of either peace or war with Israel. Syria dreaded the prospect of a succession of interim agreements between Egypt and Israel that would ignore the interests of other Arab states. As Egypt moved toward unilateral peace with Israel, Syria feared that this would limit not only Damascus's military options, but its diplomatic options as well (Rabinovich 1979, 57–59; Snider 1979, 185–86).

In sum, by the eve of its intervention in the Lebanese civil war in 1975–76, Syria's subregional stature had reached an unprecedented level. Syria could now afford to conduct an assertive foreign policy because it no longer was a state with a chronically unstable political system. Nor was it vulnerable to the foreign policy designs of stronger neighbors such as Nasser's Egypt. The Asad regime, after consolidating enough domestic support, established a network of ties in the Fertile Crescent, thereby turning Syria into a subregional power. Other Arab states, either collectively or unilaterally, did not seriously attempt to curb Syria's freedom of maneuvering in the Fertile Crescent, at least until its full-scale confrontation with the Palestinian Resistance in Lebanon.

*Palestinian Resistance*

The Palestinian Resistance to Israeli occupation emerged with the formation of Fateh in the mid-1950s in Cairo and Kuwait by Yasir Arafat, Salah Khalaf, and Khalil al-Wazir. Ideologically, the group espoused a form of Palestinian nationalism largely devoid of socioeconomic content. Fateh's goal of liberating Palestine through a Palestinian armed struggle clashed with pan-Arab formulations at the time (Brynen 1990, 23). The Arab League decided in 1964 to form the Palestine Liberation Organization (PLO) as a way of maintaining Arab and particularly Egyptian control over the Palestinian issue and therewith containing the Palestinian nationalist aspirations within manageable proportions. The Arab states thus forbade the PLO to interfere in their internal affairs. The PLO's military wing—the Palestinian Liberation Army—consisted not of guerrillas, but of regular forces attached to and controlled by the armies of Syria, Iraq, and Egypt. Notwithstanding these efforts by the Arab states to co-opt the Palestinian movement, the military wing of Fateh, al-ᶜAsifa (the storm), launched its first historic operation on January 1, 1965. Fateh's new strategy of armed struggle had three main objectives: first, to revitalize Palestinian self-identity; second, to remind Israel and the world of the Palestinians' existence; and third, to stoke the intensity of Arab-Israeli confrontation as part of a long-term war of liberation embracing both the Arab states and the Palestinian people. Over the next twenty-nine months, Fateh's Palestinian fidaʾiyyin (guerrillas) would carry out 175 military operations inside Israel (Jabber 1973, 172; Cobban 1984, 21–35). Such a rapid growth of militancy became a source of concern in most Arab capitals. The Arab states perceived fidaʾiyyin actions against Israel as uncontrolled and adventurous at least, and as dangerous invitations to Israeli reprisals at worst. Indeed, a growing number of Israeli punishing strikes against the neighboring Arab countries accompanied the escalation of fidaʾiyyin activity in the period between 1965 and 1967 (Jabber 1973, 168–173; Blechman 1972).

Yet the inability of Egypt, Syria, and Jordan to triumph on the battlefield in the 1967 war raised critical questions about the ability of a pan-Arabist approach to liberate Palestine. Such a turn of events seemed to vindicate the Fateh agenda on the necessity to liberate Palestine through a Palestinian armed struggle, thereby stimulating growth in the ranks of fidaʾiyyin. The latter increasingly became a viable alternative to the failed option of a regular interstate military confrontation. At the heart of the clash between the fidaʾiyyin's and pan-Arabist approaches was the question of a settlement with Israel. The Arab governments based their pan-Arabist posture on the issue in terms of their acceptance or rejection of UN Resolution 242. The UAR and

Jordan declared their endorsement of the resolution; Syria did not. The PLO and various Palestinian commando organizations dismissed the resolution as a sell-out, inasmuch as it signified an Arab acceptance of Israel as a sovereign state and relegated the claims of the Palestinians to a just settlement of the refugee problem (Kerr 1971, 131).

That the Palestinian Resistance was becoming an independent regional actor is evident in the events of the 1970–71 Black September episode in Jordan. This was the most dramatic challenge to post-1967 regional order (Kerr 1971, 137). Jordan, which had annexed the Palestinian West Bank in the aftermath of the 1948 war, saw virtually any expression of Palestinian militancy or nationalism as a serious political threat to its domestic stability (Brynen 1990, 24). King Hussein launched a major Jordanian military drive against Jordan-based Palestinian guerrillas on September 14, 1970. This was partly out of fear that the fidaʾiyyin's attacks on Israel would sabotage the Arab truce with Israel, but primarily because the guerrillas were becoming powerful enough to challenge his government's authority. On September 27, 1970, Hussein and Arafat agreed to a fourteen-point cease-fire under Nasser's mediation, officially ending the war. This had a strong implication for Lebanon—it became the practical base for PLO operations against Israel.

Heretofore, Jordan had been the external headquarters and main operational base of the fidaʾiyyin, accounting for over two-thirds of all cross-border guerrilla operations between June 1967 and August 1970. After the conflict with Jordan, the PLO officially moved its headquarters to Damascus—but in practice to Beirut. This, combined with Egypt's acceptance of the Rogers Plan in August 1970 and Syria's restriction of guerrilla activity on the Golan Heights the following year, made Lebanon the most important sanctuary for the Palestinian armed movement. It also made Lebanon the only state bordering Palestine within which the PLO enjoyed significant freedom of action. Over the duration of the Black September crisis, an estimated fifteen thousand to thirty thousand Palestinians displaced by the fighting in Jordan had moved to Lebanon, including several thousand armed guerrillas (Said et al. 1983, 13; O'Ballance 1974, 205). Lebanon's Palestinian population lent sympathy and provided recruits to the bourgeoning liberation movement.[6] The Palestinian movement learned a major lesson from the Jordan war. A continued survival of the Palestinian Resistance required the mobilization of a large base of popular Arab support. Such a mass support would both constrain the ability of reactionary regimes to weaken the Resistance and force them to stand by the PLO in times of need (Brynen 1990, 64).

Lebanon had already been fertile soil for the Palestinian Resistance, even before the Black September episode. The Lebanese authorities had been in firm control of Palestinian refugee camps and were determined to remain so (Turki 1972, 52–78; Sayigh 1979, 130–36). After 1967, however, the stakes for the Palestinian population in Lebanon changed dramatically. One survey of popular opinion conducted in September 1968 by the Lebanese newspaper *al-Nahar* found that 79 percent of the Lebanese population unreservedly supported the fidaʾiyyin (Brynen 1990, 47). The funeral in April 1968 of the first Lebanese Fatah volunteer to die in action, Khalil al-Jamal, also illustrates the massive popularity of the Palestinian Resistance. Between one hundred fifty thousand and a quarter of a million people attended his funeral procession from the Syrian border to Beirut. The strength and role of the Palestinian Resistance in Lebanon increased even more in the aftermath of the October 1973 War.

### *Consequences of the 1973 October War*

On October 6, 1973, Egyptian armed forces launched a successful surprise attack across the Suez Canal. The Syrians carried out an attack on Israel at the same time. Israel was able to counterattack and succeeded in surrounding the Egyptian Third Army. The UN Security Council passed Resolution 338 on October 22, 1973, calling for a cease-fire by all parties. In January 1974, Kissinger began his shuttle diplomacy between Egypt and Israel. Anwar al-Sadat and Golda Meir separately signed a first disengagement agreement on January 18, 1974, and a second one on September 1, 1975 (Bell 1974, 531–33; Bell 1977; Quandt 1977).

The 1973 war reshaped the regional order in three important ways. First, the war became a turning point in the history of Egyptian foreign policy as well as domestic politics. President Anwar al-Sadat did not fight the war to rejuvenate pan-Arabism but rather to weaken pan-Arabist Egyptian patriotism and replace it with a vision of an Egyptian Egypt, away from Nasser's pan-Arabist shadow. Egypt henceforth retreated into regional isolation and deviated from the Arab consensus by moving toward a unilateral peace with Israel (Ajami 1979, 3–30).

Second, the PLO actively participated in the war alongside the Egyptians in the west, the Syrians on the Golan Heights, and alone inside Palestine and across the Lebanese border. Thenceforth, the PLO's international status grew rapidly, and its position in both inter-Arab and international politics dramatically changed. The Arab leaders at the Rabat summit conference in October 1974 unanimously declared the PLO as "the sole legitimate representative of the Palestinian people."[7] The Arab League subsequently pushed the UN to grant the PLO an observer status in its General Assembly. The Palestinians, however, were increasingly concerned that a piecemeal Arab-Israeli settlement would leave the Palestinians' national rights unfulfilled. This became particularly alarming as U.S. secretary of state Henry Kissinger began his step-by-step diplomacy marked by the Sinai I disengagement agreement in January 1974.

Third, the war became a source of division among the Palestinians themselves. Differences over how best to respond to post-October Arab-Israeli diplomatic efforts and in particular the proposed Geneva Peace Conference undermined a sense of Palestinian unity and coordination, even within the PLO. For example, in June 1974, the Palestinian National Council (PNC) resolutions sparked fighting in Lebanon between two factions of the Palestinian Resistance (the PFLP-GC and DFLP). In September, the PFLP withdrew from the PLO Executive Committee and boycotted the meetings of the Central Council in protest over an alleged misuse of the PNC resolutions to legalize a course of deviation and surrender. The Arab Liberation Front, PFLP-GC, and PSF soon joined the Popular Front in condemning the PLO's political direction (Brynen 1990, 75).

In sum, on the eve of the May 1973–April 1975 period, the regional order was quite different from that of the pre-1967 era. Egypt withdrew from Arab politics and was in the process of building a separate peace with Israel. This had two important effects. First, Nasserism and Egyptian-led pan-Arabism disappeared from the regional political map and were not there anymore to motivate the Arab masses or force other Arab leaders to follow the Egyptian policies for the region. This in turn allowed Syria some room for seeking subregional leadership in the Fertile Crescent. Second, the Palestinian Resistance via the PLO became not only a regional actor with its specifically Palestinian agenda and strategy but also an important player in domestic politics in two states of the Fertile Crescent, Lebanon and Jordan. This, however, ultimately resulted in the Black September confrontation between the Jordanian state and the PLO. As a result, the PLO armed forces and tens of thousands of Palestinian refugees moved to Lebanon. This in turn reinforced the role of the Palestinian Resistance in Lebanon. The latter became the only practical base of armed operations against Israel. Egypt's withdrawal from the Arab scene, the rise of Syria as a would-be hegemon in the Fertile Crescent, the diplomatic strengthening of the PLO, and the reinforced presence of the Palestinian Resistance in Lebanon were all manifestations of the transformation that had occurred in the regional order—pan-Arabism was not a constitutive norm of inter-Arab politics anymore. Nor was the Arab-Israeli conflict perceived solely as a pan-Arab issue. Neither Egypt nor the PLO perceived it or dealt with it from such an angle; Egyptian and Palestinian territorial nationalism became accepted as constitutive of the regional political discourse.

An important consequence of this new regional order was that Lebanon had once again been pressured to abandon its doctrine of foreign policy neutrality on three counts. First, Syria's bid for hegemony in the Fertile Crescent reaffirmed its old aspirations to dominate Lebanon by penetrating its domestic politics. In a joint communiqué, Beirut and Damascus agreed that Syria would provide Lebanon with defensive assistance against Israel.[8] Lebanon hence lost whatever advantage a policy of neutrality might have had for maintaining a viable degree of external sovereignty. This was underscored a week later when the Israeli forces attacked and destroyed the southern Lebanese village of Kfar Chouba.[9] Second, the Palestinian Resistance undermined Lebanon's doctrine of foreign policy neutrality by launching its anti-Israeli attacks and operations from Lebanon. Moreover, the Palestinians were determined to prevent and preempt another Black September in Lebanon and hence became increasingly involved in Lebanese domestic politics. Third, Israel attempted to stop the Palestinian attacks against Israel by increasing the stakes for Lebanon to unbearable levels. Israel hoped that doing so would force the Lebanese government and army to put an end to anti-Israeli Palestinian operations from the Lebanese territory. The confluence of Syria's bid for hegemony, the presence and strong involvement in domestic coalitional politics of the Palestinian Resistance in Lebanon, and Israel's aggressive policies toward Lebanon strongly contributed to shaping an already unfolding debate in Lebanon on state governance. Whether and how to transform state governance in dealing with these challenges and imperatives became two overriding issues around which domestic politics revolved during the May 1973–April 1975 period. The debates eventually culminated in a civil war in 1975.

### *Debating State Governance, All the Way Down into the Abyss*

The collective intentionality that underpinned the form of state governance in Lebanon strongly depended on a confessional balance of state institutional power defined by the 1943 National Pact and Constitution. The debates about state governance in the period 1973–75 seriously threatened from the beginning to undermine the collective intentionality underpinning the confessional system. All debating parties—both anti- and pro-status quo forces—understood the gravity and the stakes of the debates. Yet, in contrast to the period 1957–58, collective intentionality continuously eroded through the 1973–75 period, leading inexorably to a bloody civil war in April 1975.

Collective intentionality eroded through a series of domestic debates around two key issues. First, various sectarian groups sharply differed on whether to transform the distribution of state institutional power, if not completely abolish the confessional system. Second, how to deal with the presence of an armed Palestinian Resistance in Lebanon, which was increasingly becoming an autonomous actor in Lebanese politics, widened the divide even more. The debates struck at the heart of the Lebanese polity as defined by the 1943 National Pact, raising questions about Lebanon's national identity and sovereignty. Moreover, the two issues strongly overlapped with one another, thereby making the debates feed back into one another and tremendously magnifying the difficulty of resolving any one issue to the satisfaction of any one group. Yet none of the two key issues was sufficient by itself to lead to a vanishing scope of collective intentionality; not only the debates on the two key issues but also their mutual feedback were all necessary for the scope of collective intentionality to vanish in April 1975. By early 1975, the conflicting sides were able to "persistently agree to persist disagreeing" on both key issues, thereby making it almost impossible to preserve the integrity of the polity and reinstate peaceful and accommodative coexistence and cooperation. The conflicting sides began to prepare heavily for military confrontation when it became clear that the government had become incapable of authoritatively addressing any one of the key issues. To trace the evolution of collective intentionality, I organize the discussion around a number of important events through which the debates about the redistribution of institutional power and the presence and role of an armed Palestinian Resistance unfolded.

*Debating the Distribution of State Institutional Power*

Divergent reactions to the 1967 Six-Day War between status quo challengers, epitomized by Druze leader Kamal Jumblatt, and conservative forces, epitomized by Maronite leaders Pierre Gemayel and Camille Chamoun, contributed to the widening of existing divisions in Lebanese society. The Maronite Right viewed the Arab debacle as an opportunity to renounce the Arab nationalist movement and to strengthen Lebanon's ties with the West.[10] Gemayel declared that the time had come "to internationalize Lebanon's neutrality" and make it "another Switzerland," no longer part of the Arab world.[11] Gemayel, Chamoun, and Eddé announced on August 30, 1967, their plans to form the Triple Alliance—al-Hilf al-Thulathi—as a preparation for the upcoming general elections of 1968.[12]

The Druze leader Kamal Jumblatt was drawing a substantially different lesson from the Arab defeat in the 1967 war.[13] His agenda was henceforth to seek a major revision of the Lebanese institutions to eliminate all sectarian privileges and allow Lebanon to assume its national responsibilities in the Arab world. Jumblatt and like-minded elites launched a political debate on whether and how to redistribute state institutional power in the Lebanese system. Jumblatt began to forge close political links with virtually every organization, radical and conservative alike, as long as it was seeking a change to the status quo, including of course the Palestinian Resistance.[14] He hence established in 1969 the Lebanese National Movement (LNM), a coalition of leftist and radical parties, around his own Progressive Socialist Party (PSP). The LNM demanded a thorough de-confessionalization of the Lebanese system, thereby de facto calling for an abrogation of the 1943 National Pact. This anti-status quo coalition became more determined in seeking a radical change in the system after its candidates did not fare well against traditional *zu'ama* backing President Franjieh in the 1972 parliamentary elections. The LNM candidates demanded changes in the existing sectarian distribution of seats in the Chamber of Deputies to a more truly people-based representation across sectarian lines. The LNM also called for an end to the principle of confessionalism in government employment, an amendment of the Constitution to redefine the division of responsibility among the members of the executive branch, and a reorganization of the army. In addition, the LNM called for a removal of all restrictions on naturalization, which had made it impossible for many members of some communities to acquire citizenship (Salibi 1976, 61–62, 82–83, 112–13).

However, Jumblatt and his anti–status quo alliance were not the only ones seeking to reshape the distribution of state institutional power. There also were challenges at the presidential, street, and intelligentsia levels as well as from radical political movements in the Sunni and Shiite populations, who were not necessarily allied with Jumblatt. After Fuad Shihab (1958–64) left the presidency, Presidents Charles Helou (1964–70) and Suleiman Franjieh (1970–76) endeavored to strengthen the presidency even more. Helou helped to weaken the strong "secular" character of the presidency that Shihab had established. Helou's close association with Maronite leaders such as Chamoun and Eddé strengthened the movement toward anti-Shihabism, which was later joined by Gemayel and Franjieh. In return, Helou's weak presence in the Maronite "heartland" strengthened the hands of both Gemayel and Chamoun in reasserting old notions of Maronite ideology and atavistic fears of Muslims (Goria 1985, 247). Likewise, Franjieh acted to carve out greater institutional autonomy, but in a way that would secure almost exclusive power for the Maronites at the expense of the Sunni prime minister. For example, Franjieh purposefully overlooked prestigious Sunni leaders such as Salam and Karami and appointed instead weaker, lower-ranking Sunni politicians as prime ministers. These actions helped to erode a customary intercommunal solidarity between the Sunni and Maronite *za'ims*, especially at times of crisis.

In contrast, the streets and intelligentsia sought to change radically the institutional arrangement.[15] The system of political sectarianism and the division of political posts among the various sects engendered a leadership *mahsubiya* (favoritism and corruption) system, which had become a pillar of Lebanese politics. The challenges to the positions and roles of the *za'ims* unfolded in two ways. First, emerging radical political movements in Lebanon threatened to dislodge these traditional leaders from their central political role. For example, although the outcome of the parliamentary elections of 1972 demonstrated how weighted the electoral system was in favor of these traditional leaders, the surprising victory of a young, previously unknown neo-Nasserist candidate against an established conservative rival in Beirut was an early indication of an emerging radical mood that would soon threaten seriously the Lebanese politics as usual. The vigor and intensity with which the anti–status quo forces assaulted the 1943 National Pact during the electoral campaign illustrate the mounting pressure for change (Khalidi 1979,

42). Second, the presence of the Palestinian Resistance had a strong influence on the poor Sunni people and threatened to radicalize them and cause them to drift away from their traditional leaders. This thereby forced the *za'ims* to pay more attention to Muslim rights and grievances. The *zu'ama* contended, for example, that since the Muslims clearly constituted a majority of the population, they deserved a bigger share of political power, much more than what the National Pact had guaranteed to them. This meant that since the Maronites were no longer the largest community in Lebanon, they were not entitled to continue exclusively enjoying all the political privileges they had possessed since independence. The Sunni leaders coined the slogan *al-Musharakah*—an equitable distribution of power between the president and the prime minister—to encapsulate these calls for change in the distribution of state institutional power.[16]

Likewise, the Shiite community began to organize itself more efficiently and demand its rights more strongly.[17] Although the Shiites had enjoyed official recognition since 1926 as a community separate from the Sunnis, they did not acquire an effective spokesperson until after Imam Musa Sadr established the Higher Shiite Council in 1967.[18] Mobilizing the Shiite community against the government became a core strategy of the council. Thus, on May 26, 1970, Sadr called for demonstrations and a general strike to protest against the government policy of neglect of the Shiite-populated south. In February 1974, the council formally demanded that the community receive the number of posts in government to which it was entitled under the 1943 National Pact. It also demanded that citizenship be promptly granted to the tens of thousands of Lebanese, chiefly Shiites in the deprived regions, who had long been denied it. The council also accused the state of negligence in defending the south against Israeli aggression.[19] Imam Sadr established a new organization, named the Movement of the Deprived—Harakat al-Mahrumin. This organization would ultimately become an important actor in the civil war and in its aftermath.

In sum, as the critical period of May 1973–April 1975 approached, the distribution of state institutional power was at stake for most actors in Lebanon. The coalition of leftist and Druze organizations sought to radically transform the existing distribution of institutional power by abolishing the confessional basis of the state. The Shiites first sought to acquire their rights as stipulated in the 1943 National Pact. They later joined ranks with the leftist organization to call for a transformation of a system that had made them a most deprived community. In contrast, the Maronites, particularly the Kataeb led by Pierre Gemayel and the National Liberal Party led by Camille Chamoun, opposed any change to the existing distribution of state institutional power. This position became more intransigent during the Franjieh presidency (1970–76) as the president sought to strengthen his powers at the expense of the Sunni prime minister. Although the president abided by the letter of the Constitution and the 1943 National Pact, he in fact increasingly moved away from the spirit of the confessional system.[20]

In effect, these debates on whether to transform the distribution of state institutional power unavoidably challenged the collective intentionality underpinning the Lebanese system of state governance. Because the debates on the distribution of state institutional power struck at the 1943 National Pact, the scope of collective intentionality underpinning state governance was now at stake. Hence, rejecting the National Pact, as the Jumblatt-led coalition of leftist organizations did, implied that collective intentionality was rapidly decreasing. The less agreement there was on the distribution of state institutional power, the lower the scope of collective intentionality of state governance was becoming. The erosion of collective intentionality continued even more through another crucial debate that slowly dominated the Lebanese scene, namely, the debate on the presence of an armed Palestinian Resistance in Lebanon.

### *Debating the Presence of an Armed Palestinian Resistance*

Debating the presence of an armed Palestinian Resistance in Lebanon and its repercussions on both Lebanon's relations with Israel and Lebanese domestic politics increasingly occupied center stage in the aftermath of the 1967 war because of two factors. First, in time the Palestinian Resistance grew more autonomous and became more involved in Lebanese politics, particularly after the 1970–71 Black September episode in Jordan. The issue threatened to disrupt the existing distribution of political power in the Lebanese confessional because the Palestinian refugees including the Resistance were mostly Muslims. The Maronite community and Christians at large perceived this as a threat. The 1943 National Pact had put the Christians in a clearly dominant position based on a 1932 census that the Christians were then the largest community. In addition, most of the Palestinian Resistance soon joined the coalition of anti–status quo leftist organizations.

Second, the costs of Israeli retaliations for the Lebanese societal fabric and economy became too high. This is illustrated in the following few events. On May 12, 1968, a serious exchange of shellfire erupted between Israeli and Lebanese forces. The event followed Israeli shelling of the village of Houleh in retaliation for a Palestinian rocket attack on Kibbutz Margaliot. Throughout that summer, Lebanese villages in the south came under heavy Israeli shelling. Likewise, on December 26, 1968, Palestinian commandos attacked an El Al plane in Athens. A day later, Israel retaliated by landing a helicopter-borne commando force at Beirut International Airport and destroying nearly the entire Lebanese civilian air fleet. On September 5, 1972, nine Israeli athletes and a trainer were taken hostage and later killed during the Munich Olympic Games as their captors, a Palestinian group known as Black September, clashed with West German security forces. Following a massive buildup of forces on Lebanon's southern border, the Israelis struck for three days at the Bared refugee camp near Tripoli, Rafid village in the Bekaa, Rashava al Wadi, as well as targets in Syria's Lataquia region and near Damascus. By January 14, 1974, Israeli military attacks against southern Lebanese targets began reaching a new level of intensity. The destruction of homes, and even whole villages, in the south accelerated the exodus of southern Lebanese to the relatively safe but socially and economically demoralizing "Belt of Misery" region surrounding Beirut (Kazziha 1979, 41–44).

The presence of an armed Palestinian Resistance in Lebanon became a serious source of concern for the politically dominant community in Lebanon—the Maronites—and a source of strength for the anti-status quo forces.[21] Matters began to worsen between the Resistance and the Lebanese government, ultimately leading to clashes as the objectives for the two sides collided. For the Lebanese government, maintaining its internal and external sovereignties was of utmost importance, goals that oftentimes conflicted directly with the necessity of freedom of action that the Resistance required in carrying its guerrilla agenda. The clashes were the more serious because they often had political ramifications within the Lebanese body politic. Massive popular demonstrations would usually flare up following the clashes, thereby posing a threat to the stability and integrity of Lebanon. The increase in the frequency and seriousness of clashes between the Lebanese army and the Palestinian Resistance ultimately led to the so-called Cairo Agreement.[22] The Palestinians agreed not to launch operations across the border with Israel, wear military uniforms in public, or take sides in Lebanese internal affairs. The Lebanese army in return agreed to allow the commandos free access to Syrian supply lines, relax restrictions previously placed on refugee camps, and give the commandos formal recognition of their cause.[23]

The Cairo Agreement, however, was far from effective in bringing an end to the clashes. Thus, for example, on March 17, 1970, a clash between the Lebanese army and Palestinian guerrillas near Bint Jubayl in the south left one guerrilla officer dead and two others wounded. A Lebanese Ministry of Defense communiqué issued shortly thereafter described the incident as a misunderstanding. The Higher Political Committee for Palestinian Affairs in Lebanon instead suggested that the killings were deliberate and called for an immediate investigation, a dismissal of those responsible, and an end to security forces' provocations and restrictions on the commandos' freedom of action (Brynen 1990, 58). Nor did the Cairo Agreement prevent the occurrence of violence between the Palestinian commandos and Lebanese groups that opposed the presence of an armed Palestinian Resistance in Lebanon. Only a week after the March clash between the commandos and the Lebanese army, a group of young Kataeb gunners (led by Gemayel's son, Bashir) ambushed a guerrilla funeral cortege as it was passing through the predominantly Christian village of Kahhala on its way from Beirut to Damascus. Clashes between the Palestinians and Phalange militiamen ensued in Beirut in the following hours.

The recurrence of violence between the Lebanese army and the Resistance and between the Maronites and the Resistance highlighted the difficult position of the Palestinians in Lebanon. On the one hand, the Palestinians had to protect their security and freedom of action to continue their guerrilla war against the Israelis. On the other hand, the PLO was intent on forestalling any escalation that might damage the position the Palestinian Resistance had won with the 1969 Cairo Agreement. Yet the two goals often collided with one another as the Lebanese army and the Maronites sought to maintain Lebanese sovereignty. In continuous efforts to minimize the dilemma and avoid confrontations that could only be costly to the Resistance and would thereby divert its attention and resources from its raison d'être—fighting for the liberation of Palestine—the PLO generally responded to provocations by announcing measures designed to calm tensions in the country. In addition, September 1970 marked the beginning of King Hussein's military offensive against the Palestinian movement in Jordan. Hence, the PLO had a good reason to avoid conflict with the Lebanese administration. After the conflict with Jordan, Lebanon de facto became the Palestinians' most important sanctuary and the only state bordering Palestine within which the PLO enjoyed any significant freedom of action (Said et al. 1983, 13; O'Ballance 1974, 205).

In sum, prior to the May 1973 crisis, the presence of an active, armed Palestinian Resistance in Lebanon had two effects on Lebanon: Israeli attacks at a high cost to Lebanon and violent clashes with the Lebanese government and army. Both effects had a strong impact on Lebanon's sovereignty and integrity. This was compounded by the fact that the major groups and factions of Lebanon perceived the presence of an armed Palestinian Resistance in quite different ways, as explained next.

### GOVERNMENT POLICIES AND ACTIONS

In the post-1967 period, wide and growing popular support for the Palestinian Resistance compelled the government to assume a positive attitude toward the Palestinians. For example, on April 27, 1968, some 150,000 people attended the funerals of seventeen-year-old Khalil al-Jamal. Even the Kataeb leader Gemayel and other Maronite leaders such as Chamoun and Eddé, who normally would not show much enthusiasm for the Palestinians, felt obligated to send delegates to the ceremony. Likewise, Prime Minister Abdullah Yafi promised to a big crowd demonstrating against Israel that the government "will meet your demands and give arms to volunteers who join the Lebanese army to liberate Palestine"[24]

However, this show of support for the Palestinian Resistance by government officials did not consolidate into a policy; nor did it last for long. For example, when Israel destroyed nearly the entire Lebanese civilian air fleet, President Helou opted for a mere official declaration simultaneously reaffirming Lebanon's support for the legitimate aspirations of the Palestinian people and his intention to defend Lebanese sovereignty against Israel's attacks.[25] Not only was the declaration ill received in many quarters of Lebanese society, it also magnified already mounting political and security costs for the Lebanese government. Thus, for example, large numbers of students from Beirut's four major universities began a general strike on January 2, 1969, both to protest against the Israeli raid on Beirut International Airport and to demonstrate their solidarity with the Palestinians. Five days later, the residents of the cities of Sidon and Tyre launched their own general strike and called for the introduction of military conscription for the punishment of those responsible for not repelling the Israeli attack.[26] Moreover, Prime Minister Yafi fell under enormous pressure from his Muslim constituents to adopt a militant policy on the Palestinian issue, forcing him to resign on January 8, 1969.[27] Yafi's resignation created a ministerial crisis, which Helou attempted to solve a week later by appointing Rashid Karami as premier. Karami discovered quickly enough that his effort to pursue a moderate course was not an easy course of action. Indeed, Jumblatt's demands that Karami adopt a militant policy toward Israel calling for massive allocations in the defense budget and for the institution of military conscription undermined the prime minister's ability to find a middle ground. Karami chose to step down because he was unable to directly challenge the policies of Jumblatt, upon whom he relied for political support in Tripoli and whose national stature was far greater than Karami's. Jumblatt took his pro-commando campaign even further and, for example, on April 29, 1969, accused the government of not only failing to protect Lebanon's sovereignty against Israeli aggression but also that government actions had resulted in the killing of over twenty innocent demonstrators and the injury of dozens more (Nasrallah 1969, 180–81).

Violent clashes between the Palestinian commandos and the Israelis reached a new level of intensity, prompting the Lebanese army to launch a campaign aimed at cutting the Palestinian supply line from Syria and reestablishing Lebanese authority. This led to protracted clashes between the Lebanese army and the Palestinian Resistance.[28] The Lebanese army, however, stopped short of seriously damaging the Resistance because it could not subdue the Palestinians without incurring the wrath of the Lebanese Muslim population and Syria's anger. The Lebanese government thus signed the Cairo Agreement with the PLO. Jumblatt, the anti-status quo alliance, and the bulk of the Muslim establishment welcomed the Cairo Agreement. Helou also hailed the accord as consolidating Lebanon's sovereignty and independence while dedicating Lebanon's existence to the support of the Palestinian cause. The Kataeb leader Gemayel declared the agreement to be a mistake, urging instead that the Palestinian guerrillas move from Lebanon to other Arab countries. Chamoun followed suit. Soon the NLP members of the Chamber of Deputies began demanding a full debate on the matter. Raymond Eddé was against the agreement from the outset on the ground that it compromised Lebanese sovereignty. The conservative members of the Lebanese Parliament complained of armed men in the streets, training in the camps, and incidents of cross-border shelling. They proclaimed the Cairo Agreement as a failure.

In practice, the Cairo Agreement never produced any sort of lasting truce. That matters did not improve in any major way as clashes continued to occur amid rising confrontation in the south prompted newly elected president Suleiman Franjieh to depart from his predecessor's position of support for the Cairo Agreement. He instead called on the government to take a tougher stance on guerrilla violations of the Lebanese law. Thus, the Lebanese army liaison office issued on July 5, 1971, more-restrictive regulations on Palestinian deployment in the western and central sectors. Moreover, in the wake of a three-day Israeli occupation of south Lebanon in late February 1972, the Lebanese army was ordered to occupy vacated guerrilla positions to prevent the guerrillas' return.

In sum, the government could not adopt a consistent policy toward the Palestinian Resistance. It instead remained torn between upholding Lebanese sovereignty, minimizing popular upheaval, and seeking to satisfy most parties who were at odds with one another. The government often vacillated between assuming an authoritative policy and seeking compromise on the issue with various groups. Yet such a mixed strategy only exacerbated the problem, eventually leading the main parties not to put much faith in the government, particularly the leading parties of the Maronite community. This in turn helped to undermine the collective intentionality underpinning state governance. The Maronite position is illustrative. If the Maronite community, which was at the core of the system of state governance, did not believe in the system anymore under conditions in which many other forces were already raising questions about it, one can reasonably argue that the scope of collective intentionality was rapidly vanishing. The positions and strategies of the two most important Maronite organizations, the Kataeb and the National Liberal Party, are clearly indicative in this respect.

### THE MARONITES: POSITIONS AND STRATEGIES

Until the late 1960s, the Maronites had not sensed any serious challenge to the political-institutional status quo, barring the early weeks of the 1958 civil war. The developments of the period 1967–75 thus became the first serious challenge to the privileged position of the Maronites. Two conservative parties dominated and drove the Maronite political views and actions, namely the Kataeb (Phalange), led by Pierre Gemayel, and the National Liberal Party (NLP), led by Camille Chamoun. Although the Phalange Party became national in character during the years 1967–75, it nonetheless remained very sectarian in its constituency and leadership. The NLP power base increased after it allied itself with the Phalange Party and National Bloc, particularly after the parliamentary elections of 1968. By the late 1960s, the National Liberal Party had also acquired a clear ideology, centered on the safeguarding of the free enterprise system, against incursions from the radical Left.[29] Although the Kataeb and NLP differed on various issues, they more often than not agreed on the issue of the armed Palestinian Resistance as well as on the post-1967 regional upheavals.

First, the Maronite reaction to the regional upheavals between 1966 and 1968 was not unlike their previous reaction in 1956–58 (Deeb 1980, 23; Salama 1970, 12). All their old fears reemerged, and they revived the old narrow conception of Lebanese nationalism. This culminated in the formation of al-Hilf al-Thulathi—the Tripartite Alliance—between the Phalange, Raymond Eddé's National Bloc, and Chamoun's National Liberal Party (Zuwiyya 1972, 77). The Hilf collectively focused on the government's inability to control the Palestinian commando activities and the Israeli retaliatory raids usually following them. Gemayel, Chamoun, and Eddé convened a major strategy conference for the Hilf on March 7, 1969. The conference denounced an existing disequilibrium in the delegation of constitutional authority, the sterility of the parliamentary system, a paralysis of democratic institutions, a lingering administrative corruption, and the exploitation of government offices and privileges for personal ends and oligarchic rule. As a remedy to these institutional ills, the Hilf called for the formation of a national unity cabinet. It also called for an escalation of parliamentary opposition, mass rallies and demonstrations, nationwide strikes, and specific acts of civil disobedience (Entelis 1974, 170).

Second, the Maronite parties began seriously preparing for unilaterally defending their rights and self-described best future for Lebanon. Why, asked many Maronite citizens, especially the more militant members of the Kataeb and NLP, was Lebanon to be victimized by an armed struggle movement that had largely failed to carry its armed struggle into Israel itself? As early as spring 1969, the Kataeb Party began reinforcing its existing military capabilities.[30] Soon, however, the Kataeb could not resist using their new capabilities by launching attacks on Palestinian targets. More generally, violent clashes erupted more often between the Kataeb Party militiamen and the Palestinian commandos. Once begun, such fighting would often continue for days in a row until a settlement would finally be concluded, such as the one sponsored by the Egyptian foreign minister Riad on March 31, 1969, following the Kahale crisis.

Third, the Maronites were not ready to accept any agreement with the Palestinian Resistance that fell short of curbing the commandos. Not surprisingly, most Maronites perceived the 1969 Cairo Agreement as proof that the Palestinians had become a major defiant actor on the Lebanese scene.

Fourth, the emerging confluence between the Palestinians and avowed anti–status quo radical Lebanese groups and organizations under Jumblatt's leadership alarmed the Maronite parties. The latter feared that a Palestinian alliance with Jumblatt's Progressive Front would shift the balance of power and facilitate a Muslim takeover of Lebanon (Goria 1985, 118). Hence, the more Jumblatt pressed for reforms toward state de-confessionalization, the more the Maronites would see nothing but a leftist-Palestinian conspiracy to dislodge them from their power position as guaranteed under the 1943 National Pact. The Maronite leaders saw the commandos not as the Arab vanguards in the struggle against Zionism as they claimed to be, but rather as a fifth column within the Lebanese polity. A large communist conference in January (organized by the anti–status quo forces with which the Palestinians were allied), a series of bomb blasts in Beirut during the same month, and the escalation of Israeli retaliatory raids in the south all conspired to convince many Maronites of the validity of their views.

Mobilizing the Lebanese people, and more importantly the Maronite community, against the presence of an armed Palestinian Resistance in Lebanon thus became a high priority item on the Kataeb and NLP political agenda.[31] The Maronite parties increasingly relied on three main strategies: to strengthen their popular bases and mobilize their community against the Palestinian Resistance, to step up military preparation, and to attempt to convince the government to take effective measures against the Palestinian Resistance.

### THE NATIONAL MOVEMENT: POSITIONS AND STRATEGIES

The anti–status quo movement was a broad coalition embracing the entire activist Muslim-leftist opposition. The movement led by Jumblatt included already established Lebanese parties and more recently formed ones, the Lebanese branches of pan-Arab parties, a number of popular action-oriented ad hoc groups, and student organizations. Their common goal was a revolution against the political status quo through de-confessionalism. Their common opponents were both the Maronite and the traditional Muslim establishments. Their strategic ally was the Palestinian Resistance.

Rallying around the issue of the Palestinian Resistance and its continued presence in Lebanon was a first step in bringing together various leftist and progressive parties and organizations as well as a number of traditional Muslim leaders. King Hussein's successful attack on the Palestinian guerrillas in Jordan, which began in September 1970 and ended in late 1971, strongly reinforced this alliance. While most Sunni leaders were content to verbally articulate the popular mood in Lebanon favoring the Palestinian cause, Jumblatt sought to combine verbal support with a program of action to reform the Lebanese political system (Jumblatt 1982, 94). The Palestinian Resistance movement gave Jumblatt a cause around which he hoped to exercise broad national influence as a champion of the 350,000 Palestinians living in Lebanon. He believed that the present situation required a nationalist government with a clear Arab point of view whose main objective would be a confrontation with Israel. Such a nationalist government could not "include elements, some of which have side-agreements with Israel while they verbally support the Arabs . . . it is better . . . to stay out of power and manipulate the masses to compel the rulers to execute the popular demands."[32]

In sum, in the aftermath of the 1967 war, the Palestinian Resistance increasingly consolidated its presence in Lebanon, thereafter slowly occupying center stage both in Lebanon's foreign policy with Israel and in domestic politics. This resulted in a mounting polarization of the Lebanese polity, regarding not only the presence of the Resistance itself, but also the preservation of the existing form of state governance. That many of the anti–status quo forces had existed prior to the 1967 war does not weaken the argument that the presence of the Palestinian Resistance (and ensuing Israeli actions against Lebanon) provided *the* factor that both qualitatively and quantitatively shaped the debates on the form of state governance in Lebanon. The polarization of the Lebanese polity undermined the existing scope of collective intentionality underpinning state governance. Put differently, the polarization of the Lebanese polity was about the very constitutive rules and practices of state governance as defined in the 1943 National Pact—the anti–status quo forces wanting to abrogate the National Pact with the conservative forces struggling to reinforce it. This implied that there was no collective agreement on preserving the constitutive rules and practices of state governance. The more opposed (and at times anathema to each other) were the views, strategies, and actions of the various parties in the debates on the Palestinian Resistance, the more the scope of collective intentionality decreased, eventually reaching very low levels at the beginning of the May 1973 crisis.

### *Debates in the Post–May 1973 Crisis: Toward the Abyss*

The mutually reinforcing debates on redistributing state institutional power and the presence of the armed Palestinian Resistance in Lebanon became more confrontational as the opposing actors (including the Palestinian Resistance) began to prepare for drastic measures such as acquiring weapons and military training. The spark would eventually come on April 10, 1973. An Israeli commando raid in Rue Verdun in the heart of Beirut left three major Palestinian figures dead.[33] The failure of the Lebanese security forces to intercept the raiders raised a storm of protest within the Palestinian and Muslim circles. Jumblatt accused the Lebanese government of being unwilling to defend the Palestinian movement and colluding with Israel.[34] Prime Minister Saib Salam placed the blame on General Iskandar Ghanem, the army commander, and demanded his dismissal. Salam resigned when President Franjieh refused to dismiss General Ghanem. The level of friction between the guerrillas and the security forces increased rapidly thereafter. A state of emergency was declared throughout the country.[35] On May 17, 1973, the two sides announced that they had reached an agreement—the Milkart Protocols. An atmosphere of tense insecurity nevertheless persisted in the country.[36]

The conservative Maronite forces lost almost all confidence in the government's ability to either exercise its authority over the Palestinian Resistance or protect the Maronites. Gemayel and Chamoun began to establish training camps and import large numbers of arms into the country, while keeping the channels of communication open with Israeli officials (Goria 1985, 159 n. 8). Gemayel justified his action on the ground that the Palestinian camps had their own army, police, government, and courts.[37] Chamoun retorted, "Why do foreigners and those seeking refuge in hospitable Lebanon have the right to stage military training and carry arms, while Lebanon's sons have no right to do so in defense of their homeland?"[38] Gemayel and Chamoun viewed the Syrian-backed Palestinian presence in Lebanon as a constant danger to the Maronite community and Lebanon as a whole. Because the army's attempts to curb the power of the Resistance had failed, Gemayel and Chamoun no longer believed that the state could be trusted as the ultimate safeguard of the Maronite interests, or of Lebanon for that matter. They would instead rely more heavily upon their own resources and upon the Israelis, to whom they discreetly turned for political and military support (Goria 1985, 145). This in turn made Jumblatt more disenchanted with the government's ability to regulate more closely the activities of the Kataeb and the NLP militias. Soon thereafter, the first serious clashes in four years between the Palestinian commandos and the Kataeb militiamen erupted.[39] The Palestinian commandos were convinced that the Lebanese state was now part of a conspiracy aiming at their liquidation. Fearing a repetition of the Black September episode in Lebanon, the Palestinians sought to strengthen their ties with Jumblatt's Progressive Front as well as facilitate the rapid arming of new friendly groups.

In parallel, the various sides of the mounting crisis increasingly called upon the government to intervene. Hence, when some members of the PFLP attacked a Lebanese army barrack in Tyre on January 21, 1975,[40] the Kataeb leader presented a memorandum to President Franjieh on January 24 warning that Lebanon was being "threatened by the anarchy which reigns within the Resistance," while arguing by the same token that the Cairo Agreement had proven to be a failure. It was therefore time for the commandos "to withdraw from southern Lebanon" so that a terrorizing trend could be contained.[41] Arafat issued a conciliatory statement, reaffirming his pledge not to interfere in Lebanon's internal affairs.[42] The conflict between Gemayel and Jumblatt placed Prime Minister Solh in the middle of a hard-to-resolve political dilemma. Gemayel, supported by Chamoun, demanded that the army intervene to restore order. Jumblatt strongly opposed such a measure for fear that the army, under Ghanem, might side with the Kataeb.

The final blow, which effectively plunged the country into civil war, occurred on April 13, 1975, in the Beirut suburb of Ain al Rummaneh. A group of armed men drove past a church where Gemayel was attending a service and killed four people, including Gemayel's bodyguard. The Kataeb militiamen quickly responded by ambushing a bus carrying innocent Palestinians and Lebanese from Sabra camp to Tel al Zatar, killing twenty-seven passengers and wounding nineteen.[43] As news of the incidents spread, Lebanon fell into turmoil. The Palestinian Rejection Front declared, "We proclaim very clearly and firmly our abandonment of the policy of self-restraint in the face of these attacks by Phalange gangs."[44] Arafat dispatched cables urging the Arab leaders to "strike at the malicious Phalange gangs who are conspiring with imperialism and Zionism to create sedition."[45] The next day, large-scale fighting erupted between the Kataeb militiamen and the Palestinian fighters in the suburbs of Beirut. By April 18, after the first three days of fighting, an estimated three hundred human lives had been lost and approximately fifteen hundred buildings had been destroyed or seriously damaged.[46] The government was quickly drowning in a crisis. On May 7, 1975, three Kataeb ministers and two NLP ministers resigned from the cabinet. On May 12, one Shiite and one Sunni minister also submitted their resignations. Before officially submitting his resignation, Prime Minister Solh went before Parliament and launched a bitter attack against the Kataeb, holding them responsible for the massacre at Ain al Rummaneh and for all its material and moral consequences for the country.[47] The fighting continued to spread throughout large areas of Beirut following Solh's resignation. By June 24, large-scale fighting engulfed Beirut, its suburbs, Tripoli, and the Bekaa Valley.

That the Lebanese state effectively collapsed at the end of the period 1973–75 is not a matter of dispute. That the moderate scope of collective intentionality that existed in the early 1970s had vanished is perhaps not as clear. For the reasons discussed in chapter 2, it is difficult to identify precisely the scope of collective intentionality that existed before the end of the Black September civil war in Jordan. Yet it is possible to argue with a good degree of confidence that the Franjieh regime did not succeed in launching a process of reconsolidating state governance after the 1970–71 Black September episode in Jordan and its ramifications for Lebanon. Nor did the regime fare better after the May 1973 crisis. Therefore, explaining why the Lebanese polity failed to increase its scope of collective intentionality is an important question to which I now turn. I explore the extent to which the theory outlined in chapter 3 in terms of the combination of intercommunal vulnerability, trust, and distribution of institutional power can explain the rapid decrease in the scope of collective intentionality that culminated into a civil war.

## Intercommunal Vulnerability

As the coalition of Druzes, leftists, and Palestinians consolidated its ranks, all belligerent groups began to seriously doubt the state's ability and willingness to maintain order and security. They hence began to prepare militarily for any eventuality. Under these conditions, the scope of collective intentionality underpinning the existing constitutive rules and practices of state governance as defined by the 1943 National Pact decreased very rapidly. This was partly due to a rapid increase in intercommunal vulnerability in the polity. The Maronites began to fear exploitation and exclusion from the system of state governance after the Palestinian Resistance made Lebanon its main base of operations and training and the Druze-leftist alliance increasingly closed ranks with the Palestinian Resistance. The intercommunal vulnerability (for the Maronites, at least) hence began to increase rapidly, reaching high levels during the May 1973 crisis. Moreover, as the confrontation became more intercommunally "colored" in the aftermath of the May crisis, the level of intercommunal vulnerability increased even more rapidly, not only for the Maronites and Christians in general, but also for the Muslims, including the Palestinians. The change in the level of intercommunal vulnerability from somewhat moderate to high levels during the period 1971–73 to high and rapidly increasing levels during the period 1973–75 was the result of changing levels of information complexity, predictability, and interdependence.

### *Intercommunal Information Complexity*

Information complexity began and continued to increase from the May 1973 crisis until it reached a very high level in April 1975, when the Ain al-Rammaneh massacres occurred. This is evident in the debates between the status quo defenders (for the most part the Maronites) and the challengers (for the most part the Jumblatt-led alliance) on the issues of transforming state institutional power and the presence and role of an armed Palestinian Resistance in Lebanon. Information complexity increased as the intentions of both conservatives and challengers increasingly became more opaque and their respective capabilities increasingly became harder to estimate reliably. As domestic events unfolded, both sides of the debates faced hard-to-resolve questions on their mutual intentions and (actual or projected) relative capabilities. Although each side increasingly feared that the opposite side was misrepresenting its intentions as well as not faithfully displaying its projected capabilities, the conservative Maronite parties were much more concerned than the status quo challengers were. Consequently, both the nature and level of information complexity changed as the confrontation evolved during the period May 1973–April 1975. Yet even before the May 1973 crisis erupted, information complexity had been increasing as soon as it became clear to most actors that the 1969 Cairo Agreement was a failure, especially after the Palestinian Resistance moved its base of operations from Jordan to Lebanon. Two stages thus were important in the evolution of information complexity before the April 1975 fighting erupted.

The first stage extended from the end of the civil war in Jordan in 1971 to the beginning of the May 1973 crisis. The presence of an armed Palestinian Resistance in Lebanon, as noted earlier, divided Lebanon into two main groups. The Maronite community and its main political organizations, the Phalanges and the NLP, were very critical of the Cairo Agreement, especially after the Resistance moved from Jordan to Lebanon in 1971. The anti-status quo coalition of leftists-Druzes-Palestinians, including a majority of influential Muslim leaders and a majority of the Muslim population, hailed the Cairo Agreement and embraced the Resistance. At this stage, two important questions confronted the Maronite parties. First, why was the anti-status quo not only embracing but also seeking an alliance with the Palestinian Resistance? Second, what were the Muslims of Lebanon up to?

For the conservative Maronite parties, the anti-status quo alliance was embracing and seeking to forge a strong alliance with the Palestinians because the latter had two assets that would undermine the dominant position of the Maronite community in the Lebanese polity—a large popular base and effective political and military organizations. Most Palestinians were Sunni Muslims, and, hence, if they were ever included in the political system of Lebanon, would definitely tilt the demographic balance even more in favor of the Muslims at the expense of the Christians. No wonder that Gemayal and Chamoun opposed granting citizenship to mainly Muslim inhabitants of many slum districts such as Karantina and Maslakh for fear that they would tilt the political balance in the Lebanese system against the Maronites. This fear increased after tensions developed between the Maronites and the progressive and Palestinian groups throughout the summer and fall of 1971 and thereafter. The workers' and students' unrest exacerbated these tensions for the Palestinians, and their progressive allies identified themselves as being on the side of the Muslim "have-nots" on virtually all occasions. A younger generation of Lebanese was disappointed with the Phalange support for the status quo and the way it was upholding the Christian rights, that the Phalange were well received among its traditional supporters in Beirut and Mount Lebanon notwithstanding. The Kataeb hence lost much ground to progressives slated in student elections. This became a major concern for the party, as shown in an internal report by the liberal Maronite members, who warned as early as 1971 that the Phalange doctrine was no longer attractive to Lebanese youth. According to the report, the Lebanese youth were "going through a period of awareness and doubt—awareness of the corruption of the confessional system, and doubts as to its ability to persist and progress."[48] In addition to a "cause," the Palestinians had a strong armed wing—the Palestinian Resistance—that the Lebanese government could not curb or even control, particularly after the signing of the 1969 Cairo Agreement, and even more so after the Resistance moved its base of operations from Jordan to Lebanon in 1971.

Because of these two Palestinian assets, the Maronite leaders argued that the anti-status quo forces were seeking to forge an alliance with the Palestinians in order to initiate a revolution in Lebanon that would turn the Maronites into an oppressed minority with no guarantee of political rights. Events in the aftermath of the April 1973 Verdun raid reinforced this perception. The Palestinian leadership began to feel acutely vulnerable. They consequently closed the Palestinian offices near the seashore at Ras Beirut and hurriedly withdrew to the relative safety of the Sabra-Shatila refugee camps. They also undertook a program of building fortifications in the camps, as well as acquiring heavier weaponry systems (especially antiaircraft defenses) and deploying them to defend the camps (Abu Iyad 1981, 171–72). At the same time, the PLO tried to alleviate the fears of the Maronite leadership through direct contacts and communications, most importantly through a formal dialogue with the Phalange in 1972–73 (Petran 1972, 146; Brynen 1990, 73). More generally, the Maronites believed that the Muslims were intent on abolishing the only state where the Christian minorities, particularly the Maronites, had enjoyed full political and socioeconomic rights in a sea of Arab states. The Maronites' response to Prime Minister Solh when he called for a "secularization" of a number of important posts (e.g., director general of education, director general of the interior ministry, and secretary general at the foreign ministry) traditionally reserved for the Maronites is illustrative.[49] Gemayel, Chamoun, Eddé, and Patriarch Meochi were alarmed that the Maronites' rights could be jeopardized in this manner and demanded that the president take appropriate action to block such proposals (Goria 1985, 161).[50]

The anti-status quo forces and the Palestinian Resistance did not agree with these readings of their intentions. They argued instead that the Maronites dominated the Lebanese political system in spite of the fact that the country's demographic map had changed drastically since the last official census of 1932. The Maronites had thus turned a Muslim majority into a "political minority" at any cost. As to the 1969 Cairo Agreement, Jumblatt had already concluded in January 1970 that the increasing hostility of Lebanese conservative parties was an important obstacle to successful implementation of the agreement. Similarly, Salah Khalaf of Fateh later identified "lack of trust" as the single biggest barrier to implementation of the Cairo Agreement.[51] The anti-status quo forces hence raised a set of questions that cast doubts on the intentions of the Maronite parties.

First, why were the Maronite parties seeking to abolish the Cairo Agreement? Immediately after the signature of the Cairo Agreement, Joseph Mughabghab, a deputy from Chamoun's NLP, had warned that the presence of the Palestinian movement in Lebanon threatened the stability of the Lebanese political system and that "Lebanon will then be a good soil for leftist activities and bloody armed clashes."[52] Similarly, in June 1972 Eddé called for an abrogation of the Cairo Agreement, a call that Gemayel immediately echoed (Brynen 1990, 61). The Jumblatt coalition argued that the Maronites thus were against the Palestinians and wanted to isolate Lebanon from the Arab nation. Moreover, the Palestinian Resistance was effectively the only remaining obstacle to Israel's hegemony not only in Palestine, but also in the region. This was more so after the Arab states began to seek more peaceful relations with Israel in the wake of the 1973 war, as shown by their adherence to Kissinger's step-by-step diplomacy. By calling for the abrogation of the Cairo Agreement and opposing the presence of an armed Palestinian Resistance in Lebanon, the Maronite conservatives were attempting to undermine the Resistance and its legitimate struggle, a goal that was contrary to the national identity of Lebanon itself as an Arab state.

Second, why were the Kataeb and the NLP increasing their level of military preparedness? In the wake of the May 1973 clashes, new Christian groups emerged, among them al-Tanzim (the organization) and the Guardians of the Cedars (Hurras al-Arz), led by Sa$^{c}$id$^{c}$Aql and Etienne Saqr. Both were virulently anti-Palestinian and drew their support almost exclusively from the Maronite community. Extensive military preparations were also soon visible, as massive quantities of arms flowed from abroad to conservative militias. The Maronite leaders justified these moves as appropriate Christian responses to the Palestinian armed presence and a worsening deterioration in public order. Gemayel summarized the rightist position clearly by warning that "we cannot accept the closing of our camps and at the same time allow the presence of Palestinian camps that have their own government, courts, army, and police" (Brynen 1990, 72). To the anti–status quo coalition, the Maronites were using the presence of the Palestinian Resistance only as an excuse to pursue a policy that they had been following anyway for many years, as illustrated by the history of the Kataeb Party. The Maronites were arming themselves to undermine the Lebanese political order and any peaceful transformation of state governance and to preserve the old system of confessionalism.

These charges and countercharges between the anti–status quo and conservative forces notwithstanding, the information complexity that was emerging did not have yet an intercommunal "coloration." That the alliance between Jumblatt, who was a Druze, and the Palestinians, who for the most part were Muslim, dominated most of the events and debates with the government and Maronite parties did not yet "color" the debates to make them intercommunal. The Jumblatt-led coalition was mainly leftist in ideology and called for the establishment of a nonsectarian-based political system. Likewise, the Palestinian Resistance under the leadership of Fateh made a conscientious effort not to let the issues become "intercommunal," despite the fact that most Palestinian commandos were Muslim. *Intercommunal* information complexity hence was arguably still quite low at this stage as the polity moved into the May 1973 crisis.

However, this would radically change in the second stage, which extended from the May 1973 crisis to the eruption of intercommunal fighting in the aftermath of the April 1975 massacres at Ain al-Rammaneh. As noted earlier, the conservative Maronites lost confidence in the government's ability either to exercise its authority over the Palestinian Resistance or to protect the Maronites after the May 1973 crisis. Gemayel and Chamoun believed that they should rely heavily upon their own resources and upon the Israelis, to whom they discreetly turned for political and military support (Goria 1985, 145). Conversely, the Palestinian commandos were now convinced that the Lebanese government was cooperating in a conspiracy aiming at their liquidation. Fearing a repetition of the Black September episode in Lebanon, the Palestinians decided to strengthen their ties with Jumblatt's Progressive Front as well as to facilitate the rapid arming of new groups. Each party in the debates believed that it had to be in charge of its security. Yet there was not much information on the level of military and resource preparedness that each had reached. Put differently, even though the various groups and parties became more or less convinced about their mutual intentions, no party could ascertain the level to which the "other" had prepared itself for any eventual confrontation. One consequence of this state of affairs was that the Maronites were now viewing the situation from an *intercommunal* angle. They became convinced that their identity and survival *as Maronites and Christians* were at stake, notwithstanding the fact that the anti–status quo forces never portrayed their conflict with the Maronite parties (or the government forces for that matter) as intercommunal. That on the streets most of the anti–status quo forces were Muslim (Druze, Sunni, or Shiite) was enough proof for the Maronites. These contradicting claims and perceptions of the post–May 1973 crisis thus put information complexity at a high level with an intercommunal coloration. The more the government sided with the Maronites, the more the crisis became intercommunally colored.

In sum, the complexity of *intercommunal* information began to increase significantly only in the aftermath of the May 1973 crisis, after the Maronites lost confidence in the state and began to aggressively build their own defense and security systems. The divide increasingly assumed a Muslim versus Christian character as the Sunnis, Shiites, and Druzes constituted the great majority of the anti–status quo forces, whereas the Maronites constituted for the most part the other side of the conflict, at least before Syria's intervention. Thereafter, intercommunal information complexity continuously increased to reach a very high level at the beginning of the civil war in April 1975.

*Intercommunal Predictability*

Intercommunal predictability began and continued to decrease after the May 1973 crisis until it reached a very low level after the April 1975 massacres. Prior to the period May 1973–April 1975, predictability depended on an intercommunal adherence to the 1943 Pact and the Lebanese Constitution. Any major change to the National Pact or the Constitution would create much uncertainty concerning future intercommunal relations, the integrity of the Lebanese polity, and the existing form of state governance.

As matters stood just before the May 1973 crisis, intercommunal predictability was yet to become a major issue of concern, however. The Muslim-dominated anti–status quo forces saw no imminent problem of intercommunal predictability. They were concerned but not too alarmed about the Maronite-dominated conservative forces' opposition to institutional changes. The issue of changing state institutional arrangements had yet to assume an intercommunal coloration. The unfolding of the May 1973 crisis changed the whole picture, though. Two sorts of changes—a change to the intercommunal understandings and a change in intercommunal power arrangements—would create instability, should they occur. The anti–status quo forces, as discussed earlier, were intent on abolishing the National Pact and the confessional system—that is, on initiating a radical transformation of state institutions. However, this was anathema to the conservative Maronites, for it implied to them the loss of all the political and institutional privileges that they had enjoyed since 1943. Abrogating the National Pact and the resulting confessional system hence meant an abrogation of all intercommunal understandings underpinning the Lebanese polity.

That the Maronites and the majority of the anti–status quo forces perceived these potential changes differently did not reduce the severity of the moment; intercommunal predictability was rapidly decreasing as the confrontation began to take on more of an intercommunal coloration. This situation became even worse after the government failed to impose its authority on the Palestinian Resistance during the May 1973 crisis. The Maronites thenceforth lost confidence in the state as a maintainer of order and provider of security. Predicting that a major confrontation was brewing was not far-fetched. Most groups not only were willing to rely on their own means for defense and security, but also expected that the opposing side was doing the same.

In sum, the changes in intercommunal predictability and the changes in the level and nature of information complexity during the May 1973–April 1975 period mutually reinforced one another. Intercommunal predictability began and continued to decrease after May 1973. Likewise, the complexity of *intercommunal* information began to increase significantly only after the May

1973 crisis. Yet the dynamics of intercommunal information complexity and predictability cannot explain why various opposed groups remained so susceptible to each other's beliefs and strategic actions. The answer lies in the fact that as information complexity and predictability evolved during the May 1973–April 1975 period, so did intercommunal interdependence, which I explain next.

*Intercommunal Interdependence*

Interdependence between the anti–status quo forces and the conservative Maronites during the May 1973 to April 1975 period remained high due to the confessional nature of the system. Trying to abolish this interdependence led to self-fulfilling prophecies of intercommunal confrontations. Strong interdependence (that is, a shared control over the outcomes of intercommunal interaction) among the Maronites, Sunnis, Shiites, and Druzes was entrenched in the institutional arrangements of state governance. The latter was a reflection of the stipulations of the National Pact, the Constitution, and the constraints of the sociopolitical institution of *zaʾim*. As discussed in the previous chapter, the high level of intercommunal interdependence built into the system of state governance has not always remained without serious challenges. In the period June 1957–September 1958, intercommunal interdependence wavered during the debates on the three key issues of foreign policy orientation, Chamoun's bid for reelection, and finding a way out of the summer 1958 crisis. In general, the regime and the opposition took turns attempting to undermine the high level of intercommunal interdependence inherently built in the system of governance. Both belligerents attempted more or less unilaterally to determine the outcome of the ongoing debates over the system of state governance.

The outcome of the May 1973 crisis—a weakened state authority and a reinforced armed Palestinian Resistance—quickly became the source of a security dilemma, and an atmosphere of tense insecurity prevailed in the country.[53] As discussed earlier, the Maronite parties lost confidence in the state and began to take matters of their security into their own hands. Gemayel and Chamoun actively began taking specific actions in defense of their interests, such as establishing training camps. They understood that the establishment of training camps by various parties in Lebanon was dangerous and that in normal times lethal weapons should only be in the possession of the army and national security forces. Yet they argued that they were compelled to pursue such policies, for they could not accept the closing of Kataeb camps while the Palestinian camps had their own army, police, government, and courts.[54] On January 24, 1975, the Kataeb leader presented a memorandum to President Frangieh, warning that Lebanon was being "threatened by the anarchy which reigns within the Resistance."[55] George Habash described Gemayel's memorandum as a veritable call for a massacre.[56] On the last day of January, the Progressive Front leaders organized demonstrations in Beirut, Tripoli, and Sidon as a means of showing solidarity with the Palestinians. Gemayel then submitted a second memorandum to the president three weeks later, in which he again demanded an end to the anarchy in the country and called for a referendum that would determine the status of the Palestinian commando presence in the country.[57] By now, the Palestinian Resistance began arming and training a variety of anti-status quo groups and organizations.

In sum, as discussed earlier, intercommunal predictability began and continued to decline after the May 1973 crisis until it reached a very low level after the April 1975 massacres. Likewise, the complexity of *intercommunal* information began to increase significantly only after the May 1973 crisis, as the Maronites and the Palestinians as well as the anti-status quo forces lost confidence in the state and began to organize their own defense and security systems. The sense of intercommunal interdependence between the anti-status quo forces and the conservative Maronites during the May 1973 to April 1975 period remained high due in part to the interwoven nature of the confessional system of Lebanon and in part to the security dilemma that was slowly emerging. The combination of low and declining intercommunal predictability and high and increasing intercommunal information complexity under a condition where intercommunal interdependence remained high led to a level of intercommunal vulnerability. The latter rapidly increased in the immediate aftermath of the April 1975 massacres in Ain al-Rummaneh. However, as the theory in chapter 3 suggests, high vulnerability is a necessary but insufficient condition for a collapse of state governance in times of regional change. A collapse of state governance also depends on whether and how the belligerent parties relied on trust and institutional power to address their mutual vulnerabilities. I discuss this in the remainder of the chapter.

## Intercommunal Trust

Intercommunal trust emerged and consolidated after the end of the mandate system through a process of societal construction that started before the French left and culminated in the 1943 National Pact. Although during the short civil war of 1958 intercommunal trust diminished somewhat, it bounced back significantly to reach moderate (if not higher) levels as the scope of collective intentionality increased during the Shihab era. From May 1973 to April 1975, intercommunal trust began to decrease rapidly as the Maronite parties and the Muslim-dominated coalition began clashing about whether to change the rules of state governance after the May 1973 crisis. Intercommunal trust reached a vanishing level during the fighting that erupted in the second quarter of 1975. This section is in some ways a logical continuation of the corresponding section on trust of the previous chapter, and hence often draws on much of that discussion, particularly on the role of the structure of communal cleavages, sectarian memories, and ensuing structural lock-in. In the following, I build on the previous chapter to examine the evolution of trust in the period 1973–75.

### *Structural Lock-In*

As discussed in the previous chapter, the structure of sectarian cleavages, the fabric of sectarian memories, and the constitutional arrangements of the mandate period symbiotically combined to produce a structural lock-in, reflected in the 1943 National Pact. The structural lock-in had two effects that became a trademark of the Lebanese body politic: the dominant role of the sociopolitical institution of *zaʾim* in Lebanese politics and the form and nature of post-mandate institutional arrangements of the state. These two effects of the structural lock-in defined both "normal" and "beyond-the-normal" Lebanese politics until the state collapsed in 1975. "Normal" politics in Lebanon usually consisted of rivalries or collusions among the Maronite, Druze, and Sunni *zaʾims* and government officials. Changing the 1943 National Pact was an overriding issue of "beyond-the-normal" politics.

These structural effects resulted in three important conditions—intercommunal interdependence, *ex ante* agency, and *ex post* agency—that shaped the evolution of intercommunal trust. The post-mandate arrangements to intercommunal relations created much interdependence among the major sectarian groups of Lebanon. "Normal" politics depended on this high level of intercommunal interdependence. Defining and delimiting as well as enforcing both *ex ante* communal agency and *ex post* communal agency was also at the core of the 1943 National Pact. Abiding by the first three principles of the National Pact (as discussed in the previous chapter) would circumscribe *ex ante* communal agency in deciding the fate of Lebanon and hence alleviate the fears of the Christians and Muslims. The fourth principle of the National Pact and the institutional arrangements of the state combined to define and delimit the *ex post* agency of the major sectarian communities. At a practical level, the *zaʾim* institution effectively became the mechanism through which both *ex ante* agency and *ex post* agency were exercised as well as restrained. Not only did the *zuʾama* play an important role in upholding the delimitations imposed on *ex ante* and *ex post* agency as part of playing "normal" politics, they also joined efforts to preserve these delimitations. For example, when Presidents al-Khuri and Chamoun threatened to destroy these arrangements, in 1951 and 1958, respectively, most *zuʾama* collectively revolted against each president, eventually forcing both to resign. Thus, at the time of the May 1973 crisis, the Lebanese polity faced a situation wherein the major sectarian communities shared a high sense of intercommunal interdependence while the state institutional arrangements and the *zaʾim* institution together helped to delimit *ex ante* and *ex post* sectarian agency. As long as these conditions were fulfilled, there was enough intercommunal trust among the major sectarian groups.

Conversely, any changes that would undermine these conditions had the potential to reduce intercommunal trust. As Lebanon went through the May 1973 crisis, the Muslim-dominated coalition and the conservative Maronite parties were confronted with a high level of intercommunal interdependence while they simultaneously were seeking increasingly more *ex ante* agency and more *ex post* agency. The blend of intransigent conservative Maronites, a committed anti–status quo coalition, and a weakened government conspired with the increase in *ex ante* and *ex post* agency under a condition of very high intercommunal interdependence to ultimately erode the existing intercommunal trust. Arguably, without the increase in both *ex ante* and *ex post* agency, the mutually opposed forces would have had a hard time selling their rhetoric to their respective communities. Nonetheless, what became strongly but not solely determinative of the level of intercommunal trust were the intra- and intercommunal strategies that the respective leaders opted for under the condition of high intercommunal interdependence. The latter, as discussed earlier, in combination with high and increasing information complexity and low and rapidly decreasing intercommunal predictability, created a high and increasing level of vulnerability. I now discuss how the process of deconstructing intercommunal trust evolved.

### *Deconstructing Intercommunal Trust*

This section analyzes the social deconstruction of trust between the Christians and the Muslims in the May 1973–April 1975 period. The political entrepreneurs and activists operated within and channeled existing social-structural constraints and opportunities to deconstruct the existing intercommunal trust, ultimately replacing it with intercommunal fear and violence. Intercommunal trust unraveled through a reenactment of old political myths and the routinization of new practices and discourses that redefined intercommunal relations in terms of antagonistic and irreconcilable goals. Feedback between the reciprocated strategic practices of the elites and the response of the sectarian communities at large helped to sustain the process of trust deconstruction.

The May 1973 crisis, the strong support that the anti–status quo coalition showed for the Palestinians, and the army's failure to curb the Palestinian Resistance all combined to alarm the Maronite leading parties, the Kataeb and the NLP. The leaders of these parties thus moved to revive the old Maronite, and more generally Christian, fear of Muslim domination of Lebanon, as well as the fear that Lebanon would be absorbed into the Arab world and thus lose its sovereignty. As a result, old schisms concerning the national identity of Lebanon were revived, thereby threatening to undermine the intercommunal understanding embodied in the National Pact. The Maronite leadership did not have any difficulty mobilizing its community in this respect. The Maronites by and large already saw the pro-Palestinian fervor within the anti-status quo coalition as a threat to their community.[58] The Kataeb's approach to the Palestinian issue was two-pronged. First, the Kataeb sought a resolution of the problem as part of the larger problem of the Palestinian struggle against Israel. This was evident from the party's 1974 annual three-day plenary conference. The latter concluded with a statement declaring that the party had accepted the mainstream of Arab politics with regard to the Palestinian question, the projected Arab-Israeli peace settlement, and the general issue of inter-Arab cooperation (Salibi 1976, 81). The Kataeb insisted that the settlement proposals must fully consider the Palestinian aspirations, as the establishment of a Palestinian state was an essential prerequisite for the return of political stability in Lebanon. In pursuit of this political line, Gemeyal met several times with Yasir Arafat and other Fateh leaders, declaring after each meeting that what the Lebanese in general and the Kataeb Party in particular wished for the Palestinians was no different from what the Palestinians wished for themselves. Second, taking this position ended up pitting the Kataeb Party against the Palestinian Rejection Front, which was rejecting any settlement short of an eradication of Israel (Salibi 1976, 81). Therefore, by fall 1974, the Kataeb found itself engaged on three political fronts: one against the Palestinian Rejectionists, one against the Lebanese anti-status quo coalition, and one against the traditional Sunni establishment (Salibi 1976, 84).

Although the Kataeb and the NLP were very successful in monopolizing the articulation of the Maronite interests and fears, there were some challenges within the Christian camp. These challenges did not, however, seriously counter, let alone reverse, the confrontational tide of the Maronite rightist parties. In January 1974, the Caucus of Committed Christians sought to offer the Christians an alternative to an ever more militaristic and fascistic line in the Maronite community. This initiative came from the clergy, a number of theologians and intellectuals involved in social activism, and a number of social workers who opposed the social and ideological role of the Christian institutions in which they worked. One of the Caucus's main concerns was to combat the "fear complex" that the Maronite Right was nurturing among the Christian masses by deliberately conflating the maintenance of Christian economic and political privileges with the continued existence of the Christian communities. The Caucus also tried to convince the Muslim masses about the Christian support for the Palestinian cause and the Christian rejection of church-state collusion. Hence, Orthodox Church leaders such as Archbishops Georges Khodr of Beirut, Jean Kurban of Tripoli, and Paul Khouri of Sidon assumed highly visible roles in combating the propagation of fear and sectarian strife coming from the strongholds of the Maronite Right, promoting instead coexistence among the various confessional communities on the basis of equal rights and duties (Petran 1972, 153).

Two mutually reinforcing political issues dominated and framed the political discourses of the anti-status quo coalition, namely, the Palestinian plight and resistance as an Arab cause and the Maronite domination of the Lebanese political system. Both issues had a long history within the Muslim masses in Lebanon as part of the background of "normal politics" and resonated well with the concurrent changing regional context, as discussed earlier in the chapter. Not only were most Muslims anti-Zionist, but also the Palestinian Resistance became a vindication of this belief, particularly after the 1967 defeat and more so following the Egyptian move toward peace with Israel after the 1973 war. In fact, the resonance between the leaders' self-serving strategies in combating the Maronite domination and the masses' support for the Palestinian struggle had never been stronger in Lebanon. The Palestinian cause and the government's attempt to subdue and tame the Palestinian Resistance in the May 1973 crisis provided the coalition leaders with an opportunity to strengthen their pivotal role in the Lebanese politics, if at the end by other means such as organizing their followers for fighting. That the leaders of the anti-status quo coalition used these two political issues to frame various challenges to the existing system of state governance is evident, as discussed earlier, in the events surrounding the debates on the redistribution of state institutional power and the presence of an armed Palestinian Resistance in Lebanon.

The feedback between the reciprocated strategic practices of the anti-status quo forces and of the Maronite elites and the response of their respective sectarian communities at large mutually shaped one another. The outcome was new intercommunal relations, eventually routinized in the aftermath of the May 1973 crisis. The Palestinian commandos were now convinced that the Lebanese authorities were determined not to rest until they had liquidated the Resistance, a perception much encouraged by the Lebanese anti-status quo forces. Conversely, the Christian Lebanese were now also more convinced than ever that Lebanon could not be truly sovereign until the last trace of Palestinian military presence in the country had been eradicated. These radically opposed, if mutually reinforcing, convictions eventually ended up creating a sense of mutual threat. They also created the perception that the state would not be able to maintain order by defending the status quo or by enacting political transformations that would restore order. The dynamic of confrontation had set in. The Christian Lebanese parties and factions—notably the Kataeb Party, the NLP, and Franjieh's followers in the Zgharta district—began to search in the Arab world and abroad for the means to arm their militias and their supporters. They decided to prepare themselves for what they considered to be an inevitable final encounter with the Palestinians and the anti–status quo forces (Salibi 1976, 70).

This new dynamic of confrontation is illustrated in one incident in Sidon involving the shooting of a commando by a Lebanese police officer. The incident led to a show of force by Palestinian demonstrators in that city, with an erection of barricades and explosions. This deterioration of the security situation became the source of a verbal clash between Gemayel and Jumblatt. The latter declared that the prospects for order would remain in jeopardy as long as the Kataeb blocked roads, set tires ablaze, and carried out military exercises with the full knowledge of the Lebanese authorities. He also attacked Chamoun for actively training the NLP militia units, stating, "Those who claim to be anxious to maintain security are the ones disturbing order and stability."[59] Five days later, Jumblatt increased his confrontation rhetoric and accused Gemayel and Chamoun of being "accomplices in the conspiracy against the Palestinian people" with King Hussein.[60] Gemayel replied that Jumblatt was the "biggest conspirator against the Palestinian people."[61] Chamoun added that "When Jumblatt criticizes others, he does so to ward off suspicion about himself."[62] Gemayel concluded on September 4, 1974, that Jumblatt and his left-wing allies were concerned above all with changing the system and fighting the regime with all possible means, including subversion, confusion, and chaos, something that he was determined to prevent.[63] Jumblatt, however, continued to allege that Chamoun and Gemayel were working in collaboration with certain army officers in order to bring about the final liquidation of the Resistance.[64] He cited as evidence the arrival of yet another large shipment of arms at the Aquamarina port north of Beirut.[65] Gemayel presented on December 12 and 13 three successive memoranda to the press in which he warned that Lebanon was in the process of becoming a second Palestine because of the extremists in the Palestinian Rejection Front.[66]

The coalition-Maronite strategic interaction inexorably turned into a downward-spiraling game, ultimately collapsing into violent clashes and armed confrontations. The massacres of April 1975 in Ain al-Rummaneh were the spark that transformed the debates from verbal attacks and counterattacks into violent clashes and armed conflict on the streets. At that moment, intercommunal trust had completely vanished; many Lebanese Christians could not trust their Muslim compatriots anymore, at any level. What started as a battle over constitutional changes between the anti–status quo coalition and the conservative Maronite parties and as a debate on the presence of an armed Palestinian Resistance in Lebanon became an intercommunal conflict.

Three factors contributed to this rapid worsening of intercommunal relations: the May 1973 crisis and the overwhelming support that the Muslims expressed for the Palestinian Resistance, the Maronite intransigent postures on opposing any changes to the distribution of state institutional power, and the strategic feedback between the Muslim-dominated anti–status quo coalition and the Maronite-dominated pro–status quo forces. One can assert with a large degree of confidence that the predisposing conditions of the structural lock-in and historical memories shaped the responses of the Maronites (and more generally the Christians) and the Muslim masses to the May 1973 crisis, including each other's stand on this issue. The siege mentality that the Maronites have inherited from the past and the continuous grievances of the Muslim masses against the Maronite-dominated system as reinforced by the ideology of pan-Arabism provided the propitious blend that made the May 1973 crisis a favorable context for turning the conflict between the coalition and the Maronites into an intercommunal clash, henceforth deconstructing intercommunal trust.

In sum, from May 1973 to April 1975, intercommunal trust inexorably decreased to reach a vanishing point in April 1975 as the conservative Maronite parties and the Muslim-dominated anti–status quo coalition continuously clashed with one another on whether to change the rules of state governance and on the presence of an armed Palestinian Resistance in Lebanon. The vanishing of intercommunal trust under conditions of very high intercommunal vulnerability undoubtedly helped to erode the existing scope of collective intentionality. In other words, the conservative Maronite parties were de facto refusing to play politics according to the existing rules of state governance because they felt highly vulnerable and did not trust the anti–status quo forces and the Palestinians in general. Nor would the anti–status quo forces play "normal politics" according to the existing rules of state governance. However, this is insufficient to explain a complete erosion of the collective intentionality underpinning the state governance. Indeed, the latter process also crucially depended on how the various groups used (or sought to use) institutional power in pursuing their respective goals, as discussed next.

## Institutional Power Leverage

For a given intercommunal vulnerability, the level of reliance on institutional power increases as intercommunal trust decreases, and vice versa. Likewise, for a given intercommunal vulnerability, the more rapidly the level of reliance on institutional power increases, the more rapidly intercommunal trust will decrease, and the more rapidly the scope of collective intentionality decreases. These two hypotheses can be confidently tested in this case, for, as discussed earlier in the chapter, much of the debate and conflict between the anti– and pro–status quo forces revolved around the key issue of redistributing state institutional power (and the related issues of the presence of an armed Palestinian Resistance in Lebanon). The debates shaped, and were shaped by, three key institutions: the presidency, the office of prime minister, and the army. However, the inherently pro-Maronite distribution of institutional power as defined by the 1943 National Pact and the Lebanese Constitution created a clear asymmetry in the distribution of institutional power in favor of the Maronites. Hence, during the May 1973–April 1975 period, the Maronites sought to rely on their institutional power to shape the outcomes of the debates on whether and, if yes, how to transform the rules and practices of state governance.

The conservative Maronites sought to use their institutional power in at least two ways. First, as discussed earlier, the Maronite president endeavored to weaken the premiership and strengthen the role of the presidency. This clearly aligned the presidency on the side of the conservative Maronite parties, such as the Kataeb and the NLP. In Lebanese "normal politics," the president would usually obtain (or at seek to obtain) cooperation from a majority of the *zuʾama* across various confessional communities. President Franjieh neglected this practice of Lebanese politics and instead sided with the Maronite *zuʾama.* Moreover, the president is constitutionally empowered to appoint the prime minister and the cabinet. As the highest Muslim political official, the prime minister would normally hold a significant amount of authority and institutional power. In practice, however, the power of the prime minister has varied according to his personality, his base of support, and the preferences of the president he served. After he became president in 1970, Franjieh increasingly used his powers to marginalize, or at least weaken, the Sunni prime minister. This helped to undermine an important dimension of "normal politics," that is, a good working relationship between the Maronite president and the Sunni prime minister. The following event is illustrative. In 1973, the conspicuous absence of the Lebanese army during the Israeli attacks angered the Lebanese Muslims. Prime Minister Saeb Salam claimed that the army commander, General Iskandar Ghanim (a Maronite), had disobeyed his orders by not resisting the Israeli raid. Saeb Salam resigned in protest because the president ignored the prime minister's request to fire Ghanim and decided to keep the latter as army commander. President Franjieh then chose in succession four weak Sunni leaders to head the government. This antagonized the Sunni community at a moment when the president needed good relationships with the Sunni leaders to reverse or at least minimize the drifting away of large sections of the Sunni community toward the anti–status quo coalition of Druzes, Sunnis, Shiites, and Palestinians.

Second, the Franjieh regime also relied on the Lebanese army in attempting to curb not only the Palestinian Resistance but also the anti–status quo demonstrations and unrest. This led to a polarization of the Lebanese army. The army, supposedly politically neutral and communally diverse, had been one of the most important guarantees of peaceful coexistence between the different sects and factions of the Lebanese society, as illustrated in the previous chapter. However, after 1967, any action by the army inevitably was interpreted favorably in one community and adversely in the opposing one. This effectively restricted the army's mandate and willingness to act, forcing it to opt, if in most cases unsuccessfully, for middle-course strategies. For example, in October 1969, the Lebanese army took a proactive role in restraining the Palestinian forces. However, the army could decisively defeat the Palestinians only at the risk of splitting the nation. Therefore, the army commander, General Emile Bustani, signed the Cairo Agreement in November 1969 with the Palestinian representatives in an attempt to somewhat "regulate," if not completely contain, the movements of the Palestinian Resistance. To the Maronites, however, by sanctioning the armed Palestinian presence, Lebanon had surrendered full sovereignty over military operations conducted within and across its borders and hence had become a party to the Arab-Israeli conflict.

In the 1970s, the army also failed to protect southern Lebanon against Israeli attacks and the borders with Syria against Palestinian infiltration. The issue was the source of a heated meeting of Parliament on April 16, 1974. Many deputies protested that despite the growing Israeli threat, the government was not taking any steps to strengthen the army, let alone reform it.[67] Likewise, following the Sidon incident the Muslims and the anti–status quo forces strongly denounced the behavior of the government. However, the Christian political forces fully supported the official stand taken with regard to the whole affair. Predominantly Christian sectors of East Beirut became the theater of massive demonstrations of support for the army. Thousands of students and other demonstrators acclaimed the army as the supreme vindicator of the sovereign rights of the Lebanese people. They denounced the attacks against the army command as slanderous and described the Sidon incidents as part of a plot to discredit not only the army but also the Lebanese system as a whole (Salibi 1976, 94). Conversely, sixteen Muslim leaders, including six former premiers, pressed for the reorganization of the army and threatened to escalate the crisis unless the government met their demands. They urged the government to create a "national balance" in the army command through the formation of a command council representing Muslims and Christians equally. The Christian leaderships, epitomized by Gemayel and Chamoun, strongly objected to any tampering with the army organization (Salibi 1976, 95).

More generally, until the early years of the Franjieh regime, the Lebanese army with its Maronite command had managed to retain a general popular respect by maintaining the position of arbiter on all matters with a confessional "color." The situation began to change with the disappearance of the Shihabist core within the army after 1970 and the appointment of General Iskandar Ghanem to its command in 1971. By 1973, the Muslim Lebanese began to view the Maronite army command as a political ally and instrument of the Maronite presidency. Two factors shaped this Muslim attitude. First, the Palestinian commandos encouraged and fostered anti-army suspicions among the Muslims. Second, the anti–status quo force had its problems with the army intelligence and hence encouraged anti-army feelings (Salibi 1976, 95–96). That the Muslim population did harbor negative feelings and mistrust, if not animosity, toward the Lebanese army became clear during the already mentioned Sidon incident. The Muslim demonstrators took up arms against the army in Sidon and refused to lay them down or even agree to a cease-fire until the last troops had left the city. Strong popular expressions of the Christian support for the army reinforced these Muslims' feelings toward the army. Although the Christian show of support for the army was meant to strengthen the army position and morale, it in fact had the opposite effect of branding it even more clearly as an instrument of the Christian power in the country, thereby further reducing its general acceptability within the Muslim population.

In sum, that the Franjieh regime and more generally the Maronites relied on their institutional power in attempting to shape the outcomes of the debate on the key issues of transforming state governance and the presence of an armed Palestinian Resistance in Lebanon is not disputable. This is also transparent from the fact that the anti–status quo forces in coalition with the Palestinians tried hard to contrive the Maronite control over key state institutions, first through "normal politics" and second through "politics by other means." In addition, the more the Maronites resorted to using their institutional power, the more they helped to erode the legitimacy and authority of the state. By seeking to oppose a transformation of state governance through a domination of the presidency, a weakening of the premiership, and a polarization of the army, the Maronite-dominated regime ended up hastening the erosion of what it sought to perpetuate: the form of state governance as defined by the 1943 National Pact.

## Conclusion

The collapse of state governance during 1973–75 in Lebanon evolved through a combination of two mutually reinforcing debates—the first on the confessional system as defined in the 1943 National Pact, and the second on the presence of an armed Palestinian Resistance in Lebanon. The latter was in turn rooted in the tremendous transformations that resulted from three regional events: the 1967 Six-Day War, the 1970–71 Black September episode in Jordan, and the 1973 Ramadan War and ensuing international moves toward an Israeli-Arab peace settlement. The new regional context hence reinforced domestic political debates about the state in Lebanon. State governance eventually collapsed, and the country fell into a civil war in the second quarter of 1975. That state governance collapsed was the result of a combination of moderate intercommunal vulnerability that rapidly increased, low intercommunal trust that rapidly decreased, and moderate (Maronite) reliance on institutional power that significantly increased.

The process effectively began in the immediate aftermath of the May 1973 crisis. Intercommunal vulnerability began to rise to higher levels as the Maronites began to fear losing their domination of state institutions. However, the outcome of debating state governance did not depend solely on intercommunal vulnerability. As outlined in the theory and shown in this and previous cases, intercommunal vulnerability and trust are interactive. From May 1973 to April 1975, intercommunal trust rapidly decreased as the conservative Maronites and the anti–status quo forces continuously clashed with one another about whether to change the rules of state governance and on how to deal with the presence of an armed Palestinian Resistance in Lebanon. Intercommunal trust completely vanished during the fighting that broke out in April 1975.

The outcome of the debates, in turn, depended on the interaction of intercommunal trust and the Maronites' attempt to rely on the institutional power of the presidency. As intercommunal trust was quickly eroding after the May 1973 crisis, the Maronite leaders began to have more recourse to whatever institutional power they controlled. The more the Franjieh regime resorted to its leverage over the key state institutions, the more the anti–status quo forces resorted to extra-systemic means, and the more the state legitimacy eroded. This in turn eroded further an already rapidly vanishing intercommunal trust. This cycle continued during the fighting of the second quarter of 1975. Hence, the level of reliance on institutional power increased with the rapidly decreasing scope of collective intentionality.

# PART III

# CONCLUSIONS

# Eight

# Summary, Alternative Explanations, and Implications

This book addresses the important problem of state stability in multiethnic societies under changing international conditions. This issue is complex and cuts across the disciplines of international relations and security, political science, social theory, and history. A study of this scope necessitates methodological trade-offs and selective use of historical materials. This book eschews disciplinary compartmentalization and explicitly seeks to integrate different perspectives in explaining outcomes. It addresses how international environment variables, domestic politics, and sociological and psychological variables interact in shaping the process of state stability, consolidation, and, whenever it occurs, collapse in multi-communal polities.

Two main questions drive the theoretical concerns of this book. First, what prompts domestic political actors to transform the state in deeply divided societies under conditions where the international environment is fundamentally changing? Second, what determines the final form of state governance once the process of change begins?

The central proposition of the book is that the transformation of state governance in these polities is the combined result of fundamental changes in international order and in the character of the domestic intercommunal relationship. More specifically, fundamental changes in the international order can induce pressures for adaptation to the changing external conditions through a reconfiguration of state governance. As key domestic political actors debate the issue, the form of state governance is increasingly at stake. The debate on state governance can result in one among many possible outcomes (such as collapse, failing, consolidating, or consolidated state governance), depending on a combination of intercommunal vulnerability and trust and on the distribution of institutional power among the major communal groups.

This theoretical argument implies that four questions drive the process of analyzing the transformation of a state in the four historical cases considered in the empirical chapters of the book. First, was there a fundamental change in the constitutive rules and practices of the relevant international environment, and, if yes, did such a change induce domestic debates on state governance? Second, how vulnerable did the communal groups feel or fear becoming? Third, how much did the communal groups rely on institutional power to address intercommunal vulnerability? Fourth, what is the level of intercommunal trust shared by these communal groups? These four basic questions constitute the core of the research design used to test the theory in the chosen cases.

The historical evidence is largely consistent with the theory. The outcomes of the debates on state governance for Yugoslavia in 1947–53 and 1987–91 and for Lebanon in 1957–58 and 1973–75 fit plausible readings of the independent variables. In addition, the unfolding of domestic politics in each of the four cases reveals a process of debate by and large over the kinds of issues expected in the theory. The domestic debates were responses for the most part to pressures for adaptation to changing external environments and revolved on the questions of whether to transform state governance and, if yes, how to transform it. A combination of concerns for intercommunal vulnerability, trust, and distribution of state institutional power drove these debates.

In chapter 3, I summarized the arguments of the theory in terms of ten general hypotheses. As it transpires from the cases, not every hypothesis pertains to every historical period examined in the empirical chapters. Moreover, definitive readings of each variable were not always easy or even possible. Nonetheless, the cases generally support the expectations of the theory and reinforce three themes of this book.

First, fundamental changes in the constitutive rules and practices of the international order are part of the "constitutive" context that contributes to defining the rules and practices of state governance. The failure to consider this "constitutive" aspect of the external environment by conceptualizing the latter only as either enabling or constraining opportunities seriously impairs our analysis of the phenomena of state collapse and transformation. It also biases our understanding of the causes and consequences of international politics on domestic politics and renders us conceptually insensitive to a fundamental feature of the modern state: it is a continuous process of international-domestic, two-level construction, and sometimes deconstruction. Any complete theory of state governance needs to explicitly consider this constitutive aspect of the modern state.

Second, state governance is an ongoing process of debate, the outcome of which varies along a continuum from state collapse to consolidated state governance. The failure to specify and consider alternative forms of state governance puts severe limits on our understanding of the process of transforming state governance under changing external conditions and renders us unaware of the many social construction processes that underlie the domestic debates over state governance.

Third, to explain whether and, if yes, how a deeply divided multi-communal polity would decide to transform its existing form of state governance when it is confronted with fundamental changes in the constitutive rules and practices of the external environment, we must examine all three of the principal causal variables in the theory. Intercommunal vulnerability, trust, and distribution of state institutional power are all necessary. None alone is sufficient to explain any eventual outcome of the debates over transforming state governance in a deeply divided society. In short, it is how much intercommunal vulnerability the actors are faced with, how much intercommunal trust the actors share while confronting this fear of intercommunal vulnerability, and how much they rely on institutional power to force their respective choices on one another that ultimately determine what form of state governance emerges from the debates.

In concluding, I survey the hypotheses laid out in chapter 3 in light of the post-1945 histories of the two states considered in the book. I then briefly discuss a number of alternative explanations recently suggested in extant literature. I end by examining a number of theoretical and policy implications of the analyses of the book.

## Socialist Yugoslavia and Multi-confessional Lebanon

I now survey the hypotheses laid out in chapter 3 in light of the post-1945 histories of the two states considered in the book. I illustrate each proposition with some brief references to the cases.

> $H_1$: The greater the sense of intercommunal interdependence among the politicized communal groups in the polity, the more likely they will be to seek to debate the existing form of state governance to deal with the fundamental changes occurring in the international environment.

All four cases illustrate well the effects of intercommunal interdependence on the prospects of whether to debate state governance when confronted with fundamental changes in international environments that pressure the polity for adaptation.

The emergence of the Cold War between the United States and the Soviet Union in 1947 signified major changes in the constitutive rules and practices of the international order, especially in Europe. The two superpowers began to create new patterns of practices constituted by a rule of postwar bloc politics that increasingly bounded the practice of politics throughout the international system. These fundamental changes in international constitutive rules and practices pressured Yugoslavia to seek a new international role for itself and hence induced domestic political debates about the existing form of state governance in socialist Yugoslavia. This, however, threatened to revive the old national question. Yet when the period of radical transformation began after the 1948 split with Stalin, the constituent nations of Yugoslavia were interdependent enough to realize that it was in their common interest to remain united against the Soviets' subversive maneuvers. In contrast with the interethnic massacres that occurred during the war, the immediate aftermath of the war was characterized by a respite on the national question, since most people were reluctant to be reminded of the national question. The members of the Cominform organization attempted to use the national question as a means for dividing the Yugoslav party in its support for Tito. Yet overall, this effort failed. Instead, the sense of strategic interdependence among the major communal groups in the Yugoslav polity greatly strengthened the incentives for the Yugoslav communal groups to transform the existing state governance in dealing with the fundamental changes occurring in the international environment.

In 1987–91, the transformation of one of the two blocs of the Cold War led to a fundamental transformation of the states system. The buffer role that Yugoslavia held between the two camps of the Cold War existed within and through the constitutive rules and practices of the Cold War system. The end of the Cold War thus problematized the constitutive rules and practices of the Yugoslav state. The major communal groups remained interdependent due to the mismatch created by the structure of ethnic cleavages between the constituent nations and the republics bearing their names. This situation was the more acute for the Serb leaders, as their nation was dispersed over almost all the republics, with particularly strong concentrations in Serbia proper, Croatia, and Bosnia-Herzegovina. Because these leaders rose to and remained in power positions due largely to their ultranationalistic leadership style, they would (could) not downplay the role of intercommunal vulnerability for themselves as well as for their respective communal groups. Hence, the strong level of strategic interdependence among the major communal groups in the Yugoslav polity greatly strengthened the incentives for the Yugoslav communal groups and polity to debate state governance in dealing with the fundamental changes occurring in the international environment.

In the case of Lebanon in 1956–58, the withdrawal of Britain and France and their replacement by the United States as the major Western power in the region and the rise of Nasser's Egypt as the dominant Arab state initiated a new pattern of practices in a competition over regional order in the 1950s. These entailed fundamental changes in regional constitutive rules and practices, which in turn induced domestic political debates about the form of state governance in Lebanon. Transforming state governance, however, threatened to jeopardize the stipulations of the 1943 National Pact. Yet the confessional system of state governance that was created in Lebanon had inherently built in a high sense of intercommunal interdependence. The sense of intercommunal strategic interdependence among the major communal groups in Lebanon greatly strengthened the incentives for the communal groups to reconsolidate state governance in dealing with the fundamental changes occurring in the international environment.

In 1967–75, the outcome of the 1967 Six-Day War, the expulsion of the PLO's troops and thousands of Palestinians from Jordan to Lebanon after the 1970–71 Black September episode, and the socioeconomic, political, and security consequences of the 1973 war entailed fundamental changes in regional constitutive rules and practices. This in turn induced domestic political debates about the system of state governance in Lebanon. Efforts by a coalition of leftist organizations to transform the state threatened to jeopardize the stipulations of the 1943 National Pact. Yet the sense of intercommunal strategic interdependence between the anti–status quo forces and the conservative Maronites during the period May 1973 to April 1975 remained high, due in part to the interwoven nature of the confessional system of Lebanon and in part to a security dilemma that was slowly emerging. This strong intercommunal interdependence among major sectarian groups greatly strengthened the incentives for the sectarian groups to debate state governance in dealing with the fundamental changes occurring in the region.

> $H_2$: The greater the expected intercommunal vulnerability among the politicized communal groups in the polity, the less likely they will be to engage one another in debates about the existing form of state governance to deal with the fundamental changes occurring in the international environment.

Fears of intercommunal vulnerability played an important role in the various parties' decision whether to debate the form of state governance in all four cases. Nonetheless, this is best illustrated in the cases of Lebanon in 1973–75 and Yugoslavia in 1987–91. As the debates unfolded in both cases, the communal groups became increasingly more concerned about intercommunal vulnerability. In Lebanon, intercommunal vulnerability reached a high and rapidly increasing level in the period 1973–75 as the communal leaders began making unilateral moves to protect and promote their communal interests. Under these conditions, the major communal groups increasingly became fearful of intercommunal abandonment, exploitation, or exclusion. A high and rapidly increasing intercommunal vulnerability was the result of very high information complexity, low intercommunal predictability, and high intercommunal interdependence. Information complexity became very high as the communal leaders were increasingly confronted with a lack of information on each other's intentions and actions. Intercommunal predictability was low, since there increasingly was no intercommunal commitment to the status quo arrangement and the communal leaders were increasingly sidestepping the stipulations of the 1943 National Pact. At the same time, the major communal groups remained strongly interdependent, and none sought the exit option from Lebanon.

In the Yugoslav case, intercommunal vulnerability reached a high level in the period 1987–91 as the republican leaders began taking unilateral moves to protect and promote their communal interests. Under these conditions, the major communal groups increasingly became fearful of intercommunal abandonment, exploitation, or exclusion. A high and rapidly increasing intercommunal vulnerability was the result of very high information complexity, low intercommunal predictability, and high intercommunal interdependence.

> $H_3$: The more rapidly expected intercommunal vulnerability declines with the scope of collective intentionality, the more likely the politicized communal groups are to construct a form of state governance with a higher degree of consolidation.

The rate of change of intercommunal vulnerability played a central role in every case in determining the likelihood of consolidating state governance, but its overall effect is best seen in the case of Lebanon in 1957–58. After the Maronite president manipulated the legislative elections in June 1957, intercommunal vulnerability began to rise to moderate levels as the other groups (especially the Druzes) feared exclusion. Yet after Fuad Shihab assumed the highest post in the state hierarchy, even before he officially became president, intercommunal vulnerability began to decrease significantly. The major communal groups had no serious fear of intercommunal abandonment, exploitation, or exclusion. Low intercommunal vulnerability was the result of low to moderate information complexity, moderate to high intercommunal predictability, and an important sense of intercommunal interdependence. Information complexity was low to moderate because, under Shihab's rule, the major communal groups had more or less reliable information on each other's intentions and capabilities. Intercommunal predictability was moderate to high, since there was enough mutual intercommunal commitment to the Shihab regime. As the latter increasingly succeeded in alleviating fear of intercommunal vulnerability, the likelihood of reconsolidating state governance grew steadily. In contrast, in 1973–75, the Lebanese polity became the "victim" of a seemingly unstoppable rise in intercommunal vulnerability. As the Maronites began to seriously fear exploitation and exclusion after the Palestinian Resistance made Lebanon its main base of operations and training, and as the Druze-leftist alliance increasingly closed ranks with the Palestinian Resistance, intercommunal vulnerability (for the Maronites, at least) began to rapidly increase to reach high levels during the May 1973 crisis. Moreover, as the confrontation became more intercommunally "colored" in the aftermath of the May 1973 crisis, intercommunal vulnerability increased even more rapidly, not only for the Maronites and for the Christians in general, but also for the Muslims, including the Palestinians.

$H_4$: The higher the intercommunal trust among the politicized communal groups, the more willing they will be to participate in a debate on the existing form of state governance as a response to the fundamental changes occurring in the international environment.

$H_5$: The more rapidly intercommunal trust increases, the more likely the communal groups are to construct a form of state governance with a higher degree of consolidation.

The 1947–53 Yugoslav case provides clear evidence for these two hypotheses, whereas the 1973–75 Lebanese case provides clear evidence for the converse hypotheses. In Yugoslavia, intercommunal trust increased significantly as the 1953 Constitutional Law was being formulated. The Yugoslav leaders understood that the intercommunal trust that had been developing since the end of the war was an important device that they should use to preempt any increase in intercommunal vulnerability. In fact, intercommunal trust increased with the emerging form of state governance, that is, as the scope of collective intentionality increased during the post-1948 debates. However, intercommunal trust remained somewhat moderate and increased significantly only after the 1953 Constitutional Law was formulated. In Lebanon, the level of intercommunal trust that the state institutions and policies had managed to secure under the Shihab regime quickly eroded in the pre-1975 period, particularly after the emergence of the Palestinians as an independent actor in Lebanese politics and the rise of the Shiites in South Lebanon as a force to reckon with. As the debates on state governance evolved in the aftermath of the May 1973 crisis, intercommunal trust eroded more rapidly, for the sectarian leaders not only began to talk past one another but also began to engage each other in rhetorical wars of incriminations and blame for the problems that their communal groups were facing.

$H_6$: The stronger the institutional power of the dominant group, the less likely the dominant group will be to seek to transform state governance to deal with the fundamental changes occurring in the international environment.

$H_7$: In the event that the dominant group agrees to debate state governance, the greater the expected intercommunal vulnerability, the more likely the dominant group is to rely on institutional power to shape the outcome of the debates.

The 1973–75 Lebanese case provides the best evidence for these two hypotheses. There was much asymmetry in the distribution of state institutional power, with the Maronite leadership reserving for itself the lion's share of institutional power. As intercommunal trust was quickly eroding, the Maronite leaders began to have recourse to whatever institutional power they believed they had or could muster to force their choices on the other sectarian groups. The second-best evidence for the two hypotheses is in the 1987–91 Yugoslav case. Much as in the Lebanese case, as intercommunal trust quickly eroded, the Serbians began to rely increasingly more on their institutional power to force their choices on the other republics. Both the Maronite and the Serb leaders relied increasingly more on state institutional power as a means to counter what they perceived as rising intercommunal vulnerability.

> $H_8$: The more rapidly reliance on institutional power among the politicized communal groups increases, the more likely they are to construct a form of state governance with a lower degree of consolidation.

The 1973–75 Lebanese and 1987–91 Yugoslav cases provide good evidence for this hypothesis. As the Maronite leadership relied more on its advantage of state institutional power, the opposition, most prominently the Druzes and Shiites, countered such moves by increasingly acting outside the existing rules and practices of state governance. The more the Maronite leadership resorted to its leverage over state institutions, the more the leftist alliance grouping the Druzes, the Sunnis, and the Shiites (and the Palestinians) defected from "normal politics," and the more the legitimacy of state governance eroded. Likewise, in the 1987–91 Yugoslav case, as the Serb leadership tried to increase or relied more on its existing leverage over state institutional power, the Slovene and the Croatian leaders opposed such moves by increasingly acting outside the existing rules and practices of state governance. The more the Serbian leadership resorted to its leverage over the federal institutions, the more the Slovenes and the Croats defected, and the more the legitimacy of state governance eroded. This cycle continued until fighting between the Slovenes and the YNA troops erupted in June 1990.

> $H_9$: The higher intercommunal trust is, the less likely the politicized communal groups are to rely on institutional power, and vice versa.

This hypothesis is best supported directly by the evidence in the 1957–58 Lebanese case and somewhat less strongly by the 1947–53 Yugoslav case. The converse hypothesis is supported directly by the 1973–75 Lebanese and 1987–91 Yugoslav cases. The outcome of the debates over state governance was driven by the interaction of intercommunal trust and the regime's attempt to rely on institutional power both in the presidency and in the Chamber of Deputies. After Shihab's rise, the repudiation of the Eisenhower Doctrine, and Chamoun stepped down, intercommunal trust increased significantly to reach moderate (if not higher) levels, particularly under Shihab's presidential tenure. The level of reliance on institutional power also decreased under Shihab's rule. In the 1947–53 Yugoslav case, the outcome of the debates was driven by the interaction of intercommunal trust and reliance on institutional power. The latter, however, is hard to measure unambiguously because Tito and his entourage had retreated from the more decentralized 1946 institutional arrangement to a more centralized institutional design. Consequently, the major communal groups did not have much leeway in trying to use institutional power to shape the debates on governance transformation. Instead, the Tito regime concentrated most of the institutional powers in its hand and used them as a means to carry on the transformation agenda as well as eliminate the domestic Cominformist challenge. The regime effectively used its institutional power to construct intercommunal trust as the 1953 Constitutional Law was being formulated.

In the 1973–75 Lebanese case, the outcome of the debates was also driven by the interaction of intercommunal trust and the Maronites' attempt to rely on their institutional power both in the presidency and in the army. Yet the opposite dynamic took hold. The more the Franjieh regime resorted to its leverage over the key state institutions—the presidency and the army—the more the anti–status quo forces resorted to extralegal means, and the more the legitimacy of state governance eroded. This in turn eroded further an already rapidly vanishing intercommunal trust. This cycle continued during the fighting of the second quarter of 1975. Overall, reliance on institutional power increased as intercommunal trust decreased. Likewise, in the 1987–91 Yugoslav case, state collapse was driven by the interaction of low intercommunal trust and the Serb leaders' attempt to rely on institutional power first within the Collective Presidency and then in the YNA.

$H_{10}$: The more rapidly the reliance on institutional power increases (decreases), the more rapidly intercommunal trust decreases (increases), and the more rapidly the scope of collective intentionality decreases (increases).

All four cases provide clear evidence to support this hypothesis. In the 1947–53 Yugoslav case, intercommunal vulnerability was low and decreased, intercommunal trust somewhat stagnated, and reliance on institutional power was moderate and decreased. These are close to the "most likely conditions" for a consolidating form of state governance with an increasing scope of collective intentionality. In contrast, in the 1987–91 case, intercommunal vulnerability was high and rapidly increased, intercommunal trust was rapidly decreasing, and reliance on institutional power was rapidly increasing. These are close to the "most likely conditions" for a collapsed state with a nil scope of collective intentionality.

Likewise, the two Lebanese cases also provide clear evidence for the hypothesis. In the 1957–58 case, intercommunal vulnerability was moderate and decreased, intercommunal trust increased, and reliance on institutional power decreased. These are close to the "most likely conditions" for a consolidating form of state governance with an increasing scope of collective intentionality. In contrast, in the 1973–75 case, intercommunal vulnerability was high and rapidly increased, intercommunal trust rapidly decreased, and reliance on institutional power rapidly increased. These are close to the "most likely conditions" for a collapse of state governance with a vanished scope of collective intentionality.

## Alternative Explanations

Four major approaches have dominated the recent literature on state collapse and failure in multi-communal societies: "ancient hatreds," state deformation, institutionalist, and rationalist approaches.[1] Each of these approaches individually contributes to elucidate one part of the puzzle. Yet by failing to bring together these theoretical elements, these theories have not made a sufficient effort to explicate the continuum of debates on state governance in deeply divided societies under conditions of a fundamentally changing international environment—none provides a theory of state transformation per se. While clearly building on and indebted to the existing literature, the theory developed in this book seeks to better explain the results of state change across deeply divided polities. In the following, I briefly examine the explanatory power of each of the four above approaches in light of the empirical cases.

The "ancient hatreds" hypothesis, although somewhat popular when first proposed, has since been widely rejected among academics.[2] Yet a key insight of this hypothesis—a focus on the role of historical memories in shaping the emergence of ethnic conflicts—must be incorporated into a satisfactory explanation of the transformation of state governance in multi-communal societies. The hypothesis contends that ancient ethnic hatreds burst to the surface to provoke ethnic civil war and state collapse (Kaplan 1993). The rationale is that it is very hard to preempt the long-term effects of collective memories, for they can be remembered or revived even after a majority of the group members may have "forgotten" about them for some period of time. An important shortcoming of this argument is that it does not explicate the conditions under which ancient hatreds become a potent cause of ethnic conflicts. The approach begs the question, Why do ancient hatreds dominate domestic politics in some cases but are forgotten in others? Nor does it explain what makes ancient hatreds relevant at certain times and not at others within the same country. A rounded explanation of ethnic conflicts should neither amplify the role of ancient hatreds nor reduce them to a mere tool that opportunistic leaders use to manipulate and channel the sentiments of their followers for self-serving purposes. Collective memory, as argued in chapter 3, is a social structure that shapes the elites' strategies both by creating opportunities for and by limiting the strategies of these leaders.

As the four cases show, there is an abundance of collective memories in each one of them. However, collective memories by themselves do not provide satisfactory explanations for the eruption of ethnic conflicts and state failure or collapse. The collective memories surfaced at different times, but their eruption did not always correlate with state failure or collapse, or even ethnic conflict. In Yugoslavia, there was a revival of collective memories during the Croatian crisis in the late 1960s and early 1970s, but the Yugoslav federation did not disintegrate then.[3] In Lebanon, ancient hatreds between the various communal groups never completely disappeared, but they also never completely dominated the intercommunal relations. The memories of the Maronite-Druze bloody conflict of 1860 never completely faded away. Yet they did not always cause tensions within the polity.

The state deformation approach revolves around the notion of how changes in the "constraining" role played by the international environment (particularly, security structures such as the Cold War) shape the cohesion of deeply divided states.[4] This approach focuses on the role that changing international conditions can play in undermining domestic intercommunal cohesiveness, thereby creating a strong potential for the eruption of communal conflicts in multi-communal societies and making their states more prone to collapse or failure (Desch 1996, and references therein). For example, many states created after World War II were to a large degree "externally" constructed in the wake of the colonial era through a combination of efforts by movements of armed national liberation groups, indigenous elites, and the United Nation's policies and actions that reflected the interests of the United States and the Soviet Union in reshaping the international order (Jackson 1990; Holsti 1996; Ayoob 1996). The international environment and, most importantly, the external threats played an important constitutive role and contributed to increase the coherence and stability of many among these new states. A reduction in external threat hence removes an essential element of stability, especially for those states that have significant internal tensions and cleavages. As stated by Desch (1996, 260), "States with deep ethnic, social, or linguistic cleavages facing a more benign threat environment should find it harder to maintain cohesion."

The state deformation hypothesis is insufficient to explain major events that shaped the fates of the two states considered in this book. The approach can partially account for the relevance of the emerging Cold War for the transformation of Yugoslavia's state governance. Socialist Yugoslavia reemerged in post-1945 in the image of the Soviet Union and with strong linkages to it. Yet this is underdetermining since many options were possible. Indeed, instead of severing the ties with the Cominform in 1948 and seeking an independent communist path, the Yugoslav leaders might have opted for strengthening the ties with the Soviet Union or alternatively for establishing closer relations with the Western states. Nor can the state deformation approach, for example, explain why the Tito regime decided to reconstruct state governance under the changing international conditions in the aftermath of 1948. Eliminating the Cominformist threat did not necessarily imply a radical transformation of state governance. Nor can the state deformation approach explicate the mechanisms through which the changes occurring at the end of the Cold War strongly shaped the fate of the Yugoslav polity. What linked the external threat and domestic communal cleavages so tightly that changes in international security ignited conflicts along communal lines is not explicable within the state deformation approach. The hypothesis does not, for instance, explicate the key roles that the communal elites, such as Milosevic of Serbia and Tudjman of Croatia, played in turning intercommunal relations into zero-sums.

The state deformation explanation also fails to provide a satisfactory account for the eruption of the 1958 civil war in Lebanon. Nor can it explain how pan-Arabist Nasserism and the U.S. Cold War doctrines enticed Lebanon to abandon its foreign policy of neutralism. The state deformation theory also fails to explain how the 1967 and 1973 Arab-Israeli wars and the rise of the armed Palestinian Resistance as well as the ramifications of the 1970–71 civil war in Jordan created a governance crisis inside Lebanon. The approach is mute on what linked these external conditions and the domestic confessional system so tightly that changes in regional order and security ignited domestic conflicts along lines increasingly defined as confessional in nature and a threat to the integrity of Lebanon.

The institutionalist approach explores the subversive role that state institutions play in the events resulting in a collapse or failure of state governance. The institutionalist approach argues that a state institutional arrangement, which would create and sustain state stability under certain domestic and international conditions, could become a liability to state viability under expanded opportunity structures. The latter stands for "a growing elasticity in the political environment, wherein existing political alignments are disturbed, political access widens, the policy agenda is reordered, and the costs of mobilization decline alongside the benefits of standing passive on the sidelines" (Bunce 1998, 18). The two processes—institutional rigidity and new elasticity of the political environment—push and pull the polity in opposite directions, thereby creating hard-to-resolve dilemmas resulting in state failure or collapse.

This approach provides only a partial explanation for the transformation of state governance because it does not pay attention to the collective meanings—collective intentionality—that underpin the state institutions themselves. The approach has a hard time explaining how the Tito regime succeeded in de-linking its legitimacy from Soviet communism and reconsolidating it afterward. Domestic legitimacy of the Tito regime depended on, and was defined in terms of, the legitimacy of international communism and the Soviet Union. Splitting with Moscow threatened to undermine not only the revolutionary legitimacy of the regime but also the state in its entirety. As explained in chapter 4, Tito was ultimately able to prevail in implementing his vision of a socialist Yugoslavia only after the polity, and particularly the ruling class, became the theater of political debates. These debates were the medium and resource through which a new collective intentionality emerged, independently of historical and ideological ties between the Soviet Union and Yugoslav communists.

Nor can the notion of institutional rigidity explain many of the events leading to the 1958 crisis in Lebanon. The approach does not account well for why the regime transformed the Chamber of Deputies by enlarging it to guarantee the passage of constitutional amendments that would enable Chamoun to seek a consecutive presidential term. State institutions did not become rigid; to the contrary, the effort to transform state institutions was part of what ignited the crisis in the first place. Likewise, the institutionalist approach cannot explain why the coalition of leftist-Muslim groups and organizations actively sought to reconfigure radically the distribution of state institutional power by abrogating the stipulations of the 1943 National Pact. The Maronite behavior does conform to the institutionalist expectation—they wanted to maintain the rigidity of the state institutions. The Maronite Kataeb and NLP strongly opposed any institutional transformation that might pose any threat to the privileged position and power of their community as defined by the National Pact. However, the outcome of the debates on whether to abrogate the National Pact and, hence, radically transform the state institutional arrangements is not sufficiently explicable in terms of the rigidity of state institutions. The latter were quickly marginalized or polarized during the crisis of 1973–75, thereby leading to state collapse.

According to the institutionalist explanation, changing international conditions, such as the rise of pan-Arabist Nasserism and the Cold War penetration of the Middle East, were opportunity structures that became more permissive for a governance crisis. This overlooks the fact that the rise of Nasserism and the Cold War penetration played "de-constitutive" roles in the fate of Lebanon, at both the domestic and international levels. Lebanon had to abandon its foreign policy doctrine of neutralism, which it had carefully enacted in accordance with the 1943 National Pact. This in turn undermined the collective intentionality underpinning the state governance. Similarly, the rise of the Palestinian Resistance and the ramifications of the Arab-Israeli wars as well as the Black September civil war in Jordan played "de-constitutive" roles in the fate of Lebanon in the aftermath of the 1973 war. Israel and the Palestinian Resistance increasingly pushed Lebanon to abandon its foreign policy doctrine of neutralism. However, this was possible only through a transformation of state governance within Lebanon itself, which the Franjieh regime and the Maronite community adamantly opposed. The result was a rapid and continuous erosion of the collective intentionality underpinning the system of state governance.

The rationalist (rational choice-based) approach seeks to explain domestic intercommunal conflicts that often accompany or precede many instances of state failure. The approach thus explores the strategic vulnerabilities that ethnic groups and their elites face under the condition of a weakening state. Two sorts of rationalist arguments have recently attempted to explain the rapid and widespread eruption of ethnic violence between previously peaceful ethnic communities (Lake and Rothchild 1996; Fearon and Laitin 1996; Hardin 1995; Posen 1993; Gagnon 1994–95). First, an elite-based approach argues that the elites who fear for their leadership positions might go as far as creating a situation of interethnic conflict. They would then ride on the resulting fears of their followers and co-ethnics to build popular support and demonize their opponents. Second, a group-based hypothesis argues that collective fears of future interethnic vulnerability most often cause intense ethnic conflict. As an interethnic security dilemma takes hold, ethnic groups become apprehensive and face interethnic vulnerability, thereby most likely engaging in interethnic conflict.

The empirical evidence offered in the cases considered in this book shows that the elites played important roles in the eruption of communal conflicts. However, the ruling elites did not always do so. The opposition elites or elites not holding state offices or powerful political positions also played major roles in the emergence of intercommunal conflict. Both the ruling and challenger elites appealed to communal sentiments of their communities to garner support for their strategies. Likewise, the historical cases show that the intergroup strategies chosen by the elites played an important role. They also lend support to the assertion regarding the emergence of interethnic dilemmas. The cases, however, show that the dilemmas were not unavoidable—the dilemmas were socially constructed through, first, the intergroup strategies that the communal leaders followed and, second, the feedback between these strategies.

Yet none of the two rationalist arguments can provide a satisfactory explanation for the transformation of state governance in Yugoslavia or Lebanon. Of course, ethnic politics remained an underlying condition even under the Tito regime. That the 1946 Constitution was an emulation of the 1936 Soviet solution to the problem of ethno-nationalism is testimony to this fact. However, ethnic politics during the 1947–53 period was marginally relevant because wartime intercommunal massacres had a traumatic impact on the "collective" psyche of the various communal groups; there was silence and (somewhat temporary) amnesia about the national question. Ethnic politics did threaten to become an important issue during the Cominformist challenge to Tito. Yet both variants of ethnic politics arguments fail to explain the differentiated spread of Cominformism within different national groups. The elite-based approach cannot explain why the ruling elites who belonged to different communal groups remained united under the domestic and international threats to their positions. Nor can the group-based perspective explain the debates that occurred around the Cominformist challenge to the Tito regime. Ethnic politics acquired some importance only as the national question began to reemerge in the late 1950s, and more so in the late 1960s and early 1970s.

Nor can any one of the two rationalist arguments provide a satisfactory explanation for state collapse in Yugoslavia in 1991. Ethnic politics remained an underlying condition both during and after the Tito era. That the republics' leaders would resort to using this "raw material" in the late 1980s is not surprising. Gagnon, for example, argues that the conservative Serb leaders endeavored to create a violent conflict to fend off domestic challengers (1994–95, 140). However, this is insufficient to explain, for example, the destruction of the intercommunal trust between the Serbs and the Croats and between the Serbs and the Slovenes in the period 1987–91. Trust was *deconstructed* in the late 1980s as the republican leaders began not only to talk past one another, but also to engage one another in rhetorical wars of incrimination and blame for the problems that their communal groups were facing or could face. While this book also highlights the leaders' self-serving strategies, it argues that both the Serb and Croat (and Slovene) leaders actively participated in the deconstruction of intercommunal trust. The feedback between the Serb and Croat (and Slovene) leaders inside and outside the federal institutions played an important role in stalling all federal attempts to improve the system and contributed to ignite the conflict.

Neither argument fares better in explaining the fate of state governance in Lebanon. The leaders and groups-based arguments are able to explain only some aspects of the descent toward fighting. Communal politics did threaten to become an important issue during the short 1958 civil war as the Muslims increasingly dominated the opposition militia and the Maronites dominated the militias fighting for the Chamoun regime. The elite-based approach can also partially explain why the Chamoun regime and its supporters who belonged to different communal groups feared the repercussions of the Iraqi revolution and the establishment of the UAR on the Lebanese polity. However, the conflict in Lebanon was already developing before both events took place, and the president and the Maronites were no more vulnerable than they were before. To the contrary, the opposition with its varied composition wanted the regime to preserve the stipulations of the 1943 National Pact, which meant preserving in the first place the special role that the Maronites had played since independence. It was the Chamoun regime that challenged the status quo, thereby making the Sunni and Druze leaders feel more vulnerable and politically insecure. Nor can the group-based approach explain the debates that occurred around the 1957 parliamentary elections, Chamoun's bid for a second presidential term, Chamoun's adherence to the Eisenhower Doctrine, or the eruption of fighting, to name a few. Ethnic politics was only marginally important to the whole process of transforming state governance in the period 1957–58, acquiring some importance only as the situation down-spiraled into a civil war. Before the fighting broke out, the fault line of the opposition-regime divide was not confessional; many prominent Maronite leaders such as former president al-Khuri and the Maronite patriarch joined the opposition against the Chamoun regime. In fact, most of the Lebanese political elites sided with the opposition against Chamoun's policies. Neither the Maronites nor any other major communal group feared intercommunal vulnerability before the fighting erupted; rather, the prospect of a continuing civil war is what made intercommunal fear a real possibility.

The two varieties of rationalist arguments also fall short in providing a satisfactory explanation for the second crisis of state governance in Lebanon. Of course, communal politics remained an underlying condition before and during the crisis of 1973–75. However, it became an important issue only after armed militias increasingly divided into Muslims versus Christians. The elite-based approach can in part account for how the Maronite elites in general feared for the privileges that they had enjoyed under the stipulations of the 1943 National Pact. They were willing to go as far as it takes to preserve those privileges. Likewise, the traditional Muslim establishment elite, or *zu'ama,* also came under tremendous pressure from the leftist leaders and groups and feared losing their traditional positions acquired through the practices of Lebanese sectarian domestic politics. They also were willing to do whatever it took to preserve their privileges and power positions, if somewhat to a lesser extent than the Maronite leaders. The main challengers to the system, however, were the Druze and Shiite elites. The elite-based approach can thus partially explain the Maronite-Sunni versus Druze-Shiite conflict. Yet what is missing from this picture is the Palestinian Resistance, without which the confrontation might not have begun in the first place. The presence of the armed Palestinian Resistance in Lebanon and its anti-Israeli actions and costly Israeli aggressions against Lebanon were two core issues that strongly shaped the conflict and prevented a resolution of the differences between the various antagonists. Moreover, the elite-based approach argues that threatened ruling elites will carry out major institutional transformations to preserve their power positions. However, in the case of Lebanon it was just the opposite, as the privileged Maronite and Sunni elites opposed any major institutional changes, which the Druze, Shiite, and leftist elites were demanding—the expectations of the rationalist elite-based approach are turned upside down. Nor does the group-based approach satisfactorily explain the debates that occurred around the key issues of the distribution of state institutional power and the Palestinian Resistance. The Druzes and Shiites did not fear future vulnerability but were rather seeking to increase their political power. The Druze-Shiite-leftist alliance wanted to dislodge the Maronites from their privileged power positions by radically transforming the system of state governance. Whereas the Maronites "feared for their future," the Druze-Shiite-leftist coalition was hurting from the present.

## Theoretical and Policy Implications

The modern state is a two-level social construction, and its failure or collapse, when it occurs, is a two-level social deconstruction. Fundamental changes in the international (regional) order can induce pressures for adaptation to the changing external conditions through a reconfiguration of state governance. As key domestic political actors debate the issue, the form of state governance is increasingly at stake. A combination of intercommunal vulnerability and trust and intercommunal distribution of institutional power determines the outcome of the debate on state governance as collapsed, failing, consolidating, or consolidated state. This argument has a number of implications for the research agenda on international relations, the future of the state in the post-Cold War era, and policy.

The failure to explain the rapid end of the Cold War, let alone predict it, has shaken the study of international relations. The approach of this book contributes to these ongoing debates in a number of ways. First, the book not only highlights "constitutive rules and practices" as an explanatory variable, as most constructivist works do; most important, it focuses on *changes in these constitutive rules and practices* as an explanatory variable. Because state governance is defined in terms of a collective intentionality that underpins the constitutive rules and practices of state governance, using changes in constitutive rules and practices as an explanatory variable does not, however, imply discarding the insights of approaches relying on more conventional concepts such as power structures and institutions. Relying on constitutive practices not only does not preclude the consideration of power and institutions, it also considers their founding practices and norms. As the empirical chapters show, discussing the transformation of state governance necessarily incorporates a consideration of both tangible variables such as economic and security structures and intangible variables such as ideas and intersubjective meanings. Thus, a constructivist approach is not to be opposed to conventional arguments, whether anchored in realism, neorealism, or neoliberal institutionalism. Rather, a successful constructivist argument should be able to account for the insights of these approaches and complement them with new ones. This is possible because the approach uses as its unit of analysis the notion of constitutive rules and practices, which includes both discursive and behavioral components.

Second, collective intentionality—that is, the "we take for granted" character —of state governance does not always slowly change, as conventional wisdom has it. Rather, changes in collective intentionality can be quite rapid with far-reaching effects, and thus can explain the rapid collapse of a state. As the empirical analyses show, a relatively rapid change in collective intentionality in Yugoslavia as the Cold War was winding down in 1989–91 quickly culminated in the disintegration of the federation.

Third, a recent trend in international relations (IR) theory has highlighted the importance of going beyond single-level type of theories in attempts to synthesize domestic and international variables in various types of two-level theories. Much of this work on two-level theories of IR has, however, assumed a rationalist perspective, which pays little attention to international constitutive rules and practices as independent variables. While this kind of theory has great potential, it is not the only or most comprehensive way of two-level theorizing. As the theoretical and empirical chapters of this book suggest, constructivism when simultaneously applied at two levels has much to offer us in terms of synthesizing international and domestic politics. Because constructivism fundamentally problematizes the constitutive rules and practices of states and domestic actors as well as their intersubjective meanings, it has a strong potential for bridging otherwise separated disciplines of international, comparative, and domestic politics. This is a challenge that constructivists should address.

Fourth, the recent collapse of a number of multiethnic states has highlighted once more the debate on the viability of these states. Would the current era of less intense international security competition increase the likelihood of collapse for multiethnic states? While not dismissing this line of questioning, the two-level constructivist theory of this book suggests a different though overlapping type of question: What type of international constitutive practices and rules are more conducive to the collapse of multiethnic states? The Yugoslav and Lebanese cases suggest that changes in the constitutive practices and rules of international order contributed to ignite the process of state collapse. Because the international constitutive practices and rules are social constructions that always face the prospect of deconstruction, state collapse will neither occur less nor more in the post–Cold War era. As to the specific case of multiethnic states, because the collapse of these states depends on a social construction of a domestic intercommunal debate on state governance, changes in the international constitutive rules and practices do not automatically translate to a strong potential for collapse. Multiethnic states are no more prone to collapse in the post–Cold War era than more homogeneous ones.

The two-level constructivist theory of this book has a number of policy implications. First, the collapse of states is a two-level phenomenon. Hence, the international community should deal with it as an international issue. The international community does contribute to the consolidation and dissolution of states. This contribution can be unintentional or proactive. In the case of Yugoslavia, both superpowers actively participated in the construction of the buffer position of the state, and thus to the viability of the state. However, as the Cold War was ending, the Soviet Union had no choice but not to be much concerned about Yugoslavia. In contrast, the West and in particular the United States could have opted for a different policy on Yugoslavia had they wanted to do so. Doubtless, the United States was preoccupied with other important matters such as the end of the Cold War, the collapse of the Soviet Union, and the 1991 Gulf War to liberate Kuwait. Nonetheless, the initial passive role of the United States was also the result of a misguided policy rooted in the rationale that the events unfolding in Yugoslavia in 1989–91 were the consequence of historical grievances and ethnic enmity, compounded by a domestic economic crisis. A policy rooted in a two-level constructivist understanding of state collapse would have called instead for more proactive policies. The collapse of Yugoslavia was a two-level deconstruction to which the international community and the United States in particular took part by not assuming its responsibility proactively. To use a metaphor, constructing the foundations of a building and then subsequently letting these foundations erode is de facto taking part in the demolition of the building, even if unintentionally so.

Second, the approach also implies that although the changes in the constitutive practices and rules of the global economy and the Cold War system caused strong domestic debates in deeply divided societies, the outcome of these debates is not irreversibly determined. Should the intercommunal rivalry not emerge, the collapse of the state and ensuing suffering could be averted. The international community could play a more decisive role by intervening at the right time and on the right issues. Instead of precipitating or contributing to consolidate the intercommunal rivalry as the European Union and the United States did when they recognized the newly constructed sovereignties of the Slovenes and Croats, the international community could have played a more positive role by containing the intercommunal rivalry through a combination of incentives and disincentives.

Third, even if the international community could not have averted, for example, the collapse of the Yugoslav federation, proactively contributing to construct an ethnic peace might have averted ensuing bloody ethnic conflict. A constructivist approach does not inherently call for status quo preservation but rather recognizes that states are socially constructed, deconstructed, and reconstructed. The transition phase between a deconstructed state and new constructions is also a social process to which the international community can—and in fact intentionally or unintentionally does—contribute and influence. The international community is part of the structural environment that constitutes the agency of various domestic and international actors. As such, the international community empowers certain actors and constrains others, even when it remains passive. An international community that favors international security and peace thus cannot afford not to act proactively. Not doing so only delays almost unavoidable intervention, as the tragedies of Bosnia-Herzegovina, Rwanda, and others evidence.

# Notes

## 1. Introduction

1. Seventy seven percent of the 164 wars that occurred from 1945 to 1996 were internal wars (Holsti 1996, 21).
2. The G. W. Bush administration's espousal of preemption and regime change as major components of U.S. foreign policy in the aftermath of September 11, 2001, appears to lead to a more focused interest of the United States in failing states and their consequent roles as possible breeding grounds for international terrorism. However, the jury is still out on this, since maintaining such a foreign policy agenda is strongly dependent on the nature and composition of the incumbent U.S. administration. In any case, a "hawkish" administration set on a policy of regime change and fighting international terrorism does indeed reinforce the point made in this book—understanding the failure and stability of multi-ethnic societies and states is an issue that calls for more policy and academic attention.
3. Zartman characterizes a collapsed state as "the breakdown of good governance, law, and order" (1995, 6).
4. Only eighteen complete collapses of state have occurred between 1955 and 1998 (Esty et al. 1999).

## 2. Debating State Governance

1. This chapter basically revolves around two key concepts: *collective intentionality* and *constitutive rules and practices.* Much of the conceptual and causal discussion as well as empirical validation of the book can be viewed as an attempt to set firm grounds for using these two concepts as key explanatory variables of the transformation of state governance. Moreover, although the book introduces these two concepts in the context of multi-communal states, their import goes beyond the theory and cases of this book—both concepts are indeed essential elements of any system of governance, including structures of international governance.

2. For the interested reader, see the following reference on various aspects of collective intentionality: *The American Journal of Economics and Sociology* 62, no. 1 (January 2003).
3. Ibid.
4. Put differently, I am proposing (of course, alongside many other authors) that the dilemmas of collective action cannot be satisfactorily understood and explained within an individualistic methodology. Only the use of a holistic methodology can account for and successfully explain the social dilemmas of collective action. This comes at the price of assuming that collectivities of actors can have a collective intentionality, which is not reducible to the sum of individual intentionalities of the members of the collectivity. The existence of collective intentionality then makes it possible to speak of collective rationality, making rational collective action explainable in terms of collective rationality, much like rational individual action is explainable in terms of individual rationality.
5. As defined by John Searle (1995), constitutive rules typically have the form "X counts as Y" or "X counts as Y in context C." For example, such and such counts as a legal move of a knight in chess, such and such a position counts as checkmate, such and such a person who meets certain qualifications counts as president of the United States, and so on. Such and such a person who satisfies certain conditions counts as our president, such and such a type of object counts as money in our society, and such and such a sequence of sounds or marks counts as a sentence and, indeed, counts as a speech act in our language.
6. Generally, when dealing with institutional facts from the point of view of someone who is using the rules as guides for action or as criteria of interpretation of someone else's actions one, as Wittgenstein (1974, 244) said, "can't get behind the rules, because there isn't any behind."
7. A rule can (if not necessarily always) emerge as a convention only to become later on a constitutive rule, that is, a way to define and legitimize what counts as a certain activity in a certain context.
8. Rules are either constitutive or regulative. "Constitutive rules define an activity . . . while regulative rules delimit the range of this activity's legitimacy" (Dessler 1989, 456). For example, the act of driving a car existed prior to the rule that specifies "drive on the right-hand side of the road." The rule regulates increased traffic and limits the growing numbers of accidents, an antecedently existing activity. Constitutive rules "create the very possibility of certain activities" (Searle 1995, 27; Dessler 1989). A rule is "constitutive" of an activity only when this rule becomes a taken-for-granted enabling background of the activity (Giddens 1984, 22–23, 67). In the current international system, it has become a given that states are sovereign and that their sovereignty is a right that in principle should be upheld and defended. Much of international law, for example, will be meaningless if the states are not taken for granted as being "sovereign" actors.
9. John Searle (2003) argues that political power has two characteristic features. First, all political power, though exercised from above, comes from below. This is true in dictatorships as well as in democracies. Hitler and Stalin were both constantly obsessed by the need for security because they could never take the political system as having been accepted, that is, as a given part of reality. The system

had to be constantly maintained by a system of rewards and punishments and by terror. Second, even though the individual is the source of all political power, by his or her ability to engage in collective intentionality, he or she typically feels powerless since he or she typically feels that the powers that be are not in any way dependent on him or her. This partly explains why revolutionaries always seek to introduce a new kind of collective intentionality to challenge the existing or eroding one, e.g., class consciousness, identification with the proletariat, student solidarity, or consciousness-raising among women. Because the existing entire system rests on collective intentionality, its destruction can be attained by creating an alternative and challenging form of collective intentionality.

## 3. A Theory of Debating State Governance

1. Onuf 1989; Dessler 1989; Klotz 1995; Katzenstein 1996; Finnemore 1996; Arfi 1998; Barnett 1998; Hopf 1998; Wendt 1999.
2. The capacity to organize refers to a group's ability to mobilize its members for political action. It depends on the existence of social networks connecting together the members of the ethnic communities. These networks are resources that facilitate collective action by the group.
3. Should the perception of a breach of trust emerge, the higher the mutual trust, the more likely the groups will be to give the "breaching" partner the benefit of the doubt by interpreting the case as an isolated case of misjudgment or, more generally, misguided behavior. However, a series of repeated breaches might eventually undermine the existing level of mutual trust.
4. I adopt North's (1990, 7) definition of lock-in processes with some appropriate modifications. See also Esman (1994, 31–32).
5. Kaufman (2001) presents a theory on the symbolic politics of ethnic war that explores the roots of ethnic war in psychological terms as well as considers the propitious conditions under which these psychological roots develop and evolve.
6. Horowitz (1985) argues that emotional heat comes from a fear of group extinction.
7. Generally speaking, rules are constitutive only if they are part of a set of rules. Strictly, there is no such thing as *a* rule that is constitutive in isolation. This means, for example, that the set of constitutive rules of chess is the determination of the intension of the word "chess," as the subset of constitutive rules of the rook is the determination of the intension of the word "rook" in the language game of the chess players. This feature of constitutive rules is implicit in what Wittgenstein says on the rules of chess. According to Wittgenstein (1958, §197), "chess is the game it is in virtue of all its rules." Each chessman "*is* the sum of the rules according to which it moves" (Waismann 1979, 134). A set of constitutive rules defines a logical space. A subset of these rules defines the "logical position" of a chessman *in* such space (Waismann 1979, 104). "Logical position" does not mean the actual point occupied by the chessman on the chessboard, but its "status," that is, the capacity of movement of a particular kind of object on the chessboard. Wittgenstein (1958, §563) expresses this idea when he says that "the meaning of a piece is its role in the game."
8. The external environment might contribute to the construction of the internal

attributes of some states more than others (and vice versa). Consequently, some states would be more affected by fundamental changes in the international context than others (Jackson 1990).

9. This section shares many elements with Hoffman's (2002) operationalization of trust in international politics.

## 4. Yugoslavia and the Emerging Cold War, 1947–53

1. Correspondence between the Central Committee of the Communist Party of Yugoslavia (CPY) and the Central Committee of the Communist Party of the Soviet Union (CPSU, Bolsheviks), Belgrade, 1948.
2. Tito's speech in Ljubljana on May 27, 1945; correspondence between CPY and CPSU, 3; Clissold 1975, 166.
3. Stalin and Molotov to Tito, March 27, 1948 (correspondence between CPY and CPSU, 23–28, where Stalin and Molotov are not named as the signatories of the letter).
4. Tito and Kardelj to Stalin and Molotov, April 13, 1948 (correspondence between CPY and CPSU, 29–41).
5. Stalin and Molotov to Tito and CC of CPY, May 22, 1948 (correspondence between CPY and CPSU, 66–69); Jugoslavije 1948, 251–52 ff.). The Communist Information Bureau—Cominform—was formed in October 1947 by the Soviet Union, Poland, Czechoslovakia, Hungary, Yugoslavia, Bulgaria, and Romania and French and Italian communist parties.
6. *Times* (London), August 19, 20, 21, 22, 23, 24, 26 1946, October 10, 1946; Dedijer 1953, 259–61.
7. Cannon to State Department, June 30, 1948, PRO/FO 371/72579 Disp. 936.
8. Heuser 1988, 127–29, and references therein.
9. Acheson to Fowler, February 11, 1950, *FRUS,* 1950, iv. 1370.
10. Tito, *Govori i clanci,* 5: 218–21; Kardelj, *Problemi,* 2: 223.
11. Gerskovic, *Komunist* 4, nos. 4–5 (1970): 94.
12. Ibid., 354–79.
13. Kardelj, *Problemi,* 2: 111.
14. Tito, speech of June 26, 1950, *Govori i clanci,* 5: 224.
15. Kardelj, speech of June 25, 1950, *Problemi,* 2: 45.
16. *Borba,* January 24–25, 1950.
17. *Partiska izgradnja* 2, no. 6 (July 1950): 52–56.
18. Ibid., 52.
19. Djilas, *Borba,* May 1–3, 1952.
20. *Komunist* 6 (September-December 1952): 1–8, at 7–8.
21. Statut 1952, articles 2, 7; *Statut* 1948, 51; *Komunist* 6, 103; Johnson 1972, 213–14.
22. It contained 115 articles, the last of which abolished chapters 6–10, 12, and 15 of the 1946 Constitution (Hondius 1968, 192).
23. Tito, speech of June 26, 1950, *Govori i clanci,* 5: 205.
24. On April 1, 1952, the federal Parliament adopted a General Act on People's Committees (Hondius 1968, 189).
25. Cominform journal, July 1, 1948, cited in Clissold 1975, 207.
26. *Borba,* January 22, 1949, cited in Banac 1988, 129.

27. Jelena Lovric, "Staljinizam ne miruje," *Danas,* August 16, 1983, 12.
28. At least 13,700 persons were arrested as Cominformists at the beginning of 1948 (Rankovic 1951, 387; Neal 1958, 37).
29. *Jedinstvo,* June 8, 1964, 4.
30. *Pravda,* February 24, 1950, 6, and September 12, 1952, 4.
31. *Jedinstvo,* June 15, 1964, 4; *Glas na B'ulgarite v Jugoslaviia,* June 27, 1949, 2; Shoup 1968, 138.
32. The Battle of Kosovo occurred in 1389 between advancing strong Ottoman armies and a weak and crumbling Serbian Empire.
33. The Catholic Church played a crucial role in preserving the Croats' historical memory (Ramet 1992b).
34. The Ottomans conquered Bosnia-Herzegovina in 1463, which led to profound religious changes, with a very large segment of the population converting gradually from Christianity to Islam. Under different successive post-Ottoman regimes, Muslims persistently struggled to assert a national identity, which is neither Serb nor Croat (Pinson 1993; Donia and Fine 1994; Banac 1984).
35. A 1948 party census demonstrated that of the 890,094 respondents in Bosnia-Herzegovina who said that they were Muslims, 89 percent described their identity as undetermined, 8 percent as Serb, and 3 percent as Croat (Donia and Fine 1994).
36. *Borba,* April 29, 1922, 4.
37. Sima Markovic was secretary of the Yugoslav Communist Party in the early twenties.
38. Josip Broz Tito, who became the party secretary general in 1936, gathered a group of associates from different parts of Yugoslavia, namely Mosa Pijade (a Serbian Jew), Edvard Kardelj (a Slovenian), Aleksander Rankovic (a Serb), Milovan Djilas (a Montenegrin), Rade Koncar (a Croat), and Ivo-Lola Ribar (a Croat from Serbia) (Hondius 1968, 121).
39. In the first instruction to the partisan resistance on August 10, 1941, the leadership proclaimed: "The People's Liberation Partisans Detachments in all regions of Yugoslavia—Serbia, Croatia, Slovenia, Montenegro, Bosnia and Hercegovina, Macedonia, Vojvodina, Sandzak and Dalmatia—have as their principal objective the liberation of the people from the occupiers and the struggle against the local accomplices of the occupation, who render assistance to the oppression and terror waged against our peoples" (as quoted in Hondius 1968, 122).
40. Tito 1947, 180; Burks 1971, 124–26.
41. Tito 1947, 121–30.
42. Ivo Krbek, *Narodna Republika Hrvatske u FNRJ,* 8.
43. *Novi Sad,* April 8, 1945, 1; *Oslobodjenje* (Sarajevo), April 16, 1952, 1.
44. *Jedinstvo,* June 8, 1964, 4.
45. Tito 1948, 6.
46. *Komunist* 4–5 (July–Sept 1950): 48–87. Party historians did not receive well the works that appeared in the early 1950s because they lacked ideological content (Shoup 1968, 199; *Komunist* (March 26, 1964): 4.
47. *Borba,* June 5, 1946, 1.
48. *New York Times,* December 9, 1946, 5.
49. *Nova Doba,* September 6, 1946, 1; October 2, 1946, 2–3.

50. *Oslobodjenje* (Sarajevo), January 14, 1947, 4; September 26, 1946, 4.
51. *Komunist* 10 (October 1953): 726–33.
52. *Komunist* 2–3 (March–May 1950): 258–61.
53. *Komunist* (March 16, 1963): 9.
54. *Drugi plenum Centralnog komiteta Saveza komunista Jugoslavije*, 12.
55. *Komunist* (November 5, 1964): 3.
56. An important issue of research design is involved in here (as kindly pointed out by one of the anonymous reviewers). I think that instead of just "hiding" this aspect of my empirical analysis (or by rejecting this case because it does not fully lend itself to analysis), it is important to keep this in the book so as to show the limits of the theory as well as the empirical analysis. No theory or empirical analysis is immune to some failures or shortcomings, and hence it is imperative that the author engages in a process of self-critique, even before reviewers do so. Put simply, I intentionally kept this part of the analysis to avoid falling into the trap of choosing only empirical data and cases that exactly fit the theory.
57. In 1959, the composition of the federal executive council was Serbia 10 (29 percent), Croatia 2 (6 percent), Slovenia 6 (18 percent), Bosnia and Hercegovina 4 (12 percent), Macedonia 3 (9 percent), and Montenegro 9 (26 percent) (Hondius 1968, 204).
58. Djordjevic 1963, 1–3, 12; *Osmi kongres*, 224–25; *Borba*, October 2, 1966, 1; *Komunist* (September 22, 1966); *Vjesnik*, July 27, 1966; *Ustav Socijalisticke Federativne Republike Jugoslavije*, 341.

## 5. Yugoslavia and the Waning Cold War, 1987–91

1. Important examples are the 1991 Gulf War, the threat posed by the dissolution of the Soviet Union, and the creation of weak states with nuclear capabilities.
2. In a 1989 survey, 92 percent of the Slovene and 75 percent of the Croatian youths did not wish to join the LCY, while only 42 percent of the Serbian youths did not want to become members of the LCY (Cohen 1995, 48).
3. Andrejevich 1991b, 26–29.
4. Warren Zimmermann, former U.S. ambassador to Yugoslavia (cited in Djilas 1993, 95); Glenny 1993, 36.
5. Andrejevich 1991a, 25–30.
6. Post–World War II Yugoslavia was a sort of balance of power system among the eight constituent units of the federation (six republics and two autonomous provinces) (Ramet 1992b, chapter 1).
7. Djordjevic 1963, 1–3, 12.
8. *Osmi kongres*, 224–25; articles 27 and 28 of the statute.
9. *New York Times*, February 20, 1966.
10. *Borba*, April 2, 1967, 5; *Borba*, March 26, 1967, 2.
11. *Komunist*, September 22, 1966, 1.
12. Ibid., January 13, 1966, 1.
13. Ibid., November 5, 1964, 3; ibid., September 15, 1966, 2.
14. Ibid., February 6, 1964, 1.
15. Ibid., March 3, 1966, 7.
16. Ibid., February 3, 1966, 2; ibid., March 24, 1966, 2.

17. An example of de jure exercise of *ex ante* agency is Milosevic's reduction of the Kosovo and Vojvodina statutes from autonomous provinces to provinces of Serbia.
18. *Pravloslavlje* (Belgrade), May 15, 1982.
19. Ibid., June 1, 1989, 3–4.
20. *FBIS-EEU,* August 4, 1989, 43.
21. *Politika,* September 2, 1990, 18.
22. *FBIS-EEU,* June 26, 1992, 18.
23. The LCY did not become a coveted institution for it was already increasingly marginalized.
24. John Mueller (2000) has strongly argued that in Yugoslavia in the 1990s (and Rwanda in 1994) interethnic war was "banal" in the sense that it was "by the ministrations of small—sometimes very small—bands of opportunistic marauders recruited by political leaders and operating under their general guidance. Many of these participants were drawn from street gangs or from bands of soccer hooligans. Others were criminals specifically released from prison for the purpose. Their participation was required because the Yugoslav army, despite years of supposedly influential nationalist propaganda and centuries of supposedly pent-up ethnic hatreds, substantially disintegrated early in the war and refused to fight." Although Mueller is right in his assessment of the immediate acts of killings that occurred in many instances in Yugoslavia (and Rwanda and, I would add, in Algeria in the mid-1990s) the point that is more important for the argument of this book is what made these acts possible in the first place. In fact, Mueller's argument as he described it is truly another very good refutation of the ancient-hatreds hypothesis as described in the conclusions chapter. He clearly states that "rather than reflecting deep, historic passions and hatreds, the violence seems to have been the result of a situation in which common, opportunistic, sadistic, and often distinctly non-ideological marauders were recruited and permitted free rein by political authorities." The key phrase here is "recruited and permitted free rein by political authorities." Therefore, overall Mueller's argument reinforces the need for the multidimensional analysis that this book advocates, wherein "ancient hatreds" and "ethnic vulnerability" are only two explanatory elements among many others. Moreover, the book does not attempt to specifically explain the occurrence and eruption of violence in Yugoslavia. Rather, the book offers an explanation of the general "context" that emerged as the state was collapsing and hence made violence (of all sorts) possible.

## 6. Lebanon, the Cold War Penetration, and the Rise of Nasserism, 1957–58

1. National Security Council series, n.d., 5801/1,1.
2. Ibid.
3. Ibid.
4. National Intelligence Estimate, November 15, 1955, in *FRUS* 14 (1955): 754.
5. The Kremlin's response emphasized the right of Arab states to fill the vacuum left by Britain and France (Gerges 1994, 81).

6. President Chamoun's press statement, Beirut, May 21, 1958.
7. Middle East News Agency, "Outgoing Minister's Statement," November 18, 1956, cited in *Summary of World Broadcasts,* November 20, 1956, 5.
8. *Hagerty James Collection,* July 1958, 1.
9. Tom Streithorst, "Face to Face with Camille Chamoun," *Middle East Forum* (Beirut), April 1957, 7.
10. The 1958 crisis was a direct response to foreign influence and to Lebanon's dependence on the West (Jumblatt, *Fi Majra al-siyasa al-Lubnaniya,* 57; Odeh 1985, 100).
11. *Mahadir Najkis al-Nuwwab* (Proceedings of the Chamber of Deputies), Beirut, 1957, 1: 974.
12. The Front also included the Muslim Youth Movement, the National Organization, Progressive Socialist Party, al-Ba<sup>c</sup>th, the National Call, the Constitutional Bloc.
13. The Maronite patriarch, Monsignor Paul Meouchy, sided with the opposition and accused the Chamoun regime of having failed in both its internal and external policies. *Al-Jarida and L'Orient,* April 20, 1958.
14. *Mideast Mirror,* April 7, 1957, 4–5.
15. Ibid., May 19, 1957, 15.
16. Ibid., July 7, 1957, 12.
17. Ibid., June 23, 1957, 11.
18. Ibid., February 16, 1958, 5.
19. *New York Times,* February 27, 1958; *Mideast Mirror,* March 16, 1958, 7.
20. Former president al-Khuri and the Maronite patriarch sided with the opposition.
21. *Mideast Mirror,* February 16, 1958, 5.
22. *New York Times,* March 10, 1958.
23. The Lebanese government banned Egyptian and Syrian papers and jammed Radio Cairo, Voice of the Arabs, and Radio Damascus (Qubain 1961, 80).
24. Chamoun confirmed in interviews with the correspondents of *Newsweek* and the *United Press* during the first week of July that he would step down on September 23 (*Mideast Mirror,* June 1, 1958, 6; *Mideast Mirror,* June 13, 1958, 15).
25. *Mideast Mirror,* August 24, 1958, 14; *Mideast Mirror,* August 31, 1958, 5–6.
26. Tom Streithorst, "Face to Face with Camille Chamoun," *Middle East Forum* (Beirut), April 1957, 7.
27. *Mideast Mirror,* February 16, 1958, 5.
28. *New York Times,* March 10, 1958.
29. *Mideast Mirror,* June 1, 1958, 6; *Mideast Mirror,* June 13, 1958, 15.
30. Lebanon's first president after independence, Bishara al Khuri, manipulated the parliamentary elections in 1947 and brought in a puppet Chamber. The latter adopted on May 22, 1948, a constitutional amendment that enabled him to seek a second presidential term. After the April 1951 election, which returned another puppet Chamber, opposition developed inside the Chamber known as the National Socialist Front (NSF). The NSF ultimately forced the president to resign through the "Rosewater Revolution" on September 18.
31. Before American troops landed in Lebanon, the issue of Chamoun's reelection had been settled (*Mideast Mirror,* June 1, 1958, 6).
32. The Maronites are of Aramatic origin, and until the eighteenth century they

spoke Aramaic in its Syrian form rather than Arabic. For over a thousand years, they have inhabited the northern regions of Mount Lebanon, gradually spreading southward since the latter Middle Ages over former Druze and Shiite territory (Hitti 1962).

33. The army chief of staff was supposed to be a Druze.
34. The *zu'ama* united on two occasions when politics went "beyond-the-normal" when the government attempted to exclude most of the *zu'ama* or change the stipulations of the National Pact—al-Khuri in 1952 and Chamoun in 1958.
35. The regime was able to arrange in 1958 a temporary alliance between the PPS and the Phalanges in spite of their completely mutually opposed doctrines and ideologies; whereas the Phalanges were for an independent and sovereign Lebanon, the PPS did not even recognize the independence of Lebanon and believed in incorporating it in a larger Fertile Crescent. Preserving the Chamoun regime was the common goal.
36. *Mideast Mirror,* August 24, 1958, 14; *Mideast Mirror,* August 31, 1958, 5–6.
37. The army chief feared that, if his troops were to take decisive action, the army would break up into Muslim and Christian factions, and one side would support the government and the other the opposition (Qubain 1961, 81–83).

## 7. Lebanon and the Metamorphosis of Arab-Israeli Relations, 1973–75

1. On June 9, Nasser publicly assumed responsibility for the debacle and resigned as president. The cabinet and the National Assembly rejected the resignation, and Nasser withdrew it.
2. The plan was a modification of November 1967 UN Resolution 242, which called on Israel to withdraw "from territories occupied in the recent conflict," for a termination of the state of belligerency, for the right of all states in the area "to live in peace within secure and recognized boundaries," and for a just settlement of the "refugee" problem to be attained.
3. Sadat emerged from the 1973 war with the intention of radically restructuring Egyptian domestic and foreign policies (Barnett 1998, 182–83).
4. President Asad stated on March 8, 1974, that "it will be useful to remind the Israeli leaders that Palestine is not only part of the Arab homeland but is also a principal part of southern Syria" (Dishon 1977, 28).
5. During the 1970 Jordanian civil war, Syria alone among the other Arab countries came to the Palestinians' aid.
6. In 1965, over 180,000 Palestinians were located in Lebanon, representing the second largest community of the diaspora. A combination of further immigration, the 1967 war, and natural increases in the population had raised the number of Palestinians resident in Lebanon to approximately 235,000 in 1969 and 300,000 in 1976 (Brynen 1990, 25).
7. Text of the Seventh Arab Summit Conference Resolutions, 177–78.
8. "Relations with Syria: Prior to the Lebanese War, 1973 to April 1975," *Fiches du Monde Arabe,* no. 1721 (October 22, 1980).
9. *Daily Star,* January 13, 1975.

10. Entelis 1974, 162; *Arab Report and Record,* July 28, 1967; *The Middle East Reporter* (Beirut), July 12, 1967.
11. Gemayel issued a press statement of June 22, 1967, in which he revived a four-year-old proposal for the internationalization of Lebanon in the manner of Switzerland (*Arab Report and Record,* June 22, 1967).
12. *Le Monde,* May 8, 1968.
13. "In 1967, a little revolutionary daring . . . a sense of what revolution calls for, would have transformed the battle of the Golan into an Arab Verdun, a great myth-maker in the pages of history" (Jumblatt 1982, 18).
14. These included George Habash's PFLP, Hawatmeh's PDFLP, the Syrian-supported PFLP–General Command of Ahmed Jabril, Kamal Chatila's Syrian-sponsored Union of Popular Labor Forces, Muhsin Ibrahim's Communist Action Organization, George Hawi's Communist Party, the Lebanese branches of the Syrian and Iraqi Baᶜth parties, the SSNP, and the independent Nasserist movement, al Mourabitoun (the vigilantes) (Goria 1985, 93).
15. Jumblatt interpreted the student crisis as "in every sense of the word a crisis of the political system." "From here," he stressed, "starts the revolution." *Al Amal,* March 21, 1971.
16. The "Musharakah" campaign started with a demand to make Friday, the Muslim holy day, an official day of rest (Campbell 1973).
17. The stark contrast of poor, predominantly Shiite émigrés living within walking distance of fashionable areas of the city where extravagant wealth belonged to Christian bourgeoisie accentuated sectarian as well as socioeconomic tensions (Khuri 1972, 198–209).
18. Inhabitants of the "Belt of Misery" in the suburbs of Beirut were willing to find common cause with any one party who would promise to deliver them from permanent political, economic, and social misfortune (Goria 1985, 161).
19. *Daily Star,* January 31, 1975.
20. Christian inclinations to oppose all demands that would deprive them of privileges encouraged a rapprochement between the radicals and the Muslim establishment (Salibi 1976, 83–84).
21. "Relations with the Palestinian Resistance, 1965–69," *Fichier du Monde Arabe,* no. 322 (9 July 1975).
22. General Bustani decided to accept Nasser's advice to reach an understanding with the PLO, the Cairo Agreement.
23. Annexes to the Cairo Agreement, 1977.
24. *Middle East Record* (1968), 653.
25. Speech of Charles Helou on New Year's Eve, 1969.
26. *Record of the Arab World,* January 1969, 37.
27. Seizing the moment, Jumblatt accused Helou of being indecisive (*An Nahar,* January 6, 1969).
28. "Relations with Syria during the Presidencies of Chehab and Helou 1958–1970," *Fichier du Monde Arabe,* September 24, 1980.
29. Their second platform was the struggle against the Shihabist military establishment, which was accused of allying itself with the radical Left (Mughabghab 1970, 12).
30. Gemayal appointed in January his twenty-two-year-old son, Bashir, to organize

approximately one hundred men who would be added to the Kataeb's four-hundred-strong Bekfaya section. Bashir Gemayel, *Fiches du Monde Arabe,* no. 1806 (February 28, 1981).

31. They organized a huge rally in protest on March 20, 1972, which drew an estimated sixty thousand supporters (*L'Orient le Jour,* March 21, 1972).
32. *Al Muharrir,* January 10, 1969, cited in *Record of Political Opinions,* 46.
33. These were Kamal Nasir, poet and PLO official spokesman; Muhammad al-Najjr, head of the Higher Political Committee for Palestinian Affairs in Lebanon, member of the PLO Executive Committee and Fateh Central Committee; and Kamal Udwan, a member of the Fateh Central Committee.
34. *Al Muharrir,* April 14, 1973.
35. Throughout the crisis, PLO communiqués carefully emphasized its commitment to Lebanon's sovereignty. *Al Muharrir,* May 6, 1973.
36. President Frangieh's first address before the Council of Ministers on May 23 (*Arab Report and Record,* May 23, 1973).
37. Ibid., September 17, 1973.
38. Ibid., September 19, 1973.
39. On July 27, 1974, an incident between two smugglers in the Beirut suburb of Dekwaneh turned into a series of clashes between units of the Kataeb and members of the PFLP living in the nearby camp of Tel al Zatar (Goria 1985, 165).
40. The PLO described the attack as "a premeditated and reckless act by members of the PFLP against the Tyre garrison and our brother soldiers" (*Daily Star,* January 21, 1975).
41. *Al Amal,* January 24, 1975.
42. *Egyptian Gazette,* January 26, 1975.
43. *Daily Star,* April 14, 1975.
44. Ibid.
45. *Journal of Palestinian Studies* 5, nos. 17/18 (Autumn 1975): 279.
46. "The 1975–1976 War: The Outbreak of Hostilities, April–May 1975," *Fiches du Monde Arabe,* no. 1749 (November 26, 1980).
47. *Daily Star,* May 16, 1975.
48. *Al Amal al-Shahri,* May 1977, 25–35, cited in Khater 1982, 209–12.
49. *Arab Report and Record,* February 18, 1974.
50. For Chamoun, Solh's bill "left a bitter feeling among the overwhelming majority of Maronites." *Arab Report and Record,* February 18, 1974.
51. *An Nahar,* January 4, 1970; Brynen 1990, 56.
52. *An Nahar,* December 14, 1969.
53. *Arab Report and Record,* May 23, 1973.
54. Ibid., September 17, 1973.
55. *Al Amal,* January 24, 1975.
56. *Daily Star,* January 26, 1975.
57. *Al Amal,* February 20, 1975.
58. After Israel commandos raided the heart of Beirut on April 10, 1973, to assassinate three prominent Palestinian leaders, more than 250,000 people attended the funeral ceremony of the three leaders (Petran 1972, 145).
59. *Arab Report and Record,* August 21, 1974.
60. Ibid., August 26, 1974.

61. Ibid.
62. Ibid., August 28, 1974.
63. *Daily Star,* September 4, 1974.
64. *L'Orient le Jour,* September 24, 1974.
65. Ibid.
66. *Al Amal,* December 12 and 13, 1974; *Fiches du Monde Arabe,* no. 1432 (November 21, 1979).
67. Parliament minutes, 1974/2, 2727–66.

## 8. Summary, Alternative Explanations, and Implications

1. Four illustrative books are Rubin 1995; Zartman 1995; Bunce 1998; Kaufman 2001.
2. This view has dominated journalistic accounts of the conflicts that erupted after the fall of communism. See, for example, Serge Schmemann, "Ethnic Battles Flaring in Former Soviet Fringe," *New York Times,* May 24, 1992.
3. As already pointed out in chapter 4, Mueller (2000) has strongly argued that in Yugoslavia in the 1990s (and Rwanda in 1994) interethnic war was "banal." Although Mueller is right in his assessment of the immediate "acts" of killings that occurred in many instances in Yugoslavia, the point that is more important for the argument of this book is what made these "acts" possible in the first place. Overall Mueller's argument reinforces the need for the multidimensional analysis that the book advocates, wherein ancient hatreds and ethnic vulnerability are only two explanatory elements among many others.
4. Saideman (2001) argues that domestic political concerns of leaders, as shaped by the interaction of ethnic ties and political competition, goes far in explaining why certain states and not others take sides in certain international conflicts. The focus on leaders and the political competition between them is part of my argument on intercommunal trust and vulnerability. This is also true for the effects of the distribution of institutional power in a multi-ethnic polity.

# Bibliography

## Books and Scholarly Articles


Abu, Iyad. 1981. *My Home, My Land: A Narrative of Palestinian Struggle.* New York: Times Books.

Addi, Lahouari. 1995. *L'Algérie et la démocratie: Pouvoir et crise du politique dans l'Algérie contemporaine.* Paris: Editions La Découverte.

Agwani, M. S. 1965. *The Lebanese Crisis, 1958: A Documentary Study.* New York: Asia Publishing House.

Ajami, Fouad. 1979. "The Struggle for Egypt's Soul." *Foreign Policy* 35 (Summer): 3–30.

Alamuddin, Najib. 1993. *Turmoil: The Druzes, Lebanon and the Arab-Israeli Conflict.* London: Quartet Books.

*American Journal of Economics and Sociology* 62, no. 1 (January 2003).

Anderson, Benedict. 1992. *Imagined Communities: Reflections on the Origin and Spread of Nationalism.* New York: Verso.

Andrejevich. 1991a. "Retreating from the Brink of Collapse." *RFE* 2, no. 15 (April 12): 25–30.

——. 1991b. "A Week of Great Political Importance." *RFE* 2, no. 3 (January 18): 26–29.

Arfi, Badredine. 1998. "Ethnic Fear: The Social Construction of Insecurity." *Security Studies* 8, no. 1: 151–203.

——. 2000. "'Spontaneous' Interethnic Order: The Emergence of Collective, Path Dependent Cooperation." *International Studies Quarterly* 44, no. 4: 563–90.

Arthur, W. B. 1994. *Increasing Returns and Path Dependence in the Economy.* Ann Arbor: University of Michigan Press.

Avakumovic, Ivan. 1964. *History of the Communist Party of Yugoslavia.* Aberdeen, United Kingdom Aberdeen University Press.

Ayoob, Mohammed. 1996. "State Making, State Breaking, and State Failure." In

*Managing Global Chaos: Sources of and Responses to International Conflict,* edited by Chester A. Crocker, Fen Osler Hampson, and Pamela Aall, 37–51. Washington, D.C.: United States Institute of Peace Press.

Badeau, John S. 1958. "The Middle East: Conflict in Priorities." *Foreign Affairs* 36: 232–40.

Baldwin, David A. 1993. *Neorealism and Neoliberalism: The Contemporary Debate.* New York: Columbia University Press.

Banac, Ivo. 1984. *The National Question in Yugoslavia: Origins, History, Politics.* Ithaca, N.Y.: Cornell University Press.

———. 1988. *With Stalin against Tito: Cominformist Splits in Yugoslav Communism.* Ithaca, N.Y.: Cornell University Press.

———. 1992. "Post-communism as Post-Yugoslavism: The Yugoslav Non-revolutions of 1989–1990." In *Eastern Europe in Revolution,* edited by Ivo Banac, 168–87. Ithaca, N.Y.: Cornell University Press.

———. 1995. "The Dissolution of Yugoslav Historiography." In *Beyond Yugoslavia: Politics, Economics, and Culture in a Shattered Community,* edited by Sabrina P. Ramet and Ljubisa S. Adamovich, 39–65. Boulder, Colo.: Westview Press.

Barnett, Michael. 1998. *Dialogues in Arab Politics.* New York: Columbia University Press.

Bell, Coral. 1974. "The October Middle East War: A Case Study in Crisis-Management during Détente." *International Affairs* 50: 531–33.

———. 1977. *The Diplomacy of Détente: The Kissinger Era.* London: Martin Robertson.

Benderly, Jill, and Evan Kraft. 1994. *Independent Slovenia: Origins, Movements, Prospects.* New York: St. Martin's Press.

Bennett, William L. 1980. "Myth, Ritual, and Political Control." *Journal of Communication* 30: 166–79.

Berger, Peter L., and Thomas Luckmann. 1966. *The Social Construction of Reality: A Treatise in the Sociology of Knowledge.* New York: Doubleday.

Bicanic, Rudolf. 1973. *Economic Policy in Socialist Yugoslavia.* Cambridge: Cambridge University Press.

Blechman, Barry. 1972. "The Impact of Israeli Reprisals on Behavior of Bordering Arab Nations Directed at Israel." *Journal of Conflict Resolution* 16, no. 2 (June): 155–81.

Bokovoy, Melissa K. 1998. *Peasants and Communists: Politics and Ideology in the Yugoslav Countryside, 1941–1953.* Pittsburgh: University of Pittsburgh Press.

Brands, H. W., Jr., and William H. Henry Jr. 1986. "What Eisenhower and Dulles Saw in Nasser: Personalities and Interests in US-Egyptian Relations." *American-Arab Affairs* 17: 44–54.

Brynen, Rex. 1990. *Sanctuary and Survival: The PLO in Lebanon.* Boulder, Colo.: Westview Press.

Bukovansky, Mlada. 1997. "American Identity and Neutral Rights from Independence to the War of 1812." *International Organization* 51, no. 2: 209–43.

Bunce, Valerie. 1998. *Subversive Institutions: The Design and the Destruction of Socialism and the State.* New York: Cambridge University Press.

Burg, Steven L. 1983. *Conflict and Cohesion in Socialist Yugoslavia: Political Decision Making since 1966.* Princeton: Princeton University Press.

Burks, R. V. 1971. *The National Problem and the Future of Yugoslavia. Rand Report No. P-4761.* Santa Monica, Calif.: The Rand Corporation.

Campbell, Robert. 1973. "Le problème du chômage du vendredi au Liban." *Travaux et Jours* 49 (October).

Carr, Edward H. 1961. *What Is History?* New York: Vintage Books.

Charef, Abed. 1994. *Algérie: Le grand dérapage.* Paris: Editions de l'Aube.

Clissold, Stephen. 1966. *A Short History of Yugoslavia.* Cambridge and New York: Cambridge University Press.

———. 1975. *Yugoslavia and the Soviet Union, 1939–1973: A Documentary Survey.* New York: Oxford University Press.

Cobban, Helena. 1984. *The Palestinian Liberation Organization: People, Power, and Politics.* Cambridge: Cambridge University Press.

———. 1985. *The Making of Modern Lebanon.* London: Hutchinson.

Cohen, Lenard J. 1995. *Broken Bonds: Yugoslavia's Disintegration and Balkan Politics in Transition.* Boulder, Colo.: Westview Press.

Cohen, Warren I. 1993. *America in the Age of Soviet Power, 1945–1991.* Cambridge History of American Foreign Relations, vol. 4. New York: Cambridge University Press.

Collingwood, Richard G. 1956. *The Idea of History.* New York: Oxford University Press.

Connerton, Paul. 1994. *How Societies Remember.* New York: Cambridge University Press.

Dann, Uriel. 1969. *Iraq under Qassem: A Political History, 1958–1963.* Jerusalem: Israel University Press.

Davis, Eric, and Nicolas Gavrielides. 1991. *Statecraft in the Middle East: Oil, Historical Memory, and Popular Culture.* Miami: Florida International University Press.

Davis, John B. 2002. "Collective Intentionality and Individual Behavior." In *Intersubjectivity in Economics: Agents and Structures,* edited by Edward Fullbrook, 11–27. New York: Routledge.

Dawisha, Adeed. 1983. "Jordan in the Middle East: The Art of Survival." In *The Shaping of an Arab Statesman: Abd al-Hammid Sharaf and the Modern Arab World,* edited by Patrick Seale, 69. New York: Quartet.

Dawisha, Karen, and Bruce Parrot. 1994. *Russia and the New States of Eurasia: The Politics of Upheaval.* New York: Cambridge University Press.

Dedijer, Vladimir. 1953. *Tito Speaks: His Self-Portrait and Struggle with Stalin.* London: Weidenfeld and Nicholson.

———. 1972. *The Battle Stalin Lost: Memoirs of Yugoslavia, 1948–53.* New York: Gossett.

Deeb, Marius. 1980. *The Lebanese Civil War.* New York: Praeger.

Denitch, Bogdan. 1994. *Ethnic Nationalism: The Tragic Death of Yugoslavia.* Minneapolis: University of Minnesota Press.

Derderian, Richard L. 2002. "Algeria as a *Lieu de Mémoire*: Ethnic Minority Memory and National Identity in Contemporary France." *Radical History Review* 83 (Spring): 28–43.

Desch, Michael C. 1996. "War and Strong States, Peace and Weak States?" *International Organization* 50, no. 2: 237–68.

Dessler, David. 1989. "What's at Stake in the Agent-Structure Debate?" *International Organization* 43, no. 3: 441–73.

Dishon, Daniel. 1977. "The Lebanese War—An All Arab Crisis." *Midstream* (January): 25–32.

Djilas, Aleksa. 1991. *The Contested Country: Yugoslav Unity and Communist Revolution, 1919–1953.* Cambridge: Harvard University Press.

———. 1992. "The Nation That Wasn't." *The New Republic,* September 21, 25–31.

———. 1993. "A Profile of Slobodan Milosevic." *Foreign Affairs* 72, no. 3: 81–96.

———. 1995. "Fear Thy Neighbor: The Breakup of Yugoslavia." In *Nationalism and Nationalities in the New Europe,* edited by Charles A. Kupchan, 85–106. Ithaca, N.Y.: Cornell University Press.

Djilas, Milovan. 1962. *Conversations with Stalin.* New York: Harcourt, Brace and World.

———. 1969. *The Unperfect Society: Beyond the New Class.* New York: Harcourt, Brace and World.

———. 1980. *Tito: The Story from Inside.* New York: Harcourt Brace Jovanovich.

———. 1983. *Vlast.* London: Nasa Rec.

Djordjevic, Jovan. 1963. "The Socialist Federation and the Republic." *New Yugoslav Law* 1–3: 12.

———. 1970. *Ustavno pravo.* Belgrade: Savezna Admistracija.

Dolenc, Ervin. 1994. "Culture, Politics, and Slovene Identity." In *Independent Slovenia: Origins, Movements, Prospects,* edited by Jill Benderly and Evan Kraft, 69–90. New York: St. Martin's Press.

Donia, Robert J., and John V. A. Fine Jr. 1994. *Bosnia and Hercegovina: A Tradition Betrayed.* New York: Columbia University Press.

Duchacek, Ivo D. 1991. "Comparative Federalism: An Agenda for Additional Research." In *Constitutional Design and Power-Sharing in the Post-modern Epoch,* edited by Daniel J. Elazar, 23–40. Lanham, Md.: University Press of America.

Dyker, David A. 1990. *Yugoslavia: Socialism, Development and Debt.* New York: Routledge.

Edelman, Murray. 1971. *Politics as Symbolic Action: Mass Arousal and Quiescence.* New York: Academic Press.

Emmert, Thomas A. 1990. *Serbian Golgotha Kosovo, 1389.* New York: Columbia University Press.

Entelis, John P. 1974. *Pluralism and Party Transformation in Lebanon: AL-KATA'IB, 1936–1970.* Leiden: E. J. Brill.

Esman, Milton J. 1994. *Ethnic Politics.* Ithaca, N.Y.: Cornell University Press.

Esty, D. C., J. Goldstone, T. R. Gurr, B. Harff, M. Levy, G. D. Dabelko, P. T. Surko, and A. N. Unger. 1999. "State Failure Task Force Report: Phase II Findings." *Environmental Change and Security Project Report* 5 (Summer): 49–72.

Ezrahi, Yaron. 1997. *Rubber Bullets: Power and Conscience in Modern Israel.* Berkeley and Los Angeles: University of California Press.

Fearon, James D., and David D. Laitin. 1996. "Explaining Interethnic Cooperation." *American Political Science Review* 90, no. 4: 715–35.

Finnemore, Martha. 1996. *National Interests in International Society.* Ithaca, N.Y.: Cornell University Press.

Finnemore, Martha, and Kathryn Sikkink. 1998. "International Norm Dynamics and Political Change." *International Organization* 52, no. 4: 887–917.

Freedman, Robert O. 1975. *Soviet Policy toward the Middle East since 1970.* New York: Praeger.

Fromkin, David. 1989. *A Peace to End All Peace: The Fall of the Ottoman Empire and the Creation of the Modern Middle East.* New York: Avon Books.

Gaddis, John L. 1987. *The Long Peace: Inquiries into the History of the Cold War.* New York: Oxford University Press.

Gagnon, V. P., Jr. 1994–95. "Ethnic Nationalism and International Conflict: The Case of Serbia." *International Security* 19: 130–66.

George, A. L., and R. Smoke. 1974. *Deterrence in American Foreign Policy: Theory and Practice.* New York: Columbia University Press.

Gerges, Fawaz A. 1994. *The Superpowers and the Middle East: Regional and International Politics, 1955–1967.* Boulder, Colo.: Westview Press.

Giddens, Anthony. 1984. *The Constitution of Society.* Berkeley and Los Angeles: University of California Press.

Gillis, John Red. 1994. *Commemorations: The Politics of National Identity.* Princeton: Princeton University Press.

Gilmour, David. 1987. *Lebanon: The Fractured Country.* London: Sphere Books.

Glenny, Misha. 1993. *The Fall of Yugoslavia: The Third Balkan War.* London: Penguin.

Goodwin, Jeff. 1994. "Toward a New Sociology of Revolutions." *Theory and Society* 23: 731–66.

Gordon, David C. 1980. *Lebanon: The Fragmented Nation.* Stanford, Calif.: Hoover Institution Press.

Goria, Wade R. 1985. *Sovereignty and Leadership in Lebanon, 1943–1976.* London: Ithaca Press.

Gourevitch, Peter. 1978. "The Second Image Reversed: The International Sources of Domestic Politics." *International Organization* 32, no. 4: 881–912.

Gow, James. 1992. *Legitimacy and the Military: The Yugoslav Crisis.* New York: St. Martin's Press.

———. 1997. *Triumph of the Lack of Will: International Diplomacy and the Yugoslav War.* New York: Columbia University Press.

Greene, Owen. 1988. "The Balkans in a Divided Europe: Yugoslavian Security in the Context of the NATO-Warsaw Pact Confrontation." In *Yugoslavia's Security Dilemmas: Armed Forces, National Defence and Foreign Policy,* edited by Marko Milivojevic, John B. Allcock, and Pierre Maurer, 213–60. New York: Berg.

Grouch, Harold. 1978. "From Alliance to Barisan National." In *Malaysian Politics and the 1978 Election,* edited by Harold Grouch, Lee Kam Hing, and Michael Ong, 1–10. Kuala Lumpur: Oxford University Press.

Gurr, Ted R. 1993. *Minorities at Risk: A Global View of Ethnopolitical Conflicts.* Washington, D.C.: United States Institute of Peace Press.

Haddad, Wadi A. 1985. *Lebanon: The Politics of Revolving Doors.* Washington, D.C.: Praeger Special Studies.

Halbwachs, Maurice. 1992. *On Collective Memory.* Chicago: University of Chicago Press.

Hall, Rodney B. 1999. *National Collective Identity: Social Constructs and International Systems.* New York: Columbia University Press.

Hamroush, Ahmed. 1984. *Qissa Taura 23 Yulio: Kharif Abdel-Nasser* [The story of the 23 July revolution: The autumn of Abdel-Nasser]. Vol. 5. Cairo: Maktaba al-Madbuli.

Hardin, Russell. 1995. *One for All: The Logic of Group Conflict.* Princeton: Princeton University Press.

Heikal, Mohamed. 1978. *The Sphinx and the Commissar.* New York: Harper and Row.

Herbst, Jeffrey. 1996–97. "Responding to State Failure in Africa." *International Security* 21, no. 3: 120–44.

Heuser, Beatrice. 1988. "Yugoslavia in Western Military Planning, 1948-53." In *Yugoslavia's Security Dilemmas, Armed Forces, National Defense and Foreign Policy,* edited by Marko Milivojevic, John B. Allock, and Pierre Maurer, 126–63. New York: Berg Publishers.

———. 1989. *Western "Containment" Policies in the Cold War: The Yugoslav Case, 1948–53.* New York: Routledge.

Hitti, Philip K. 1962. *Lebanon in History from the Earliest Times to the Present.* New York: St. Martin's Press.

Hoffman, Aaron M. 2002. "A Conceptualization of Trust in International Relations." *European Journal of International Relations* 8, no. 3: 375–401.

Hoffman, George W., and Fred W. Neal. 1962. *Yugoslavia and the New Communism.* New York: Twentieth Century Fund.

Holsti, Kalevi J. 1996. *The State, War, and the State of War.* New York: Cambridge University Press.

Hondius, Frits W. 1968. *The Yugoslav Community of Nations.* Paris: Mouton.

Hoopes, T. 1973. *The Devil and John Foster Dulles.* Boston: Little and Brown.

Hopf, Theodore. 1998. "The Promise of Constructivism in International Relations Theory." *International Security* 23, no. 1: 171–200.

Höpken, Wolfgang. 1997. "History Education and Yugoslav (Dis-)Integration." In *State-Society Relations in Yugoslavia, 1945–1992,* edited by Melissa K. Bokovoy, Jill A. Irvine, and Carol S. Lilly, 78–104. New York: St. Martin's Press.

Horowitz, Donald L. 1985. *Ethnic Groups in Conflict.* Berkeley and Los Angeles: University of California Press.

Horvat, Branko. 1976. *The Yugoslav Economic System.* White Plains, N.Y.: M. E. Sharpe.

Hosking, Geoffrey, and George Schöpflin, eds. 1997. *Myths and Nationhood.* New York: Routledge.

Hottinger, Arnold. 1966. "Zuʾamaʾ in Historical Perspective." In *Politics in Lebanon,* edited by Leonard Binder, 85–105. New York: John Wiley and Sons.

Howe, Herbert M. 1996–97. "Lessons of Liberia: ECOMOG and Regional Peacekeeping." *International Security* 21, no. 3: 145–76.

———. 2001. *Ambiguous Order: Military Forces in African States.* Boulder, Colo.: Lynne Rienner Publishers.

Irvine, Jill A. 1993. *The Croat Question: Partisan Politics in the Formation of the Yugoslav Socialist State.* Boulder, Colo.: Westview Press.

Ismael, Tareq Y. 1986. *International Relations of the Contemporary Middle East: A Study in World Politics.* Syracuse, N.Y.: Syracuse University Press.

Jabber, Fuad. 1973. "The Palestinian Resistance and Inter-Arab Politics." In *The Politics of Palestinian Nationalism,* edited by William B. Quandt et al., 168–73. Berkeley and Los Angeles: University of California Press.

Jackson, Robert H. 1990. *Quasi-states: Sovereignty, International Relations, and the Third World.* New York: Cambridge University Press.

Johnson, A. Ross. 1972. *The Transformation of Communist Ideology: The Yugoslav Case, 1945–1953.* Cambridge, Mass.: MIT Press.

Jugoslavije, Arkiv. 1948. *Minutes of Politburo,* Belgrade, June 13.

Jumblatt, Kamal. 1959. *Tabiʿatu al-haqiqiyah Li al-thawrah al-lubnaniyah* [The true nature of the Lebanese revolt]. Beirut: Dar al-Nashr al-ʿArabiyyah.

——. 1982. *I Speak for Lebanon*. London: Zed Press.

——. N.d. *Fi Majra al-Siyasa al-Lubnaniya* [In the course of Lebanese politics]. Beirut: Dar al-Tali'a.

Jureidini, Paul, and Ronald McLaurin. 1979. "The Hashemite Kingdom of Jordan." In *Lebanon in Crisis,* edited by P. Edward Haley and Lewis W. Snider. Syracuse, N.Y.: Syracuse University Press.

Kaplan, Robert D. 1993. *Balkan Ghosts: A Journey through History.* New York: St. Martin's Press.

Kardelj, Edward. 1982. *Reminiscences.* London: Blond and Briggs.

Katzenstein, Peter J. 1996. *The Culture of National Security: Norms and Identity in World Politics.* New York: Columbia University Press.

Kaufman, Stuart J. 2001. *Modern Hatreds: The Symbolic Politics of Ethnic War.* Ithaca, N.Y.: Cornell University Press.

Kazziha, Walid W. 1979. *Palestine in the Arab Dilemma.* London: Croom Helm.

Keohane, Robert O. 1986. *Neorealism and Its Critics.* New York: Columbia University Press.

Kerr, Malcolm H. 1971. *The Arab Cold War.* New York: Oxford University Press.

——. 1972a. "The Lebanese Civil War." In *The International Regulation of Civil War,* edited by E. Luard. New York: New York University Press.

——. 1972b. "Regional Arab Politics and the Conflict with Israel." In *Political Dynamics in the Middle East,* edited by P. Y. Hammon and S. S. Alexander. New York: American Elsevier.

Kertzer, David I. 1988. *Ritual, Politics, and Power.* New Haven: Yale University Press.

Khalidi, Rashid. 1989. "Consequences of the Suez Crisis in the Arab World." In *The Crisis and Its Consequences,* edited by W. R. Louis and R. Owen, 377–92. New York: Oxford University Press.

Khalidi, Walid. 1979. *Conflict and Violence in Lebanon: Confrontation in the Middle East.* Cambridge: Center for International Affairs, Harvard University.

Khater, Tony. 1982. "Lebanese Politics and the Palestinian Resistance Movement, 1967–1976." PhD diss., State University New York, Buffalo.

Khuri, Fuad I. 1972. "Sectarian Loyalty among Rural Migrants in Two Lebanese Suburbs: A Stage between Family and National Allegiance." In *Rural Politics and Social Change in the Middle East,* edited by Antoun Harik and Illiya Harik, 198–209. Bloomington: Indiana University Press.

King, John. 1999. *Algeria: A Society Divided.* Cheltenham, England: Understanding Global Issues.

Kirschbaum, Stanislav J. 1995. *A History of Slovakia: The Struggle for Survival.* New York: St. Martin's Press/Griffin, 1995.

Klotz, Audie. 1995. "Norms Reconstituting Interests: Global Racial Equality and U.S. Sanctions against South Africa." *International Organization* 49: 451–78.

Koslowski, Rey, and Friedrich V. Kratochwil. 1994. "Understanding Change in International Politics: The Soviet Empire's Demise and the International System." *International Organization* 48, no. 2: 215–47.

Kratochwil, Friedrich V. 1989. *Rules, Norms, and Decisions: On the Conditions of Practical and Legal Reasoning in International Relations and Domestic Affairs.* New York: Cambridge University Press.

Kuran, Timur. 1995. *Private Truths, Public Lies: The Social Consequences of Preference Falsification.* Cambridge: Harvard University Press.

Lake, David A., and Donald Rothchild. 1996. "Containing Fear: The Origins and Management of Ethnic Conflict." *International Security* 21, no. 2: 41–75.

———. 1998. *The International Spread of Ethnic Conflict.* Princeton: Princeton University Press.

Lambrose, R. J. 2002. "The Abusable Past." *Radical History Review* 83 (Spring): 211–14.

Lampe, John R. 1996. *Yugoslavia As History: Twice There Was a Country.* New York: Cambridge University Press.

Lampe, John R., Russell O. Prickett, and Ljubiša S. Adamovic. 1990. *Yugoslav-American Economic Relations since World War II.* Durham, N.C.: Duke University Press.

Lang, Nicholas R. 1975. "The Dialectics of Decentralization: Economic Reform and Regional Inequality in Yugoslavia." *World Politics* 27, no. 3: 309–35.

Leff, Carol S. 1988. *National Conflict in Czechoslovakia: The Making and Remaking of a State, 1918–1987.* Princeton: Princeton University Press.

Leffler, Melvyn P. 1984. "The American Conception of National Security and the Beginnings of the Cold War, 1945–48." *The American Historical Review* 89, no. 2: 346–81.

Lemarchand, René. 1994. *Burundi: Ethnocide As Discourse and Practice.* New York: Cambridge University Press.

Levi, Margaret. 1997. "A Model, a Method, and a Map: Rational in Comparative and Historical Analysis." In *Comparative Politics: Rationality, Culture, and Structure,* edited by Mark I. Lichbach and Alan S. Zuckerman, 19–41. Cambridge: Cambridge University Press.

Levinshohn, Florence H. 1994. *Belgrade: Among the Serbs.* Chicago: Ivan R. Dee.

Lewis, Bernard. 1975. *History: Remembered, Recovered, Invented.* Princeton: Princeton University Press.

Lewis, J. D., and Andrew Weigert. 1985. "Trust As a Social Reality." *Social Forces* 63, no. 4: 967–85.

Lijphart, Arend. 1977. *Democracy in Plural Societies: A Comparative Exploration.* New Haven: Yale University Press.

Linz, Juan, and Alfred Stepan. 1992. "Political Identities and Electoral Sequences: Spain, the Soviet Union and Yugoslavia." *Daedalus* 121, no. 2: 123–39.

Lowenthal, David. 1985. *The Past Is a Foreign Country.* New York: Cambridge University Press.

Lustick, Ian S. 1979. "Stability in Deeply Divided Societies: Consociationalism versus Control." *World Politics* 31, no. 4: 325–44.

———. 1993. *Unsettled States, Disputed Lands: Britain and Ireland, France and Algeria, Israel and the West Bank–Gaza.* Ithaca, N.Y.: Cornell University Press.

Marenin, Otwin. 1987. "The Managerial State." In *The African State in Transition,* edited by Zaki Ergas, 61–82. London: Macmillan.

Martínez, Luis. 1998. *The Algerian Civil War, 1990–1998.* New York: Columbia University Press, in association with the Centre d'Etudes et de Recherches.

McClintock, Robert. 1967. *The Meaning of Limited War.* Boston: Houghton Mifflin.

McVicker, Charles P. 1957. *Titoism: Pattern for International Communism.* New York: St. Martin's Press.

Means, Gordon P. 1991. *Malaysian Politics: The Second Generation.* New York: Oxford University Press.

Meo, Leila T. 1965. *Lebanon: Improbable Nation—A Study in Political Development.* Bloomington: Indiana University Press.

Mistzal, Barbara. 1996. *Trust in Modern Societies.* Cambridge, Mass.: Polity Press.

Mosse, George. 1990. *Fallen Soldiers: Reshaping the Memory of the World Wars.* New York: Oxford University Press.

Mozaffar, Shaheen. 1995. "The Institutional Logic of Ethnic Politics: A Prolegomenon." In *Ethnic Conflict and Democratization in Africa,* edited by Harvey Glickman, 33–69. Atlanta: The African Studies Association Press.

Mueller, John. 2000. "The Banality of 'Ethnic War.'" *International Security* 25, no. 1: 42–70.

Mughabghab, Joseph. 1970. "Hizb al-Wataniyyin al-Ahrar." In *Al-Qiwa al-Siyasiya fi Lubnan.* Beirut: Dar al-Tali<sup>c</sup>a.

Nasrallah, George. 1969. *Palestinian Arab Documents.* Beirut: Institute for Palestinian Studies.

Nasser, Gamal Abdel. 1954. *The Philosophy of the Revolution.* Cairo: Ministry of National Guidance Information Administration.

Neal, Fred Warner. 1958. *Titoism in Action: The Reforms in Yugoslavia after 1948.* Berkeley and Los Angeles: University of California Press.

Neustadt, Richard E., and Ernest R. May. 1986. *Thinking in Time: The Uses of History for Decision-Makers.* New York: The Free Press.

Noble, Paul. 1984. "The Arab System: Opportunities, Constraints and Pressures." In *The Foreign Policies of the Arab States,* edited by Bahgat Korany and Ali E. Hillal Dessouki, 48. Boulder, Colo.: Westview Press.

North, Douglass C. 1990. *Institutions, Institutional Change and Economic Performance.* New York: Cambridge University Press.

Novak, Bogdan. 1990. *Trieste, 1941–54: The Ethnic, Political, and Ideological Struggle.* Chicago: University of Chicago Press.

O'Ballance, Edgar. 1974. *Arab Guerrilla Power, 1967–72.* London: Faber and Faber.

Odeh, B. J. 1985. *Lebanon: Dynamics of Conflict: A Modern Political History.* London: Zed Books.

Onuf, Nicholas G. 1989. *World of Our Making: Rules and Rule in Social Theory and International Relations.* Columbia: University of South Carolina Press.

Pattee, Richard. 1953. *The Case of Cardinal Aloysius Stepinac.* Milwaukee: Bruce Publishing Co.

Pauljevic, Slobodan. 1982. *Strasno budjenje.* Rijeka.

Pavlowitch, Stevan K. 1971. *Yugoslavia.* New York: Benn.

Peled, Yaov. 1992. "Ethnic Democracy and the Legal Construction of Citizenship: Arab Citizens of the Jewish State." *American Political Science Review* 86, no. 2: 432–43.

Peleg, Ilan. 1997. "The Peace Process and Israel's Political Cultures: The Intensification of a KulturKampf." In *The Role of Domestic Politics in Israeli Peacemaking,* edited by A. Dowty et al., 13–24. Jerusalem: Leonard Davis Institute, Hebrew University of Jerusalem.

Pennebaker, James W., Dario Paez, and Bernard Rime. 1997. *Collective Memory of Political Events: Social Psychological Perspectives.* Mahwah, N.J.: Lawrence Erlbaum Associates.

Perinbanayagam, R. 1985. *Signifying Acts: Structure and Meaning in Every Day Life.* Carbondale: Southern Illinois University Press.

Petran, Tabitha. 1972. *Syria.* London: Benn.

Petrovich, Michael B. 1976. *A History of Modern Serbia, 1804–1918.* Vol. 1. New York: Harcourt Brace Jovanovich.

Pierson, Paul. 2000. "Increasing Returns, Path Dependence, and the Study of Politics." *American Political Science Review* 4, no. 2: 251–68.

Pinson, Mark. 1993. *The Muslims of Bosnia-Herzegovina: Their Historic Development from the Middle Ages to the Dissolution of Yugoslavia.* Cambridge: Harvard University Press.

Pipes, Richard. 1980. *The Formation of the Soviet Union: Communism and Nationalism, 1917–1923.* Cambridge: Harvard University Press.

Podeh, Elie. 1995. *The Quest for Hegemony in the Arab World.* New York: E. J. Brill.

Posen, Barry R. 1993. "The Security Dilemma and Ethnic Conflict." *Survival* 35: 27–47.

Quandt, William B. 1977. *Decade of Decisions: American Policy toward the Arab-Israeli Conflict, 1967–1976.* Berkeley and Los Angeles: University of California Press.

Qubain, Fahim I. 1961. *Crisis in Lebanon.* Washington, D.C.: The Middle East Institute.

Rabinovich, Itamar. 1979. "Limits of Military Power: Syria's Role." In *Lebanon in Crisis,* edited by P. Edward Haley and Lewis W. Snider, 55–74. Syracuse, N.Y.: Syracuse University Press.

Ram, Uri. 2000. "National, Ethnic or Civic? Contesting Paradigms of Memory, Identity and Culture in Israel." *Studies in Philosophy and Education* 19: 405–22.

Ramet, Sabrina P. 1992a. *Balkan Babel: Politics, Culture, and Religion in Yugoslavia.* Boulder, Colo.: Westview Press.

———. 1992b. *Nationalism and Federalism in Yugoslavia, 1962–1991.* Bloomington: Indiana University Press.

———. 1995. "The Serbian Church and the Serbian Nation." In *Beyond Yugoslavia: Politics, Economics, and Culture in a Shattered Community,* edited by Sabrina P. Ramet and Ljubisa S. Adamovich, 102–22. Boulder, Colo.: Westview Press.

Rankovic, Aleksander. 1951. *Izabrani govori i clanci, 1941–1945.* Belgrade: Kultura.

Reiter, Dan. 1996. *Crucible of Beliefs: Learning, Alliances, and World Wars.* Ithaca, N.Y.: Cornell University Press.

Reyntjens, Filip. 1995. *Burundi: Breaking the Cycle of Violence.* London: Minority Rights Group.

Richter, James G. 1992. "Perpetuating the Cold War: Domestic Sources of International Patterns of Behavior." *Political Science Quarterly* 107, no. 2: 271–302.

Ridley, Jasper. 1994. *Tito.* London: Constable.

Roberts, Hugh. 2003. *The Battlefield: Algeria, 1988–2002, Studies in a Broken Polity.* New York: Verso Books.

Roeder, Philip. 1991. "Soviet Federalism and Ethnic Mobilization." *World Politics* 43 (January): 196–232.

Rogel, Carole. 1977. *The Slovenes and Yugoslavism, 1890–1914.* Boulder, Colo.: East European Quarterly.

———. 1994. "In the Beginning: The Slovenes from the Seventh Century to 1945." In *Independent Slovenia: Origins, Movements, Prospects,* edited by Jill Benderly and Evan Kraft, 3–21. New York: St. Martin's Press.

Rosenau, James N. 1992. *Turbulence in World Politics: A Theory of Change and Continuity.* Princeton: Princeton University Press.

Rotberg, Robert I., Erick A. Albaugh, Happyton Bonyongwe, Christopher Clapham, and Jeffrey Herbst. 2000. *Peacekeeping and Peace Enforcement in Africa: Methods of Conflict Prevention.* Washington, D.C.: Brookings Institution Press.

Rubin, Barnett R. 1995. *The Fragmentation of Afghanistan: State Formation and Collapse in the International System.* New Haven: Yale University Press.

Rubinstein, Alvin Z. 1989. *Soviet Foreign Policy since World War II: Imperial and Global.* 3d ed. Glenview, Ill.: Scott and Foresman.

Ruggie, John G. 1998. "What Makes the World Hang Together? Neo-utilitarianism and the Social Constructivist Challenge." *International Organization* 52, no. 4: 855–85.

Rusinow, Dennison. 1995. "The Avoidable Catastrophe." In *Beyond Yugoslavia: Politics, Economics, and Culture in a Shattered Community,* edited by Sabrina P. Ramet and Ljubisa S. Adamovich, 13–37. Boulder, Colo.: Westview Press.

Said, Edward, et al. 1983. *A Profile of the Palestinian People.* Chicago: Palestine Human Rights Campaign.

Saideman, Stephen M. 2001. *The Ties That Divide: Ethnic Politics, Foreign Policy and International Conflict.* New York: Columbia University Press.

Salama, Rashad. 1970. "Hizb al-Kataʾib al-Lubnaniyya." In *Al-Qiwa al-Siyasiya fi Lubnan.* Beirut: Dar al-Taliʿa.

Salibi, Kamal. 1976. *Crossroads to Civil War.* New York: Caravan Books.

Sayigh, Rosemary. 1979. *Palestinians: From Peasants to Revolutionaries.* London: Zed Press.

Schöpflin, George. 1997. "The Functions of Myth and a Taxonomy of Myths." In *Myths and Nationhood,* edited by Geoffrey Hosking and George Schöpflin, 19–35. New York: Routledge.

Seale, Patrick. 1987. *The Struggle for Syria.* New Haven: Yale University Press.

Searle, John R. 1995. *The Construction of Social Reality.* New York: The Free Press.

———. 2003. "Social Ontology and Political Power." Mimeo. University of California, Berkeley. February 4.

Sekelj, Laslo. 1993. *Yugoslavia: The Process of Disintegration.* New York: Columbia University Press.

Shoup, Paul. 1968. *Communism and the Yugoslav National Question.* New York: Columbia University Press.

Siber, Ivan. 1994. "Central and Eastern European Political Cultural in Transition: From Communism's Decline to Nationalism Triumph." In *Nationalism, Ethnicity, and Identity: Cross-national and Comparative Perspectives,* edited by Russell F. Farnenm, 371–99. New Brunswick, N.J.: Transaction Publishers.

Silber, Laura, and Allan Little. 1997. *Yugoslavia: Death of a Nation.* New York: Penguin Books.

Singleton, Fred. 1985. *A Short History of the Yugoslav Peoples.* Cambridge, Mass.: Cambridge University Press.

Smith, Anthony. 1997. "The 'Golden Age' and National Renewal." In *Myths and Nationhood,* edited by Geoffrey Hosking and George Schöpflin, 36–59. New York: Routledge.

Smolanski, Oles. 1965. "Moscow and the Suez Crisis 1956: A Reappraisal." *Political Science Quarterly* 80, no. 4: 581–605.

Snider, Lewis W. 1979. "Inter-Arab Relations." In *Lebanon in Crisis,* edited by P. Edward Haley and Lewis W. Snider, 179–206. Syracuse, N.Y.: Syracuse University Press.

Snyder, Jack, and K. Ballentine. 1996. "Nationalism and the Marketplace of Ideas." *International Security* 21, no. 2: 5–40.

Starr, Frederick S. 1994. *The Legacy of History in Russia and the New States of Eurasia.* New York: M. E. Sharpe.

Stein, Janice Gross. 1996. "Image, Identity, and Conflict Resolution." In *Managing Global Chaos: Sources of and Responses to International Conflict,* edited by Chester A. Crocker, Fen Osler Hampson, and Pamela Aall, 93–111. Washington, D.C.: United States Institute of Peace Press.

Stokes, Gale. 1993. *The Walls Came Tumbling Down: The Collapse of Communism in Eastern Europe.* New York: Oxford University Press.

Streich, Gregory W. 2002. "Is There a Right to Forget? Historical Injustices, Race, Memory, and Identity." *New Political Science* 24, no. 4: 525–42.

Talbot, Strobe. 1971. *Khrushchev Remembers.* London: Book Club Associates.

Thompson, Mark. 1994. *Forging War: The Media in Serbia, Croatia, and Bosnia-Herzegovina.* London: Bath Press.

Tito, Josip Broz. 1947. *Borba za oslobodjenie Jugoslavije 1941–1945.* Zagreb: Kultura.

——. 1948. *Nationalismus and Internationalismus.* Belgrade.

Turki, Fawaz. 1972. *The Disinherited: The Journal of a Palestinian Exile.* New York: Monthly Review Press.

Vodopivec, Peter. 1994. "Seven Decades of Unconfronted Incongruities: The Slovenes and Yugoslavia." In *Independent Slovenia: Origins, Movements, Prospects,* edited by Jill Benderly and Evan Kraft, 23–46. New York: St. Martin's Press.

Waismann, F. 1979. *Wittgenstein and the Vienna Circle.* Oxford: Blackwell.

Walt, Stephen M. 1987. *The Origins of Alliances.* Ithaca, N.Y.: Cornell University Press.

Waltz, Kenneth N. 1979. *Theory of International Politics.* New York: McGraw-Hill.

Wendt, Alexander. 1999. *Social Theory of International Politics.* New York: Cambridge University Press.

Williams, Suzanne S. 1955. "The Communist Party of Yugoslavia and the Nationality Problem." Master's thesis, Columbia University.

Wilson, Duncan. 1979. *Tito's Yugoslavia.* New York: Cambridge University Press.

Wittgenstein, Ludwig. 1958. *Philosophical Investigations.* Oxford: Blackwell.

——. 1974. *Philosophical Grammar.* Oxford: Blackwell.

Woodward, Susan L. 1995a. *Balkan Tragedy: Chaos and Dissolution after the Cold War.* Washington, D.C.: The Brookings Institution.

——. 1995b. *Socialist Unemployment: The Political Economy of Yugoslavia, 1945–1990.* Princeton: Princeton University Press.

Wrong, Dennis H. 1994. *The Problem of Order: What Unites and Divides Society.* Cambridge: Harvard University Press.

Yamak, L. Zuwiyyu. 1966. *The Syrian Social Nationalist Party.* Cambridge: Harvard Middle Eastern Monograph Studies.

Zartman, I. William. 1995. *Collapsed States: The Disintegration and Restoration of Legitimate Authority.* Boulder, Colo.: Lynne Rienner.

Zimmerman, William, 1987. *Open Borders, Nonalignment, and the Political Evolution of Yugoslavia.* Princeton: Princeton University Press.

Zuwiyya, Jalal. 1972. *The Parliamentary Election of Lebanon, 1968.* Leiden: E. J. Brill.

## Newspapers

*Al Amal*
*Al Amal al-Shahri*
*Al Muharrir*
*Al Sayyad*
*Al-Jarida and L'Orient*
*An Nahar*
*Borba*
*Borba za oslobodjenje Jugoslavije*
*Cominform Journal*
*Daily Star*
*Danas*
*Drugi plenum Centralnog komiteta Saveza komunista Jugoslavije*
*Egyptian Gazette*
*FBIS-EEU*
*Glas na B'ulgarite v Jugoslaviia*
*Govori i clanci*
*Jedinstvo*
*Journal of Palestinian Studies*
*Komunist*
*L'Orient le Jour*
*Le Monde*
*Middle East Forum*
*The Middle East Reporter*
*Mideast Mirror*
*New York Times*
*New Yugoslav Law*
*Nova Doba*
*Novi Sad*
*Oslobodjenje* (Sarajevo)
*Osmi kongres*
*Partiska izgradnja*
*Politika*
*Pravda*
*Pravloslavlje*
*Problemi*
*The Times*
*Ustav Socijalisticke Federativne Republike Jugoslavije*
*Vjesnik*

## Documents

Acheson to Fowler, 11 February 1950, *FRUS*, 1950, iv. 1370.

Annexes to the Cairo Agreement: Memorandum—Top Secret—Urgent Lebanese Republic—Ministry of National Defense, High Command of the Army, General Staff of the Supreme Command—Second and Third Bureau no./72/3.S Classification 1000-1; 120-1 Subject: Circulation of the Fedayeen Inside Lebanese Territory Including Military Zones, *Fichier du Monde Arabe,* March 9, 1977, no. 580.

*Arab Report and Record*

Cannon to State Department, June 30, 1948, PRO/FO 371/72579 Disp. 936.

Correspondence between CPY and CPSU

Fiches du Monde Arabe

*Fichier du Monde Arabe*

Foreign Office, October 1, 1949, PRO/FO 371/78823/UN 2021.

Government of Malaysia. 1971. Second Malaysia Plan, 1971–75.

Hagerty James Collection

*International Documents on Palestine.* Beirut: The Institute for Palestinian Studies, 1972.

Joint Strategic Plans Committee. "The Position of the United States with Respect to Yugoslavia." April 7, 1951 (USNA/JSPC 969/2, Enclosure E., par. 14, p. 16).

*Mahadir Najlis al-Nuwwab* (Proceedings of the Chamber of Deputies). Beirut, vol. 1, 1957.

*Middle East Record*

Ministry of Foreign Affairs, White Book [Yugoslavia]

Narodna Republika Hrvatske u FNRJ
National Intelligence Estimate, November 15, 1955, in *FRUS* 14 (1955): 754.
National Security Council Series, n.d., 5801/1,1.
Parliament Minutes [Lebanon]
Peake to Foreign Office, October 1, 1949, PRO/FO 371/78823/UN 2021.
President Camille Chamoun Press Statement. Beirut, May 21, 1958 [Summary of World Broadcasts, May 23, 1958, p. 10].
PRO/DEFE 4/46 JP(51) 139 (Final), Annex, August 21, 1951.
*Record of the Arab World*
*Record of Political Opinions*
Speech of Charles Helou on New Year's Eve, *Record of the Arab World,* January 1969. Beirut: The Research and Publishing House, 1969, pp. 30–31.
Statut
Summary of World Broadcasts
Text of Seventh Arab Summit Conference Resolutions in *Journal of Palestine Studies* 4, no. 3 (Spring 1975): 177–78.

# Index

**Badredine Arfi** is Assistant Professor of Political Science at Southern Illinois University at Carbondale. He has previously taught at the University of Illinois at Urbana-Champaign. He holds a PhD in political science and a PhD in theoretical physics. He is the author of several articles in leading journals on international relations theory, comparative politics, and physics.

www.ingramcontent.com/pod-product-compliance
Lightning Source LLC
LaVergne TN
LVHW040202080826
844660LV00001B/82